Evangelical Gotham

I0876592

HISTORICAL STUDIES OF URBAN AMERICA

Edited by Lilia Fernández, Timothy J. Gilfoyle, and Amanda I. Seligman
James R. Grossman, Editor Emeritus

RECENT TITLES IN THE SERIES

Thomas J. Sugrue, ed., *Segregating Cities: An Arnold Hirsch Reader*

Terrence J. McDonald, *Nearly Neighbors: Jane Addams, Johnny Powers, and the Progressive Political Imagination*

Tikia Hamilton, *Nothing Less Than Equality: The Battle over Segregated Education in the Nation's Capital*

Joshua B. Freeman, *Garden Apartments: The History of a Low-Rent Utopia*

Emily Lieb, *Road to Nowhere: How a Highway Map Wrecked Baltimore*

Ruby Oram, *Home Work: Gender, Child Labor, and Education for Girls in Urban America, 1870–1930*

Daniel Wortel-London, *The Menace of Prosperity: New York City and the Struggle for Economic Development, 1865–1981*

Stephen M. Koeth, *Crabgrass Catholicism: How Suburbanization Transformed Faith and Politics in Postwar America*

A. K. Sandoval-Strausz, ed., *Metropolitan Latinidad: Transforming American Urban History*

Alexander Wood, *Building the Metropolis: Architecture, Construction, and Labor in New York City, 1880–1935*

Leslie M. Harris, *In the Shadow of Slavery: African Americans in New York City, 1626–1863*, With a New Afterword by the Author

Tim Keogh, *In Levittown's Shadow: Poverty in America's Wealthiest Postwar Suburb*

Nicholas Dagen Bloom, *The Great American Transit Disaster: A Century of Austerity, Auto-Centric Planning, and White Flight*

Sean T. Dempsey, *City of Dignity: Christianity, Liberalism, and the Making of Global Los Angeles*

Claire Dunning, *Nonprofit Neighborhoods: An Urban History of Inequality and the American State*

Tracy E. K'Meyer, *To Live Peaceably Together: The American Friends Service Committee's Campaign for Open Housing*

Additional series titles follow the index.

Evangelical Gotham

Religion and the Making of New York City, 1783–1860

KYLE B. ROBERTS

The University of Chicago Press

CHICAGO AND LONDON

PUBLICATION OF THIS BOOK HAS BEEN AIDED BY A GRANT
FROM THE BEVINGTON FUND.

The University of Chicago Press, Chicago 60637
The University of Chicago Press, Ltd., London
© 2016 by The University of Chicago
All rights reserved, including rights for text and data mining and training of artificial intelligence technologies or similar technologies. No part of this book may be used or reproduced in any manner whatsoever without written permission, except in the case of brief quotations in critical articles and reviews. For more information, contact the University of Chicago Press, 1427 E. 60th St., Chicago, IL 60637.
Published 2016
Paperback edition 2026
Printed in the United States of America

35 34 33 32 31 30 29 28 27 26 1 2 3 4 5

ISBN-13: 978-0-226-38814-4 (cloth)
ISBN-13: 978-0-226-85454-0 (paper)
ISBN-13: 978-0-226-38828-1 (e-book)
DOI: https://doi.org/10.7208/chicago/9780226388281.001.0001

Library of Congress Cataloging-in-Publication Data

Names: Roberts, Kyle B., author.
Title: Evangelical Gotham : religion and the making of New York City, 1783–1860 / Kyle B. Roberts.
Other titles: Historical studies of urban America.
Description: Chicago : The University of Chicago Press, 2016. | Series: Historical studies of urban America
Identifiers: LCCN 2016026514 | ISBN 9780226388144 (cloth : alk. paper) | ISBN 9780226388281 (e-book)
Subjects: LCSH: Evangelicalism—New York (State)—New York—History—18th century. | Evangelicalism—New York (State)—New York—History—19th century. | New York (N.Y.)—Church history—18th century. | New York (N.Y.)—Church history—19th century. | City churches—New York (State)—New York—History—18th century. | City churches—New York (State)—New York—History—19th century.
Classification: LCC BV1642.U5 R63 2016 | DDC 277.471/081—dc23
LC record available at https://lccn.loc.gov/2016026514

♾ This paper meets the requirements of ANSI/NISO Z39.48-1992 (Permanence of Paper).

Authorized Representative for EU General Product Safety Regulation (GPSR) queries: **Easy Access System Europe**—Mustamäe tee 50, 10621 Tallinn, Estonia, gpsr.requests@easproject.com
Any other queries: https://press.uchicago.edu/press/contact.html

To Cris
and my parents
for everything

Contents

Evangelical Gotham was a hymn, a plea, a vision, a melted heart, a network, a marketplace, an imagined community, an abdication, a vector of modernity. Evangelical Gotham was the sacred and the profane, storefront churches and converted stables, meetinghouses and countinghouses, half-orphan asylums and floating bethel chapels, "upper room" prayer meetings, revivals, and baptisms in the East River. The inhabitants of this renowned and not-so-ancient holy city were housewives and prostitutes, masters and slaves, merchants and clerks, missionaries and drunkards, native born and immigrant. They were also deacons, elders, and Mothers-in-Israel; ordinary hearers and sermon gadders, enthusiasts, visionaries, backsliders, the born again. This is a history of their efforts to create an urban religious community of like-minded individuals in the midst of a modernizing city. Here is the story of how they made New York.

Introduction

To twenty-first century viewers conditioned to think in terms of a strict divide between the sacred and the secular, a church spire appears to be the only ostensible religious element in an illustration of the intersection of Ann and Nassau Streets from an early September 1830 issue of the *New-York Mirror* (fig. I.1), and even it looks consigned to the margin. But to the congregation worshipping under the spire of the Old Brick Presbyterian Church, the structures on this block were part of the warp of urban evangelicalism. They knew the three-story structure in the center of the block as the national headquarters of the American Bible Society (ABS), a nondenominational publisher that annually produced hundreds of thousands of Bibles in various languages and distributed them through global networks the city provided. They knew they could procure pamphlets and books for various reform and benevolent societies from Jonathan Seymour, a commercial printer, at the end of the block. Some likely attended meetings of antislavery and moral reform associations in Clinton Hall, the four-story structure to the right of the ABS. The residents of the three small townhouses, vestiges of an earlier age, might have been fellow congregants or potential converts. In each of these spaces urban religion was formed, negotiated, and not infrequently contested.

If churches, publishing houses, rental halls, and private homes were the warp, then evangelical New Yorkers were the weft, deftly weaving together disparate strands into the fabric of urban evangelicalism. Without the women and men sitting in the pews, binding Bibles, attending antislavery meetings, leading family worship, or knocking on doors to deliver tracts,

FIGURE I.1 "View of a section of Ann and Nassau Streets—taken from the south corner," in the *New-York Mirror, and Ladies' Literary Gazette,* September 4, 1830. Courtesy, American Antiquarian Society

there would have been no Evangelical Gotham. The city's evangelical community actively competed in the urban spiritual marketplace by mastering the tools of commercial culture to attract new and retain old congregants. They innovated and borrowed marketing and advertising techniques, branded their churches in a recognizable architectural style, invested in the latest printing technologies, and devised new organizational structures. They funneled the wealth they made in the growing market economy into the construction of new churches, the publication of texts for gratuitous distribution, and the sponsorship of urban missions. Evangelicalism provided a common culture on which to draw, but local churches and national denominations developed ways to differentiate themselves. They proved remarkably successful. By the mid-nineteenth century, Evangelical Gotham claimed hundreds of churches and tens of thousands of congregants within the city. That influence extended across the nation and around the world.

"Evangelical Gotham" sounds like an oxymoron. What does "evangelical," with its connotations of pious converts and reform movements have to do with "Gotham," "the wonder-loving city" populated with foolish and sinful people, as characterized by native son (and nonevangelical) Washington Irving? Contemporary observers and modern-day historians alike have discounted the influence of religion on the life and development of the nineteenth century's most bustling and rapidly growing commercial center. James Fenimore Cooper concluded in 1850 that it would not be in religion but "in their trade, their resources, their activity, and their influence on the rest of the world, as well as in their population, that the towns of Manhattan will be first entitled to rank with the larger capitals of Europe."[1] A century and a half later, Edwin Burrows and Mike Wallace concurred in their Pulitzer Prize–winning history of the city, stating that "despite the formidable number of churches established here, Mammon ruled, not God."[2]

Scholarly oversight in recognizing the important role religion played in the development of the modernizing city reflects larger shortcomings within both urban history and American religious history. When urban historians think of the forces that shaped modern New York, immigration, commerce, and real estate scarcity come to mind more immediately than religion. When religion is considered, it is often portrayed as antithetical to modernization.[3] At the same time, when religious historians think of the forces that shaped American religion, the urban context is typically discounted as hostile. Our understanding of late eighteenth- and early nineteenth-century evangelicalism continues to be a rural story, of camp meetings and dramatic expansion across the hinterland, despite the fact that denominations owed their ability to undertake this expansion to networks of communication, transportation, funding, and cultural production located in urban centers.[4] The few studies of religion in general and evangelicalism in particular in nineteenth-century New York City tend to focus narrowly on specific churches and denominations or on fringe figures and movements.[5]

We ignore the role of the urban evangelical community in the development of New York between the American Revolution and the Civil War at our peril. Looking more closely reveals a world in which the astonishing rise of the early nineteenth-century nation's leading city and dominant Protestant religious movement were intricately intertwined. New York's evangelical population was never large, certainly never approaching a majority of the overall population (see the appendix for specific detail), but it had an unmistakable influence on urban life and development. As developers prepared to open new neighborhoods uptown, evangelicals stood ready to build meetinghouses. As the city emerged as a commercial center, evangelicals capitalized on the resultant wealth, technology, and resources to expand their missionary, tract, and benevolent causes. And when evangelicals felt the city's morals had degenerated, they turned to temperance, Sunday schools, antislavery, and other initiatives to reform its residents, who, in turn, responded variously with indifference, occasional violence, and, less frequently than evangelicals would have liked, conversion. The result of their efforts was Evangelical Gotham, a complicated and contradictory world whose influence spread far beyond the shores of Manhattan.

URBAN EVANGELICALISM

Etymologically, *evangelical* comes from the Greek word *euangelion,* meaning "good news." The term was commonly used as shorthand for the good news or gospel (from an Old English translation) of Jesus Christ. From the Protestant Reformation onward, Protestants used the term *evangelical* to distinguish, as a leading scholar explains, between what they believed to be their "faithful adherence to the gospel message of the New Testament" and "Catholic perversions of that message." Evangelical became code for everything Roman Catholic was not: justification by faith instead of works, the triumph of Christ's death on the cross over the repetition of his sacrifice in mass, a priesthood of believers rather than a class of priests.[6] While the Reformation's legacy of anti-Catholic bias persisted, the movement to which evangelical New Yorkers subscribed was a product of the eighteenth-century Protestant Atlantic World. Evangelicalism has long eluded simple definition because it does not neatly act the part of an institutional religion but ebbs and flows with all the vigor and unpredictability of a religious movement.[7] Like puritanism and pietism, two seventeenth-century movements often credited with influencing its emergence, evangelicalism developed no creed or institutional body to arbitrate what it was or was not. Instead, evangelicalism proffered a small core of principles that converts grafted onto the beliefs, practices, and worldviews of a broad range of Protestant denominations and sects.[8]

At the heart of evangelicalism's core principles is an inherent tension between individual-focused conversion and community-based activism. Conversion (the belief that all must experience spiritual regeneration), biblicism (a reliance on the Bible as the source of all spiritual truth), and crucicentrism (a stress on the atoning death of Christ on the cross) placed a premium on the discovery of an individuated, subjective self and the development of a personal relationship with God. These principles predated evangelicalism, having deep roots in puritanism and pietism, even if those movements put them to different ends.[9] Activism (the expression of faith through efforts toward others) and revivalism (an expectation of seasons of grace for the renewal of the church) anchored the converted in a community of faith. One was not born again into isolation but into a new family of brothers and sisters who were, early on at least, more often fictive than actual kin.[10] Each of these principles understood sin as a pervasive danger to the individual and the broader society, and proposed a powerful alternative. Evangelical tenets affirmed that the good news of Christ provided the *only* hope to regenerate individual lives, reconcile relationships, restore community, and rebuild the world by the standards of God's design. Evangelicals reiterated the concerns of Protestant reformers and frequently claimed precedent in the primitive church, but these principles took on distinctly new meanings in the eighteenth and nineteenth centuries.

Evangelicalism's appeal and the emphasis placed on its different core principles varied over time and space. In Great Britain, for example, evangelicalism remained safely within the bosom of the Church of England in the eighteenth century and did not gain widespread acceptance among dissenters until the nineteenth century. In North America, the opposite was the case. Eighteenth-century Anglicans turned a cold shoulder to evangelical itinerants. Baptists, Congregationalists, Methodists, and Presbyterians offered a warmer embrace that expanded in the nineteenth century. Most reconciled their evangelical and denominational identities, although some were caught betwixt and between. On both sides of the Atlantic, eighteenth-century evangelicalism tended to place greater emphasis on individual conversion than on community activism; by the early nineteenth century, the reverse was the case.

For postrevolutionary New Yorkers, evangelicalism's appeal lay in its fundamentally modern nature. Evangelicalism emerged simultaneously with the conditions associated with modernity. Scholars have gone so far as to identify evangelicalism as a "vector of modernity, a creative response to the transformations that were reshaping everyday life."[11] Few places experienced as momentous a change in politics, economics, social conditions, and intellectual life as New York. As an Atlantic World seaport, the city was ethnically, nationally, and religiously plural from its founding. New arrivals were taken aback by the diversity of peoples they discovered living within the city. Transatlantic and international trade networks connected the urban seaport to the broader world and exposed its inhabitants to new ideas, technologies, and economic and social practices. Large-scale participatory politics emerged as relations with Crown and Parliament broke down and set the stage for a new political order following a war that at its heart was a contest over where power and sovereignty rightfully lay among a free people. What emerged from the confluence of these and other factors was nothing less than a distinctly new society.[12]

This new society impelled women and men to seek a new kind of Christianity, one better suited to their increasingly individualistic spiritual needs. They did this rather than abandoning religion altogether.[13] The importance evangelicalism accorded to an individual's firsthand experience of assurance as the basis of knowledge of salvation and the mandate it gave to create a personal relationship with God proved to be incredibly empowering for women and men looking to exert a modicum of control over their personal destinies. In an age that saw authority challenged from all directions, evangelicalism offered to all, regardless of gender, race, class, or marital status, the opportunity to stand as equals before God, a luxury rarely afforded before their neighbors. At the same time, evangelicalism's emphasis on the community of faith offered a crucial difference from what we often think of as the secular, modern version of self emerging simultaneously in the eighteenth century.

Evangelicalism's success can also be attributed to its effectiveness as a popular religion. The experience of religion for most women and men was far more popular than scholars have previously acknowledged, found less in the unquestioned adoption of official church doctrine as formulated by institutions and clergy and more in the creation of a rich personal syncretism, blending the oral and the written, the orthodox and the folk.[14] Drawing from "a central zone of religious symbols, values, and beliefs—many of them provided by official, formal religious traditions," scholar of religion Charles Lippy explains, women and men "erect for themselves worlds of meaning, they create identities for themselves, they engage in the age-old task of religion by finding a way to make sense out of their lives."[15] Evangelicalism allowed converts to draw just as readily on urban secular influences as on spiritual ones in shaping their spiritual journeys and forming religious communities.

From the start of an individual's spiritual journey, evangelicalism demanded active improvisation rather than passive acceptance, a hallmark of popular religion.[16] All evangelicals were expected to have a conversion experience. Manuals of devotion, concerned clergy, and pious laity might provide guidance, but ultimately the journey was one's own. Evangelicalism also demanded, to some degree, syncretism. Converts were expected to incorporate its small core of principles into the broader matrix of beliefs, practices, and worldviews that they learned from the city's denominations. As a result, evangelicalism found acceptance within Protestant faiths along a broad theological spectrum that ranged from Arminianism to strict Calvinism. Denominations sometimes put a distinctive spin on these principles, such as specifying who might actually be saved by conversion, what a conversion entailed, who were appropriate subjects for activism, or how to interpret the Bible. But a common evangelical culture grounded in these core principles emerged nonetheless. And because evangelicalism remained in flux, that common culture incorporated new ideas over time.

In addition to being a fundamentally modern and broadly popular religion, evangelicalism succeeded because it was a highly effective urban religion. Urban religion "does not refer simply to religious beliefs and practices that happen to take place in cities (and that might as well take place elsewhere)," historian Robert Orsi perceptively explains. "Urban religion is what comes from the dynamic engagement of religious traditions . . . with specific features of the industrial and post-industrial cityscapes and with the social conditions of city life. The results are distinctly and specifically urban forms of religious practice, experience, and understanding."[17] Evangelicalism provided a very useful religion for New Yorkers. Its core principles helped New Yorkers respond to, and locate themselves within, the city because they spoke to the very challenges of the urban experience, of pervasive individualism on the one hand and the desire for community amid overwhelming anonymity on the other. Evangelicals did not just live in New York; they lived through it. In the eighty years between the end of the American Revolution and the onset of the Civil War, evangelicalism served as a resource for the dislocated, provided a moral code, and drove community and city growth.

SPIRITUAL MARKETPLACE

Evangelicalism wrought an internal renovation in tens of thousands of New Yorkers, melting their hearts of stone through conversion, but it also brought about an external transformation of the city through the efforts of the converted who lived, moved, and had their being within it. Many studies of urban religion look at how immigrant religious groups located themselves within a built environment constructed by others; this study seeks to understand the role played by, and motivations of, evangelicals in the construction of the nineteenth-century nation's greatest metropolis in the first place.[18] While some of the city's earliest evangelical communions struggled to find a place in an already densely built-up colonial city, they stood at the end of the Revolution alongside their fellow New Yorkers ready to grow and expand with the city, to be partners in the development of the unsettled twelve miles of northern Manhattan. As New York's built environment expanded from Chambers and Roosevelt Streets, the boundary of the settled city in 1783, all the way to the base of Central Park by 1859, evangelicals were among the most active of city builders.

Evangelical willingness to compete in the city's spiritual marketplace made this growth possible. Disestablishment in the 1777 New York State

Constitution laid the foundation for the postwar spiritual marketplace. Pluralism characterized New York's colonial religious landscape, but the city's Anglican and, to a lesser extent, Reformed Dutch churches enjoyed power and prominence in excess of other denominations. After the Revolution, the state ceased to tax the populace for the support of the church and extended the legal benefits of incorporation to all faiths. This allowed them to enjoy the benefit of a democratically elected body of trustees who took financial responsibility for overseeing property and transacting related business. The underlying premise of the spiritual marketplace was free choice: women and men could choose the faith that most meaningfully spoke to them. Longstanding preferences grounded in ethnicity and family were swept away and replaced by a new spirit of voluntarism. Evangelical churches made a conversion experience the primary criterion of membership and stood ready to accept all who qualified. In fact, they developed a notorious reputation in the late eighteenth century for breaking up natural families by luring away converted spouses and children.

Evangelicals positioned themselves well for the spiritual marketplace by rethinking what made space sacred and experimenting with new kinds of religious places. Following practices that dated back to the Reformation but had more immediate origins in the architectural choices of seventeenth- and eighteenth-century dissenting English Protestants, they stripped sacred space down to its essential components. Sacredness was understood to come not from the physical space itself but from the actions of believers who gathered there to hear the gospel preached. Evangelicals embraced the fluid possibilities of sacred space but also realized the importance of making a recognizable mark on the urban landscape through purpose-built or converted structures. They proved particularly willing to blur the line between commercial and religious culture, building denominational and ecumenical publishing houses, orphan and deaf-mute asylums, seaman's bethels and Magdalen hospitals. They became masters of adaptive reuse and converted secular structures to sacred uses when they could not secure an empty lot or desired to make a pointed message. Storefronts, stables, theaters, and breweries became churches while hospital wards, counting rooms, prison cells, parlors, and the decks of merchant ships became chapels. Few spaces were beyond reclamation and reformation.

But the spiritual marketplace also exacted a toll. In some quarters competition could be particularly brutal, hinging more on the politics of personality than differences of doctrine. Missionaries undercut the efforts of comrades from competing societies, charismatic preachers attracted listeners away from less eloquent ministers, and the religious press engaged in vitriolic debates on some topics but was conspicuously silent on others. The problem stemmed, in part, from the fact that the theological message of the dominant Protestant churches, especially those that identified as evangelical, had progressively grown similar while their preferred audiences constricted to the same group of consumers.[19] Denominationalism represented one attempt at rationalizing the religious economy, by pooling financial resources, sharing bureaucracies, and crafting a distinctive brand for the faith. The very nature of their faiths, however, limited the effectiveness of denominational consolidation and the spiritual marketplace grew more fragmented in the middle decades of the nineteenth century.[20]

As the spiritual marketplace grew larger and more impersonal, it fell prey to the same concerns that dogged the secular marketplace. The residents of America's modernizing cities felt an acute crisis of identity that came with living in a fluid social environment. Churches should have, and in many cases did, provide a sense of community and a stable identity for those buffeted by change. But the proliferation of options in the spiritual marketplace just as easily provoked crises of confidence. Celebrated urban preachers proved to be fallible men. The best-intended missions rarely achieved the goals set for them, regardless of how realistic they might have been. Walking around the city, many asked: how can I know which is the one true church in the midst of so many?

In the end, consumers in the spiritual marketplace did not cease consuming and vendors did not stop selling their brand of faith. They adapted. No amount of rationalization overrode the fact that consumers' decisions in the spiritual marketplace were just as subjective as those they made in the secular marketplace. To that end, producers adapted as well. They built new churches, in new styles, in new parts of the city, and with new amenities. They modified their preaching, emphasized different messages for different audiences, and used new techniques to get people in the door. Even more important, they continued their program of rethinking sacred space and continued to blur the boundaries between the sacred and the secular. The emergence of evangelicalism as the city's dominant faith by the early nineteenth century was their reward.

EVANGELICAL GOTHAM

This study divides the period between the American Revolution and the Civil War into three phases, with the War of 1812 and the Panic of 1837 marking the transitions between them. Throughout, as the city experienced unprecedented demographic and geographic expansion, so, too, did the evangelical community.

During the period between the end of the American Revolution and the outbreak of the War of 1812, much of the city's population arrived from elsewhere around the Atlantic World. Evangelicalism provided an important resource in their crossings and dwellings, helping them to make sense of their experience of migration and to locate communities of the like-minded when in port. This generation emphasized the importance of conversion and established a number of meetinghouses across the city; it also proved slow to look beyond the threshold of those structures. Individual evangelicals initiated efforts to aid the city's most vulnerable residents, those who fell between the cracks of the patchwork of state, private, and denominational benevolence. The published journals of one missionary introduced New Yorkers to the voices of the city's most vulnerable. None made a greater impression than a young fallen woman who may or may not have been what she seemed, an increasing reality in the atomized city.

In a period of economic boom between the end of the War of 1812 and the Panic of 1837, evangelicals optimistically shifted their focus from their own salvation to that of their neighbors. They formed voluntary associations that initiated domestic missions, seamen's bethels, monthly tract distribution, and other innovations to bring the light of the gospel into corners of the city where it rarely shined. They embraced the newest technological innovations in printing and advances in distribution to foster local, national, and global communities dedicated to the perfection of man and society. Through their efforts, New York emerged as an international center for the production and distribution of evangelical culture. They also rethought their role in urban church building and pushed evangelical principles of conversion and the missionary spirit into new understandings of individualism, reform, and church polity. But in so doing, they ran into the limits of what their neighbors, evangelical and otherwise, would accept.

In the period of recovery that followed the Panic of 1837 and lasted until the Civil War, a generation of native-born evangelical New Yorkers came of age. They faced new spiritual crises grounded in an increasing emphasis on childhood conversion and gendered ideologies of domesticity. Working within conventions allowed some women to carve out new, public roles for themselves as theologians, authors, and revivalists. At the same time, the city's dramatic demographic and geographic expansion overwhelmed evangelicals. They had to make careful decisions about where to place new congregations as the urban landscape increasingly segmented into zones residential and commercial, native born and immigrant, rich and poor. Many churches faced the painful (and contested) decision of whether to follow their congregants uptown or to reinvent themselves downtown.

By the eve of the Civil War, evangelical commitment to individual salvation and community-based social activism had produced a profound ambivalence, which allowed New Yorkers to engage with their city in unprecedented ways yet also to withdraw from it in order to focus on their own salvation. Such a stance turned New York into a national center for the production of evangelical culture—exported across the country and around the world—but also helps explain its reticence on hot-button issues like slavery in the decade leading up to the Civil War. Through hundreds of churches, scores of voluntary associations, and tens of thousands of converts, evangelicals profoundly shaped the development of early nineteenth-century New York, and were equally shaped by it in the process.

PART I

1783-1815

CHAPTER ONE

Crossings and Dwellings

In late spring 1789, the captain of the *Lord Middleton*, en route to New York from London via Halifax, Nova Scotia, approached one of the ship's passengers with an unusual request: he wanted the young man to preach the following Sunday. What made the request unusual was that the young man was not a minister but an estate agent, traveling to North America to adjust some financial matters among the relatives of his deceased English employer. Equally surprising, the ship already had a young Anglican clergyman on board. What could possibly make an obscure layman a more desirable preacher than an ordained minister of the Church of England? Charles Lahatt, the estate agent in question, certainly wanted to know. "That R—l shall preach no more on board of my Ship," the captain told Lahatt. "He will gorge, and drink, and go on deck and vomit into the sea, come down and eat again, play cards with fellows untill midnight, get drunk &c." Besides, the captain continued, Lahatt appeared to possess more vital religion and, in his opinion, must be a member of "Lady Huntingdon's Connection," a group of British evangelical itinerants. "You appear to know more than I do," the young man protested, but in vain. The captain insisted, telling him not to deny his calling. The following Sunday, the young man complied.[1]

Lahatt's decision raises important questions about the relationship between religion and mobility at the end of the eighteenth century. Why would he agree to preach, especially when he was under the eye of the Established Church, even if that eye was bloodshot and its beholder intoxicated? The answer can be found in Lahatt's faith. As the ship's captain correctly surmised, Lahatt was an evangelical. His spiritual and terrestrial journeys had begun several years earlier when he traded the German town of his youth for the bustling metropolis of London and a communal Lutheranism modeled on adherence for an individualistic Protestant evangelicalism predicated on active piety. When he rose to preach that fateful day, he prepared to make another spiritual crossing. Conversion had implanted in him the desire to live a life of grateful obedience and service. It also had endowed him with the self-assurance to believe he could be an agent for spreading the gospel when the situation necessitated. The geographical dislocation of his Atlantic crossing, far from the judging eyes of orthodox society, and his destination's radically new way of envisioning religious freedom did not hurt. Lahatt's experience represents an increasingly common occurrence at the end of the eighteenth century that would have profound implications for the development of evangelicalism in the nineteenth century.

Charles Lahatt was just one of many evangelical New Yorkers who experienced a spiritual crossing in the midst of a terrestrial one in the generation following the American Revolution. This period proved one of unprecedented mobility, both voluntary and forced, throughout the Atlantic World. Revolutions in British North America, France, and Haiti at the end of the century and in Spanish America at the beginning of the next, mobilized large numbers of soldiers and created streams of refugees. The Atlantic Slave Trade carried 1.8 million African women, men, and children into chattel slavery in the Caribbean, Brazil, and North America in the last quarter of the century alone.[2] Many turned to religion to help them make sense of their movements through the world. The primacy evangelicalism placed on individualism especially appealed to a generation of women and men set adrift from their families and the close-knit communities of their youth as they navigated a world of revolution, upheaval, and modernity. Evangelicalism resonated—and stood in dialogue—with contemporary intellectual developments in secular society often associated with the Enlightenment. Making the transition from crossing to dwelling helped women and men orient themselves in unfamiliar places, build communities, and inhabit religiously remade selves in new homes and homelands.

In New York City, patriots fled for exile when the British entered the city in the fall of 1776; loyalists beat an equally hasty retreat under the British-ordered evacuation seven years later. A remnant population of around 12,000 in late 1783 nearly tripled to more than 33,000 by 1790, and nearly tripled again to 96,000 on the eve of the country's second war with Great Britain.[3] This rapid growth came not from natural increase but from new arrivals. Whether they came on commercial vessels from Europe, schooners plying the North American coast, or slavers from Africa, members of New York's postrevolutionary generation understood what it meant to actively engage in crossing. Once in the city, evangelical New Yorkers embraced and quickly mastered the postrevolutionary spiritual marketplace. They looked beyond the compact colonial city to the edges of urban settlement when they planted new congregations. In the end, all evangelicals experienced New York differently. Some saw it as a city of deliverance or the Celestial City and settled down; others saw it as Vanity Fair, or worse, and kept moving. Regardless, all contributed to the rise of Evangelical Gotham.

CROSSINGS

Narratives of travel often functioned simultaneously as narratives of conversion among evangelical New Yorkers in the generation following the American Revolution. The surviving fragment of Charles Lahatt's spiritual autobiography, for example, begins with its protagonist foundering in a gale off the southwestern coast of England, buffeted by waves until Providence directed his broken ship back into Plymouth Sound. To convey to his readers the precariousness of his position, Lahatt invoked a familiar image from Protestant devotional literature: Christian at the beginning of John Bunyan's *The Pilgrim's Progress*, a "man clothed with rags" standing with his face from his house, a book in his hand, and a great burden on his back.[4] The storm-tossed Lahatt's burden was the "convictions and uneasy Conscience" that came with the realization of his unregenerate nature that had haunted him "ever since the danger of the Ships foundering." Bunyan—and the Bible before him—might have provided the model, but Lahatt personally located himself in a narrative that was all his own. Over twenty-five closely written pages, Lahatt traveled on a journey of spiritual self-discovery through the Atlantic World.[5]

Most postrevolutionary New Yorkers began life somewhere else. In the midst of their travels, they turned to religion to negotiate an uncertain world. The appeal of evangelicalism lay in how it helped this generation order their interior lives through a more active engagement with their faith. Conversion forced them to trade passive adherence for vital piety. To make sense of their personal experience, they wrote about their lives in autobiographical narratives and spiritual journals. They drew on the interpretive framework and often directly employed the lexicon of imagery and tropes Bunyan provided. They recorded their own journeys from awakening to sin and likened conversion to a dangerous passage through a world of temptation and persecution before ultimately arriving, or at least hoping to arrive, at the gates of the Celestial City, or, as luck would often have it, a wharf in New York harbor.[6]

A range of motivations—commercial, military, political, and social, as well as religious—underlay the journeys of this generation. Commercial opportunities motivated Charles Lahatt.[7] The garrisoning of Isabella Marshall Graham's husband, an army surgeon, at Fort Niagara in the 1760s first brought her to North America; his death in Antigua a few years later set in motion the events that led her to settle in New York.[8] The promise of political freedom attracted others. "When the French Revolution had fairly commenced, and the pulpit and the press were teeming all over Britain with reform," Grant Thorburn joined the radical "Friends of the People" in Dalkeith on the outskirts of Edinburgh, only to find himself later imprisoned. Salvation awaited on the auspiciously named *Providence* bound for New York.[9] Not a few sought to escape their families. Mary Morgan fled a lapsed Methodist shoemaker father and a mother who, "having imbided the infidel sentiments of Thomas Paine and his contemporaries, used her talents in open opposition to religion."[10] Virginia-born freed slave George White simply sought freedom. "I felt anxious to become more acquainted with Christian people," he recalled, "and hearing that the Africans were treated with less severity and contempt in the northern, than in the southern states, I resolved to evade these scenes of brutal barbarity . . . and so set off for the city of New-York."[11]

For this highly mobile generation, religion enabled and constrained terrestrial, corporeal, and cosmic crossings by providing a valuable means of orientation and, as one theorist has put it, of coming "to terms with the ultimate significance of one's place in the world."[12] In the process of finding their place in the world and moving through space, the devout drew on human and suprahuman forces to guide their journeys. More than anything, religion allowed people to respond and adapt to change. Given the confluence of economic, political, social, and religious currents flowing throughout the Atlantic World between the end of the American Revolution and the outbreak of the War of 1812, crossings that ostensibly began with one purpose often took on other meanings. Unsure of their place in the world and no longer able to rely on the security of their place in tight-knit communities, men and women like Charles Lahatt became aware in the midst of these journeys of their need for a faith not of adherence but of active piety.

Evangelicalism provided many denizens of the eighteenth-century Atlantic World with just such a faith. It had been created in the crucible of the North Atlantic and refined through the travels of George Whitefield, the century's most famous Anglican itinerant minister, and John Wesley, the founder of Methodism. Their published *Journals* literally embodied a life spent in crossing.[13] Each documents evangelicalism's portability and adaptability: it dispensed with the need for consecrated space for its performance, it provided a variety of textual materials to support the faithful, it required the embrace of only a handful of core principles—conversion and social activism foremost among them—that could be grafted onto a range of Protestant denominations, and it could just as easily be sustained by a gathering of two or two thousand. Evangelicalism's greatest strength lay in the premium it placed on personal discovery of an individuated experience. Anyone, regardless of race, gender, class, or denomination could remake their spiritual selves by renouncing sin and placing their reliance in the Lord, giving evangelicalism a radical, and potentially subversive, edge. This especially appealed to those unmoored by the upheavals of the eighteenth-century Atlantic World. Alienated from the stable, close-knit communities of their youth—in the valley of the Rhine, the highlands of Scotland, the plantations of Virginia—they found a faith sustained primarily through the discovery of their subjective selves and the creation of a personal relationship with God. Not surprisingly, evangelicalism developed parallel to, and in dialogue with, the conditions associated with modernity.[14]

Spiritual autobiographies exemplify this new sense of individualism within evangelicalism. The genre dates back to seventeenth-century English Puritans and Continental Pietists but grew in popularity over the course of the eighteenth century.[15] The focus of the narratives shifted over time from conversion as entry into community toward discovery of the individual. Inspired by Enlightenment practices, reflective writing offered eighteenth-century evangelicals a means of examining their hearts for signs of corruption, strengthening their relationship with God, and making sense of events that stretched the limits of their understanding. It transformed their lives into "texts" that could be "read" during times of trouble or despair for rational proof of God's presence in their lives and existence in the world. In these autobiographies, as one scholar has explained, evangelicals emerge from the "silent throng of lay people with a name, and a voice, and a story."[16]

Process was as important as product for scribbling evangelicals. "One of my most delightful mental exercises has been that of endeavoring to recollect my earliest religious impressions," wrote Sarah Sergeant Miller, "so as to form a series, which should connect my own ideas on this subject in some order, and make them more intelligible to others." Such was easier said than done. Miller struggled with her autobiography and revised it numerous times over a sixteen-year period. "I have written over and over again many parts," she told her husband, a New York Presbyterian minister, "and have not now satisfied myself with it."[17] Charles Lahatt waited until the end of his life to write his account, and even so it bears evidence of reworking.[18] Divie Bethune recited a concise summation of his experiences during periods of crisis and despair over a twenty-five-year-period in his voluminous diaries. Bethune's repetition comes closest to the oral relations of experiences, now lost to us, that evangelicals regularly made.[19]

At the core of all evangelicals' narratives is a journey toward conversion. They imagined conversion not only as a spiritual crossing, from the world of sin to the holiness of heaven through the assurance of salvation, but also as a corporeal one, transforming the body of the believer. Conversion quickened the soul and remade the individual, one New York minister explained, turning him "from darkness to light, from the power of Satan to the living God: he feels, hears, sees, tastes, loves objects, the very reverse with which he was conversant before; and thus he differs from his former self, in his approach before God, and as he is in his temper and conduct before mankind."[20] The central trope of conversion, the renewed heart, was imagined in terms of a physical transformation: as stony and hard until "melted" into fleshy and pliable by the infusing power of the Holy Spirit.[21] Conversion was a gift of God, initiating a new, ideally unmediated, relationship between human and Supreme Being, in which the former professed perfect dependence on the latter in return for the assurance of salvation.

Publications attempted to make concrete the abstract stages of awakening, conversion, and holy living. These are often modeled on the biblical narrative and follow a common pattern that begins with prosperity, descends into suffering and humiliation, only to conclude with redemption and a return to prosperity. Printers and publishers repackaged works by seventeenth-century English nonconformist divines, titles that David Hall refers to as Protestant "steady sellers," and their eighteenth-century heirs for evangelical audiences.[22] One of the most popular, Philip Doddridge's *Rise and Progress of Religion in the Soul* (1742) guides readers step by step through the conversion process and provided prayers to help seekers along the way.[23] Evangelicals came to depend on Bunyan, Doddridge, and other authors. "I borrowed *Pilgrim's Progress,* with Scott's notes, and read it with prayer; but I could not get out of the 'Slough of Despond' with Christian," Joanna Graham remembered in frustration before conversion.[24] Personal narratives written by postrevolutionary New Yorkers bear witness to the influence of these publications and illustrate how people interpreted the process found within them.

Like Bunyan's classic, evangelical personal narratives tend to begin in medias res. They commence with their authors' search for the New Birth, when as pilgrims they received forgiveness from the guilt of sin through the imputation of Christ's righteousness and commenced their journeys toward a life of holiness. Since eighteenth-century evangelicals typically experienced conversion in adulthood, everything that came prior, no matter how significant it might seem today, received summary treatment. George White, for example, dispensed in two pages with the first twenty-six years of his life, which included his birth into slavery, meeting his mother at age nineteen for the first time since infancy, and his unexpected manumission.[25] Lahatt provided even less information. The careful reader must reconstruct his previous experience by closely reading for clues in the narrative that follows.

Awakening to the burden of one's sins, but also to the possibility of attaining salvation, initiated the conversion process. Following his shipwreck, Charles Lahatt made his way to London, which must have seemed impersonal and overwhelming.[26] The scare of an interrupted oceanic crossing reminded Lahatt of how ill prepared he was to cross the ultimate horizon. An invitation to hear speak Rowland Hill, a noted evangelical preacher and protégé of Whitefield, kindled his hope for salvation. Like Whitefield, Hill warned his auditors that an inflated sense of one's own morality derived from public religious observance stood as the main impediment to the experience of the New Birth. "The Christian World swarms with these Professors," Whitefield warned, "who think, because they can perform the outward Parts of Religion, God will regard them: But let such People know that this Politeness, this negative Goodness, will never bring their Souls to Heaven."[27] Salvation required the discovery of a private religious experience, evangelicals argued, demonstrated through an active piety, instead of passive adherence.[28]

The impression of being personally addressed by an evangelical minister is common in these narratives and underscored the impact of evangelicalism's individualistic rhetoric. "In his Discourse," Lahatt remembered, Hill "told me all things that ever I did, and I fancied that he had singled me out, yet on reflection this could not be possible, for I was a stranger, as much as if I had dropt out of the clouds."[29] Daniel De Vinné had a similar experience. "Every word seemed like an ounce bullet that hit the spot," he remembered after going into a Methodist Watch-night meeting one cold evening in the hope of warming up. "The very thoughts and intents of my heart [were] laid open; and it really seemed as if everybody was looking at me."[30] Lahatt and De Vinné took the message to heart. "I was slain, my youthful sins came up before me, my soul trembled, my mortality looked very doubtful," Lahatt reflected. "I knew not how to pray, my German prayer book and psalm book I had always kept with me, but the prayers it contained did not speak my feeling . . . I felt perplexed, yea vile and guilty."[31] De Vinné felt more relief: "Directly it came into my mind, as if some invisible one was present, and saying, '*These are the people*, these are the people you have been looking for.' "[32]

Awakening often involved crossing out of one's community and into another, which could happen as easily during a walk across the city as a voyage across the ocean. Born to Swiss immigrants on the eve of the American Revolution, Philip Milledoler was raised in New York's German Reformed Church, a congregation of German-speaking Calvinist Lutherans.[33] Later Milledoler remembered in vivid detail the moment Catherine Snyder, a fellow congregant, burst into his parents' house while he was eating breakfast. "My Mother supposing she had met with some great temporal windfall (for She and her Husband had been prosperous, and lov'd this world quite well enough), said to her remember Catherine, it is but the World," he recalled. But Snyder quickly revealed that she and her husband had "found mercy with God" at the Methodist church in John Street the night before. "It had pleased God to open their Eyes—to convince them of Sin, righteousness, and judgment—and to lay them down stricken at the foot of the Cross." Snyder's words, "we must be born of God—we must be born again," sunk deep into the fourteen-year-old's mind. "For days it was like the sound of a bell ringing in my ears, and from which I could not escape."[34]

Milledoler was determined to attend a service at the English-speaking Methodist church to investigate further. What he found disgusted him: "The House was fill'd to overflowing—some to hear, and others to mock. After service had commenc'd, there was great confusion—some praying, others exhorting—and many were exceedingly agitated. Can this, I thought, be acceptable worship? God is a God of order and not of confusion—This thought was immediately follow'd by another. The Galleries were crowded. If a shingle should break, or a cry be uttered that they were coming down—What a cry of terror would follow, and what a rush to the Doors for safety?" Despite his revulsion to what he saw, it irrevocably affected him. "I do remember leaving the house under strongly excited feelings," he wrote, "hastening Home, and when I had reach'd my Bed chamber throwing myself upon my face on the Floor, and pouring out my soul to God in language dictated by what I felt."[35]

For late eighteenth-century evangelicals, the road to conversion was often a long one. New York Baptist minister John Stanford gave an extended example of this journey in *The Conversion of Juvenis* (1794). His titular protagonist had reached the age of twenty-two having lived a life neither "moral nor profane." He had been preserved from "those open notorious vices to which many unhappy youths have been devoted" in cities like New York. But he also slid through life, falling "infinitely short" of the Lord's expectations.[36] Over a period of a few months, he felt an awakening in his heart sparked not by external factors but by a God-given inner spirit. Initial attempts to reconcile himself to the Lord led to failure and despair. When he prayed, clouds of doubt formed over his mind. When he read the scriptures, he only saw threats for sin, not promises for salvation. When he heard the gospel preached, his heart was not warmed. And when he heard the conversation of the serious, he was happy for them but sad for himself. "There are some moments when I think I have a glimpse of the glory of Jesus and the freeness of his salvation," he explained, but then it is "suddenly driven back." Patience, faith, and optimism were key, his mentor Evangelicus told him. Read the sacred word, pray constantly, attend the most evangelical minister he could find, and wait. "In general, the delay of divine manifestations is not because he loves you not," Evangelicus promised, "but that your heart thereby may be proved and tried."[37] Three months later, Juvenis began to see the world through new eyes.

Conversion could manifest itself as a vision, an assurance, an intuition, a wish, or a nagging suspicion. Only the awakened individual was party to the sign. As Rowland Hill spoke of the "Shepherd nursing a Lamb in his bosom" while officiating the Lord's Supper, Charles Lahatt discovered "Christ on the Cross" and realized the significance of his atoning death for the salvation of mankind. "My burden of Mind left me almost suddenly," he remembered, "my heart filled with Joyfull emotion."[38] Joanna Graham experienced conversion through a series of visions, although fear of being accused of enthusiasm led her to claim she witnessed them "not with bodily eyes, but with [her] mind." As the image of Satan taunted her, Graham's mother read aloud from the Bible of Paul's temptation. Within a short time, Graham's mind "seemed transported" from her New York bedroom to the foot of the cross on Mount Calvary. A little while later, she witnessed Christ's agony in the Garden of Gethsemane. There, "the fullness and sufficiency of Christ's atonement blazed on my mind" and the burden "which had so long pressed on my shoulders rolled off at the feet of my Jesus."[39] Milledoler was not so sure about his experience. "I have never been able certainly to determine whether this was the beginning or the ~~signal~~ powerful furtherance of a [*inserted*: previous] work of God upon my soul," he wrote later in life.[40] His textual revisions reinforce the uncertainties of evangelical conversion and storytelling.

Evangelicals populated their accounts with characters who sought by turns to help and hinder their progress. Sarah Sergeant Miller took solace in the support of her childhood friend "M____." "She exhorted me against yielding to my feelings, and was a means, under Providence, of rousing me from my first distress," Miller remembered. But M____ bore resemblance more to Bunyan's Pliable, Christian's unconverted fair-weather friend, than to Evangelist, an experienced traveler who ultimately directed Christian's journey. "The blind cannot lead the blind, and this was and is her pitiable condition," lamented Miller. "Oh, that I may yet see her a fellow-worker with thee, and of the household of faith!"[41] Lahatt found a more helpful friend in the Widow Carr, "a solemn reserved lady" who boarded in the same house. She lent him a volume of "truly orthodox sermons" that belonged to her deceased husband, a Baptist minister. These works implanted in his mind the importance of adult baptism, although it would be several more years before he acted on it.[42]

Throughout, evangelicals read terrestrial landscapes through a spiritual lens as they journeyed over dangerous lands and across threatening oceans, seeking to understand which real spaces and places might be their metaphoric Cities of Destruction, Vanity Fairs, or Doubting Castles. Christian's journey through the Valley of the Shadow of Death in *The Pilgrim's Progress* especially captured evangelical imaginations. Soon after conversion, George White described a "frightful dream, or night vision" of passing by "a lake burning with fire and brimstone" and witnessing a "coach, with horses richly furnitured, and full of gay, modish passengers." His dream ended with his guide telling him, "Go, and declare what you have seen," which he promptly did.[43] Bethune likened the two years he spent in Tobago on his brother's plantation before his arrival in New York to an actual experience of the Valley. He recounted being one of the only young Englishmen with whom he had shipped out who remained alive after two years in the slaveholding colony. This, coupled with the brutality of mid-eighteenth-century Caribbean slavery, made the island literally strewn, in Bunyan's words, with "blood, bones, ashes, and mangled bodies of men."[44]

Conversion brought evangelicals into a new relationship with the Lord but did not save them from the temptations of the world. As much as evangelicals envisioned the spiritual journey as a transition out of the secular world, with its temptation to sin, into a new world of godly living through spiritual rebirth, the reality could often be quite different. Cities were notorious for the temptations they put in the way of the converted. In the summer following his conversion in London, little fell under Charles Lahatt's notice other than "seeing, and hearing novelties in this great Babilon."[45] An inability to break with the world stood as the major impediment for many. In New York, Juvenis reported that after attempting to pray for the first time, he arose and found himself "surrounded with temptation, inducing me if possible to erase the terrors of my heart, by plunging afresh into the delusive charms of the world."[46]

Persecution proved another challenge for the newly converted as they wended their way through the world. "There must and will be a War between the People of the World, and the People of God," George Whitefield warned his followers. The Lord put enmity between Eve and the serpent at the fall of man, he explained, prefiguring a polarity that would persist in evangelicalism, starkly dichotomizing grace and nature, righteousness and sin, holiness and unholiness, the New Birth and the fallen world.[47] "It is hard for youth, in the present age, to follow our christian pattern," Isabella Marshall Graham reflected in a letter about her brother's spiritual condition. She knew that "every real christian, every Bible christian, must lay his account with being branded with the name of enthusiast" but insisted that "the opinion of the world cannot alter the nature of holiness, nor the maxims of Christ."[48] She recommended all evangelicals read, think, and judge for themselves; be confident in the strength of their relationship with God; conform to his will in all things; and avoid entangling conversations with those unsympathetic to their spiritual plight. The best way to convert the scoffing was to humbly present an exemplary character to the world rather than to cleverly show one's persecutors the error of their ways.[49]

The accumulated experience of evangelicalism—the uncertain path to awakening, the joyful assurance of salvation, the threat of temptation, the sting of persecution, and throughout it all the guiding hand of Providence—came together for many evangelicals in their Atlantic crossings. Ships have long been acknowledged as notorious sites of mixing.[50] In the middle of the ocean, far from the rules of civil society, passengers and crew from a range of backgrounds and faiths converged. Grant Thorburn found a cacophony of religious voices among the one hundred passengers and crew on the *Providence*. "We had also some warm contests on religious points, there being in our number, Presbyterians, Methodists, Universalists, Burghers, Cameronians, Deists, and an Anti-burgher minister," Thorburn remembered. "It was not uncommon to see the minister preaching on the quarter-deck, and singing the old version of David's psalms, and at the same time the Universalists, consisting of eight or ten members, chanting Winchester's hymns on the forecastle. At last the captain put a stop to this public contempt, by declaring the Presbyterian religion to be the established religion of his ship."[51] In the absence of stable religious communities, ships challenged the identities of individual passengers. Many found that evangelicalism better prepared them for the challenges these crossings posed than more passive faiths.

Whether evangelicals like Thorburn and Lahatt realized it or not, the individualistic focus of their faith and their religiously remade selves marked them as evangelicals on their Atlantic crossings. They might have demonstrated their faith by praying on deck, reading the Bible, abstaining from profanity, or sharing the captain's disgust at the Episcopalian missionary's inability to control his carnal appetite. Perhaps their ships' captains might have been evangelical themselves and, like a certain Captain Swinburn, sought out "a few of the despised followers of Jesus" among his crew and passengers to go "on very steady in our little sphere on shipboard."[52] It might even have been even subtler than that. Eighteenth-century evangelicals likely exuded a sense of self-assurance and self-awareness that came with the radical act of forging an individual relationship with God.

One crossing thus opened the way for others. When Lahatt arose to preach on shipboard that fateful Sabbath, he confirmed the suspicions of the ship's captain in a moment that served as a logical extension of his experiences over the past five years. He chose Acts 26:18 as his sermon text, the apostle Paul's explanation to King Agrippa in Jerusalem of the mandate he received to preach on the road to Damascus.[53] Perhaps Lahatt anticipated a similarly hostile audience.[54] Standing on the deck of the *Lord Middleton*, Lahatt hoped to convince his hearers to seek salvation. Lahatt's choice of sermon text seems fitting. Both he and Paul received their commissions to preach in the midst of life-changing crossings, in the absence of suitable clergy, and accepted out of a sense of obedience and service. Afterward, the captain thanked Lahatt for his efforts. The rest of the voyage proved "boisterous and plagued by thick fogs," curtailing any further preaching. "Glad was I to be exonerated from doing," Lahatt later wrote, "what I considered myself incapable of doing."[55] This, however, was not the end of Charles Lahatt's career preaching the gospel; it was only the beginning. He found plenty more opportunities in his new home in New York.

DWELLINGS

Making the transition from crossing to dwelling was not without its challenges, especially for a stranger in a new city. Many found postrevolutionary

New York a disorienting place. John Moss immediately felt overwhelmed and unprepared to navigate his new environs. "I found I was a stranger to all, and being, I thought, as one alone in the world," he later wrote, "I began to be tired of myself, for I had been on the roving scale some years." Already anxious about his lack of clothes, money, and friends, he feared he entered a "critical situation" upon discovering that smallpox had broken out in the city. He had been raised in the country and grew concerned that his lack of acquaintance with "the customs of the city" might accidentally lead him to "some house of ill fame." Trusting in Providence seemed like a good idea, Moss thought, but "I did not know what it meant, for I was a stranger to God and myself." Desperate, Moss found salvation in the form of a cousin living in the city. Taken under wing, given shelter, and helped to find a job, Moss found another kind of salvation by the end of the year, conversion.[56]

Dwelling as an evangelical in postrevolutionary New York required finding a community of faith. This need marked a crucial difference between evangelical notions of individualism and the secular, modern version of the self that emerged at the same time. The goal of the spiritual journey for evangelicals might have been to locate themselves ultimately at the right hand of the Lord on the day of Resurrection, but in the interim, they had to situate themselves within their homes, churches, and homelands. To do this, they created domestic spaces for the care of their families and sacred spaces for communing with like-minded others. They deployed artifacts across the landscape to "anchor the tropes, values, emotions, and beliefs" of their community, marking their own social location and prescribing expectations for proper use. The creation of a homeland was also central to their collective identity.[57] Religion provides three overlapping processes—mapping, building, and inhabiting—through which to dwell.[58] Each of these processes were revealed in the narratives left by women and men of the postrevolutionary generation.

Upon arrival in the city, evangelicals surveyed the landscape. John Moss was not the only one to find this difficult. For a decade after the war, New York remained a city of destruction. Seven years of British wartime occupation left whole segments of the city unrecognizable, even to former inhabitants. "We poor ruined Yorkers returned to our disfigured houses," remembered Baptist minister John Gano. "My house needed some repairs, and wanted some new furniture; for the enemy plundered a great many articles." Not only were their prized material possessions gone but so, too, were their friends, neighbors, and congregants. Gano could only locate thirty-seven out of "upwards of two hundred" prewar congregants of his First Baptist Church. "Some were dead, and others scattered into almost every part of the union," he recalled. Nevertheless, Gano commenced rebuilding his congregation.[59]

Economic depression slowed the recovery of New York's built environment, sacred and secular, and hindered the resumption of the foreign trade that furnished the city's prewar wealth. Samuel Breck was struck by what he saw around him in 1787. "I arrived at that city, and found it a neglected place, built chiefly of wood, and in a state of prostration and decay," he later remembered, "for although the war had ceased during that period, and the enemy had departed, no attempt had been made to rebuild them. In short, there was silence and inactivity everywhere."[60] Yet amid the rubble, new signs of life sprouted. Selection of New York as the seat of the federal government in 1789 and 1790, the rise of an important new market for American agricultural production as a result of crop failures in Europe, and the arrival of tens of thousands of new residents who needed housing served as catalysts to economic development.[61] By the middle of the first decade of the nineteenth century, New York resumed its place among the thriving ports of the Atlantic World.

Self-taught artist William Chappel captured the transformation of the city's built environment from the colonial city of its past to the republican city of its future. His paintings document the persistence of seventeenth-century Dutch buildings alongside eighteenth-century English Georgian mansions and nineteenth-century American townhouses in older parts of the city (fig. 1.1). They also illustrate the feverish building of wooden houses and shops for artisans on the northern and eastern edges of urban settlement. In his best-known painting, an outdoor meeting of the Tammany Society takes place against the prominent backdrop of the evangelical Brick Presbyterian Church (fig. 1.2). But most evangelical churches, like the Elizabeth Street African Methodist Episcopal Meeting House, were tucked away at the backs of lots on side streets (fig. 1.3). In the colonial period, these structures stood in a landscape that featured institutions of political, economic, and religious authority in close proximity. Separately, statehouses, markets, and churches oversaw functions key to running a colony; together they embodied the comprehensive power of the state.[62] After the war, churches spread out across the urban landscape as it expanded away from the core of the colonial city.[63]

The 1777 New York State Constitution's guarantee of "the free exercise and enjoyment of religious profession and worship, without discrimination or preference" rewrote the rules of the spiritual marketplace.[64] Where established churches once benefited from the political and economic support of the state, all now stood on equal footing. Legislation passed in April 1784 allowed for the incorporation of any congregation, regardless of confession,

FIGURE 1.1 William P. Chappel, "No 2 / the Lamp Lighter / in Broad St the lower End west Side / 1806 N York," ca. 1870s. The Metropolitan Museum of Art, The Edward W. C. Arnold Collection of New York Prints, Maps, and Pictures, Bequest of Edward W. C. Arnold, 1954, www.metmuseum.org

as long as it democratically elected a body of trustees to oversee its property and transact related business.[65] As the now disestablished Anglican Church, keen to the political sentiment and legal reality of the time, declared itself independent of the Church of England and refashioned itself as the Protestant Episcopal Church, other churches lined up to apply for incorporation.

Postrevolutionary evangelicals sought fellowship with like-minded others. Here they could unburden their souls among the converted who shared their experience and the seekers who still sought assurance. When they could not find a community to their liking, they did not hesitate to create their own. "I seldom had any Christian company," Charles Lahatt recalled of his new neighborhood; "quite the reverse, I was almost always surrounded with ungodly men &c. I more than once felt such emotions of conscience that I literally ran away from alluring Company."[66] Lahatt needed somewhere to run *to*, so he began a prayer meeting. The city's African American Methodists knew how he felt. Increasingly marginalized within the city's predominantly white

FIGURE 1.2 William P. Chappel, "Tammany Society Celebrating the 4th of July, 1812," 1869, oil on canvas, 18½ × 21½ in., 1940.961, New-York Historical Society. Photography © New-York Historical Society

Methodist meetinghouses, they founded the African Society so that "they might have an opportunity to exercise their spiritual gifts among themselves, and thereby be more useful to each other," in the words of their nineteenth-century historian Christopher Rush.[67] A prayer meeting would be a beacon, "something like a religious standard," in Lahatt's words, around which the like-minded might rally.[68]

Prayer meetings offered the most basic form of evangelical community. As large or small, formal or informal as participants desired, prayer meetings did not require ministerial oversight: an articulate layperson, male or female, experienced in spiritual regeneration and possessed of the patience necessary to guide others on their spiritual journeys proved sufficient. Nor did they require any specific type of space and hence occurred in a range of domestic, commercial, civic, and religious places. On any given night, prayer meetings could be found in back kitchens, over carpenters' shops, and in schoolhouses throughout the city. Lahatt referred to his prayer meeting location as "an upper room," a reference to where Christ and his disciples celebrated the Last Supper.[69] Channeling that connection imbued the space with extraordinary power. On Sunday and Wednesday evenings, Lahatt practiced his skills at exhorting, prayer, and scripture explication first tried out on the deck of the *Lord Middleton*. Committed to fostering evangelicalism within his

FIGURE 1.3 William P. Chappel, "No 13 / One of the City Watchmen / & his Watch Box in Elisabeth St / West Side house No 41 on the left Occupyed [illeg.] / Bedstead Maker named John [Jungerick] Next No 43 By / A Mr. Mount an Inspector of Ward No 45 by a / Quaker Lady Named Piggot kept a [illeg.] Grocery at the Present Time is Built the Working Womans [?] House / Little to the Right is the Old Methodist Meeting House / Where [preached?] Lorenzo Dow / 1809," ca. 1870s. The Metropolitan Museum of Art, The Edward W. C. Arnold Collection of New York Prints, Maps, and Pictures, Bequest of Edward W. C. Arnold, 1954. www.metmuseum.org

community, he extended use of the space to local Methodists for their own fortnightly meetings.[70]

Building for evangelicals meant not only gathering community in informal prayer meetings but also converting or constructing physical structures as spaces for formal worship. The city's tight real estate market placed restrictions on what was available to religious groups, but evangelical willingness to rethink sacred space gave them an advantage. For evangelicals, space became sacred through the animating work of the Holy Spirit, not through rituals of dedication or the presence of fixed material features like altars. This emphasis on preaching over liturgy changed the requirements for worship. Any space in which people could hear the Word preached without impediment qualified.

When prayer meetings outgrew the confines of their domestic settings, evangelicals turned to schoolhouses, barns, and storefronts. Ten years after Mrs. John Coutant began a Methodist prayer meeting in her own "upper room" over her husband's grocery store in Bowery Village, the nascent congregation erected a two-story building that housed a schoolroom on the first floor and a worship space on the second. This civic structure fit the needs of the neighborhood as well as the growing religious community. Even the city's most marginal structures—barns and sheds—could be repurposed. When the ardor of the Bowery Village congregation cooled to such a degree that some dubbed the schoolhouse/meetinghouse an "ice house," detractors walked down to the "Christie Street Prayer Meeting." Here in a large open shed, a mid-nineteenth-century minister remembered, "Under less restraints, perhaps, than they felt in their churches, the people could exercise their gifts with all the freedom, if not all the grace of primitive simplicity." Structures could just as quickly transition back to secular uses. After worshippers returned to the Bowery Village congregation, the Christie Street Prayer Meeting reverted to its less illustrious former role.[71]

Storefront churches offered one of the most important, and lasting, innovations in evangelical sacred space. They typify the intersection and accommodation of the secular and the sacred within urban settings. The cost of purchasing a lot with a meetinghouse or building a new one in the compactly settled city proved prohibitive for many new congregations. They could, however, afford to rent a commercial structure. In the 1760s, a rigging loft on Horse-and-Cart (now William) Street (fig. 1.4) became one of the city's first storefront churches, housing, successively, a Baptist, Methodist, and a schismatic Anglican congregation.[72] In the structure's open loft, designed for craftsmen working with rope for ships, evangelicals found a convenient space for

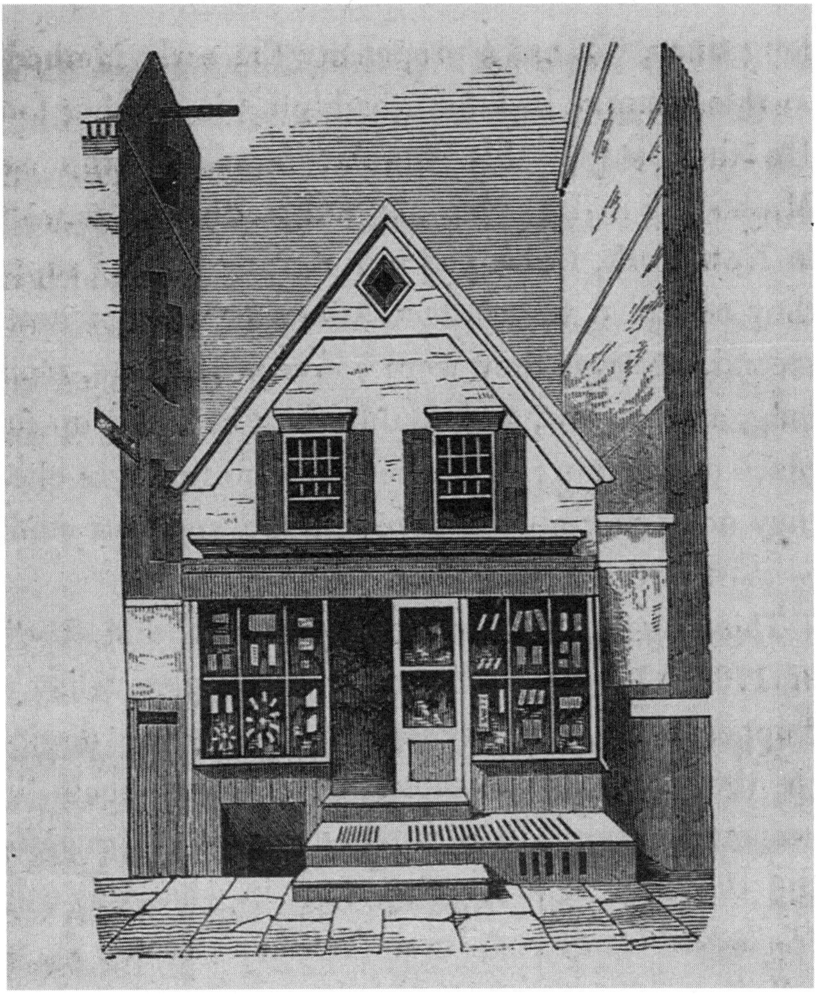

FIGURE 1.4 Joseph Beekman Smith, "Old Rigging Loft," in J. P. Wakeley, *Lost Chapters Recovered from the Early History of American Methodism* (New York, 1858)

worship and set about distilling an auditory church down to its constitutive elements: an unobstructed room, a pulpit, and seats. Storefront churches were a temporary means to an end; when the congregation raised enough money to build a new meetinghouse elsewhere, they moved out. By the antebellum period, storefront churches were ubiquitous throughout the city. For most new congregations, they offered the only affordable means of securing space.

The goal for every evangelical congregation was to build its own house of worship. Evangelicals eschewed the rituals of sacralization common among nonevangelical Protestants and Roman Catholics. They preferred to call them meetinghouses, preaching houses, or chapels, rather than churches, the term they reserved for the people who met within them. An evangelical analogized the church as a structure in 1796: "The owner, the builder and maker is God, and it is his peculiar treasure. Christ is the foundation and *chief corner-stone*, and his house are we, built upon him, cemented together, a spiritual building; the foundation cannot fail, the corner-stone can never give way; neither can we fall to pieces or be separated from him."[73] A meetinghouse presented the congregation's public face to the world. It was a material embodiment of beliefs, practices, and people. Such structures demonstrated to the urban community the legitimacy of the congregation worshipping within.

New Yorkers deployed an emerging evangelical vernacular that came to dominate the design of their meetinghouses for decades to come.[74] The quintessential evangelical meetinghouse was a wooden, brick, or stone structure with a tripartite two-and-a-half story, gable-end façade fronting the street. It might have a cupola but very rarely a steeple. Cost and aesthetic preferences led congregations to eschew ostentatious detailing in favor of a pared-down Georgian or Federal style. Interiors often had little more than a wooden pulpit and pews (or, among the Methodists, movable benches). Meetinghouses like the Elizabeth Street African Methodist Episcopal Church (see fig. 1.3) made a much different statement on the landscape than nonevangelical churches like St. Paul's Chapel (1764–1766) (fig. 1.5).[75] They typically stood on side streets and at the backs of lots, rather than in places of prominence. Well suited to poor urban congregations, the evangelical vernacular could be built quickly and cheaply, provided an auditory conducive to preaching, and fit the constraints of the urban landscape.

Having surveyed the landscape and constructed spaces for worship, women and men settled into inhabiting the city as evangelical New Yorkers. One way of maintaining their relationship with God was by joining a church. When asked by the newly regenerate Juvenis which church he should join, John Stanford's Evangelicus dodged making a recommendation. Eighteenth-century itinerants owed their success to their ability to transcend denominational differences. They avoided advocating for any specific church in favor of the larger movement's goal of mass conversion.[76] But they did offer precepts to guide the selection process. First and foremost, Evangelicus argued, selection must be a matter of free inquiry, just as the decision to seek the New Birth had been. "Apply, therefore, to the New Testament, which contains the mind of Christ, for there alone you can find direction," he counseled. Find a

FIGURE 1.5 St. Paul's Protestant Episcopal Chapel in the *New-York Mirror, and Ladies' Literary Gazette,* October 20, 1827. Courtesy, American Antiquarian Society

congregation that best exemplifies the uncorrupted model of the primitive church, then "examine your affections, and see if the members of that church are likely to prove, in the general, of one heart and of one soul with yourself; for this will in a great measure determine your future happiness with them."[77] While the lives of converted New Yorkers could be as transitory as those of itinerant ministers, many eventually made their way into a church.

Some competed outright for new members. When James Kent, Chancellor of the State of New York, took up an appointment as professor of law at Columbia in the mid-1790s, many congregations hoped to have him as a member. One man imposed on Kent to attend a service at the fashionable Grace Protestant Episcopal Church. "It was a fine day, and the congregation was well represented," another later reminisced of that visit. "All the interior arrangements were not only convenient, but elegant: the aisles richly carpeted; the pews furnished in luxurious style; with gilt and purple-velvet prayer-books; the organ music of the most artistic kind, and the most celebrated opera singers to lead in the choir." Everything was calculated to make a good impression. When asked what he thought, Kent replied, "That sir, is what I should call very genteel worship" and soon after joined an evangelical Presbyterian church.[78]

A ritual of incorporation often served as a prerequisite for joining a church. In November 1791, Charles Lahatt met Rev. Adam Hamilton of the Second Baptist Church on the banks of the East River to make a spiritual crossing to secure admission into a higher state of dwelling. Hamilton baptized Lahatt by immersion in a ritual that looked backward to Christ's baptism at the hands of John the Baptist (Mark 1:4) and forward to Lahatt's taking a place among a church of believers. Most late eighteenth-century evangelicals embraced infant baptism, a reflection of high infant mortality rates as much as theological preference. Yet for Baptists, the sacrament signified a public confirmation of an individual's salvation through conversion and hence could only be performed on adults professing such assurance.[79] William Chappel's painting of an adult baptism at Corlaers Hook confirms just how public this ritual could be within an urban setting, as church members, family, friends, and gawkers gathered to watch (fig. 1.6).

Evangelicals settled into inhabiting their new congregations by purchasing a pew or, among Methodists, joining a class meeting. Pew ownership provided the laity with a demarcated and legally protected place within the meetinghouse as well as a stake in running the church.[80] Pews had different prices based on their locations in the sanctuary, often reinforcing a class-based hierarchy. The persistence of "negro pews" into the early nineteenth century became a point of significant contestation among black and white churchgoers over the message it relayed. Methodists, in contrast, rejected (initially at least) pew ownership for its overtones of class privilege. Realizing the value of material signs of ownership, they distributed quarterly class tickets to the faithful. Lay Methodists preserved these tickets as evidence of their belonging, of their right to inhabit a spiritual community.[81]

FIGURE 1.6 William P. Chappel, "No 29 / Baptising at the End of Water St / Corlies Hook N York on Sunday Mornings / 1811 / W P Chappel / No 29," ca. 1870s. The Metropolitan Museum of Art, The Edward W. C. Arnold Collection of New York Prints, Maps, and Pictures, Bequest of Edward W. C. Arnold, 1954. www.metmuseum.org

Inhabiting an urban religious community was not without its challenges. Tensions sometimes unfolded within the meetinghouse, the very space designed to nurture community. Upon returning from a trip to Great Britain in 1805, Divie Bethune discovered that his brother-in-law Andrew Smith's financial mismanagement had brought their firm into serious debt. An ensuing civil suit in city courts and an ecclesiastical trial in the Scotch Presbyterian meetinghouse caused significant anguish. Bethune was particularly aggrieved by Smith's ability to win over to his side their minister, Rev. John Mitchell Mason, and their beloved mother-in-law, Mrs. Isabella Marshall Graham. Mrs. Graham, in turn, used her influence to sway several leading members of the congregation against Bethune. It pained him that the "dear Mother whom I have always cherished & honoured, who hath known & approved my uprightness all along" would turn against him "thru warmth weakness & impatience of temper." In the end, he realized there was only one on whom he should depend. He credited the Lord with his deliverance, as the civil suit was decided in his favor and he was restored to full communion in the church.[82]

Sometimes tensions pitted whole factions against each other within a congregation, as African American evangelicals knew all too well. Enslaved New Yorkers flocked to hear Whitefield and other evangelicals preach before the Revolution, eagerly embracing the opportunity to exert, through conversion, a measure of autonomy denied to them by their owners in so many other facets of their lives. Within the protective walls of the meetinghouse, they found the same opportunities for connection with the Lord that white converts enjoyed. In fact, urban African Americans appear to have responded more favorably to evangelicalism than their white counterparts (see the appendix). Despite the fervent dedication of John Wesley to antislavery, the American Methodist Episcopal church's commitment slipped soon after its formation in 1784.[83] Other evangelical denominations similarly wrestled with their stances. This, of course, reflected larger societal trends. Unlike other northern states, New York politicians balked at talk of emancipation in the 1777 Constitutional Convention and again in a 1785 bill put forward by the New York Manumission Society. An emancipation act did not pass until 1799, and even then, it granted only gradual freedoms.[84] Spatial marginalization in "negro pews" reinforced African Americans' sense of spiritual marginalization within the life of the community. Before long, evangelicals began to found autonomous, if not fully independent, black Baptist, Methodist, and Protestant Episcopalian congregations in the first two decades of the nineteenth century.[85]

Inhabiting the city also required learning how to be in the world but not of it. As a bustling commercial entrepôt with a heterogeneous population drawn from all over the Atlantic World, New York offered vibrant spiritual and secular marketplaces full of opportunities for godly living as well as temptations to fall away from it. The narratives of urban evangelicals remind us that their selves were profoundly situational. "City people think with each other," one scholar explains. "They tell complicated stories about their neighbors that are also stories about themselves, about their own fears, hopes, needs, and desires."[86] The diverse ideas circulating around the city's parlors and workshops stood in dialogue with broader commercial, recreational, and spiritual trends. They forced New Yorkers to define their subjective selves in ways they had not while in the homogenous communities from which they often hailed. While interactions with fellow New Yorkers outside of the meetinghouse could be the cause of significant anxiety, they ultimately strengthened rather than weakened their faith.

Some found themselves torn between their evangelical religious communities and the city's vibrant social world. As Joanna Graham walked up Broadway each Sunday to attend the Scotch Presbyterian church on Cedar Street, she passed the fine homes of her mother's students in which she socialized during the week. "I was trying to serve God and Mammon," Graham later recalled of her balancing act. That changed in the winter of 1793–94 when Divie Bethune convinced her to attend evening prayer meetings and lectures at city churches with him instead. One weeknight, when a minister canceled his lecture, Graham found herself with no excuse to turn down an invitation to a ball. As soon as she arrived, her host railed her for being overly religious. Increasingly self-conscious, Graham tried to dance but could only think about her spiritual state. When the master of the house joked before dinner that he had said grace coming down the stairs "to save time," a joke "heartily" enjoyed by many of the other guests, Graham reached her tipping point. "I almost feared to look around, and feared lest the earth should open and swallow us up," she recalled; "but I thought myself the most guilty of all, for I knew better, had been trained in the nurture of the Lord from my youth up, nay, had professed at the table of the Lord to renounce the pomps and vanities of this world."[87] Graham later married Bethune and became one of the city's most active evangelical reformers.

Others found that the spiritual and the sacred collided in their very spaces of work. Samuel Seabury III, grandson of the first Episcopal Bishop in the United States and son of an Anglican minister who had fallen on hard times, resented being put out as an apprentice to a Presbyterian cabinetmaker "in a place that abounded [with] dissenters and sectaries of every description."[88] Despite his lowly surroundings, Seabury never lost his high-church disdain for popular religion, but his outsider's view is valuable. New York's artisan community tended to embrace faiths—such as evangelicalism but, by the same token, also deism—that reinforced a sense of workshop egalitarianism and distance from the mercantile elite, many of whom worshipped in Protestant Episcopal or Reformed Dutch churches.[89] Seabury's master professed devotion to evangelical family prayer and Sabbath worship, but "his religion never reached as far as his workshop." Obscene songs and profane language were the idiom of Seabury's fellow laborers, which included a journeyman "deist of the Tom Paine school" and a temperamental apprentice whose evangelical conversion turned him "suddenly from singing songs and swearing to quoting scripture and repeating aloud all prayers and collects in the prayerbook." In the end, Seabury's exposure to evangelicalism and other faiths only strengthened his own Episcopalianism.[90]

Through their strategies for dwelling, evangelical New Yorkers built not only congregations but the very city itself in the generation following the American Revolution. By orienting the disoriented, constructing and gathering churches, and inhabiting spaces sacred and secular, they situated themselves within the city and created the loci around which it grew. All faced the challenge of maintaining their individual relationship with God on the one hand while learning how to be in the world but not of it on the other. Neither proved easy, but there were ever-increasing numbers of congregations to support them by the outbreak of the War of 1812.

EVANGELICAL GOTHAM

Evangelical Gotham began to emerge in the midst of New York City in the generation following the American Revolution. Those responsible for its growth were not elite real estate developers but common laborers and artisans. They had been displaced and pushed into the northern wards by merchants building up the city's import and export trade along Manhattan's waterfront docks. Their new neighborhoods, such as the one at Bowery Village, constituted a "plebeian belt" that girded the northern boundary of the city.[91] Anchoring these communities were evangelical churches, like the Bowery Village Methodist Episcopal Church, in which tradesmen, rather than merchants, served as trustees, class leaders, and elders. "The main source of authority for artisan [evangelicals], especially men from the poorer trades, lay closer to home," reflects one historian. "Tradesmen ran the New York chapels and appeared to do so with bravado."[92] Over the coming decades, there would be scores more for them to run.

Most of the city's twenty-eight churches in 1790 were located south of Chambers Street, no more than a mile from the tip of Manhattan (map 1.1). These overwhelmingly Protestant churches—the city had only one synagogue and one Roman Catholic congregation—served a population of 33,131. Their construction predated the Revolution and made up nodes in a tight-knit world where no point was more than a fifteen-minute walk from another.[93] All were arranged in relation to a residual colonial order that gave established national churches—typically nonevangelical—prominent sites. (Most of the ten evangelical meetinghouses were relegated to the margins.) Only one evangelical church stood north of Chambers Street in 1790, a Methodist Episcopal Church erected the previous autumn on Second (now Forsyth) Street on land confiscated from the loyalist Delancey family and recently opened for settlement.[94] Minutes of the Methodist General Conference justified construction

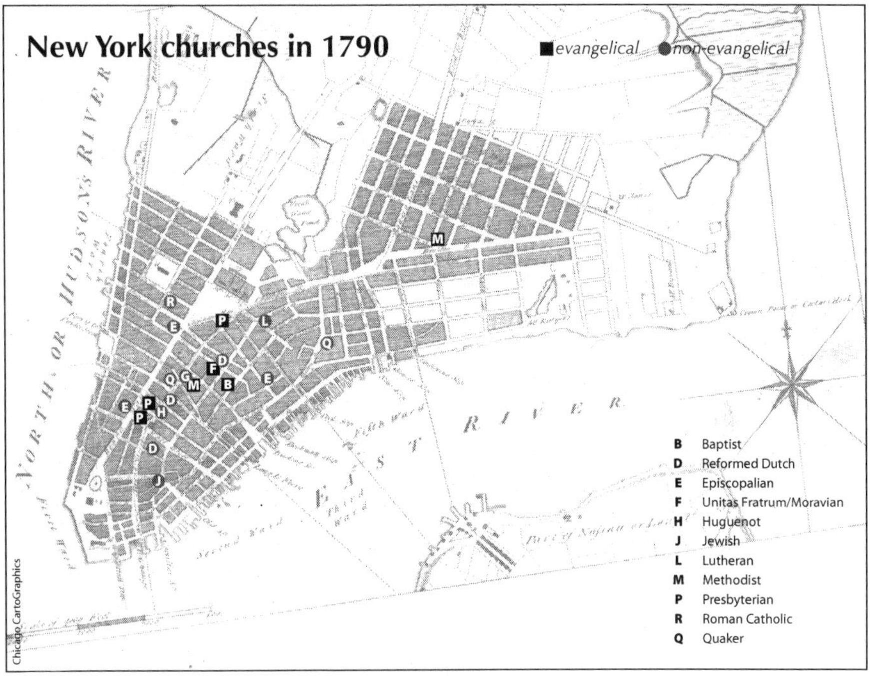

MAP 1.1 New York City in 1790, by Dennis McClendon

of a second church in response to a "great revival and a great increase" in interest in Methodism. The decision to locate in the "north or north-east part of the city" reflected the denomination's response to the expense and scarcity of land, its appeal to laborers and artisans who populated the new northern neighborhoods, and its desire to be on the forward edge of urban growth.[95] Other evangelical denominations followed suit.

Nearly every one of the two dozen new churches constructed over the next twenty years opened north of Chambers Street. Most were built by evangelical denominations. Part of this northward shift was practical: the city had experienced dramatic population growth, tripling to 96,373, and much of the available space for building below Chambers had been taken. More important, however, was the desire of the religious to take an active role in city building. Urban settlement expanded along two northward axes into what had once been farmland. One axis ran parallel to the Hudson River along the line of Greenwich Street, eventually connecting the city with the small community at Greenwich Village. The other ran through the center

MAP 1.2 New York City in 1810, by Dennis McClendon

of the island along the Bowery Road up to Bowery Village. Comparing the tight clustering of churches in the prewar city with the diffusion of churches along these axes reveals the extent to which these churches sought to provide the nucleus for new urban communities (map 1.2). Microclusters of two or three churches remind us that these congregations saw themselves in competition with each other. Evangelical denominations dominated this process of city building, planting most of their eighteen new churches in this area. Quite simply, they provided the shock troops of urban settlement.

Two distinct emplacement strategies—planting and schism—drove the expansion of the postrevolutionary urban spiritual landscape. Ambitious denominations with strong, centralized, and hierarchical denominational leadership structures—namely, the Methodist Episcopals, Protestant Episcopals, and Presbyterians—used their organizational arrangement to make coordinated decisions about where to plant new congregations. They deputized ministers and well-connected laity to gather the necessary financial resources to build what were often speculative structures, houses of worship without congregations. Records of the meetings of the annual Methodist General Conference and the Presbyterian Synod detail these efforts to expand their place within the urban spiritual marketplace. When the Methodist Conference, for example, wanted to start a new church, the bishops and constituent ministers appointed one of their own to raise a subscription and secure a location.[96] Methodists tended to build on the furthest edge of urban settlement. Aware of the typically speculative nature of meetinghouse building, they first fostered prayer meetings in private homes and shops to make sure a potential community existed.[97] Presbyterians did not go as far out or put so much effort into antecedent prayer groups. Their new meetinghouses stood in closer proximity to more settled communities, hoping to attract congregants from older churches.

Schism provided the other dominant mode of religious expansion. The challenges of trying to serve diverse urban audiences within a competitive spiritual marketplace made evangelical churches particularly susceptible to internal dissension. The frequent concentration of Baptist churches within a few blocks of each other reflects such a history.[98] The settlement of Rev. William Parkinson at First Baptist Church in spring 1805 ushered in several years of congregational growth but also brought acrimony, inspiring schisms. In 1807, African American members of First Baptist requested permission to form their own church but were denied. Two years later, eighteen men and women walked out and formed the Abyssinian Baptist Church in a meetinghouse formerly used by a Scotch Baptist congregation.[99] That same year, women and men in the northwest section of the city broke away to form the North Baptist Church instead of walking downtown.[100] After Parkinson was exonerated from accusations of adultery and improper advances toward several female parishioners in 1812, a group of outraged members formed the Zoar Church a few blocks away on Rose Street. All drew on the confidence imparted by conversion to question the authority of their ministers and established their own congregations, purified of distracting influences.

Building new meetinghouses was one thing; filling the pews, something else entirely. The speculative nature of this enterprise is nicely illustrated by

Rev. Stephen N. Rowan's salary dispute with the Reformed Dutch church at Greenwich Village in 1818. When Rowan was settled as the church's first minister in the autumn of 1807, there were only thirty-one members in full communion. The number of "ordinary hearers," adult women and men who attended worship but were not in full communion, was so small, he dramatically commented, "you might have planted a cannon, and firing it off in almost any direction, it would scarcely have killed any body."[101] Ten years later, however, every pew was taken—and in some pews, he proudly noted, sat more than one family. The number of members in full communion stood at 164, and the number of ordinary hearers had greatly increased as well.[102] He carefully gave the Lord the credit for this "*favorable* change" in temporal and spiritual affairs, but reminded readers of his resignation sermon that "still the fact exists" that it happened under his watch.[103] Soon after, Rowan began the whole speculative process again when he led a small faction out of the church to form the Eighth Presbyterian Church a few blocks south.[104]

Rowan's recollection of the growth of the Greenwich Village congregation under his ministry reminds us of the assiduous quantification undertaken by New York's religious communities and the challenges—then and now—of how we count the religious. Each of the major evangelical denominations collected statistics on their membership and reported them to various local, regional, and national associations. Rowan argued that when counting a church's membership, one has to take into account not only the number of individuals who had some form of conversion experience and joined in full membership but also their families and those adults who regularly attended but had not yet experienced conversion. Yet the numbers reported by the Methodists, Baptists, and Presbyterians reflect only those in full communion, a fraction of the actual number of evangelical worshippers.[105]

Reported membership data does reveal a boom in evangelical church membership in the first decade of the nineteenth century. All three of the city's leading evangelical denominations witnessed significant growth between 1800 and 1816 after the relative stasis of the 1790s. Baptists and Methodists saw their numbers more than triple, while Presbyterians grew fourfold (see table A.4 in the appendix). This growth speaks to two unrelated but mutually reinforcing factors: the recoalescing of the evangelical community into churches after the upheaval of the revolutionary period, and an extended period of economic unpredictability that began with Jefferson's Embargo of 1807.[106] In fact, accessions occurred most rapidly between 1807 and the outbreak of war in 1812. The growth of evangelical church membership significantly outpaced the overall urban population, which increased by only 54 percent.[107] By 1816, an estimated one in ten adult New Yorkers were members of an evangelical church.

Revivalism, a period of heightened religious activity marked by an outpouring of the Holy Spirit, brought new converts into urban churches during this time. Evangelicals believed that revivals typically began when the Lord allowed the influence of the Holy Spirit to move a few pious people and then spread through entire congregations. The real gain came when the Holy Spirit began to convert significant numbers from the outside world. "Wherever God is pleased to manifest his power and grace, in enlarging the views, in enlivening and invigorating the graces of his own people, and in turning the hearts of considerable numbers of his enemies, at the same time to seek and secure his pardoning mercy, there, is a revival of religion," explained Gardiner Spring of the Brick Presbyterian Church.[108] The Lord controlled the influence of the Holy Ghost on people's hearts and decided whether to send down a single drop or an entire shower, converting one or one thousand. Early nineteenth-century evangelicals, raised on their parents' and grandparents' memories of the colonial revivals under Whitefield and the Wesleys, spent much of their time praying for a new era of revivals, often tinged with millenarian expectations.

Historians have treated late eighteenth- and early nineteenth-century revivalism as a frontier phenomenon, slighting what was actually happening in urban America. A massive camp meeting at Cane Ridge, Kentucky, in early August 1801 has been celebrated as the starting point of an extended period of revivalism known as the "Second Great Awakening." Revivals in rural communities running along the line of settlement from Maine to Kentucky followed in its wake over the next few decades.[109] Urban revivals that do receive scholarly attention tend to date to a much later period, often in the wake of the Panics of 1837 or 1857.[110] Yet nineteenth-century evangelicals knew better. Urban revivals had been happening from the 1780s onward.[111] Early ones tended to occur within specific congregations, but in time revivalism spread citywide across all denominations.

Speculative churches, like the Rutgers Street Presbyterian Church, depended on revivalism. The Rutgers Street Church was initiated in 1797 when wealthy landowner Col. Henry Rutgers, Esq., donated a lot in the Seventh Ward. Soon a "handsome, well proportioned and capacious" wood frame meetinghouse with "suitable cupola or steeple, and excellent clock and bell" arose on the eastern edge of urban settlement.[112] Presbyterian churches at that time operated within a collegiate system, meaning that all connected churches shared a common body of ministers who rotated their pulpit assignments each week. Rutgers Street thus had no settled minister for its first few years, languishing as an outlier to the centrally located Wall Street and Brick churches. That changed in November 1805 with the installation of Philip Milledoler as its settled minister. Within a matter of months, the congregation emerged as one of the fastest growing and most active in the city.

New Yorkers who failed to heed the call during times of peace and prosperity filled meetinghouses in times of adversity, especially in the lead up to a second war with Great Britain. In late February 1808, Milledoler noted that the prospects for a revival seemed brighter than at any time since he took charge of the congregation. He was in a good position to know. The revival that came that winter was the third of five major revivals he oversaw between 1805 and 1813.[113] It occurred on the heels of Jefferson's Embargo, which had gone into effect that winter and hit the maritime neighborhood surrounding the Rutgers Church particularly hard. "How shall I describe the melancholy dejection that was painted upon the countenances of the people, who seemed to have taken leave of all their former gaiety and cheerfulness?" English traveler John Lambert asked in that spring. The previous fall, "the port was filled with shipping, and the wharfs were crowded with commodities of every description," he wrote. "All was noise and bustle." No longer. Closed-up countinghouses, dismantled shipping, and vacated coffee houses blotted the new landscape. Grass had even begun to grow on the wharves.[114] Local residents flocked to the Rutgers Street Church in the midst of the downturn. In March, twenty-five women and men joined the church on examination of their oral confessions of faith.[115] For all who made the life-changing decision to subject their religious experiences to examination for membership, scores more participated in revival but did not formally join the church.

Urban revivalists like Milledoler created a variety of opportunities for seekers to encounter the gospel message. In an average week during the winter 1808 revival, Milledoler preached three times on Sunday, sometimes to crowds numbering 1,800 to 2,000. On Wednesday evenings he delivered a lecture on some aspect of spiritual rebirth or holy living in the "Welsh Church," an abandoned meetinghouse across the street.[116] Thursday evenings were left free for "enquiry" meetings, informal support groups for those under conviction. Finally, on Friday evenings he returned to the Welsh Church for an evening prayer meeting. He also went out into the community to meet the awakened and curious in their homes. Mrs. Freelove Britain invited him to her house to meet with a group of young persons concerned for their souls. A week later that number grew even larger. "Some of them were members who thought they were not invited to come under various pretexts to be witnesses of what the Lord is doing for us," he reflected in his diary, "upwards of 20 persons came to enquire what they should do to be saved, and we have heard since of others who on that evening were not present with us."[117] As the revival grew, all eagerly anticipated the upcoming communion season, the first opportunity for the newly converted to make formal professions and take their place among their new spiritual family.

The spiritual community that formed inside the walls of the Rutgers Street meetinghouse reflected and reinforced the economic and social webs found in the neighborhood outside. New converts were predominantly female, about twice as many married as single, and only three joined with their husbands. The smaller number of male converts was evenly split between single and married. This gender imbalance reflects the larger trajectory of Milledoler's tenure, and antebellum urban evangelicalism more generally, during which more than 70 percent of new converts were female.[118] Most lived within a few blocks' radius of the church. Their employments reflected the economic reality of life on the edge of urban settlement: shoemakers, carpenters, cartmen, laborers, and widows constituted the body of Milledoler's church, a far cry from the merchants and other professionals who dominated the older Presbyterian churches in the city's core. They lived in large households, composed of members of their extended family, servants, slaves, and apprentices. Yet for all who found conversion during the seasons of revival, there were many others, including the husbands of many congregants, who slipped by without an experience.

Revivalists preferred to channel the newly converted into church membership but some invariably spilled out of the meetinghouse and into the street, forcing ministers to move quickly to curtail their efforts. Emboldened by the confidence that came with conversion, a handful of men and women even began to exhort the world that had yet to beat a path to evangelicalism's door. During the winter 1808 revival, Philip Milledoler discovered that two lay members had taken up exhorting. Acknowledging that "what they have done, they have done in Zeal and simplicity of their hearts," he still let it be known, through mutual friends, that they should confine themselves to Christian conversation and prayer.[119] William Parkinson of the First Baptist Church similarly tried to rein in three young men in November 1809 who had been "speaking at the Alms house from passages of scripture." When the offenders acknowledged their wrongdoing and promised to be more obedient, the normally punitive congregation "chastised them and let them go."[120] Evangelicals preferred to kindly, but firmly, redirect the enthusiastic, rather than suppress them entirely.

City residents were more than willing to step in when evangelicals failed to keep their renegade exhorters in line, often through less humane tactics.

Johnny Edwards, a Welsh scale-beam maker who had been variously affiliated with Anglican, Methodist, Baptist, and Quaker congregations, joined efforts with Dorothy Ripley in the spring of 1810 to host an outdoor revival. Still upset about the "Church of Christ" that Edwards had convened in his house the previous year, mobs of nonevangelical New Yorkers rioted. Walking a fine line between preserving public order and respecting freedom of conscience, the Common Council sought to defuse such situations without angering either side. It passed a law against "disorderly assemblies of persons in the City of New York" in the hope of eliminating mobs by removing the cause for disorder. When Ripley rose to preach, city officials arrested her.[121]

Even more notorious evangelical Amos Broad set up a church on Rose Street, near the city's new Baptist meetinghouses, around the same time and met a similar end. Broad was widely known for his trial and conviction for beating his slave Betty and her three-year-old daughter. He sought licensing as a Baptist preacher but tried to circumvent the city's churches by applying to an out-of-town church for sponsorship. When First Baptist got wind of his request, it made sure he was denied. The Common Council continued to protect Broad's freedom of conscience, but when the mobs surrounding his meetinghouse grew to upward of a thousand strong, its patience ran out. Broad plea-bargained and escaped conviction in return for selling his meetinghouse.[122] Edwards and Broad represented the disorder that evangelicals feared from zealous converts not content to just look inward.

By the eve of the War of 1812, Evangelical Gotham had emerged as a thriving network of churches, pious converts, anxious seekers, and a handful of renegade preachers who refused to seek denominational approval. They preferred to locate themselves on the edges of urban settlement, although they also had congregations in the core of the city. Revivalism often provided the engine for expanding the membership rolls of their speculative meetinghouses. In general, they waited for converts to come to them, rather than going out and looking for them, although this changed in the coming generation. As the postrevolutionary generation who brought this world into being approached the ultimate horizon, they often looked back on what they and God had accomplished.

CELESTIAL CITY OR VANITY FAIR?

At some point in the construction of their autobiographical narratives, evangelical New Yorkers invariably reflected on the place of New York in their spiritual journeys. While they were united by a shared affection for John Bunyan's narrative, many saw it as a lexicon on which to draw rather than a template to follow. The wide variance in their engagement reminds us that their narratives are not hagiographies but truly popular tales written by ordinary folk.[123] For Charles Lahatt, New York was one of many stops along a lifetime's journey. Like so many, he kept moving after a few years' residency in the city. George White saw New York through the lens of the biblical narrative of Exodus, as did so many fellow African American evangelicals. For him, New York was a land of deliverance, although it held its share of disappointments.[124] And for Divie Bethune, New York was the Celestial City. "Thou alone knowst O Lord, what great things Thou hast done for me; Thou hast led me from that sink of iniquity, that blackness of darkness, Tobago, & brought me into the light of the liberty of thy children in the midst of a favor'd church, & a highly privileged City," he repeated throughout his adult life.[125] Bethune and White spent the remainder of their lives in the "highly privileged City." For a generation made mobile by war, ambition, enslavement, and privation, New York was more than a Vanity Fair. It was a safe harbor in a storm, a conflicted land of deliverance, and even a heavenly reward.

Narratives of postrevolutionary New Yorkers reflect the ironies of evangelical storytelling. For all the insight they provide into their writers' subjective selves, they are silent on one important element. Bunyan cleverly structured his narrative around a dream in which the reader witnesses not only Christian's lifetime journey but also his passing over to the Celestial City. No living evangelical could pen as complete a narrative, however, for none could assume the voice of an omniscient narrator. Charles Lahatt wrote his spiritual autobiography near the end of his life in the hope of discerning whether he had achieved salvation, but he could never record if he made it to the other side. George White responded to this dilemma by publishing deathbed narratives for two others. The pious death of his wife Mary Henery gave him hope for his own successful passage to the world to come, while the death of an impious husband served as a cautionary tale. As Henery greeted death with joyous shouts—"the chariot is coming—are you all ready? Are you all ready? Now! Now! Here it comes. Glory! Glory! Glory! . . . Mother, are you shouting? Jane, are you shouting? Are you all shouting?"—the impious husband attempted to run away, convinced that he saw death coming for him.[126] Evangelicals utilized these narratives to anticipate what they (and their readers) might expect when the time came to cross the ultimate horizon.

In the end, the faithful could only rest on the assurance that came with conversion and the knowledge that they had spent their lives devoted to crossing and dwelling. "I am now waiting for the common pale messenger at God's bidding to call me hence to where peace, and pure heavenly pleasure reigns for ever," Charles Lahatt wrote at the end of his spiritual autobiography.[127] In the interim, Lahatt, George White, Sarah Sergeant Miller, Divie Bethune and Joanna Graham Bethune, and many others crossed over into a state of salvation through conversion and transformed New York City into a place where they could dwell with like-minded others. They did so as church builders, lay exhorters, ministers' wives, supporters of voluntary societies, and in many other capacities. Their legacy lay in Evangelical Gotham, a dynamic evangelical community in the midst of the nation's fastest growing city. Others would soon take up the charge to convince fellow New Yorkers to join the work.

CHAPTER TWO

The Widow, the Missionary, and the Prostitute

When an eminent minister scheduled to address "a large and respectable audience" at the Presbyterian Church on Cedar Street failed to show in October 1810, a young minister seized the unexpected opportunity to speak. Though he had prepared no comments, Ezra Stiles Ely spoke of what he had come to know all too well during his short time in New York, and what his audience, to his dismay, failed to comprehend: the spiritual suffering of the city's destitute. In the aftermath of Jefferson's Embargo, most New Yorkers acknowledged the necessity of public relief and institutions to alleviate the physical suffering of the less fortunate but ignored their souls. Ely reminded the gathered that in the almshouse resided paupers "too old, or too lame, or too blind, or too feeble to go from their rooms to the Churches in the city" and for whom no provision had been made to hear the gospel. Patients in the hospital fared little better; "while their worm-eaten bodies have been objects of attention, their immortal souls have been wholly neglected!" Ely's audience hardly believed him, he later recalled, but pressed him to publish the substance of his comments. "You attend public and private worship regularly, instruct your families, associate in religious societies, and do much for Christ," Ely concluded; "Very well: but you might do more."[1]

"Doing more" for the city's destitute was something evangelical New Yorkers generally left to others. Few would have denied the obligation to charity under which all men and women labored as Christians; the well-known parable of the Good Samaritan (Luke 10:25–37) pervaded eighteenth-century sermons and devotional manuals.[2] One of the great contributions of British preachers to the nascent evangelical movement was to couple individual conversion with social activism. Conversion obliged the regenerate to embrace the missionary spirit, as evangelicals called it, the responsibility to spread the gospel to the unconverted. George Whitefield, John Wesley, and others pointed to Christ's "great commission" to Matthew (Matt. 28:19)—"Go ye therefore, and teach all nations"—to justify itinerant preaching and the creation of benevolent institutions.[3] But postrevolutionary evangelical New Yorkers concentrated more on rebuilding meetinghouses and regathering scattered congregations than ministering to those beyond their religious communities.

Evangelical activism emerged in fits and starts in the generation following the American Revolution. New Yorkers depended on state-sponsored institutions, private associations, and denominational support to care for the destitute immediately after the war. More a patchwork than a safety net, many fell through the cracks. Isabella Marshall Graham, a widow with young daughters, knew firsthand the privations facing the city's most vulnerable. She founded the Ladies' Society for the Relief of Poor Widows with Small Children, the city's first evangelical benevolent association, to provide temporal and spiritual support to keep these women in their homes. Ezra Stiles Ely, a recent graduate of Yale, arrived two decades after Graham. He saw in the almshouse and hospital a more pressing field of labor. If Graham provided evangelical New Yorkers with a model for voluntary association building, then Ely, though his published *Journals*, offered a nuanced introduction to the objects of their charity. Recording scores of encounters with almshouse residents and hospital patients, Ely preserved an unparalleled window into popular urban religiosity. Yet he did more than that. His *Journals* represent a deliberate effort to transform the responses of his evangelical readers to the city around them. The uncontested star of Ely's account was a young prostitute named Caroline, who may or may not have been what she seemed. Together, Graham, Ely, and Caroline transformed how evangelical New Yorkers thought about the women and men outside of their meetinghouses and inspired a rising generation to attempt to convert the city following the War of 1812.

THE SCATTERED ORIGINS OF EVANGELICAL BENEVOLENCE

Life in New York proved anything but stable in the decades immediately following the American Revolution. Those who fell on hard times often found limited sources of benevolence. The Common Council, the city's ruling body,

FIGURE 2.1 Arthur J. (Arthur Joseph) Stansbury (1781–1865), City Hall Park from the Northwest Corner of Chambers Street, ca. 1825. Watercolor from the collections of the Museum of the City of New York. 52.100.16

supported the indigent through outdoor relief and an expanding complex of public institutions. It preferred to provide the basic necessities—food, fuel, clothing, and sometimes money—that allowed the needy to live in their own homes or neighboring households. For those exceptionally burdensome cases incapable of caring for themselves and wanting friends or family, the city built an almshouse in 1736 on the common, then the northern edge of settlement (now City Hall Park). Sixty years later, overcrowding prompted the construction of a massive new structure, three stories high and 260 feet long (fig. 2.1). At a cost of $130,000, the new almshouse was a major capital expense. The spare structure blended into the urban landscape, indistinguishable, except in its austerity, from blocks of row houses and counting-houses going up all over the city.[4] Nearby stood the public hospital.[5]

Often the Common Council depended on private associations to provide benevolence. An English visitor listed thirty-one benevolent associations in the city in November 1807.[6] Most had as their mission either to provide funds, such as the House Carpenters' Society (instituted 1806), for "the relief of sick and infirm members, and their widows and children," or to support institutions, such as the New York Dispensary (founded 1795), which provided services to the disadvantaged.[7] Private associations typically coalesced around specific categories of affiliation, such as ethnicity, vocation, or political affiliation, or around a certain type of institutional offering, such as education or medicine.[8] Some, as the English visitor surmised, were "mere benefit societies," the forerunner of modern-day life insurance companies, which allowed men and women to contribute annually to a fund on which they might draw someday.[9] Channeling the republican spirit of the day, these voluntary associations wrote constitutions, elected officers and boards of directors, and were frequently chartered by the state.

Churches also offered support to indigent members. Record books of the city's Presbyterian, Baptist, and Methodist congregations document that collections were regularly taken up for the poor. Sometimes these came at the request of the Common Council or specific benevolent associations, but more often they reflected the churches' sense of duty and obligation to sick and needy congregants. Records of the Methodist Poor Fund reveal an active system of benevolence that primarily aided women. In 1795, for example, fifty-two out of sixty-seven recipients of aid, mainly cash or firewood, were women. They included servants, former slaves, and widows; most, however, were white and of childbearing age. Young Methodist laymen formed an "Assistance Society for relieving and advising sick & poor persons in the city of New York" when Jefferson's Embargo strangled the city. They divided New York into five different walks and set about visiting poor Methodists within those districts. They made their first disbursements in January 1809 and continued for several years.[10] Urban Methodists offered their followers a generous helping hand, regardless of status, and even paid for funerals when required.[11]

Into this mix of state, private, and denominational support appeared the Ladies' Society for the Relief of Poor Widows with Small Children (SRPW). Initiated by Isabella Marshall Graham in November 1797 at the behest of her daughter Joanna and incorporated by the state in April 1802, the SRPW was the first association in the city run by and for women, the first explicitly evangelical voluntary association, and one of the few that offered relief regardless of affiliation. As the name suggests, the subjects of its benevolence were some of the city's most vulnerable residents. Like other benevolent associations, the society sought to keep its recipients out of the almshouse by providing them with clothing, fuel, and employment. Contemporary observers marveled at its organizational structure and noted, with interest, the unusual financial responsibility placed on its female officers. Equally important, the society offered its recipients both temporal and spiritual support.[12]

Isabella Marshall Graham's personal experience of widowhood made her sensitive to the importance of benevolent relief for women in a similar position. Born in Scotland in 1742, Graham arrived in North America in August 1767 with her husband, John, a surgeon in the Royal American regiment. She spent four years at Fort Niagara, a period that proved a spiritual as well as a literal time in the wilderness. With no religious services to speak of in the isolated garrison, she turned to the Bible and to evangelical classics like Doddridge's *Rise and Progress of Religion in the Soul* to sustain her.[13] The outbreak of hostilities forced the removal of her young family to Antigua, via a short visit in New York, in 1772. She gained in religious conviction among the Methodist and Moravian missionaries on the Caribbean island but lost her husband to "the putrid fever" within a year. Widowhood left her with three daughters under the age of five in a foreign port and little temporal support.[14] Like other similarly situated women, Graham turned to teaching, first back in Scotland and later in New York. The young ladies' academy she established in the city in 1789 allowed her to support her growing family. It also gave her the administrative skills and social contacts indispensable to running a voluntary association.[15]

Widowhood provided Graham with a powerful sense of her duty to work on behalf of others. "My whole life, from fifteen till the thirtieth year of my age, was one continued succession of departure and backsliding on my part; of chastening, forgiving, restoring, and comforting on the part of my God," she wrote in September 1800 to a young woman undergoing the throes of conversion. "When lighter afflictions proved ineffectual," she remembered, "He at last, at one blow, took from me all that made life dear, the very kernel of all my earthly joys, my idol, my beloved husband. Then I no longer halted between two opinions; my God became my all." Thirty years on, Graham saw a spiritual silver lining to her loss, although her writings at the time of her husband's death suggest that she possessed anything but clarity.[16] Graham devoted her life to helping others seek rebirth in the Lord, who was, in the language of one of Graham's favorite scriptural passages, "a father to the fatherless, a husband to the widow, the stranger's shield and orphan's stay."[17]

Graham followed with interest the news coming off English ships docked at New York wharves about rising evangelical interest in the missionary spirit. Laid up at home with a sprained ankle one day in 1796, she read imported missionary magazines and reminisced about the formative impact of her time at Antigua. "How many such stragglers as I, may be wandering in both East and West Indies, and may be restored by these precious missionaries," she wrote to a friend; "I owe them, of my labours, more than others."[18] Graham was among the earliest supporters of the New-York Missionary Society and attended the first of the society's monthly prayer meetings in February 1798, happy to be there even if the meetinghouse "was far from full."[19] The missionary spirit flourished in her heart during these heady days. "I wish to serve religion some way," she confided to the same friend. "I feel very useless; the Lord does not give me fruit among my pupils."[20] Benevolence offered Graham another outlet for her evangelical impulses.

Devastating outbreaks of yellow fever terrorized New York in the 1790s and laid bare the weaknesses of the city's patchwork of state, private, and denominational benevolence. The 1795 outbreak killed upward of 750 over three months and smaller flare-ups followed in subsequent summers.[21] Unable to flee the city, Graham witnessed the devastation firsthand. "I have now in my house a girl who lost both father and mother, and many whole families were cut off;" she wrote to a friend in Scotland. "My house was emptied; my school broken up; we confined to town, and heavy duty laid upon us."[22] Hardship overwhelmed the city's benevolence sources. Private ethnic associations did what they could, but their beneficence was limited to certain applicants. Graham's son-in-law, Divie Bethune, was one of the distributing managers for the St. Andrew's Society, the association for Scottish immigrants. Frustrated by the association's tribalistic boundaries in the face of widespread suffering, Graham's daughter (and Divie's wife) Joanna, collected small sums for the excluded. Graham consulted with a few friends on the propriety of proposing a female society for the support of poor widows "without limitation" and agreed to host an organizational meeting.[23]

The SRPW mobilized a broad coalition of evangelical women. Just as widows and small children were to be relieved "without the shadow of regard either to national distinction, or to religious persuasion," so, too, the women involved in the association came from a range of denominational backgrounds. A study of the officers and managers of the society over its first forty years reveals nearly equal numbers of Presbyterian and Protestant Episcopal women, followed by smaller numbers of Reformed Dutch, Methodist Episcopal, and Quaker women.[24] The leadership tended to be exclusively white and enjoyed a genteel standard of living, many of them married to merchants, physicians, lawyers, ministers, and others of professional position.[25] Sarah Ogden Hoffman was representative of their number. Born the same year as Graham, Hoffman also started a family at a young age and knew what it was like to suffer disappointment and affliction. Those afflictions, remembered Hoffman's biographer, "taught her the evils to which humanity is subject, [but] she learned the charming art of feeling for another's woe; and how to stretch forth the maternal hand of kindness to relieve."[26] The death of Hoffman's husband and daughter-in-law after protracted illnesses placed her at greater liberty to devote herself to helping others.

The SRPW's constitution, published in 1799, clearly laid out the conditions and nature of relief. Every manager was to list in a common record book the names, addresses, and circumstances of all widows and children served. Twice a month officers and managers of the society met to review the running record of granted aid and to receive a portion of the "society's bounty" to distribute among the widows for whom they had responsibility.[27] Any application for support began with an investigation of the widow's abode. The manager also inquired among her neighbors about her character; any indication of immorality excluded her from patronage. The society explicitly stated it only funded the distribution of items necessary to the support of the household. Afraid of fostering dependency, it strove to provide widows with employment that allowed them to remain within their homes and eventually support themselves.[28] While widows worked, their children either attended charity schools or were placed in a suitable trade; or, in cases of extreme disorder, were sent to live with other families. The ordered domesticity of a widow's own home, the society reminded applicants, was far preferable to the disordered domesticity of the city's almshouse.

Graham fantasized about the power of an idealized domestic encounter between the SRPW's agents and their recipients. "To us, our comfortable dwellings, cheerful fires, and convivial parties, give to winter its charms," she explained. "Alas, for her! the new-made widow! to whom all these are lost forever—to her, the approach of winter is as the approach of death!" While husbands sit down to dinner prepared by their wives, surrounded by their children, the widow "staggers to her dreary dwelling, and wakes to all the realities of her widowed state. The once cheerful chimney scarcely emits a taper blaze. Her children cry for bread, but her empty pantry affords it not." Managers might not be able to restore what was lost, but they could impart even greater gifts. Hope allowed the widow to dream once again of "schemes of industry" and to exert herself to become "father and mother to her orphans." Temporal resources helped her to regain her independence.[29] "How often, like angels of mercy commissioned from above," reflected another speaker, have the society's managers and officers "broken in upon the gloom that surrounded whole families, and brought a timely and most acceptable relief to their bodies and to their souls!"[30]

Despite their fantasies, these "angels of mercy" often discovered a different reality. The work of managers could be grueling and the needs of widows greater than anticipated. During a typical season of winter visiting, Graham and Hoffman met at ten o'clock in the morning and wandered the city until dusk looking for widows. "These were sometimes found in garrets, cellars and other places of obscurity, half-starved, destitute of clothing, and perishing with cold; while their infant children were clinging to the breast, and others looking wishfully for a morsel of bread to satisfy the cravings of hunger," their biographer explained.[31] The SRPW's optimism that every widow could be made independent and self-sufficient did not take into account the debilitating prevalence of disease or the city's tumultuous economy. Restrictions on what the SRPW would fund forced many managers to draw on their own resources. Some raided their own pantries or arranged to have meals cooked and delivered on a daily basis.[32] Others helped to pay widow's rents, even though the SRPW's constitution forbade it. In the aftermath of the 1799 yellow fever outbreak, many widows sold their best clothing and furniture to survive.[33] Others lucky enough to flee the city returned to find "nothing remaining but naked walls" and landlords clamoring for rent. In all, managers contributed upward of $300 from their own pocketbooks to address harsh realities that season.[34]

Spiritual sustenance, often through the distribution of religious tracts, accompanied temporal support. This happened as much, if not more, for the benefit of the managers as the widows. In private writings and public sermons, leaders and supporters of the society reinforced a vision of managers as active agents of evangelicalism's principles of conversion and social activism. "With the people of the world christians have much to do: they are fellow-members of society with them; they have many duties to perform to them, with them, and by them," Graham wrote in 1801.[35] Sermons preached by the city's leading evangelical ministers on behalf of the society encouraged managers in their benevolent work for its spiritual rewards. Philip Milledoler exhorted the society to be like the Christians of the primitive church, who knew "that love of God and benevolence toward man were inseparably connected."[36] Samuel Miller argued that women had both a proclivity toward and a responsibility for providing charity. His emphasis on the performance of good works as a sign of "vital union" with Christ through faith was a favorite evangelical theme.[37] "The simple fact is," wrote Gardiner Spring, "that the faith of the Gospel, and the works of the Gospel, necessarily and inseparably co-exist."[38] To be a good manager was to be a good evangelical.

Toward the end of their lives, Isabella Marshall Graham and Sarah Ogden Hoffman reflected, with varying degrees of candor, on their experiences within the city's first evangelical association. The SRPW had prospered, catalyzing the founding in 1806 of an Orphan Asylum Society to support the children of the widows they served. For Hoffman, all had gone well. "Unwearied in her long exertions to nourish and instruct these distressed objects," Hoffman's biographer recalled about her final days, "it was impossible but that her mind should review the scenes of her benevolence with satisfaction, that she had thus far served her generation by the will of her God."[39] But Graham's writings reveal a nagging fear that she had not done enough to convert the widows. The SRPW encouraged managers to offer religious advice and distribute tracts but stopped short of condoning active proselytizing. "How seldom have I endeavored to rescue my friend from sin and Satan, by leading her to the Friend of sinners, the source of happiness!" she lamented two years before her death in 1814.[40] That tension would persist within evangelical benevolence far into the future. Regardless, the work of Graham, Hoffman, and other members of the SRPW opened the door for other reformers and voluntary associations to venture even further into the city and to reach broader audiences.

PREACHER, POET, POLEMICIST

New York City in the spring of 1810 was a world apart from the rural Connecticut of Ezra Stiles Ely's youth. Even New Haven, where Ely spent four years as a student, could hardly compare to the great commercial seaport to its south. Ely's time in Connecticut awakened him not only to his own salvation but also to what opportunities the city might offer. New Englanders tired of farming stony ground were eager to cultivate new commercial ventures in New York after the end of the Revolution. In April 1810, the young minister joined their number. He entered the city with a satchel full of poems, a mind quick to debate, and a heart burning to convert. He expected to make an indelible mark.

Ezra Stiles Ely was born in 1786 in Lebanon, Connecticut. Son of the minister of the First Congregational church, he found in Lebanon a supportive community in which he experienced spiritual rebirth but also witnessed tensions simmering beneath the surface in an increasingly backwater, politically divided, one-church town.[41] At fourteen, he followed his father's footsteps into Yale with the intention of becoming a minister and studied under Timothy Dwight.[42] An aspiring poet, Ely would have known Dwight's paean to a pastoral New England town, *Greenfield Hill* (1794), as well as his anonymous rant against heterodoxy, *The Triumph of Infidelity* (1788).[43] In the classroom, Dwight sharpened the minds of his students with weekly debates on a range of historic and contemporary topics, while in the sanctuary he ignited their hearts to seek conversion through revivalism.[44] In this charged evangelical atmosphere, a generation of students (re)discovered the missionary spirit and committed themselves to converting the heathen on the frontier and in foreign lands. Some even made their way to the city. Ely later rejected Dwight's theological and political leanings but shared the divine's love of preaching, poetry, polemic, and revivalism.

Why Ely took a pulpit in rural Colchester upon graduation, after having experienced all New Haven had to offer, is unclear. Whether seeking a more fertile field for soul conquering or nursing a broken heart, Ely arrived in New York City in April 1810. He likely stayed with his younger brother Elisha, a merchant who had been in the city for several years.

Applying to the Presbytery of New York gave Ely insight into New York's religious landscape and an unexpected opportunity to test his college-honed debating skills. An unavoidable competition for congregants existed among the city's nine Presbyterian churches. Most ministers with city pulpits hailed from mid-Atlantic seminaries and looked with suspicion on the "New Divinity" of Yale and Andover. Given the paucity of evangelical New England ministers in the city, Ely might have welcomed the sight of another recent Yale graduate, Gardiner Spring, who had received a call from the Brick Presbyterian Church a few months earlier. In fact, just the opposite happened. When certain conservative ministers detected New Divinity sentiments in Spring's trial sermon, Ely quickly went on the attack against his former classmate. Through the intercession of a senior minister, Spring's confirmation eventually succeeded, but an unsatisfied Ely published a few months later *A Contrast between Calvinism and Hopkinsianism* (1811), a five-hundred-page polemic aimed at Spring, which forever earned Ely the scorn of New England ministers.[45]

The ambitious Ely soon had other productions rolling off city presses. A few months after *A Contrast*, Ely published a volume of poems. Perceiving a pattern in the work, one critic commented, "His poems were so lucky in the article of flattery, to certain great men he wished to please, that they effectually did his business for him."[46] Assuming the posture of a "son of Columbia," Ely offered a nationalist rationale for his work instead, arguing that Americans were just as well suited to write poetry as the British. He admitted his hope to make money off the publication, not for his own benefit but that of "a little child, whom the author, after repeated solicitation, consented to accept of a dying woman, that [his] mother might fall asleep in peace."[47] Appearing in one edition each, Ely's poetry and polemic were not very profitable.

Ely's preaching, not his polemics or poetry, cemented his memory in New York's evangelical circles. Ely was a preacher; his heart burned to spread the gospel (and his body needed the financial stability of a pulpit if he were to remain in the city). His brash challenge to Spring failed to secure him the only unfilled Presbyterian pulpit in the city. A call to a Reformed Dutch or Baptist church might have been attractive, although his now well-publicized doctrinal views likely gave congregations pause. Looking for a pulpit, Ely gambled on an unconventional and untried congregation—the destitute residents of the city's almshouse and hospital. Here, preaching was not unknown. Ministers such as the beloved Baptist Rev. John Stanford had occasionally preached in the city's public institutions for years.[48] No one, however, had succeeded in securing a full-time calling to this uniquely urban pulpit. Ely was about to change that.

The Journal of the Stated Preacher

Every Sunday and multiple times during the week, Ezra Stiles Ely preached the gospel just like ministers across rural Connecticut and urban New York, but in a far different sanctuary. He preached to people not neatly sitting in pews, subtly ranked by social and spiritual criteria, but stretched out on beds, crouched on the floor, or packed around the perimeter of the ward. Such conditions might have proven an indignity to many urban ministers and churchgoers, but for evangelicals like Ely bent on conversion, it only added to the allure. "To stand in a confined atmosphere, before a warm fire, amidst the sick, who are attentive," wrote Ely, "is not so painful to the heart as to preach in a spacious church, to empty seats, or to thoughtless people, who either whisper, cough needlessly, examine faces, or slumber."[49] Those who dared not cross the threshold of public institutions could live vicariously through his experiences by reading the two published *Journals* of his time there.[50]

The pew system of rural and urban churches ensured that ministers saw the same faces week after week, but Ely had no such luxury.[51] Each week he preached to a different ward in the almshouse and hospital. He might recognize the familiar faces of his more mobile followers, but he primarily addressed audiences confined to their beds by infirmity or old age. (Those who had no interest in his preaching lay doubly captive.) Competition occasionally arose among his hearers. "After public worship was concluded, a warm debate arose about the nomination of the ward where I should preach next," a flattered Ely recorded one day. "Seven or eight aged women were entreating for their turn next, and naming the number of their sick for arguments." The decision to plead mortality is an important reminder of the turnover in these institutions. In any given week, his auditors might pass on to the next world, be restored to life in this one (and not infrequently lose their religious convictions), or disappear back into the city. There were always more who desired his attention than could be served. "What can I do but serve them all in rotation?" he asked.[52]

The impermanence of life in the almshouse and hospital made the creation of a permanent congregation impractical, if not impossible. Ely not only lacked a dedicated sanctuary and a stable audience, but he also potentially jeopardized his base of support by gathering a formal congregation, an endemic problem for evangelical missionaries. The same catholic spirit that inspired ecumenical missionary organizations made gathering the fruit of their efforts near impossible. Forming a congregation required crafting a covenant, adopting a creed, and settling on admissions qualifications, all the distinct domain of denominations. Colonial missionaries sidestepped this problem; their support typically came from the state or a specific denomination with the explicit expectation that congregations would be gathered. After the Revolution, however, evangelicals created broader, more ecumenical organizations. When a Presbyterian minister under the aegis of the New-York Missionary Society baptized Tuscarora Indians by sprinkling instead of immersion, Baptist members walked out and formed their own organization.[53] Lacking the support of any denomination, Ely could not risk alienating potential sponsors.

A new, distinctly urban form of religious community emerges in the pages of Ely's *Journals*. This community reflected the city from which it was drawn: it was heterogeneous, religiously plural, transient, buffeted by the market economy, and not always harmonious. His congregation of strangers—women and men "providentially allotted" to his ministry because no other church would have them—somehow managed to work in spite of, or perhaps because of, its diversity.[54] "When we attempt to praise God in the Almshouse, the dialect of almost every nation is heard; for the English, Scotch, Irish, Dutch, German, French, Spanish, and Italian, as well as American poor, have met together," he reflected. "What some of the foreigners want in pronunciation, they more than make up in their musical notes. I have become, now, so accustomed to this confusion of dialects, that it does not disturb my devotion."[55] His warmest reception came from white women and African Americans, the same groups most attracted to evangelicalism outside these institutions.[56] Yet, also like the city's broader population, far more rejected his evangelical message. Not more than "half, or even a fourth part of the thousand people in this Institution," he calculated, "are disposed to pay constant attention to the preaching of the Gospel."[57]

A new form of urban religious community required a different pastoral approach. In New England villages, preaching often took precedence over pastoral work. The demand for three sermons each Sunday consigned many ministers to their desks for days on end.[58] As their ministers wrote, congregations took on the role of supporting and policing the community, enabled to do so by their small size and tight bonds of kinship. New York's rapid expansion made such an approach difficult. Moving to the city sundered many of these social ties; the competitive spiritual marketplace undercut the ability of any one congregation to enforce morality over a geographic area. Ely understood this reality. Instead of building up the community through public discourses, he focused on the conversion of individuals through personal conversations.[59] "A popular sermon resembles a note of hand," he explained, invoking the language of the market; "and the private application which should follow is like the endorsement, which often proves the most important part of the instrument."[60] Endorsing his gospel message made it personal and increased its efficacy. Ely recorded little or nothing in his *Journals* about what he preached, but he did, however, preserve scores of personal conversations in detail, providing an unparalleled window into the popular religiosity of poor New Yorkers.

Missionaries had long recorded their experiences with the objects of their endeavors, and more recently British poets and authors had begun to celebrate exemplars of piety in unexpected places. In the writings of Experience Mayhew, John Eliot, and David Brainerd, Ely found pious men struggling to bring the gospel to heathen audiences in a foreign setting and to make sense of their failures and successes in light of God's plan.[61] When Ely signaled in his first *Journal* his intention to record "the short, and simple annals of the poor," a reference to Thomas Gray's popular pastoral poem, "An Elegy in a Country Church-yard" (1751), he, too, sentimentalized the poor while criticizing a complacent establishment indifferent to their suffering. Other eighteenth-century pastoral poets, such as George Crabbe, contested such a view and refused to absolve the poor of their vices and faults.[62] Ely wrestled with their conflicting views. British evangelical writers, such as Rowland Hill, Hannah More, and Legh Richmond, channeled this complicated pastoral tradition into works that highlighted the piety of the poor, rural and urban.[63] The structure of their popular texts, essentially anthologies of fictitious narratives or dialogues between a narrator and a pious individual, provided Ely with another model for his writing.

Tracts, poetry, and fiction not only shaped how Ely located himself within the almshouse and hospital but also set expectations for his encounters with their denizens. "A preacher here resembles a guide-post indeed," he reflected, "for he stands beside a public road, multitudes pass him; he points them to the path which leads to a better country, and they are soon out of sight."[64] Like Eliot and Mayhew, he effaced his own story in favor of the objects of his missionary attention in order to assume a neutral stance. At one point, he referred to himself as a modern-day Charon, ferrying souls over to the world to come, for many of Ely's encounters took place over the deathbed.[65] Yet neither a guidepost nor Charon are neutral postures: both are predicated on the power to distinguish between correct and incorrect paths. In the dynamic yet uneasy dialogues that Ely preserved, missionary and potential convert employed scripts drawn from a range of sources and endeavored to make themselves comprehensible to the other. Ultimately, however, the power to record the discourse lay with Ely. His "short and simple annals of the poor" often proved anything but.[66]

In his conversations, Ely deployed a script derived from his Calvinist upbringing. For him, only the awesome power of God rivaled the inherent weakness of man. Actual sin compounded the imputed sin of Adam, regardless of one's moral performance.[67] An all-powerful and benevolent God, however, freed men and women from their burden of sin through the atoning death of Christ. Through faith, not works, God justified man by imputing Christ's righteousness, so that man might enter heaven. Ely's was a ministry of hope. Historians have long emphasized the dark and foreboding nature of early nineteenth-century Calvinism, but Ely and his followers viewed salvation as a glorious gift from a loving God. As he assured a downcast sailor struggling with intemperance, "Jesus Christ came into the world to save sinners from themselves and from hell, and the greatness of your sin cannot exclude you from heaven, if you truly believe and repent."[68]

Ely's evangelical dedication to spreading the gospel tempered the love of Calvinist doctrine so evident in his published polemics. Like many evangelicals, he sought to regularize the process of conversion into identifiable stages. He emphasized the universality of the Protestant experience and left the theological niceties to be parsed out by those within denominations, as Philip Doddridge had done in *The Rise and Progress of Religion in the Soul.* At the same time, he made conversion more comprehensible by placing it in the context of the lifelong spiritual journey, familiar to many from John Bunyan's *The Pilgrim's Progress.* The men and women that Ely met came from a broad range of theological backgrounds, and most had veered off the straight-and-narrow path more times than they cared to remember, but he offered them the hope of a successful crossing to the world to come.

Ely insisted on repentance as the cost of passage and found that New Yorkers had much to repent. His *Journals* read like a catalog of urban sins: intemperance, infidelity, theater going, and prostitution all figure prominently. For many, residence in the city only exacerbated the temptation to sin. After nine years in New York and another four in New Orleans, one man feared that "by degrees his faith was unhinged, and he learned the wicked ways of the people with whom he lived." A dying sailor read the Bible regularly and admitted that he knew the cost of sin, but could not resist getting drunk whenever he was in port. "Sir, when I am in here," he said, "and you preach, or I read the Bible, I believe every word, and determine [to do] well; but when I go out into company, if I will not swear and drink as my messmates do, I am nobody. It's a hard thing for an old sailor to get to heaven." Months of meeting sinners convinced Ely that innate instinct had as much to do with the proclivity to sin as environment. "I consider that in nine cases out of ten, premature sickness comes in consequence of making a god of animal appetite." Sometimes the difficulty went even deeper. Some appeared to "have more damning ingredients put into their composition than others."[69]

Admitting one's inclination to sin represented the first step to repentance. "O Lord Jesus! I am a vile sinner: I deserve hell; but, Oh! pardon me! pardon all my sins! Lord Jesus, I come to thee, I confess to thee, I trust in thee!" one aged woman repeated, Ely recorded, "for three or four days, with the intermission of only a few moments, besides those of sleep." Again and again, Ely encouraged people to confess their sins, although the process never proved easy. "Oh! Sir, I have a hard, hard heart: it will not break, it will not burst," a young Scottish woman explained. He assured her that God could soften the hardest heart, but she would not hear it. She felt she had more to answer for, having been raised in the church—Ely wondered if she had been a "systematic theologist from her childhood"—and knowing the proper path but refusing to follow it. Her grief often exceeded his ability to provide comfort. Less than three weeks later she passed away, only at the end expressing some hope in her spiritual worth. "If Jesus is ready to receive me, I am ready to die," she told her fellow companions.[70]

True repentance could lead to a transformation in the sinner. "The complex emotion of hatred against all unbelief" coupled with an "earnest desire to live a life of faith on the Son of God" manifested itself both internally and externally. Nothing better illustrated this than the change in a "bold, profane, rampant tar" whose heart burned for conversion after the death of his beloved grandmother. "I must say, that my messmates were afraid of me, because I was so blasphemously wicked, but HE has made me like a little child," the sailor recalled. "I, who always desired a boxing-match, have since been more pleased to be smitten on both cheeks without retuning it, than I should be to receive a hundred dollars."[71] Spiritual regeneration proved life altering for many.

Judging whether a sinner was truly saved proved tricky. Deathbed conversions had long been suspect. "When men expect death in less than a week, and their sins arise in horrible array against them, it is difficult to distinguish *filial fear* from the *slavish dread* of God," Ely noted after counseling two men headed to the gallows. Many hoped a former experience of piety might suffice, but Ely found such hopes suspect as well, for if the heart had been truly transformed, it would not have backslid. He had the greatest faith in those who exhibited "a holy hatred of sin" and who found their time in the almshouse and hospital a blessing. "I can truly, Sir, declare, that I have had more happiness since I have been sick, than I ever had in my whole life before," explained Richard Neal, a dying freed black man, whom Ely believed "God has taught . . . sounder practical divinity than is to be found in many ponderous volumes of Christian Doctors."[72]

These, of course, were the ideal encounters. Others proved more complicated. More often than not, men and women proved wary of parting with beliefs, practices, and worldviews developed over their lives. Many understood salvation in terms of some variation of works righteousness, to Ely's chagrin. The captain of a gunboat felt he had done "good deeds enough to balance all the criminality of swearing a little."[73] When a woman stood by the integrity of her heart, Ely demanded to know if she thought herself better than the apostle Paul, who readily confessed his sin.[74] A widow on the verge of death shared with Ely the grounds on which she felt she was saved. "She did not fear hell, she said, because there was no such place as hell; but she believed that all would in future have some punishment, and some reward, according to their deserts. She added, that she had always done as well as she could, and was therefore persuaded that God would not punish her much." Ely pushed back, arguing that faith, and not works, was the basis of salvation, and told her he doubted she had lived as good a life as she believed. "These were hard doctrines, but if they are not blessed of God, to her spiritual life," he concluded, "she must remain proud of her own performances, dead in trespasses and sins."[75] She disagreed, preferring to await her just deserts.

The enthusiasm African American New Yorkers displayed for evangelicalism delighted Ely, although he found their syncretism of Christian and African beliefs at times troubling.[76] New York had one of the largest enslaved urban populations in the north in the eighteenth century. The disproportionate number living in segregated wards within the almshouse speaks to their vulnerability.[77] Entering a cellar in late February 1813, Ely met a woman whom he thought might be pious until she spoke about "the strange visions which she saw long ago" of Christ. For those from non-Christian faiths that valued the spiritual power of visions, the identification of a "glorious personage" with Christ represented an understandable way of comprehending Christianity. For Ely, "a vision of myriads of angels," "prophetic dreams," even seeing "Christ in the flesh" too much resembled superstition and had absolutely no efficacy in furthering spiritual regeneration. Ely proved equally dismissive of other religious retentions. An African in the hospital "who said a few rational things" captured Ely's attention until he told the young minister that his disease derived from a spell that another man placed on him. "It was useless to converse with him any longer," Ely wrote, "and I turned to others."[78]

In contrast to his zeal on questions of spiritual concern, Ely exhibited less certainty over what sort of critique to make of the impact of urban growth on the social and economic existence of the poor. Early in 1811, Ely met a woman "moral in deportment" who had been an industrious and independent servant until she fell ill. The medical treatment she received consumed all the "industry she accumulated" and landed her in the almshouse. This clearly frustrated Ely, although he expressed some relief with her resignation and happiness at being able to hear him regularly preach the gospel. A conversation with a widowed mother of ten who tried, with little success, to support herself by making "nankeen pantaloons and common shirts" angered Ely. "All who sell ought to have lawful gain," he blasted, "but the poor, who perform the work, ought to receive at least half of that sum which is charged for making of apparel." He documented other failures of social justice, yet never did much more than express outrage.[79]

These issues of personal responsibility and environmental causation collided in one person. Ely first spied this young woman, with "a fair complexion, a soft eye, a fine form, agreeable features, and hands more delicate than they should be," reading a Bible in a hospital ward. She said her name was Caroline, and tears welled up in her eyes when she spoke of a "fascinating" man who brought her to the city from her rural boarding school under the promise of marriage. Caroline believed he loved her until, in the words of Ely, "the spoiler came, found the sweet flower of the mountains, plucked it in wantonness, rifled it of its fragrance, and cast it away to perish with noxious weeds." As a parting indignity, her inconstant lover "contaminated his prey," necessitating her removal to the hospital. Caroline's fervent repentance only made Ely angrier with her seducer. And when she confided that if God had not suffered her to be afflicted she would never have met him, she had Ely right where she wanted him. "If this person acts the part of a hypocrite," Ely reflected, "she must be a consummate mistress of her art." As it turned out, he was not all that far off.[80]

Ely went to lengths on behalf of Caroline that surpassed his efforts for any other hospital or almshouse resident. Convinced her recovery would be accelerated by a reunion with her mother, he hurried off a conciliatory letter to Vermont. When the only reply forthcoming was "no such person resides in that town or vicinity," Ely could hardly conceal his hurt. "You have done evil in this affair," he blasted in a letter, unable to confront Caroline directly. But he refused to give up on her. "Tell me your name, your wants, your trials in relation to your friends, and you will find me one who can pity and pardon a thousand times," Ely wrote, sounding as much like her lover as her minister. Three days later, "foolish Caroline" ran away from the hospital.[81] She soon came back, and the lengths to which Ely was willing to go only grew more ridiculous. He traveled 350 miles to Vermont to track down her mother (unsuccessfully) and convinced a group of benevolent leaders to found a Magdalen society.[82] And this was just in the span of the first *Journal*. In the second, Ely appended a narrative of her adventures from 1812 to 1815, including her time among the Shakers at New Lebanon, her masquerades around Philadelphia under an alias, and her marriage ultimately to a farmer in upstate New York.[83]

The story of Caroline reveals just how complex the encounter between the missionary and the almshouse or hospital resident could be. Caroline knew she needed to perform to an expected model to gain Ely's favor and manipulated his script through language, emotion, and gesture. At the same time, she employed her own script, one to which Ely proved sympathetic. Caroline channeled Charlotte Temple, the eponymous protagonist of the best-selling novel by Susanna Rowson, and a host of other heroines of seduction stories that had become standard fare in the popular print of early national New York.[84] Every aspect of Caroline's seduction and abandonment conformed to literary antecedents, right down to her name: two different tales of seduced Carolines appeared in American newspapers in as many decades.[85] Seduction stories can be interpreted as either cautionary tales for women or critiques of male sexual license, yet both are predicated on a fundamental understanding of women as the inevitable victims of male sexual power.[86] Caroline, however, inverted this formula and found a way to empower herself through these texts, to turn the tables and reclaim her own agency.

Seduction narratives typically offered one of two possible endings for the fallen woman, prostitution or death, although Caroline took her chances with a third: redemption. Popular literature reinforced the premium that postrevolutionary society placed on the sexual purity of unmarried women. In most cases, seduction necessitated a separation from the family and a turn to prostitution, the only viable means of economic livelihood in a period already lacking options for women.[87] Novels like *Charlotte Temple* presented death as a more virtuous end, although for the prostitute active long enough, venereal disease effected a similar, though less romantic and certainly less honorable, conclusion.[88] A new movement to reform prostitutes gained traction in the United States toward the close of the eighteenth century, though New York lagged about a decade behind Philadelphia in founding a Magdalen society.[89] Gossip in the hospital ward swirled around the unmarried twenty-five-year-old stated preacher's weakness for beautiful young prostitutes and likely gave Caroline encouragement to seek his assistance with her redemption.[90] With Ely by her hospital bed, she performed a dramatic repentance that captured his attention throughout the summer and into the fall.[91]

Ezra Stiles Ely knew to be wary of tales told by fallen women, but his heart burned to redeem Caroline's soul, and possibly more. "So many romantic tales are told by the patients of this sort, that few of them can be trusted," he wrote after their second meeting, although he paid his own admonition little heed. Caroline's past might have been suspect, but her repentance seemed as genuine as any that he had seen, and that was what ultimately mattered. Going against popularly held beliefs about the inherent sexual weakness of women, he did not blame Caroline for her seduction or question her motives, a benefit of the doubt that many others, including her fellow prostitutes in the hospital and his critics in the Presbytery, did not grant.[92] In fact, Ely's poem "William and Ellen" revealed an interest in the redemption of prostitutes that went beyond saving their souls to vindicating their honor in a court of law.[93] He surely would have known of the contemporary successes of Philadelphia's Magdalen society in redeeming and placing young prostitutes back in society as teachers, servants, and wives.[94] Perhaps the unmarried young minister, so long unlucky in love, even thought he had found a suitable wife.

Of all the encounters Ely recorded, his interaction with Caroline reveals the most complex negotiation between competing scripts, expectations, and outcomes; it illustrates the quintessential urbanness of his encounters in the almshouse and hospital. Large, anonymous New York allowed Caroline to perpetuate a ruse that would have been impossible in tight-knit Lebanon or Colchester. Unmoored from kinship ties and community memory, urban individuals had to decide who they would be and in which urban community they would locate themselves. Because New York was so vast and unknowable, residents had to accept one another on their word. It is tempting to read Caroline as an early confidence woman, but she was also a woman intimately shaped by the exigencies of the urban experience. Young, unmarried, and female, she represented an urban demographic that disproportionately joined evangelical churches. Posing as a repentant evangelical—perhaps even striving to be one—Caroline found attention and acceptance, at least for a while.

A question, however, remains. Caroline receives more discussion, not to mention more financial resources than any other figure in Ely's *Journals*, and ultimately with no success. Given the ambiguity surrounding her life and repentance, why did Ely choose to make her story so central to his narrative? It might be because she was more like Ely and his readers than they cared to acknowledge.

Visits of Mercy

When Philip Milledoler, Ely's old ally in the Presbytery, wrote a prefatory address for the first *Journal of the Stated Preacher* in the early autumn of 1812, he made it clear that Caroline and the other residents of the city's almshouse and hospital were not the publication's intended audience. That honor fell to the city's "religious public," a broad community of evangelicals from a range of denominations with the dedication, influence, and most important, resources, to spread the gospel. "Abundantly furnished with the means of grace for ourselves, brethren," Milledoler pointedly asked, "are we not called by every consideration that can influence the human mind, to extend these blessings to the poor, the destitute, and the friendless?"[95] Ely certainly thought so. He intended his *Journals* to convince New Yorkers to play just such a role.

Scholars have increasingly argued for the importance of understanding what missionaries attempted to convey to audiences of their works. In his two *Journals*, Ely sought to craft an evangelical identity for his readers out of an urban encounter.[96] Three distinct goals underlie his project. The first two—cultivating benefactors and warning readers of the dangers of the city—proved relatively straightforward; the third—enlisting the city's evangelical population in social activism—required urban evangelicals to do nothing less than rethink their relationship to God, to each other, and to their city. To accomplish this, Ely had to convince them that his *Journals* were more than a simple record of his activities; they were, as his London publishers packaged them, *Visits of Mercy*, in which readers should want to participate.

The first goal for the *Journals* was clearly financial. To survive in the field, missionaries depended on the support of benefactors, typically from a specific denomination or voluntary association. Colonial missionaries, for example, enjoyed the support of the Society for the Propagation of the Gospel (SPG) and the Society for Promoting Christian Knowledge (SPCK). Ely's mission, however, predated the formation of a society to support him. At first, he thought the State Legislature might be amendable to "doing more," although Milledoler, who was more attuned to the tenor of the times, dispelled such hopes.[97] Ely managed to collect a small subscription in November 1810 from individual evangelicals, principally Presbyterian and Reformed Dutch, but it did not go far. "Solely dependant on a precarious subscription, which he has now entirely relinquished, his receipts have never exceeded half the necessary support of a single man," Milledoler wrote of Ely's "radically defective" plan.[98] Eventually Ely sold his books "to procure the necessaries of life," a point skillfully publicized to garner sympathy.[99]

The appearance of the first *Journal* in November 1812, two years into his mission, succeeded in generating financial support for the young missionary. People "expressed their astonishment, that, in such a benevolent city as this, any preacher to the poor should fail of receiving maintenance," he later reflected. "It was supposed by many that I received a competence; and others, (few, however, in number,) from some doctrinal differences, wished that penury might drive me from the city." In December 1812, the nondenominational "Society for Supporting the Gospel among the Poor in the City of New York" formed. It immediately granted Ely two hundred dollars for past services and funded him until he departed the city six months later.[100] An initial lack of benefactors made life difficult but had a positive effect: it freed him to imagine his audience broadly. For Ely, his audience could be the entire city.

Ely felt his time in the almshouse and hospital made clear the need to warn his audience of the dangers of sin proliferating in their city, the second goal of his *Journals*. The printed page became the pulpit from which he admonished young men "on the brink of ruin" and young women "who have almost passed, for some favourite individual, the boundaries of decorum." Through the relation of his encounters, Ely put a human face on abstract problems of sin and temptation. An Irish woman deserted by her drunken husband or a blaspheming old sailor hardly surprised readers, but the stories of an English journeyman who ended up in the hospital after being duped and beaten on May 1, the city's moving day, or of the seduced young country girl Caroline drove home the precariousness of urban life for all, regardless of gender, ethnicity, or class. Story after story exacted a toll on its narrator. "Reader, are you not fatigued with going over the same ground repeatedly?" Ely asked in the second *Journal*. "If you are not, I am weary with leading you, for thus I twice visit the dying and the dead. But if you may learn to die [to sin], I will proceed."[101]

A keen observer of the human mind, Ely offered an extended discussion of the "moral causes of mental derangement" exacerbated by urban living. "A blow to the head, a fever, intense heat, *coup de soleil*, and lunar changes, may affect the brain and whole nervous system," he explained, "but intemperance in drink, inordinate attachments, and vicious indulgences, are the most common sources of mental disorder." He cataloged cases of insanity among city residents attributable to poor moral choices: a wealthy landlady learned the cost of refusing mercy to a tenant; a West Indian planter who moved to the city after commercial failure found that with each subsequent failure, "the strange notion came into his head, that the citizens thought him black"; and an Englishman accustomed to malt liquor went mad after refusing to refrain from consuming "ardent spirits cheap and much in fashion." Urban living might increase temptation to sin, but sin could be prevented.[102]

Beyond raising funds and warning of the dangers of vice, Ely wanted to convince evangelical New Yorkers to desire something they did not know they wanted—the conversion of their neighbors—and, by so doing, restore the centrality of social activism to their understanding of evangelicalism. This was his third, and most important, goal. "Who can forbear to drop a tear / On scenes of woe recorded here!" the author of "Lines occasioned by reading Ely's Journal" asked in the poem's opening line. While shedding "a tear" might seem a stock and meaningless gesture today, it was full of import in an age of literary sentimentalism. Invoking such a response in his readers went straight to the heart of what Ely wished to accomplish: their involvement in his work. It was not as easy as it seemed, but it had the potential not only to convert the poor but also to transform the city. To effect this change, Ely appealed to emotion.[103]

Before evangelical New Yorkers could embrace responsibility for the spiritual welfare of others, they needed a language in which to understand that responsibility. Ely took his lead from popular British literature. Sentimentalism's emphasis on the individual emotional response encouraged readers to be more sensitive to the experience of those around them. Yet sentimentalism tended to privilege feeling over action. In Henry MacKenzie's popular *The Man of Feeling* (1771), the protagonist Harley relies on instinct, intuition, and his own sense of things, measuring the value of personal experience in its own terms, not for its social or religious ramifications. Harley's heightened capacity to feel inspires him to display sympathy, the ability to imagine someone else's suffering, but he knows not how to act on it.[104]

For Ely, "the man of *feeling*" without religion was nothing better than an "unrestrained libertine." Feeling had to be balanced with action, and sympathy with benevolence, which he defined as a "consistent, habitual regard for the welfare of others," manifested through corresponding deeds.[105] In the early nineteenth century, benevolence derived from pity, the acknowledgment of obligation and duty, and not from a feeling-based sympathy.[106] London publishers recognized his semantic project when they repackaged the *Journals* as the *Visits of Mercy*, although Ely sought to dispel any confusion. "In every page of the work we recognize 'the man of feeling'; but it is the feeling of the renewed heart, enlarged as is the range of human wretchedness, purified by the indwelling Spirit of God, and ennobled by the model on which it is formed," he carefully explained.[107] Duty, ultimately, not shared feeling, motivated Ely.

Ely's *Journals* gave readers a model for emulation as well as a new understanding of emotion and responsibility. The great popularity of *The Life of David Brainerd* among evangelicals lay in its account of the long-suffering missionary, not in the piety of his Native American audience. Isolated far from society among a "heathen" people who often resisted his gospel message, Brainerd approached the limits of human benevolence, exhausting himself and transforming from an individual into an example of a Christian ideal.[108] Ely hoped for a similar transformation, or at least to make himself the beneficiary of collective feeling.

Laboring in a virtual "Second Sodom," Ely detailed the filth, overcrowding, and even smells of the almshouse and hospital to emphasize his own suffering. Preaching in the schoolroom to avoid "the loathsome effluvia of old beds, cookery, and drugs," he wrote in March of his first year, "the room was full; the scorching sun could not be excluded from the windows; and all the swine of the place, which are not few, surrounded the building." He was loath to take a necessary breath in the height of August's heat due to the bodies "in such a putrescent state," which "would have caused vomition" had the nurses not burned linen and aromatics. By the end of the year, the corpse of a typhus victim left in a hospital ward sickened a devoted nurse and a pious woman. It disgusted Ely. So "weary with writing the history of human miseries," he took the following year off from writing.[109]

Descriptions of the foreignness of the almshouse and hospital inmates heightened readers' identification with Ely. Deists provided one of the hostile "others" against which he constructed himself. Early national evangelicals harbored a fear of the influence of Deists far in excess of their actual numbers.[110] Ely liked to take them on as theological sparring partners, although they often had the last word. "If I frequented the grog-shops, I did not myself drink to excess, nor partake with those who blasphemed their maker," a dying Deist told Ely. "On the Sabbath I sat and smoked in a friendly way with my neighbours, while others were running to this and that church, to show their new clothes, to hear a new preacher, and to criticize his discourse." Ely disliked the man's unwillingness to acknowledge himself a sinner; but the dying man took comfort in the belief that he, at least, "spent his time in a rational way!" A week later, he frustrated Ely even more by telling some visitors that after his death, he would stand at the door of hell to call them in, "that he might have the pleasure of raking open the coals of the bottomless pit, to warm them."[111]

Roman Catholics provided another important foil in Ely's narrative. In 1810, the city's Catholic community was small, poor, and marginal, with only one parish.[112] Most Catholics—in and out of public institutions—had little interest in his evangelical message. "Sir," a sick Catholic once roughly told him, "when I want a priest I will send for one. We are of different religions." Ely sought to reassure him "that I claimed no right to teach him, and had in no case imposed my services upon any one, contrary to his inclination," before going on to give him a lesson about the "one religion that leads to heaven." Ely played on age-old Protestant prejudices to present Catholics as not only personally rebuffing his ministry but also impeding the devotion of others. "Figure to yourself, readers, a room almost full of Roman Catholics, smoking, talking, washing, patching old rags, walking from one end of the room to the other, counting and repeating 'pater nosters' as they go," he shared after witnessing an old Protestant woman unable to hear a Bible being read to her. Ely's revulsion toward Roman Catholics, common among evangelicals, only reinforced religious tensions that erupted in violence in later years.[113]

To encourage emulation of his efforts, Ely populated his *Journals* with examples of how readers might participate in the larger work. Leonard Bleecker, a pious Baptist businessman and founding trustee of the society that later supported Ely, sometimes joined him on his rounds to read the Bible, converse with the sick, and offer advice.[114] Blind George, an African American almshouse resident with a fine singing voice and a remarkable memory made an even more important contribution. Ely appointed George his clerk and gave him a hymnbook (for others to read to him) and a new suit of clothes. George, in turn, gathered other blind members of the almshouse's African American community to sing in the wards, providing Ely with something of a Greek chorus.[115] Ely's supporters did not always coexist peacefully. When an aged blind woman overheard Bleecker say one day that "perhaps many of these persons are more blind in spirit, than in their bodily organs," she exclaimed, with considerable resentment, "Perhaps we are not so blind, neither!"[116]

Ely also recorded how his work intersected with the city's nascent evangelical and secular voluntary associations, which his readers might join. Two city Bible societies "honourably supplied" books to an audience eager for print. Sometimes inmates competed with each other for access to these texts. Ely relayed how a man "whose countenance indicates past intemperance" privately inquired about procuring a hymn book in the hope of avoiding his rivals, only to have "two or three aged women," who overheard him, express their hope not to be forgotten. The Dorcas Society, a group of benevolent women, gathered to make clothes for the poor in the almshouse and hospital. They even elicited a "hymn" in their honor that Ely reprinted in the first *Journal*.[117] These early benevolent organizations paled in comparison to the scope and scale of those that followed but provided readers with a range of ways in which they might become involved.

In the end, Ely's most effective argument might have been the most self-serving for his readers. The title of his 1810 appeal, *A Sermon for the Rich to Buy, That They May Benefit Themselves and the Poor*, confirms his willingness to put the needs of potential patrons before the objects of his mission. Duty and eternal reward served as his stick and his carrot. The renewed Christian, he argued, demonstrated his faith not only through conversion and personal devotion but also through his concern for the spiritual well-being of his fellow man. Earthly labors, he argued, would lead to an eternal reward. To this end, he even offered his own theological refinement, explaining, "There is a *higher* and *lower* seat in heaven, but although it would be bliss to abide for ever on the threshold of glory, yet he is a mean spirited believer who would not humbly aspire to eminence among the luminaries that surround the throne of God."[118] This bold bit of theology should have gotten Ely in trouble with local orthodox clerics, but it nicely illustrates the lengths to which he was willing to go to promote social activism.

Ely thus wrote of his endeavors on behalf of Caroline and others as part of a larger project to enlist evangelical New Yorkers in the work of urban benevolence. Duty required him to reach out to Caroline, and her apparent openness to his gospel message made her all the more attractive. She had more in common with Ely and his readers than other figures in the *Journals*: her struggle with a sincere repentance rang true for many city residents, while her seduction focused attention on the dangers of her urban experience. Ultimately her story sold well. Repackaged as the *Visits of Mercy*, the two *Journals* appeared in five editions over twenty years, circulating in more than ten thousand copies throughout America, England, and Ireland.[119] In the process, Ely's telling of Caroline's story enlisted readers' sympathy for himself as much as, if not more than, for her. And that sympathy absolved him of criticism for being duped in attempting to convert her.

LOOKING TO THE FUTURE

A little over three years after first settling in New York, Ezra Stiles Ely traded the wards of the almshouse and hospital for the sanctuary of a leading Presbyterian church in Philadelphia.[120] His love of polemics, if not poetry, continued, leading him, most famously, to call for the creation of a "Christian Party in politics" during the 1827 campaign to end delivery of the mail on the Sabbath.[121] Caroline, interestingly, followed in his footsteps, although not, ostensibly, to find him. She reinvented herself as Sarah How, a victim of seduction, and sought the support of the benevolent women of Philadelphia. Ely kept track of her comings and goings but made no more efforts to save her.

Ely might have failed to convert Caroline and many others that he met, but he refused to let that deter him from his (and Isabella Marshall Graham's) larger project: to reveal a new audience for evangelical proselytizing and to mobilize evangelical New Yorkers to action. Residents of the almshouse and hospital could not have looked more different from those in the rural villages from which they hailed. Ethnically, racially, and culturally heterogeneous, many held (and tenaciously defended) complex, syncretistic religious beliefs and practices developed from a broad range of sources. Dependent on the fluctuating market, these men and women could not be boarded in the houses of friends and family when they fell on hard times, for they had no such support networks. New York was a city of strangers, but the almshouse and hospital provided membership in a new, distinctly urban congregation.

By reading the *Journals*, evangelical New Yorkers awoke, or so Ely hoped, to their duty to "do more" for their neighbors. He provided a new language of benevolence, offered himself as a model for emulation, and promised an eternal reward. Described as "constitutionally indiscreet," full of "ardent feelings," and wanting "mature judgment" by both his critics and his supporters, Ely alienated many.[122] Nonetheless, his efforts helped restore to evangelicalism the characteristic principle of social activism that had been deficient.

Evangelical New Yorkers could no longer afford to overlook their neighbors, for Ely had revealed what was at stake: their own salvation. "If any religious community, or evangelized city, provides not the Bread of Life for the indigent members of its own family," he warned, "it has denied the faith, and exhibits the worst kind of practical infidelity."[123]

Over the next generation, evangelical New Yorkers embraced and acted on that realization through an explosion of Bible, tract, missionary, reform, and benevolent associations. New Yorkers, in fact, grew so generous that the same men who tried to limit the licensing of taverns in 1809 reformed as the Society for the Prevention of Pauperism less than a decade later in the hope of curtailing benevolent giving, fearing it was creating a permanent class of paupers.[124] Evangelicals did not fully embrace either tactic, remaining focused on the salvation of the individual. Where Ely taught New Yorkers the value of mercy, a fellow Yale graduate and emigrant from the country named Ward Stafford took them out of the almshouse and hospital and into a whole "New Missionary Field," inaugurating a generation of unprecedented efforts to convert New York.

PART II

1815–1840

CHAPTER THREE

The New Missionary Field

"If the piety of a nation is estimated according to the number of its religious institutions, then, indeed, may the citizens of New-York be considered a pious and religious people," Edmund Blunt gushed in his 1817 *Stranger's Guide to the City of New-York*. Counting no less than fifty-three churches, chapels, and meetinghouses, Blunt wondered if any European city of similar size could exhibit so great a number. He believed these ecclesiastical structures in their republican simplicity surpassed their European counterparts, bearing more resemblance to "what may naturally be supposed formed the temples of the primitive Christians" than the "magnificent cathedrals" of Europe. All the more impressive, these structures existed in a nation that rejected an established church in favor of safeguarding the freedom of conscience of every man, "whatever may be his religious sentiments." New York's houses of worship stood amid its grid of streets, its busy port and commercial districts, and its steamship-navigated waters as yet another indication of the success America achieved by throwing off the shackles of Europe. Edmund Blunt might have been a shameless city booster, but so were many New Yorkers in the heady years that followed the War of 1812.[1]

Yet where Blunt saw cause for celebration, Ward Stafford saw cause for alarm. Stafford had also studied the city but came to a different conclusion. He passed the same churches, chapels, and meetinghouses, but rather than debating their architectural merit, he lamented their uneven distribution. "While almost all the churches are in the lower, the great mass of the people are in the upper part of the city," he wrote. This was especially the case in the city's wards along the East River, which had been opened for settlement following the American Revolution. A solitary church in the Seventh Ward, for example, ministered to the spiritual needs of a district with over nine thousand inhabitants. The results, in Stafford's opinion, were disastrous. Freedom of conscience was now a license for licentiousness as taverns replaced meetinghouses as the place of resort on the Sabbath. "Souls are perishing in the midst of us," he concluded; "the work has been too long delayed."[2]

Blunt and Stafford represented two sides of a long-forgotten debate about the spiritual health of New York City following the War of 1812. Freed from the threat of European encroachment on the continent and flush from wartime profiteering, the city and its spiritual marketplace rebounded quickly, if unevenly. Evangelical denominations emerged as the most active producers in the marketplace, but their emplacement strategies led them to ignore whole swaths of the city. To rectify this situation, Ward Stafford devised an ambitious blueprint for a "New Missionary Field." Evangelical laity traditionally on the margins of church decision-making—women and young men—formed voluntary associations in which they pooled their financial resources and organizational talents to sponsor missionaries to implement Stafford's plan. Along the edge of urban settlement, they focused on gathering people into missions that became the basis of neighborhood churches. On the waterfront, they engaged sailors and their families on the decks of ships and in boardinghouse parlors. Not content to be passive recipients of missionary attention, local residents took an active role in shaping missionary activities to suit their own needs.

QUANTIFYING THE LANDSCAPE

Early nineteenth-century New Yorkers placed great faith in numbers. Blunt's *Stranger's Guide* reads as an elaborate exercise in counting. He enumerated anything and everything in the city that he thought might prove its greatness, from the number of rooms in city hall to the number of hides annually produced by city tanneries to the number of different species of animals for sale in the markets.[3] Ministers took stock of the number and capacity of their meetinghouses just as assiduously as merchants counted the tons of raw materials exported and finished goods imported. All agreed that numbers could speak; they disagreed, as it turns out, over what those numbers had to say.

On July 4, 1823, Jonathan Weeden published the most elaborate religious contribution to this quantification mania. His "Summary View of the Houses of Public Worship, in the City and County of New York" meticulously documented the city's spiritual marketplace. Neatly arranged in orderly columns, the impressive broadside lists the name, location, denomination, dimensions, materials, and square footage of the city's houses of worship in order of their founding. His conclusions were more in line with Blunt than Stafford. "From the above exhibit," he explained, "it is clearly to be seen that the places for public worship have kept full pace with the population of this great metropolis, for if it required 21 houses in 1790, to contain the then population, (say, 33,000), it would require only 82 houses now to contain (130,000) the supposed population; whereas we have 87, including those now building." His conclusions should be accepted, he argued, because of the veracity of his data, derived from six months of worshipping in, and speaking to the clergy of, city churches. "No sectarian considerations" influenced his presentation, he assured his audience.[4]

Weeden's "Summary View" provides a snapshot of a thriving urban spiritual marketplace. It lists twenty-six houses of worship built since the end of the War of 1812, as well as another six "now going up." This represented a nearly two-thirds increase in city churches. The spiritual marketplace's growth is impressive given that the War of 1812 halted new meetinghouse construction and suspended the momentum of the 1790s and 1800s. (The massive St. Patrick's Roman Catholic Cathedral on Mott Street proved a noteworthy exception when it opened in 1815, but its construction had languished since before Jefferson's disastrous Embargo.)[5] After the war, construction of new houses of worship resumed unabated through the Panic of 1819 and into the next decade. Even as the economic market took a battering, the spiritual market thrived.[6]

New York exhibited a diversity of faiths found only in the largest of the young nation's cities. Eighteen different denominations are represented as well as three institutions—the almshouse, the state prison, and the Mariner's Church—that eschewed a denominational affiliation. According to Weeden's count, Episcopalians had the most meetinghouses (15), followed by Presbyterians (14), Methodists (13), Baptists and Reformed Dutch (10 each). These denominational categories, however, often masked important variations in theological thought. Baptists, for example, embraced a range of viewpoints on doctrinal issues, while Episcopalians divided into high church and low church (evangelical) factions. Weeden lumped the African Methodist Episcopal Zion Church under the Methodist denomination even though it had severed its ties with the white-dominated New York Conference two years earlier. In all, evangelical faiths dominated. Baptists, Methodists, low church Episcopalians, and Presbyterians (the last breaking ground on no less than eight new meetinghouses in this period) made up nearly half the churches in the city where, a generation earlier, they made up barely a quarter. Non-evangelical and non-Protestant faiths—Swedenborgians, Universalists, Unitarians, Jews, and Roman Catholics—possessed only a single or a few houses of worship.

A new way of thinking about the urban landscape facilitated this dramatic expansion. In 1811, a state-appointed Streets Commission unveiled a plan for the future settlement of Manhattan Island. Three years earlier the commission had hired John Randel Jr. to survey all 11,400 acres of Manhattan and draw up a plan for its development. Randel and his team plotted a rigid grid of twelve north-running avenues and scores of smaller perpendicular streets crossing every two hundred feet. Where the colonial city had been based on a landscape of symbolic power reified in the close connection of the established church, the state house, and markets, the early national city instituted a rigorously systematic landscape of (ideally) evenly distributed structures. The grid eradicated natural inequalities of topography and led to the leveling of hills and the filling of swamps in a massive municipal effort to extend equal access to all city residents. Private property was subjected to the common good by conquering space and properly regulating it. In all, New Yorkers believed circulation could be improved, waste eliminated, and land brought into more regular and productive use. War delayed the implementation of the Commissioners' Plan, but once peace returned, surveying and new construction continued apace along the eastern and northern edges of urban settlement.[7]

The location of new houses of worship followed the expansion of the city's gridded landscape. Before the War, houses of worship concentrated in three zones: in the core of the colonial city (south of Chambers Street and mostly east of Broadway) or on either side of the northward axes of development that ran parallel to the Hudson River (in the direction of Greenwich Village) or along the Bowery Road (toward Bowery Village) (see map 1.2). The eastern corner of the city had very few churches within it, despite having been recently surveyed and beginning to be built up with the homes, workshops, and shipyards of artisans and laborers. After the war, new houses of worship arose primarily north of Chambers Street all the way to Houston Street (see map 3.1). These structures continued to follow the Hudson River and the Bowery Road but also filled in much of the newly surveyed areas in between. The few meetinghouses that arose east of Bowery, as we will see, were founded primarily through lay-sponsored missions.

Denominational initiative and congregational schism provided the two dominant modes for new church growth before and after the War of 1812. Evangelical denominations embraced the grid as a tool for situating new

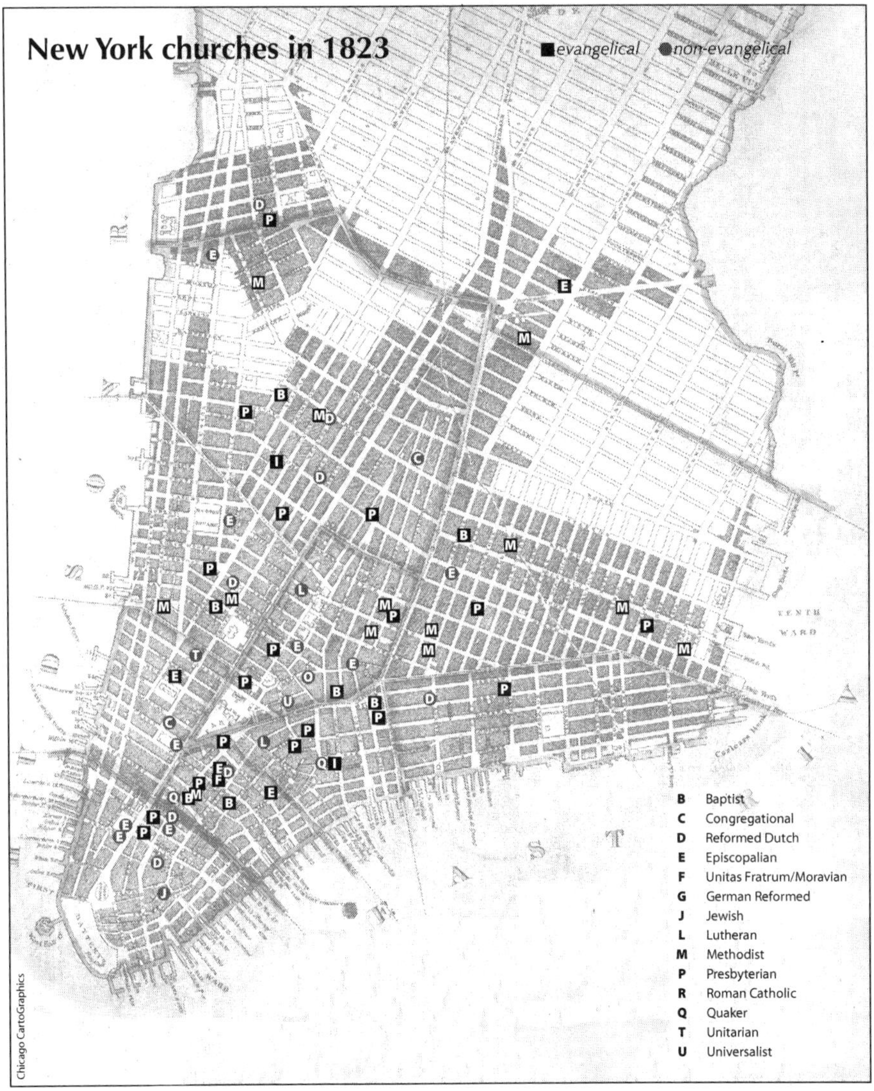

MAP 3.1 Houses of Worship in New York City at the time of Weeden's "Summary View" (1823), by Dennis McClendon

congregations. The Methodist New-York Conference, for example, placed houses of worship on the edge of settlement, spaced anywhere from one-third to two-thirds of a mile apart. Baptists had no such centralizing authority and their new congregations emerged as a result of schism or as a colony from an established church. As a result, they tended to be located much closer together, sometimes only a block or two apart. Congregational schisms need not be thought of as negative phenomena. They caused significant anxiety as they unfolded, but strengthened the bonds that held different factions together while providing the impetus for new church growth.

Geographic naming patterns reinforced the relationship between the spatiality of the grid and congregational identity. Thirty-three of the eighty-seven churches on Weeden's list bore the name of the street on which they stood. Others referenced neighborhoods, such as Bowery or Greenwich Villages. The Reformed Dutch used relational naming practices—South, Middle, North, Northeast, and Northwest—to distinguish their churches. Reference to a specific geographic location not only provided a crucial mechanism for wayfinding in a rapidly growing city but also signaled something of the congregants' character, such as downtown respectability or a willingness to place oneself on the forward edge of settlement. When a congregation moved, as many frequently did, it typically renamed itself after its new location. The presence of Zion, Bethel, Beriah, New Jerusalem, and Abyssinian churches reveals that for some evangelical New Yorkers the most important spatial coordinates transcended space and time. Naming practices also remind us what denominations chose not to do. Evangelicals refused to dedicate churches to particular saints, a practice extensively employed by the city's Episcopalians and Roman Catholics.[8]

Evangelicals extended this mania for quantification into their pews. Every major evangelical denomination annually published its membership numbers by 1825.[9] The number of Methodists doubled while Presbyterians again grew fourfold between 1816 and 1840 (see the appendix, table A.4). Methodists had two periods of growth during this time: a long, steady rise between 1821 and 1832 and then a rapid spurt between 1837 and 1843, the period of the Panic of 1837 and the economic depression that followed. Membership numbers are a conservative estimate of evangelicals, since the number who worshipped in but did not join evangelical churches—unconverted spouses, children, and the curious—was perhaps five times the number of converted. Tens of thousands of New Yorkers likely identified as evangelical at the end of the first quarter of the nineteenth century.

Revivalism provided much of this membership growth. Low church Episcopalians at St. George's and Christ Church, for example, enjoyed a period of revivalism in 1816, with the former nearly doubling its membership and the latter increasing by a third. For most, revivalism could be hard to sustain, but under Rev. James Milnor, known for his engaging preaching within a denomination not known for such, St. George's sustained multiple revivals.[10]

Itinerant revivalists made New York a stop on their regional and transatlantic tours. The arrival of British Methodist John Summerfield in the early 1820s generated excitement throughout the city's churches. John Pintard, a decidedly nonevangelical Episcopalian, regularly split his Sundays between St. du Esprit on Pine Street (the French Episcopal Church) and Grace Church on Broadway. Yet after hearing Summerfield preach at the annual meeting of the American Bible Society—"I think I never heard a more original or more elegant speaker," Pintard wrote to his daughter—he resolved to take his wife and other daughter to hear the revivalist preach the following Sunday.[11]

The city's spiritual marketplace expanded and diversified rapidly over the years following the War of 1812, but it did not grow evenly. In some wards, especially in lower Manhattan, New Yorkers had a wide variety of churches from which to choose. But in the upper part of the city east of the Bowery Road, women and men had to walk long distances to find a meetinghouse. A recently arrived Yale graduate soon embraced their plight as his calling.

THE NEW MISSIONARY FIELD

Ward Stafford knew when he presented his quarterly report to the Female Missionary Society in March 1817 that he had stepped beyond the bounds of what was expected. Instead of a dozen paragraphs summarizing his work among the city's less fortunate, Stafford presented fifty-five pages of observations, recommendations, and justifications for work yet to be done. "It may be thought improper by some, that one who has been a labourer in the vineyard for so short a period, should attempt to point out the means by which the temporal and eternal welfare of these people is to be promoted," Stafford confessed.[12] He looked at New York through a lens refined in the hill country of New Hampshire, where he was born in 1788, and the evangelical classrooms and sanctuaries of Andover and Yale, where discussions of conversion and missionary spirit dominated his ministerial training.[13] It was "not unreasonable to suppose," he thought, that he had advantages for judging "not in the possession of others." What did he see in New York? "A new missionary field has opened to my view," he told his sponsors, and urged them to join him in cultivating it.[14]

In *The New Missionary Field,* Stafford differed from Blunt and Weeden in his estimation of the city's spiritual health. Development of the city's religious landscape, he revealed, had been uneven, overly concentrated in older wards and largely ignored in newer ones. If anything, the Commissioners'

Plan only exacerbated his fears: the city was rapidly expanding and the distribution of churches failed to reflect the distribution of the population. This was especially glaring in the northeastern corner of the city. Nearly one-third of the city's population lived in this sprawling region bounded by the Bowery Road on the west and the East River on the south and east, but only one-sixth of the city's churches had been erected there.

Not only did New York not have enough churches in the right locations; it did not have enough churches to serve its growing population. Even though the rate of church growth was higher than that of the population, as Weeden later noted, Stafford believed the ratio of people to churches was still too high (see the appendix, table A.3). "Allowing that one minister ought not to have the immediate charge of more than a thousand souls," he explained, "there will be 60,000 people destitute of the stated ministry of the gospel, or of proper religious instruction." Conversations with ministers suggested even this ratio might be too high and should be reduced to six hundred to one.[15] New York potentially had eighty-nine thousand inhabitants not receiving proper spiritual guidance, although Stafford admitted some adjustment must be made for "children, invalids, and others necessarily detained."[16]

Conditions within extant meetinghouses and outlying homes made the problem worse. Those who traveled from regions without churches into the settled part of the city for religious worship found few, if any, seats available to them. "The seats in the Presbyterian and in most of the other churches are owned or hired by private persons," Stafford explained. Many pews were underutilized yet rarely shared with others. Little provision was made for free or cheap seating.[17] Denied the opportunity to worship, the poor returned to crowded homes, typically containing four to twelve families, where they were corrupted by the impious among them. "The simple fact, that people live together in the manner described, and without the restraints of religion," Stafford harshly concluded, "is strong evidence that they are immoral."[18]

For Stafford, individual conversion offered an antidote to urban disorder. He recounted meeting a fifteen-year-old girl who "came to one of the Sabbath Schools, who had never been within a church, had never heard of a Bible or a Saviour, knew not that she had a soul, and supposed that when she died it would be the end of her existence."[19] Many more just like her, he assured his readers, lived across the city. Evangelical conversion could properly order her and others' naturally disordered hearts through the intervention of the Holy Spirit. What they needed was the Bible, the "sun of the moral world," to cast its illuminating rays on the disorder of the natural world, revealing and hopefully eradicating it. "It is that light to which natural man will not come, 'lest their deeds should be reproved,'" Stafford explained, but exposure to that light was the only way to "open the eyes of the understanding, and purify the heart, so that men shall not only see but love that light, and rejoice in it."[20]

Stafford drew inspiration not only from the Bible but also from the grid. More than just a plan for economic development, the grid presented a vision of the city as a system that could be reformed and reorganized into a single, centralized, rational order. It could make New York transparent, neutral, and nonhierarchical, not just spatially but also politically, economically, and culturally. Republicanism similarly shared this vision of ordering the country's citizenry while removing impediments to their advancement. Yet the grid also transcended these categories. For evangelical New Yorkers, it offered a template for expansion and also the scaffolding for an articulation of self that extended deep into the moral world. New Yorkers held great faith that natural and moral orders could be placed in parallel.[21]

To affect internal transformations first required external renovations. Walking the city, Stafford saw plenty of evidence of what Dell Upton calls the "myth of the shadow landscape," a perceived parallel geography of "unseparated, unclassified spaces [that] threatened to spread social disorder throughout society."[22] Where the systematic landscape of the grid promoted transparency and moral order, the shadow landscape sought to subvert that order through ambiguity and immorality. Taverns, theaters, and brothels represented visible embodiments of the shadow landscape, but other threats, even such seemingly trivial superstitious practices like nailing horseshoes to the bottom of doors, lurked in more mundane spaces.[23] The light of the Bible provided a torch for this darkened landscape. "We must carry it to them; we must cause it to shine in their dark abodes," Stafford explained; "If they flee from it into a cavern more dark, we must follow them; till there shall be no place in the city or in the world, to which they can retreat."[24]

As the Bible shined a light into the darkest recesses of the heart, a meetinghouse stood as a beacon within an unenlightened community. Meetinghouses provided perpetual monitors and visible symbols of moral order and piety that could affect visceral reactions in even the most "grossly vicious." "Erect a church, and the moral atmosphere will be purified," wrote Stafford. "The mists of darkness and death will vanish—the harsh gratings of discord and blasphemy will be changed into the sweet songs of Zion—the habitation of cruelty and vice into a Bethel—the sink of pollution into a fountain of life—the desert into the garden of God."[25] The temptation to provide makeshift structures instead of permanent meetinghouses in poor neighborhoods was understandable, but to be avoided. "When we consider the natural pride of the human heart, in connexion with the fact that these people live in a city, and in the midst of other churches," Stafford argued, "it is unreasonable to expect, that people of this description should go to a school-house or a private room to worship on the Sabbath."[26]

Meetinghouses offered unmoored urban individuals a form of community.[27] Here the city's new grid both hindered and helped Stafford. On the one hand, the grid promoted an individualism that tended toward anonymity and isolation: one could disappear into the grid, to the detriment of stable communities of longstanding residents who knew the character and circumstances of everyone in the neighborhood. Evangelicalism had long been pervaded by this tension between individualism, as exemplified in the conversion process, and community, manifest through the missionary spirit's focus on social activism. Yet evangelicals of Stafford's generation came to value community-based social activism because it served as an important means for fostering individual-focused conversion. On the other hand, the grid's embrace of transparency offered the promise of systematically finding the lost, street-by-street, house-by-house. Historians have criticized Stafford's plan for its focus on the promotion of community, judging it rural, old-fashioned, and woefully inadequate for the challenges of the city.[28] In reality, Stafford knew urban evangelicals hungered for a supportive community and innovated ways of fostering it.

Stafford had few qualms about enlisting the laity to undertake work traditionally done by the clergy. "The very sight of the moral and pious is a check to the wicked," he argued. "Should respectable persons simply pass through particular streets every day, and look at those who now exhibit in those streets all the degradation of their character, it would soon cause them to hide their heads." Stafford balanced the need to provide inspiration by example with the value of surveillance. "If the people are visited and instructed in their own dwellings," he explained; "if, in addition to this, they are assembled together in little circles for social worship; if they are followed from day to day, and week to week; if all is done in a manner so kind, so affectionate, so faithful, that they shall be convinced, that you have no object in view but the glory of God, and their own best good, we cannot doubt, that a powerful effect will be produced." Evangelicalism has rightly been critiqued for incorporating elements of social control within its practices, but it is important to remember that evangelicals held themselves to these standards.[29]

In the end, Stafford based his rallying cry on the interests of civil society and his readers' responsibility as urban evangelicals. The city was a destination for young people seeking new vocational and social opportunities and it set the trends "in the way of fashion" that the hinterland followed. Thus, Stafford exclaimed, "how immensely important, that they should be free from ignorance, error, and immorality! That they should set an example of holiness and of every good work!"[30] Stafford insisted that the missionary spirit mandated that urban evangelicals, ministers and laity alike, go out and solve these problems. *The New Missionary Field* provided a blueprint for making New York a religious center on par with the great financial and cultural center it was fast becoming.[31] Before Stafford knew it, his evangelical neighbors tripped over each other to stake their place in the new missionary field.

THE FIELD OPENS

The year 1816 was a watershed for the formation of evangelical voluntary associations in New York. Where evangelicals in the preceding generation, with notable exceptions, hesitated to reach out to those beyond their meetinghouses, the generation that came of age following the War of 1812 embraced the cause of the unconverted wholeheartedly. While clergy and older men dominated the leadership of newly formed or expanded national Sunday school, Bible, and tract societies, women and young men established their own local voluntary associations that year to support urban missions and church building.[32] They recruited recent college graduates to distribute Bibles and tracts, converse with local residents, and gather congregations in the eastern part of the city, Stafford's "new missionary field." Bitter competition wracked some of their early efforts, and their missionaries often found their idealism tested by the reaction of area residents, which ranged from acceptance to indifference to outright hostility. For those who persevered, reward came as mission congregations blossomed into some of the most active evangelical churches in the city.

The Society for the Prevention of Pauperism (SPP), begun in December 1817, is often considered the first significant organized voluntary response to the city following the War of 1812. Pauperism—defined as dependency on public assistance and private charity—had long been a reality of urban life. But for some concerned citizens the threat it posed to the economic and moral health of the city magnified in the economic depression of the late 1810s.[33] "I am tired assisting them in their distress," wrote Thomas Eddy, one of the SPP founders, to Governor DeWitt Clinton; "It appears to me more wise, to fix on every possible plan to *prevent* their poverty and misery."[34] The SPP's strategy for amelioration focused on legislative chambers rather than city streets. It lobbied for a dramatic restructuring of public assistance (cutting off all but the most helpless) and an aggressive system of municipal reforms and regulations. Its proposals included laws on marriage, taxes on the theater, licenses for taverns and grog shops, restrictions on immigration, and even limits on the sale of billiard tables and playing cards. It hoped the imposition of a system of moral values might transform the undeserving poor into useful and productive members of society. Ultimately their efforts fell short.[35]

The evangelical sisters, wives, and daughters of the city's bakers and merchants, carpenters and shipmasters who made up the Female Missionary Society for the Poor in the City of New-York and its Vicinity (FMS) could not have been more different than the distinguished civic, commercial, and professional leaders, many of them Quaker, who composed the board of directors of the SPP.[36] Their brothers, husbands, and sons, who formed the Young Men's Missionary Society of New York (YMMS) and the New-York Evangelical Missionary Society of Young Men (NYEMS), were also more at home in the workshop than the state house. These evangelicals shared a common vision and refused to see gender, age, or class as an impediment to their benevolent efforts. For them, evangelicalism's emphasis on soul equality applied as much to their efficacy as activists as to their ability to achieve conversion.[37] Their ultimate goal was not to legislate but to sponsor stable, permanent neighborhood churches on par with those in other parts of the city.

As these nascent societies sought suitable candidates to sponsor as missionaries, they benefited from a rising generation of educated young ministers enthusiastic about missionary work. Men like Ward Stafford, Samuel Mills, and Elihu Baldwin grew up in pious families in rural farming communities that early enkindled within them the importance of conversion and social activism. Revivals, family worship, and the biographies of Protestant missionary martyrs shaped their worldview. "How many Christians," Stafford asked of his generation, ". . . when reading the history of some self-denying missionary; when tracing the footsteps of a Brainerd, a Buchanan, a Newell, have desired to share with them the trials, the joy, and the glory of their work!"[38] Mills' interest came from his mother. "She was a *Missionary woman*, and frequently spake of Brainerd, and Eliot, and other Missionaries," his biographer recorded; "and as she dwelt upon the glorious cause in which they were engaged, [Mills] once heard her say respecting himself—'*I have consecrated this child to the service of God as a Missionary.*'"[39] Early impressions never faded.

These pious young men converged on the nation's colleges, where they found peers who shared their missionary fantasies (and others who dismissed them as "the offspring of over-heated zeal"). Under a haystack at Williams College in the midst of a thunderstorm in 1808, Samuel Mills famously covenanted with fellow classmates to become missionaries. At Yale the next year, he met Obookiah, a young Sandwich Islander brought back by British missionaries, who inspired him to later found the American Board of Commissioners for Foreign Missions. Some hesitated in the face of opportunity. The call for a missionary to labor among the Six Nations Iroquois made Elihu Baldwin wonder if his love of God was strong enough "to devote myself to the most difficult and unpleasant calling in his service."[40] He eventually overcame his unease, but classmate Gardiner Spring did not. "I once thought even of becoming a missionary to the heathen," Spring reflected later in life; "but it was the dream of the moment. I had not piety enough to look at so self-denying a question."[41] Missionary life on the North American frontier or in foreign lands required a level of devotion sufficient to offset the knowledge that it could also be an early death sentence. Cities provided a less fatal outlet for missionary zeal, although not without their own challenges.

Finding interested candidates was often easier for these new associations than agreeing on which to hire. Despite its ostensibly nondenominational status, the YMMS suffered a highly public schism when rival factions put forward competing candidates in November 1816. A majority supported Arthur J. Stansbury, a minister of the Associate Reformed Church, while a minority desired the selection of Samuel Hanson Cox, a recently ordained Presbyterian minister. Each side questioned the other's motives. The minority saw the nomination of Stansbury as a rejection not only of Cox but also of their theological views. (The majority all but confirmed this when they refused to promise that future missionaries "with Cox's sentiments" be employed.)[42] After a month of wrangling, the minority was offered a proportion of the YMMS's funds if it would secede "without wasting time and creating scandal by prolonged debate."[43] Ultimately one hundred members formed the NYEMS, but not without first resorting to the press to alert the city's evangelical community of the recent turn of events.[44]

All three missionary societies focused their efforts on the underserved eastern part of the city, which stretched from Franklin and Chatham Squares to Corlaers Hook. Laid out on confiscated loyalist land in the late 1780s, this was one of the first sections of the city to boast a regular grid and was a precursor to the Commissioners' Plan. Shipbuilding and related crafts occurred along the waterfront, while the people engaged in those industries lived in neighborhoods to the north. Yet church building lagged behind, as Stafford revealed in *The New Missionary Field*. Only three churches—the Oliver Street Baptist (1795) and Forsyth Street Methodist (1789) in the northwest corner and the Rutgers Presbyterian Church (1796) in the center—served this diverse area before the War of 1812 (see map 1.2).[45]

In rapid succession, the new evangelical societies initiated their missions. In October 1817, the Union Mission Church opened on the corner of Catherine and Bancker (now Madison) Streets under the direction of the FMS's missionary Ward Stafford. The NYEMS's missionary, Elihu Baldwin, also worked in this neighborhood for a few months, apparently without any tensions with Stafford. In November, he moved out to Corlaers Hook, a settlement that had sprung up during the War of 1812 around a handful of shipyards on the East River. Baldwin discovered a Methodist Sunday school in operation when he arrived, but plenty of work remained to be done. He preached in a variety of makeshift rented spaces as he worked to gather a congregation. The YMMS, despite being the first society organized, was the last to enter the field. Its first missionary lasted only a few weeks, but his successor, John E. Miller, served for several months. Miller carved out a niche geographically between Stafford's and Baldwin's missions, preaching in a house on Norfolk Street and at the Free School on Henry Street.

Competition between the two young men's societies flared up when their missionaries began to organize formal congregations. Baldwin's mission took shape as the Seventh Presbyterian Church in a little wooden meetinghouse on Sheriff Street in 1819.[46] Col. Henry Rutgers offered a lot of land to the YMMS in the area where Miller had been laboring, but instead it leased two lots and built a meetinghouse a block away from Baldwin's preaching house. Baldwin was devastated. "The time,—I can truly say, the much-dreaded time—has come, when the designs of men who have come into this field of labor, with the apparent object of destroying this little congregation and church, are to have their sway," he lamented in his diary. "His meetings for the evenings are appointed at the same time with my meetings. Thus minister is arrayed against minister, and people against people."[47] The YMMS's perceived victory proved short-lived. According to his biographer, Baldwin killed his competitor with kindness, so cheerfully cooperating with Robert Steel, Miller's successor, that he resigned within a few months. (The real cause might have been a lack of market demand.) The YMMS soon after rented the mission house to Methodists and retired from the field.[48]

Such competition likely amused residents, not a few of whom appreciated the distance the area afforded from the watchful eye of city churches. For many, the Sabbath offered their only day off. Rather than walking downtown to church, Stafford reported with dismay, they "calculate to have better food and more liquor than on other days; to associate together, and to make of this blessed day, which to the Christian is better than a thousand, a day of mirth and rioting." Grocers, often the leading purveyors of alcohol on the Sabbath, outnumbered any other profession on Catherine Street by five to one.[49] Such conditions only strengthened the resolve of missionaries. Samuel Mills found numerous families on Front Street destitute of Bibles, although many for want of interest. One bluntly told him she had no Bible and did not want one. When he insisted, "she observed it was not necessary for me to continue my 'preachment' any longer, for she would not receive a Bible." Later in the month, another threatened to burn the Bible if he left one.[50] Mills, however, was lucky. Another Bible distributor in the area was attacked, knocked down, had his clothes torn off, and lost considerable blood.[51]

Residents of Corlaers Hook seemed only slightly more receptive. The area had a reputation as a resort "for [the] lewd and abandoned of both sexes."[52] Baldwin first attempted to reach sinners in the spaces of their sin by preaching in a local ballroom. The owners soon feared the young missionary's presence would drive away their business, and compelled him to move to another venue.[53] He wrestled not only with finding a space to preach but with tailoring his message. A conversation with a "sprightly colored man" has overtones of the same doctrinal rigidity Ezra Stiles Ely exhibited in the almshouse. The man acknowledged he was a sinner but expressed hope "to do better in time to come." Baldwin quickly pushed back and insisted on salvation by faith instead of works, telling him in no uncertain terms that "future obedience would not compensate for past transgression." Incredulous, the man responded, "If they are true, I do not see what will become of the generality of people." Bemused, Baldwin reflected on his conversation (and nodded to the universality of contemporary missionary efforts): "While most of them speak of Christ as a Saviour, the majority expect salvation by their good works, (which, by the way, are not superlatively good,) as really and entirely, as the pagans of India."[54]

After the initial flurry of church construction, missionaries found growth to be frustratingly slow. New meetinghouses did not always have the immediate impact that Stafford predicted. Membership rolls at Seventh Presbyterian reveal that congregants came from the ranks of local artisans and small shopkeepers, many pushed out of the city's core by an expanding mercantile elite.[55] Women dominated, making up, on average, 70 percent of new members each year, similar to the ratio in other evangelical churches across the city (see the appendix, table A.6).[56] A greater percentage joined the church by profession than certificate or letter of dismissal from another church, strong evidence that revivalism brought them through the door. Eventually Seventh Presbyterian enjoyed a steady increase in members, but the Union

Mission Church did not. "If the people in Bancker-street (probably not the worst street in the city) have not been reformed," a missionary reflected as he rethought his strategy, "there is great reason to persevere in the good work begun, and perhaps retreating to a more convenient and salubrious location is an important preparatory step to a more vigorous effort to benefit their precious souls."[57] In 1823, the Union Mission Church closed its doors and moved two blocks east and six blocks north to Allen Street to start again.

Seventh Presbyterian's wooden meetinghouse, a scaled-down version of the evangelical vernacular, exerted a perceptible influence over the neighborhood. Calling on seventy-seven out of eighty families on a nearby street in 1823, Baldwin found that fifteen regularly attended religious worship, twenty-five occasionally, and the rest were "entirely neglectful of the house of God." He readily admitted this might not be the renovation for which he and his sponsors had hoped, but it was an improvement nonetheless. Change manifested itself in even more surprising ways. "Some among us, who cannot be persuaded to unite themselves with Christians of a more evangelical character, are forced by the increasing light, into the society of Unitarians and Universalists," Baldwin reported to his sponsors. "It is becoming more necessary for every man to take his stand with some denomination."[58] But he had more to fear from other evangelical faiths. The former YMMS Mission House was rented first by Methodists, who laid the cornerstone for a new meetinghouse on Willett Street in October 1825 (fig. 3.1), and later by a Baptist mission. A Methodist Society congregation undertook a structure a block to the north on Delancey Street. Baldwin feared that if his church did not soon build a new meetinghouse, "the erection of more commodious and beautiful edifices by other denominations should swallow us up."[59]

The concern for respectability that underlay Baldwin's call to construct a new meetinghouse also played out in the politics of the pews. Seventh Presbyterian's session remained cautious about initiating discipline against church members in its early years, fearful of alienating those whose allegiance already seemed tenuous. Only three cases of discipline made it into the session's records between 1818 and 1825, and only the complaint against Mrs. Sarah Morson for "the habitual sin of intemperance" warranted an extended discussion, culminating in her suspension.[60] Yet as the congregation's numbers grew and the walls of a new "large, neat, and convenient" brick meetinghouse rose on Ridge Street, the session went after a more "respectable" habitual offender.[61] Dr. Elias Badeau was a founding member of the church, along with several other members of his family, but also "long suspected of being addicted to the sin of intemperance." Baldwin privately admonished him, re-

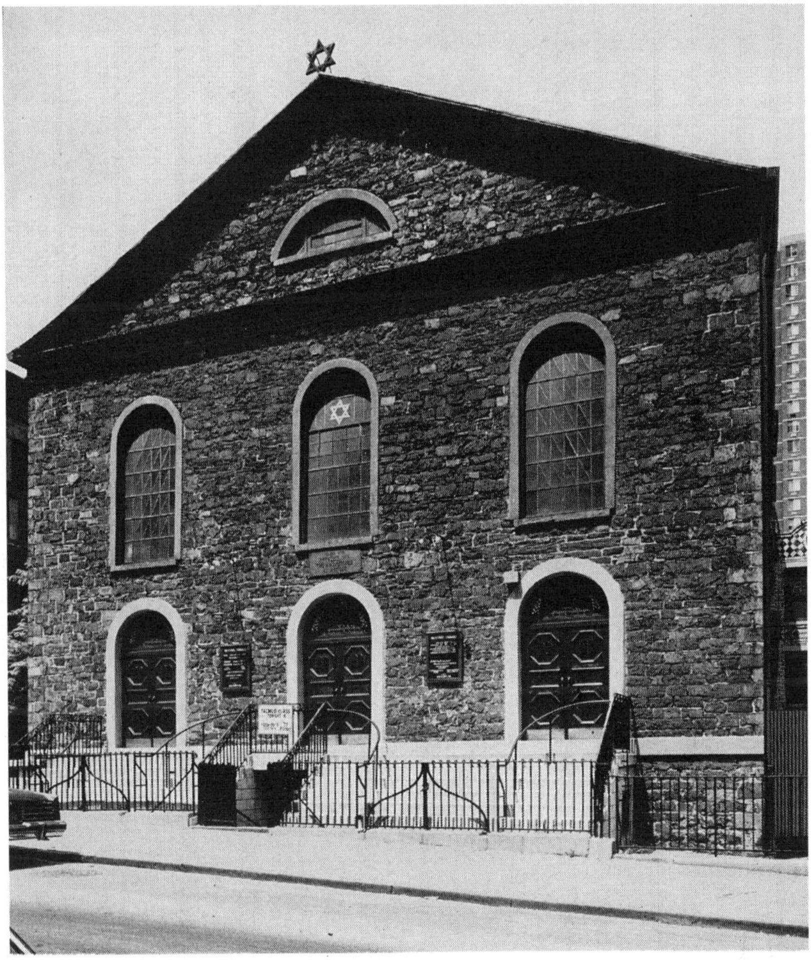

FIGURE 3.1 Willet Street Methodist Episcopal Church (built 1826), later sold and became the Bialystoker Synagogue. Edmund V. Gillon, [Bialystoker Synagogue, 7–13 Bialystoker Place / Willett Street], ca. 1977. Photograph from the collections of the Museum of the City of New York. 2013.3.1.619

luctant to publicly compromise his professional reputation, but the lay members of the session finally decided to act. Badeau's social position had lent the mission a level of respectability few other members could offer. Yet with a new material sign of respectability rising around them, Badeau became a liability instead of an asset. "The public voice called for prompt and decided measures," and the session suspended Badeau in June 1827.[62]

FIGURE 3.2 Beecher Ogden, Third Meetinghouse of the Seventh Presbyterian Church, 1831, Broome Street at Ridge Street, n.d., photograph, from PR020 (geographic file), box 57, f: Seventh Presbyterian Church; neg. #90832d, New-York Historical Society. Photography © New-York Historical Society

The opening of the Seventh Presbyterian Church's new meetinghouse in 1827 marked its final transition from mission to neighborhood church (fig. 3.2). The large brick meetinghouse staked its claim to prominence and permanency by rebuilding on the corner of a busy commercial street rather than in the middle of a residential side street, like its predecessor. Membership records confirm its influence in fostering a community around it. Those joining by letter of dismissal from other churches outnumbered those by profession of faith in the second half of the 1820s. According to their letters, they hailed from congregations in New York State, New England, and New Jersey, as well as other parts of the city.[63] They had previously belonged to a range of faiths, illustrating the fluidity within urban evangelicalism. The presence of well-off men, such as George Stoughtenburgh, a dry goods merchant, and David Hale, editor of the *Journal of Commerce,* reveals the extent to which new middle-class residents found the previously dodgy area increasingly attractive.[64] Yet by and large Seventh Presbyterian continued to be a congregation of cartmen, shoemakers, and carpenters. "There are almost none among them that were not dependent on their daily labor for subsistence," Baldwin's biographer remembered.[65] As Stafford predicted, the physical presence of Seventh Presbyterian Church played no small role in the area's transformation.

The importance of the missions undertaken by the FMS, the NYEMS, and the YMMS lay as much in the churches they planted as in the new mode of congregation building they pioneered. A partnership of evangelical voluntary associations, urban missionaries, and neighborhood residents proved a viable solution to filling absences in the spiritual marketplace. Three additional missions undertaken in the early 1820s, all of them in the neighborhoods west of the Bowery, ran into challenges common to the urban missionary field. Samuel Cornish, a freeborn black Presbyterian minister and later editor with John Russwurm of the pioneering African American newspaper *Freedom's Journal*, had no difficulty in attracting a devoted following among the city's African American community but could not sustain it financially.[66] Within two years of building one of the finest small meetinghouses in the city, the First Colored Presbyterian Church saw it sold under foreclosure to a Jewish congregation.[67] Missions up on Bleecker Street and in the Bowery had the opposite problem. There, missionaries attracted an upscale audience who could easily attend other churches rather than their stated audience of the underserved poor. "Originally a purely missionary enterprise," a nineteenth-century historian candidly remembered of the Bowery Mission, before long "it had come to be a gathering of intelligent and cultivated people drawn from a distance, some of them to sustain a sinking enterprise, and others to enjoy the brilliant oratory of [Rev. Joseph Stubbs] Christmas."[68] Despite these challenges, all three developed into settled congregations. Many others followed in the coming decades.

CONVERTING THE WATERFRONT

Not every mission lent itself to a process of church building. Congregations require permanency, but transiency has long been a hallmark of urban life. The city's competitive real estate market created conditions in which men and women moved residences with frequency. May 1 was the city's annual moving day—a chaotic tradition that stretched back to the eighteenth century as the majority of the city's rental properties turned over and families competed to relocate themselves. For every family that moved, another stood ready to take its place.[69] In fact, the city's phenomenal population growth derived not from natural increase but from the continued arrival of men and women from around the Atlantic World. Some put down roots, while others drifted through, enjoying the excitement and opportunity that the city offered before shipping out again. Among the most visible of the final category were sailors.

Sailors presented a distinct challenge to evangelical proselytizing. New York emerged as a dominant North American port in the early nineteenth century, making sailors ubiquitous within the city. Writers then, as now, commented on their behavior, or more often their misbehavior, in port. After months within the tightly packed, strictly ordered, homosocial world of commercial and navy ships, sailors savored the liberty they found on the waterfront. An informal economy of taverns, brothels, and other amusements catered to those with hard-earned money to spend.[70] Many found sailors' ability to pass "between sea and land without ever fully committing to either" puzzling.[71] Yet anyone who actually spent time with them realized the complexity of their liminal position. Situated not only between land and sea, sailors also acutely felt what it meant to be between this world and the next. To navigate that experience, sailors created a rich world of belief and practice.[72] Rather than being dismissed as irreligious, sailors might be better understood as differently religious. Sensitivity to those differences was crucial to missionary success. "That vast republic of men who have their dwellings on the sea, constitutes in many respects a world by itself," Rev. Edward D. Griffin reflected in 1819, "governed by different laws, connected by a different language, and not likely to fall under the influence of any of those plans which are set on foot for the reformation of landsmen."[73] Evangelicals hired missionaries and experimented with a range of innovative spatial solutions—bethel and boardinghouse prayer meetings, domestic visitations, and a Mariner's Church—to reach this other world. In the process, they attracted an active audience, but not necessarily the one they intended.

As domestic missionary associations fought for turf along the edges of the expanding city, marine missionary associations turned their attention to the city's wharves. When a few keepers and lodgers of sailors' boardinghouses began to show up at prayer meetings on Water Street after the War of 1812, evangelicals capitalized on their interest to form a prayer meeting just for sailors. Over the coming years, they founded several voluntary associations to distribute Bibles, hire preachers, and organize prayer meetings.[74] Like their domestic sisters and brothers, these marine missionary associations eschewed denominational affiliations. They, however, figured out how to be more complementary and less competitive in their efforts.

Evangelical merchants, rather than women or young men, provided the driving force behind these new associations. Annual sermons and reports drove home the message that maritime missions touched their sponsors' temporal and spiritual well-being. "A city containing so many merchants, so many Christians, and so distinguished for its benevolent institutions, cannot, will not, be the last to accomplish a work which promises such a revenue of good to man, and of glory to God," the New York Marine Society reasoned in 1817.[75] Use of the term *revenue* is important, for society organizers expected these missions to pay economic and spiritual dividends. Reports spoke of sailors as ambassadors for the United States and Christ, whose bad behavior jeopardized globalizing commercial and sacred economies. Rev. Edward Griffin asked his auditors to consider "how much we are indebted to [sailors] for our wealth and prosperity" and how "it is for our service that they forego [*sic*] the moral and religious advantages which we enjoy." This "great emporium of commerce," he pronounced, must support missions to sailors as an "act of sacred justice in sight of all who live upon the labour and deprivations of seamen."[76]

To reach sailors, evangelical merchants sought to enlist those ostensibly with the most influence over them: ship captains. Over half of the founding managers of the Marine Bible Society in 1817 were or had been ship captains, although only one, Christopher Prince, held an office.[77] "More than forty shipmasters of this city have voluntarily given their opinion, that the spread of the Bible among seamen has made them better men," the Society adverted, hoping that captains might see the utility, while feeling the obligation, of spreading the gospel.[78] In reality, most captains showed little interest in the work. An initial meeting to raise money for a Mariner's Church in 1819 started late because so few captains appeared.[79] Within a few years, merchants significantly outnumbered sea captains among the officers and directors of the New York Port Society.[80]

Early on, these associations agreed that the reformation of sailors had a better chance on land than on sea. "Even in the Millennium," Ward Stafford remarked, "we cannot suppose that the Gospel will, to any great extent, be preached on the ocean."[81] Awaiting them in port, he insisted, must be spaces, formal and informal, dedicated for their worship. Many would be induced to attend these places, he thought, "by the influence of early education, by curiosity, a desire to see their companions and to be like other people, or the pride with which they would take in an institution of their own."[82] Carefully customizing the message was crucial. Rather than analogizing the Bible as a light illuminating the deepest recesses of sin, Stafford used the more familiar image of a compass and pole star guiding sailors back to God, and, by implication, to port, whether terrestrial or heavenly.

Stafford devoted considerable space to highlighting the distinctive needs of sailors in *The New Missionary Field,* but the real work of bringing them to conversion and building a community fell to the young Methodist minister Henry Chase. Born in rural Rensselaer County, Chase was not a product of New England's evangelical colleges and seminaries. He did value religious education and arrived in the city in the late 1810s to serve as the first superintendent of the Wesleyan Academy. Methodists had long been reluctant to embrace a learned ministry, and this early initiative in denominational training ended in failure. Chase reveals little in his private diaries about what drew him to be a missionary on the waterfront. Somehow he found his calling and ministered to the city's maritime community from 1821 until his death in 1854, a longer tenure than any other urban missionary of his generation. His Methodism distinguished him from the mass of Presbyterian missionaries working in the same wards of the city, and caused occasional tension with his sponsors on the one hand and fellow Methodist ministers on the other. Ultimately neither impeded his work.[83] If anything, his selection helped marine missionary associations maintain broader interest and participation across the city's evangelical community.

Where Elihu Baldwin went to his target audience's site of sin, the ballroom, to convert, Chase went to sailors' site of work, the ship. Prayer meetings on the decks of New York's commercial and naval vessels, known as bethel meetings, sought to transform (if only temporarily) a secular space that bridged the order of land and the disorder of sea into a sacred one that mediated between this world and the next. On June 22, 1821, a blue bunting flag emblazoned with the word "BETHEL," an image of a dove with an olive branch below and a small star above, was hoisted up the masthead of the ship *Cadmus,* docked at Pine Wharf, signaling a new effort to bring the gospel to the secular waterfront. The gift of a British society, the bethel flag, as it came to be known, signified the location of a sacred space, and, at the same time, competed with a profusion of national flags, furled sails, and towering masts.[84] Evangelical merchants, "several friends from the shore," and a "considerable number" of sea captains and sailors gathered under the flag that evening for the first of a series of hour-long prayer meetings sponsored by the New York Bethel Union.[85] Those who missed these meetings could read about them in Journal of the Bethel Flag, a regular column written by Chase and his fellow missionaries in the *Christian Herald and Seaman's Magazine.*[86]

At Coffee House Slip, Steven's Wharf, and dozens of other piers, the bethel flag announced the nightly transformation of the decks of schooners, sloops,

FIGURE 3.3 "Bethel Meeting, Quarter Deck of the Receiving Ship, Fulton, Navy-Yard, New-York, July 18, 1828." Illustration in *The Sailor's Magazine, and Naval Journal*, October 1828. Courtesy, American Antiquarian Society

brigs, and ships into evangelical chapels. The captains of these ships served as hosts and put their crew to work clearing the deck, lashing awnings to the masts, and laying out seats for the evening's meeting. At the stated time, participants assumed assigned places for a service of prayer, hymn singing, scripture reading, and personal testimony. Newspaper accounts reveal as much about efforts to locate the evening's nonmaritime guests symbolically as they do about accommodating the ostensible target audience.[87] An engraving of a bethel meeting on the quarterdeck of the receiving ship *Fulton* illustrates this concern with reinforcing the order of the ship and the shore (fig. 3.3). To the left, carefully segregated, the officers of the ship and female guests are gathered, and a man, likely from the Bethel Union, leads the meeting. Crowded to the right sit sailors. Published reports of turnout vary, but on particularly popular nights sailors spilled out onto the wharf. Chase and other missionaries liked this overflow, reflecting one evening that "after many hundreds were collected, it seemed the Lord enclosed us in on every side; he made a hedge around us, so that Satan could not come near us."[88]

Order proved important, and ships remained a contested space. Fear of disorder almost prevented on-deck prayer meetings from happening in the first place. "When it was considered that seamen, not withstanding their characteristic frankness and generosity, were from that very source frequently rash and inconsiderate; that these meetings would be held under the shades of night, and within the borders of that empire which Satan had for ages claimed as his own, the timid Christian might well be pardoned, if he felt some anxious forebodings," a missionary confessed.[89] Intoxicated and rowdy men appeared at prayer meetings, whether out of sport, curiosity, or to deny the space's transformation from secular to sacred. Typically, though, missionaries invoked drunken sailors in published reports only to foil their intemperance with the gospel.[90] Solemnity, not enthusiasm, ultimately proved the criteria for judging that God was in their midst. "Some were as solemn as death, and others were lifting their eyes to heaven, adoring and praising redeeming love," wrote a missionary; "and in leaving the ship there was the same silence; not a word was heard; all walked off the wharf with slow and solemn steps."[91]

Bethel meetings moved into the kitchens and parlors of sailors' boardinghouses when the weather grew cold. A by-product of the city's residential development, boardinghouses emerged in the early nineteenth century.[92] Some catered to specific populations, while others, including many poor widows, rented any available space in their homes out of economic necessity. In the winter, standing meetings on Tuesday and Friday evenings at specific boardinghouses drew a more regular, if smaller, crowd.[93] The confined domestic space created a different kind of spiritual environment than open-air meetings, one that brought to mind the bonds of the household rather than the structured order of work. Women occasionally attended bethel meetings, but they seem to have participated more actively and in greater numbers in boardinghouse prayer meetings. Their presence and participation was likely encouraged as a means to bring their struggling husbands to conversion. In his private diaries, Chase hinted at the potential for disorder that lurked in these less hierarchical and more intimate gatherings. "A little sailor spoke some things rather unadvisedly and a woman also addressed the meeting," he wrote in December 1822. "Rather an unusual time."[94]

For rank and file sailors unaccustomed to having their voices heard at sea, bethel and boardinghouse prayer meetings provided a platform, an audience, and the spiritual authority to counsel others of all ranks. "I know not how to be silent on such an occasion," a sailor excused himself one evening. "I must declare the goodness of the Lord to my own soul, in bringing me, I trust, from darkness into light." His conversion occurred while on a voyage to Curaçao, when, "without human agency, that blessed book, the Bible, which has now been so earnestly recommended to our attention, was in the reading of it sanctified to my soul." Diffusing potential objections from his fellow sailors, he explained, "I was awakened to see my true condition, not that I was better than my shipmates, but that I was a guilty sinner, lying at the mercy of a holy God." He spoke out of gratitude for that "gracious change" and to reassure others that he knew the dangers with which they wrestled.[95]

Different factors made sailors susceptible to evangelicalism's influence. The transition back to life on land created social and spiritual crises for some. One sailor, after spending sixteen years in the China Sea trade, came home only to contend with a younger brother, whom he had never met, "who often told me I was going to hell! For I was a heathen."[96] Others returned to wives, daughters, and even perfect strangers concerned about their salvation. Testimonials reprinted in Journal of the Bethel Flag showed confident sailors who had achieved the New Birth. Chase's diaries reveal a far more anxious lot, men struggling under the weight of spiritual distress in a land with a different set of rules. Peter De Coux put it to Chase bluntly: "He wanted to know how to get rid of his sins."[97] The overwhelming attention sailors placed on confessing sins reveals the extent to which they accepted evangelicals' stress on such reformation as key to restoring order to their lives.

If sailors would not come to the bethel and boardinghouse prayer meetings, then Chase would go to them. In fact, most of his time, as his public reports to his sponsors and private diaries confirm, was spent canvassing the waterfront. "I have walked through the streets in search of them, and wherever I found them, whether in the street, in the church, at their homes, or at their boarding-houses, I endeavored to persuade them to forsake their sins and turn to God," he explained.[98] In his first few months, he entertained a fantasy about that interaction, as captured in his account of a visit to a boardinghouse on Water Street:

> Having ascertained that entertainment for mariners was kept at the house, I rapped at the door, and was invited in. Passing through a kind of hall, I came to a back room in which was sitting the mistress of the house, and half a dozen mariners, who were conversing together cheerfully, but not rudely. I had a bundle of tracts under my arm. I walked leisurely towards a table there was standing in the room, at the same time taking off my hat, and using the customary words of salutation. The mariners all respectfully imitated me by uncovering their heads.

> I then stated to them my errand, gave each a few tracts, which they received, and thanked me a thousand times, promised to read them, and to attend the Mariners' Church the next Sabbath.[99]

Doffing his hat and using "customary words of salutation," Chase tried to exhibit an air of familiarity in an altogether unfamiliar territory. His naïveté is perhaps not surprising. In time, he learned to stay and speak with those he encountered instead of leaving some tracts on the table and moving along.

The grid of the East River waterfront provided both the ethos and the template for Chase's early visitations. Between November 1821 and January 1822, Chase moved systematically through the neighborhood. Starting on Bancker near the corner of Catherine, where Stafford's Union Mission Church stood, he worked his way east down to Rutgers Street, doubled back to Pike Street, and then traveled west along Henry, back to Catherine. Finally, he worked west along Lombardy (later Monroe) from Henry Rutgers's mansion on Jefferson to Catherine Street. Some of the sailors he met proved receptive to his evangelical message. Young John Malison said he was "very attentive to church" and recently impressed by the experience of a young man washed overboard only to be "saved almost miraculously." Chase encouraged him to "depend constantly on God" and "not be laughed out of his religion." Others proved less interested. Silvanus Gifford, a sick mariner in the same house, told him he was "unconcerned about his soul" and had "always lived a moral life and needs nothing more."[100]

Three-quarters of the sailors Chase called on, however, were at sea, moved away, or just "not in." In their place he encountered a community of wives, widows, and mothers solicitous of his attention. True to his mission, he began by asking them about the spiritual state of the sailors in their lives. Some spoke highly of their husbands' religious devotion when in port, while others revealed anxiety over their lack of conversion. The wife of John Morgan, a rigger, confessed her husband "got drunk every night" and that she "had trouble enough with him."[101] Invariably, though, the conversation turned to the spiritual state of these women. The wife of John Smith, a mariner, spoke of her "serious and inquiring state." She had never been converted, despite her prayers, and coped with the vicissitudes of a husband who was "not a man of religion but of strict morality" and a mother who had been confined to bed for nearly seventeen years."[102] Others needed more serious comfort. Mrs. Mansfield's husband had been missing for three weeks and "from certain circumstances, is thought to have drowned in the East River by falling from dock in a dark night." When asked whether she had any friends or family, she shook her head and told him, as the tears flowed, "I was left to the wide world when I was but a child and am now left again." He left her some tracts, his standard response early in his career.

Before long, Chase's daily visitations forced him to crisscross the neighborhood rather than process in a more orderly way up and down the gridded streets. Three households—Mrs. Mansfield at 21 Pike, Mrs. Smith at the corner of James and Cherry Streets, and the store of John Potwine on Pearl near Oak Street—provided the nodes for his travels in January 1823. Mrs. Mansfield's suspicions about her husband's drowning proved true. In his absence she opened her house to Chase, allowing him to converse with her boarders and to run a Thursday evening prayer meeting. He, in turn, acquired information on her behalf about receiving support from the Society for the Relief of Poor Widows and Orphan Children.[103] Mrs. Smith's husband went off to sea, and her mother appeared on the point of death, so Chase checked in every other day.[104] And when Chase arrived to comfort the dying Miss Starr in the household of John Potwine, he found a whole household waiting for him. "I had quite a religious conversation with all of them," he recorded. "Miss Starr, the sick daughter, very comfortable in mind. Mrs. Star, Mrs. Potwine, Mrs. Adams, enjoying themselves very well in religion. Mrs. Comstock quite anxious, and Mr. Potwine in an interesting state of mind. Spoke to each one on the subject of religion, and then prayed with them."[105] Chase's audiences chose him as often as he chose them.

Henry Chase might have spent his weekdays in the ships, boardinghouses, and households of the waterfront, but he insisted that on the Sabbath all converge at the Mariner's Church at 65 Roosevelt Street. A dearth of churches along the waterfront made it difficult for sailors to attend worship services. While the poor who walked to downtown churches competed for the few free pews available, sailors found even less provision for their accommodation. If seats were available, Stafford argued, sailors would not use them anyway. "When they enter a church, they are known and marked as sailors," he explained. "They attract the notice of no small part of the congregation; and most of them would sooner face the cannon's mouth than the thoughtless, supercilious gaze, which betrays equally a want of civility to the stranger, and of reverence in the house of God."[106] To solve this problem, the New York Port Society (NYPS) rented a large schoolroom for Chase to preach in between Franklin Square and Roosevelt Street in 1818. Soon after, it secured land around the corner and built a Mariner's Church, which opened the following year.

The Mariner's Church represented a new form of meetinghouse, clothed in a familiar evangelical vernacular. The laying of the cornerstone in October 1819, one observer recorded, piqued the curiosity of between four and five hundred.[107] Over the next year, the nearly square brick structure arose on Roosevelt Street, symbolically sited among the homes of the city's ship captains. An illustration on the cover of the *Christian Herald and Seaman's Magazine* suggests this structure dedicated to the spiritual needs of common sailors towered over the surrounding two-story dwelling houses of their masters, although in reality it probably was not so imposing (see fig. 3.4). The exterior echoed the gable-end, tripartite façade common among other urban evangelical meetinghouses. Two entrances initially graced the street level, one leading to the sanctuary and a basement lecture room, and the other to the galleries. Exterior ornamentation was limited to a central Palladian window and dome-topped windows on the second floor, and some decorative quoins and architraves. The bethel flag waved at the gable's peak.[108]

The interior of the meetinghouse combined innovative and traditional evangelical approaches to space. The basement story consisted of a large lecture room for Wednesday evening prayer meetings and Sunday schools. The sanctuary sat six hundred, while the gallery accommodated a few hundred more. Most evangelical city churches by 1820 promoted family seating by pews, but the Mariner's Church insisted on gender-segregated seating. Sanctuary seats were explicitly limited to "seafaring persons and the male friends of the institution." In a move more common to Jewish synagogues than evangelical meetinghouses, women sat in the galleries. The NYPS explained this policy removed a barrier "to the attendance of many who might otherwise from diffidence or backwardness decline entering a more mixed assembly." It suggested concerns about respectability and the belief that sailors desired a homosocial worship experience. But such an arrangement also had a practical function: it kept women, to whom evangelicalism disproportionately appealed, from crowding out sailors.[109]

From its opening on the first Sabbath in June, 1820, the Mariner's Church quickly became an integral part of the waterfront neighborhood. "In the evening I went to the Mariners Church, it was so full many could not get in," Christopher Prince recorded in his diary a week after it opened. "It was a pleasing sight—many ship mates were there as well as seamen."[110] The vast majority of people Chase visited between November 1821 and January 1822 mentioned attending services in the new church, their frequency ranging from "always" and "constantly" to "sometimes" and "not often." Attendance varied by season, and the church was not immune to the occasional false alarm of "fire" from a rowdy sailor. The Mariner's Church succeeded so well, in fact, that some worshippers wished to become full members. This was not possible, however, because the NYPS had agreed not to incorporate under a

FIGURE 3.4 The Mariner's Church, 65 Roosevelt Street, New York, 1820. Illustration in the *Christian Herald and Seaman's Magazine,* August 2, 1823. Courtesy, American Antiquarian Society

specific denomination. Robert Green and his wife approached Chase about this issue one Sunday. "They wish to join the Church and partake of ordinances. They are unwilling to join any other church because they say the Mariner's Church seems so much like home to them," Chase recorded in his diary. "The difficulty, I told them might be obviated, by their receiving the ordinances where they should join, and attend the Mariner's Church still."[111]

Within a few short years, the combined efforts of voluntary associations, missionaries, and residents of the city's maritime community created an evangelical presence in the midst of an area long considered a world apart. Evangelicalism spread through nightly prayer meetings on the decks of ships and in boardinghouses, daytime visitations to maritime households, and services in a specially designed meetinghouse. Marine missionary associations embraced the spirit of the grid and hoped to bring order to what otherwise appeared a disordered region. The missionaries they sponsored took advantage of the wide latitude given. When Henry Chase wrote Journal of the Bethel Flag or preached in his gender-segregated meetinghouse, he reinforced a public performance ostensibly about converting the individual sailor. His daily domestic visitations, however, reveal evangelicalism's much broader appeal to the maritime community. These women and men did not passively accept the gospel. Instead, they actively embraced it and, in the process, put Chase to work.

CONCLUSION

Following the War of 1812, a host of new missionary societies sponsored ambitious young ministers who coupled the transformative power of evangelical conversion with the potential of community-focused social activism. Instead of shipping out as missionaries to foreign lands, Ward Stafford and Henry Chase turned to the rapidly growing city, a mission field that many Americans found equally foreign. Stafford's *The New Missionary Field* brought to the attention of evangelical New Yorkers whole districts that had been overlooked as the city expanded. Taking his inspiration from the ethos of the grid recently proposed in the Commissioners' Plan, he offered a series of recommendations for how an internal renovation of New Yorkers' hearts might be effected through an external renovation of their neighborhoods. His report captured the imagination of evangelical laity and ministers alike. Where the postrevolutionary generation looked inward to their own conversion, the rising generation looked outward to the conversion of the city. Years later, Stafford's alumni biographer remembered *The New Missionary Field* as an "epoch-making report in the history of city missions."[112]

The number of mission churches, bethel meetings, and boardinghouse prayer groups in the city never came close to the number of taverns, ballrooms, and brothels, but in time they became equally integral components of the urban landscape. These missions were not one-directional endeavors, where the missionary delivered the gospel to the unconverted and they unquestioningly accepted it. Instead, the interaction involved a far more complex negotiation. Sometimes, as the Union Mission and First Coloured Presbyterian churches learned, their efforts did not succeed as planned. Other times, as Elihu Baldwin in his nearly eighteen years at the Seventh Presbyterian Church and Henry Chase in his thirty-two years at the Mariner's Church both discovered, they surpassed their expectations. As Henry Chase's public writings hint, and private writings confirm, flexibility proved key. Over the 1810s and '20s, aspirations collided with realities as Stafford's plan for a "new missionary field" was embraced and adapted, setting the course for urban evangelicalism's reform efforts over the next four decades.

CHAPTER FOUR

Practicing Faith through Reading and Writing

Returning home from a day spent up at the family's Harlem farm, Michael Floy Jr. met with the unexpected news that John Mather Jr. was "very low" and had repeatedly asked for him to visit. Floy knew the young boy from the Sunday school at the Bowery Village Methodist Episcopal Church, where he served as a teacher and later superintendent. With Charles Davis, the boy's current teacher, Floy made his way to Mather's home. "There I saw what I shall never forget," he recorded in his diary, "the dear little boy almost in the agonies of death, but happy and resigned to God's will." Before parting, he had a brief conversation with Mather about his spiritual state at this important moment of transition. The boy valiantly labored under the pain of a "locked jaw" to answer his questions. "The idea of losing him whom I had so often seen at school with pleasure and delight, affected me strangely," Floy admitted, "and I could sleep but little after coming home." Young Mather entered his eternal rest that evening. As Floy struggled with the loss, he found solace in a perhaps surprising activity: he wrote an account of the boy's final hours that he later published.[1]

Michael Floy's decision to write about the passing of his Sunday school scholar is a reminder of the centrality of print to antebellum evangelicalism. Participation in the urban evangelical community conditioned Floy to desire to connect a private encounter with a larger social experience. New York, which was emerging as a national and international center for evangelical cultural production, offered him the means to do so. Evangelical magazines had long memorialized the last moments of pious residents, but the subjects of those accounts were more often ministers and matriarchs than eleven-year-old boys with tetanus.[2] Floy had come to know the forms, styles, and genres of evangelical print intimately through his work with the Bowery Village Sunday School, his visits to the Methodist Book Concern on Mulberry Street, and his voracious reading of hundreds of magazines and books upon which he commented in his remarkable diary. His account of Mather's death might strike modern readers as formulaic and sentimental, but it reveals the influence of books as diverse as seventeenth-century devotional guides and contemporary secular biographies. Even more significantly, it reflects his belief that individual textual practices could be spiritually transformative, sanctifying individuals as well as the broader community. City publishers made Floy's account accessible to audiences far beyond Manhattan.[3]

Scholars have traditionally interpreted evangelicalism and the market as fundamentally at odds, despite the experiences of Michael Floy and others. They assume nineteenth-century transformations in market culture, felt first and most intensely in cities, made evangelicals reject urban centers as immoral and irreligious and long for a rural ideal.[4] Yet evangelical print culture reveals that rather than fueling a decline in religious devotion and practice, urban commercial culture stimulated it. Evangelicalism thrived by appropriating aspects of the new urban market capitalism and embracing trends within popular literary culture, print technology, and trade organization. Cities provided sites for this rich experimentation as well as the financial and organizational resources for its production and distribution, first across the country and later around the world. Religious and commercial culture existed in an ongoing, if occasionally volatile, relationship. Throughout, they exhibited a greater degree of collaboration than has typically been acknowledged.[5]

Coalescing an audience around print was the ambition, and the challenge, for evangelicals throughout the eighteenth and nineteenth centuries. Before the American Revolution, itinerant ministers published sermons, journals, and devotional guides to foster and sustain textual communities after they left town. In the postrevolutionary city, local ministers tried to create a conversation that transcended denominational difference to spread the gospel and to counter threats posed by temptations to sin and other religious traditions. New printing technologies, modes of distribution, and organizational structures revolutionized evangelical print culture following the War of 1812. Bibles, tracts, and periodicals poured forth from nondenominational, denominational, and commercial presses and traveled over roads, down canals, and across oceans in search of readers. Michael Floy's decision to write an account of his Sunday school scholar's death embodied this textual culture.

NATIONAL ASPIRATIONS, LOCAL FAILURES

"While the presses throughout the union are teeming with literary and political journals," publisher Cornelius Davis wrote at the opening of the nineteenth century, many "have lamented that no convenient medium is found for conveying to the public information relative to the state of the Church, and the prosperity or decline of that kingdom whose interests they esteem more important than those of any temporal sovereignty."[6] Davis was correct that postrevolutionary New York was awash in newspapers and magazines, but his assumption about those papers' ability "to call forth a unified public to act the role of a national public" was more fantasy than reality. Regardless, evangelical publishers believed the periodical press was key to turning the loose, discordant voices of a dispersed community into a common, unified discourse that might advance the cause of evangelicalism and counter its most pressing threats locally, nationally, and globally. Their efforts proved short-lived, but this rich period of experimentation set the stage for the emergence of longstanding and far-reaching evangelical magazines after the War of 1812.

New York's periodical press rebounded quickly following the American Revolution. Six newspapers competed for the attention of city residents in 1785. Thirty years later that number rose to sixteen.[7] Postrevolutionary newspaper editors dreamed of fostering a nationalist consciousness, yet their dedication to oppositional politics had the effect of limiting their appeal to narrower, more local audiences.[8] Federalist, Anti-Federalist, and later Democratic-Republican editors exploited tumultuous political strife over the adoption of the Constitution, the launching of the new national government, Alexander Hamilton's plan for the nation's economic recovery, and ongoing tensions with France and Britain to engage the attention of readers—and to alienate others.[9] Contemporary magazines fared little better. Between 1787 and 1810, New York printers published forty-one different magazines, most short-lived. Some, such as Noah Webster's *American Magazine* (1787) sought to unite citizens through a national literary discourse, while others, such as the *Monthly Military Repository* (1796–1797) courted more specific readerships.[10] Nearly half (18 out of 41) were addressed to religious audiences. Most, like the quarterly *Free Universal Magazine* (1793), could not rise above sectarian differences.[11] That particular magazine's editor filled its pages with biblical exegesis and defenses of Universalism, such as a dialogue between a Baptist congregation and a "dissenting sister" who had lately joined the Universalists.[12] The magazine lasted only four issues.[13]

Material conditions also limited print's reach during this time, despite assumptions by scholars to the contrary.[14] Costs of equipment, shortages of paper, and difficulties of collecting subscriptions ensured that over two-thirds of American newspapers launched before 1821 lasted for three years or less.[15] Magazines proved even more difficult to sustain.[16] Their format, limited (and in many cases, lack of) advertising, and reliance on paid subscriptions made them more vulnerable. In general, publishers had to wait until after 1816 for the internal improvements necessary for the mass circulation of print and until after 1830 for the technologies that sustained mass production.[17]

Editors of evangelical magazines were aware of these realities. Their need to unify an evangelical audience by transcending sectarian differences, however, compelled them to try anyway. The metrical psalms of the Scotch Presbyterians, the learned sermons of the Strict Baptists, and the call-and-response of African American Methodists testified to the diversity of the city's evangelical sects every Sabbath. As the evangelical community expanded within the rapidly growing city, print offered the promise of generating a new comparative consciousness—an imagined community—across local, national, or even international boundaries.[18] Following the example of their British cousins, they focused on the basic principles of individual conversion and community activism that united evangelicals, rather than the theological distinctions that divided them.

Running throughout evangelical magazines in the 1790s and 1800s was a persistent concern about participation in a larger discourse about morality and virtue taking place as the young nation struggled for political stability.[19] The editor of the *United States Christian Magazine* (a title that reveals its ambition) explained in 1795 that he aimed to fight the "growing ignorance of true religion, and the sensible decline of vital piety." He warned that "when others are industrious in disseminating poison," evangelicals must not be "remiss in circulating the antidote."[20] Danger lurked, another editor detailed, with "the intemperate pursuit of wealth, with the gradual relaxation of every social bond; with the violence of political ferment; and with the approach of those fearful days which are coming upon earth." His magazine, he promised, would be "a standard round which the friends of truth may rally," an evangelical beacon in a sea of economic, social, and political turmoil.[21] The challenge was how best to raise this standard. Editors experimented with three different strategies to bring individual evangelicals into community through print, each with varying degrees of success.

The first, and most widely attempted, strategy was to unify evangelicals around a discourse on holy living. This approach harkened back to the pioneering efforts of eighteenth-century British itinerants George Whitefield and John Wesley. They published sermons, journals of their preaching tours, and even magazines to provide men and women with models of conversion and exemplary piety. They aimed for practicality, providing examples of real people and addressing common problems faced in the quest to lead pious lives. Their extensive catalogs of religious titles united the Anglo-Atlantic's first evangelical public around the doctrine of the New Birth. While the Calvinist Whitefield and Arminian Wesley occupied opposite ends of the mainstream Protestant theological spectrum, both delivered evangelical messages that transcended the boundaries of their confessions.[22]

In the *Experienced Christian's Magazine,* William Phoebus sought to foster holy living by appealing to the universal church. The introduction to the magazine's first run (1796–1797) announced its intention to provide examples of "some of the most worthy persons, after a life of exemplary devotion, and exalted virtue, bearing their dying testimony to the excellency of the gospel, and the pleasure of religion."[23] The value of such models, Phoebus explained, lay in the cues they gave about proper conduct, the deliverance one might expect by emulating them, and the evidence they displayed of the power of the gospel. He drew on exemplary men and women from classical antiquity and the Reformation as well as the recent past. In the first issue, for example, he held up Polycarp, bishop of the Church of Smyrna, and Mrs. Bartine, a New York housewife, as comparatively valuable models for emulation.[24] Their inclusion created a sense of simultaneity across space and time that allowed readers to imagine themselves as part of a larger translocal (and transhistorical) community. Phoebus, a Methodist minister, reached out to evangelical Protestants of all sects. "Religion in theory and form, has been more or less different in all denominations, in all ages;" he explained, "but the religion of the heart has been the same in every age, and denomination of orthodox Christians."[25]

Nearly a decade passed before Phoebus had the means to issue a second run of the *Experienced Christian's Magazine* (1805–1806). In the interim, he shifted the magazine's focus away from the universal church to the church of the new American nation in order to highlight the advance of evangelicalism in the United States. The *United States Christian Magazine* had tried this a decade earlier but failed after three issues. Phoebus's prefatory comments acknowledged the ongoing reality of partisanship in the city's newspapers but noted that something else distinctive was happening in the religious realm. The "hydra of a party spirit" was stunned by the lack of controversy with which the magazine was received. American Christians, he said, could be "restorers of the breach." Among them, "you will find one a follower of St. Peter, of Paul, of Apollos, of Luther, of Calvin, of Fox, of Wesley, &c. but all I trust of Christ." If denominations only dropped their divisions, he argued, Americans might be recipients of a great outpouring of Grace from the Lord.[26] Despite Phoebus's optimism, the second run failed after a year as well.

What interested Presbyterian bookstore owner and publisher Cornelius Davis was not the need to provide exemplary models for conversion and holy living but to engage Americans in a rational-critical discourse about religion, the second strategy of the period. Much like the partisan secular press, Davis had no qualms about taking a controversial stance. In the *Theological Magazine* (1795–1799), he placed himself firmly on the side of evangelicalism and expected all other forms of religious expression to be proven inadequate or insufficient through debate. Through an ongoing, open discussion between contributors and subscribers, on and off the page, religious truth would prevail, and those "still enslaved to vice" would be emancipated from their errors.[27]

Letters to the editor, however, raised the possibility that Davis's ideal discourse might have excluded and alienated more than it engaged. Some did not dispute the "associating nature" of the magazine but expressed concern over the inaccessibility of its content. A letter from "a constant reader" objected to the inclusion of Latin phrases without translation in several essays. "*The Theological Magazine* is published with a professed design to serve the public, unlearned as well as learned. And must it not rather be an insult upon an unlearned reader to accost him in the manner complained of?"[28] Others took issue with the tone of the discourse. "It is thought by many, it seems, that *The Theological Magazine* is too metaphysical," another commented. The writer went on to refute that notion, arguing it was only inaccessible to those who failed to take the time to read it closely and carefully. "The most useful citizens" among us, he explained, are those "willing to use all the means assiduously, which are necessary to make them wiser and better." And how many "useful citizens" might there have been out there? A thousand to fifteen hundred the writer estimated. In a new nation of several million, the *Theological Magazine* foundered on the shoals of exclusion and failed after three volumes.[29]

Undaunted, Cornelius Davis rebounded with a third strategy that tapped into resurging interest in the missionary spirit and fostered in its readers a sense of being part of a global evangelical community. His inspiration came from a recent popular English import, the *Evangelical Magazine*. As opposed to the *Theological Magazine*'s emphasis on disputation of weighty theological topics, the *Evangelical Magazine* focused on the importance of practical piety but expanded its discussion beyond the necessity of personal salvation to the missionary spirit's emphasis on the conversion of others. Exciting tales of missionaries performing the Lord's calling in foreign lands encouraged readers to imagine themselves as part of a larger movement working to bring the kingdom of Christ to earth. The magazine urged like-minded men and women to pray for the success of missionary endeavors and to raise money to support the spread of the gospel around the world. Davis discovered that entrusting the laity with the responsibility for missionary activism could lead to local, national, and even global conversion and proved more rousing than theological disputations.

In January 1800, Davis published the first issue of the *New-York Missionary Magazine and Repository of Religious Intelligence*, a new bimonthly magazine devoted to the spread of the gospel. International news was hardly novel reading matter for New Yorkers. What made the *New-York Missionary Magazine* different was its focus on the spread of Christianity. "Never, since the days of the apostles, has there been so much and such general attention paid to the great object of spreading the gospel as at the present day." The author of an early, short article with an auspicious title—"On the Coming of the Redeemer's Kingdom; and the Publication of Religious Magazines as the Most Likely Mean to Promote That Event" thought ushering in the second coming of Christ might seem a tall order for religious magazines, but he was confident of their efficacy. In his opinion, they were "the counterpart of the good news and glad tidings of salvation sent from Heaven to all people. . . . While the gospel sets before us the precious promises, Magazines acquaint us with the performance. The former is good news from Heaven, the latter from earth."[30]

In the pages of the *New-York Missionary Magazine*, the first of its kind in America, Davis believed he could organize, connect, and make productive the disparate places and people not only of North America but also of the wider world. Evangelical New Yorkers could follow the efforts of missionaries in places as diverse as western New York, Tahiti, and Canton through extracts from their letters and journals. They could learn about revivals of religion in towns stretching from Maine to Kentucky. Alongside the standard accounts of the conversions of American housewives appeared the more exotic narratives of Naimbanna, "an African King's Son," and Levi P——and Catharina M——, converts from Judaism.[31] Davis eschewed time over space, thus promoting a different kind of simultaneity than Phoebus had done five years earlier.

But the *New-York Missionary Magazine* also preserved evidence of the limitations of early nineteenth-century evangelical missionary activity. Careful readers could not help but notice the scattered nature of evangelical initiatives and realize that the gaps between the stories in the magazine reflected far greater geographic gaps in missionary coverage. This only reinforced the consequent enormity of the project of global conversion. One way Davis tried to counter this was to enjoin readers to make their own contributions to the record of this imagined community. "Some can compose essays," wrote a contributor, "and they who cannot compose, can read. Might not, should not, will not some saint, in your next, give us an account of some remarkable dispensation of providence, which has had unspeakable influence on his lot in the world?"[32] In the end, however, the *New-York Missionary Magazine* did more to reveal the difficulty—perhaps the impossibility—of evangelicals' stated goals than to achieve them.[33]

The *New-York Missionary Magazine* achieved the closest to a national readership of any of New York's early evangelical magazines. At the end of the first volume's run, Davis must have been ecstatic to have 2,434 subscriptions—an astonishing number in a time when the *Medical Repository* bragged about having almost three hundred subscribers. (The country's most popular literary magazine, the Philadelphia-published *Port Folio,* had a subscription of only 2,000 in the same year.)[34] Even more impressive was the broad network of clergy and laity Davis assembled to solicit subscriptions across the country. Every other month, fifty copies went to Rev. G. Blackburn in Maryville, Tennessee, twenty-one to Rev. Eliphalet Gillet in Hallowell, Maine (then Massachusetts), and twenty-six to Mr. Jeremiah Ross in Providence, Rhode Island. Two hundred and fifty subscribers lived in New York City, perhaps carryovers from the supporters of the *Theological Magazine,* and the rest of his subscribers were spread out over at least fourteen different states.[35] The *New-York Missionary Magazine* might not have coalesced a truly national audience, but it had achieved more than the *United States Christian Magazine* and other ambitiously titled magazines ever did.

Yet the *New-York Missionary Magazine* was on the wane by its fourth volume. Fewer and fewer original submissions appeared on Davis's desk, and more and more pages were filled with reprinted excerpts from the *London*

Evangelical Magazine, the *Edinburgh Missionary Magazine*, the *Christian Observer*, and other British magazines. Davis tried to rationalize the impending failure. "This is not to be considered as indicating that [Davis's] patrons want the ability to write," he explained, "but is rather to be ascribed to their numerous avocations; to their modesty; to the high opinion they entertain of foreign essays, and an impression that such are perused with great pleasure and profit than our domestic productions."[36] In reality, as Davis knew all too well, it was an indication of the fickle American market. Favorable prospects time and again fell victim to delinquent subscribers.[37] "It is astonishing that they have had so little success in America," wrote one puzzled contributor. "Surely in America there are many religious people. Have these no desire to be quickened themselves, or to hear what God is doing in this eventful period for the souls of others?"[38]

Ultimately Cornelius Davis suspected his competitors in the spiritual marketplace had bested him. They had, in fact, but not for the reason he suspected. In the nineteenth century, the backing of a religious organization would determine the success or failure of evangelical newspapers and magazines. The *Connecticut Missionary Magazine* (1800–1815) and the *Massachusetts Missionary Magazine* (1803–1808), which Davis believed captured part of his audience, were sponsored by robust regional missionary organizations. The *New-York Missionary Magazine* was not.[39] As Isabella Marshall Graham noted in her diary, few showed up for one of the New-York Missionary Society's early meetings. In time, the society's annual meeting would become a permanent fixture on the city's religious and social calendar, foreshadowing the popularity of the anniversaries of national benevolent, missionary, and reform organizations a few decades later. Unfortunately for Davis, that was still a while off.

The *New-York Missionary Magazine* was a financial failure for Davis, but his decision to tap into the missionary spirit marked an important development in evangelicalism in New York. Efforts to constitute an evangelical public around a discourse on holy living or a distinctly "American" debate on theological truths had failed. All around, Davis saw signs that the new spirit had begun to capture the evangelical imagination. Laity and clergy on both sides of the Atlantic formed missionary societies to organize, fund, and pray for the Lord's blessing on their endeavors to spread the gospel. The missionary spirit backed up by a robust organizational structure offered the promise of a more understandable discourse, of working together to bring about mass conversion, and perhaps even of ushering in the return of Christ's kingdom on earth. This first generation of evangelical magazines paved the way for more successful efforts following the War of 1812 that shaped the local, national, and global direction of evangelicalism over the nineteenth century.

NEW YORK'S EMERGENCE AS A NATIONAL PUBLISHING CENTER

The first *Annual Report* (1812) of the newly reorganized New-York Tract Society (NYTS) laid out the value evangelicals placed on the printed word, while unwittingly revealing a curious paradox. The medium of the press, the *Report* explained, served as a "powerful auxiliary" to the preached word and had, in fact, some "peculiar advantages" over it. The printed word was a permanent word. Repeated reading guaranteed the resolution of any potential misreadings or perversions of judgment, unlike oral communication, which displayed "a tendency to excite powerful emotions." Mindful of this, the NYTS proposed to print large numbers of brief tracts to extend "knowledge of evangelical truth" to those bereft of religious instruction. Yet the *Report* admitted that religion's enemies had also taken notice of these advantages. The press could also be wielded in the "cause of error and licentiousness" through the "poisoned productions" of history and romance, philosophy and poetry. In the NYTS's call to arms against the secular press, it sought to wage war with the very commercial infrastructure that made its own publishing initiatives possible.[40]

Evangelical New Yorkers embraced the press with a vigor that surpassed most others' in the early nineteenth century. Their publishing initiatives blossomed alongside efforts by secular New York publishers to outpace rivals in Philadelphia and Boston to capture a larger share of the growing national market for book and magazine publishing. The American book trade at the time was profoundly regional, although New York enjoyed a decided advantage as a spoiler to the New England and Philadelphia markets.[41] Technological innovations, such as stereotype plates (introduced 1813, cost-effective by 1825), cylindrical papermaking machines (1817, widely used by the 1830s), case and cloth bindings (mid-1820s), and steam-powered printing presses (1821), helped reorganize the trade, even if they did not give any one city a decided advantage.[42] Internal improvements facilitated distribution across the nation. The opening of the Erie Canal in 1825 gave urban publishers direct access to one of the country's most active hinterland book markets.[43] By 1840, New York had more than double the number of men employed in the printing and binding trades as its next closest rival, Philadelphia (2,029 versus 925).[44] No single national market emerged until after the Civil War, although New York publishers enjoyed a brisk business within the region as well as through a growing network of middlemen across the country.

Evangelicals paid close attention to developments across the Atlantic. They saw in the efforts of their British cousins the potential the press offered for spreading the gospel through large-scale and inexpensive printing of tracts and Bibles. British Independent minister George Burder had been impressed by the popularity of Hannah More's *Cheap Repository Tracts* but regretted they did not contain a "fuller statement of the great evangelical principles." To rectify this, he invited fellow ministers and laymen to form the Religious Tract Society of London (RTS) in May 1799. By printing short (generally four- to twelve-page) original essays or abridgements of larger works for free or cheap distribution, the RTS discovered a way to spread the gospel to broad audiences and to engage evangelicals in the work of distribution.[45] Five years later, Burder attended another auspicious founding. The British and Foreign Bible Society was initiated in 1804 to place Bibles in the hands of women and men across Great Britain and around the globe. "Nations unborn will have cause to bless God for the meeting this day," Burder recorded in his diary.[46] Before long hundreds of thousands of evangelical tracts and Bibles annually rolled off British presses and were distributed far and wide.

Word of these new British evangelical initiatives spread quickly. In New York, they first captured the attention of the laity. Cornelius Davis reprinted the RTS's first tract, "An Address to Christians, Recommending the Distribution of Cheap Religious Tracts," in the *New-York Missionary Magazine* in the fall of 1802.[47] Divie Bethune promised that if the Lord delivered him from a bitter legal dispute with his former business partner he would print religious tracts and distribute them among the poor in the hospital and almshouse. In November 1804, he personally paid for the printing of ten thousand tracts on a variety of subjects (table 4.1).[48] He could not resist the temptation to write a tract himself, exemplifying the excitement tract societies generated among evangelicals and the fluid and flexible canon that emerged from them.[49]

A few years later, Bethune counted himself among the founding members of the New York Bible Society (NYBS, 1809) and the NYTS (1809; reorganized 1812). These local associations undertook evangelical publishing and distribution on a scale Bethune could only imagine.[50] Like the RTS, they assumed a nondenominational stance.[51] They hired local commercial printers to reissue titles from the RTS catalog and to print Bibles, rather than import British imprints. Paralleling trends in secular publishing, the RTS's efforts were centered in London with auxiliaries for distribution across the

TABLE 4.1. Tracts printed by Divie Bethune, November 1804

Title of tract	*No. in RTS series*	*No. printed*
Important subjects of consideration	3	500
Letter from a Mother to her daughter at a Boarding School	64	500
Poor Joseph, with reflections	143	1000
Fulfilment of Prophecy in the destruction of Jerusalem	71	500
The death of Altamont	58	500
The evil of a late attendance on divine worship	60	500
Parental Duties	62	500
Five minutes consideration	55	500
Address to parents from persons who support Sabbath schools	59	500
Friendly Advice to all whom it may concern	65	1,000
Sin no trifle	66	1,000
The well spent day	57	500
The Travellers or the Broad & narrow way	[unclear]	500
The Prisoner	10	1,000
Donation to Poor Widows w. small children—this last written by myself		1,000
Total		10,000

Source: Divie Bethune, Diary (October 9, 1803 to January 6, 1805), Collection of the William Clements Library, University of Michigan

country, while, initially at least in the still decentralized United States, every American state or major city with access to a printing press formed its own tract society. Bibles and tracts were made available in a variety of bindings, at a range of prices, and offered to as broad a market as possible. New York's location between Boston and Philadelphia ensured that the distribution patterns of the NYTS and NYBS often overlapped with those of neighboring societies.[52] Unlike secular publishers, evangelical associations expressed less concern about poaching. To them, the more production and distribution, the better.

These associations were early adopters of the newest developments in printing technology and institutional organization. Early on, Matthew Carey discovered how to dominate American Bible publishing by assembling standing type for his most popular editions, thereby significantly reducing the labor, time, and expense of reprinting. In 1812, the Philadelphia Bible Society imported from England a set of stereotyped plates, a new and relatively untested innovation, which proved a less costly alternative to standing type. The Bible held the honor of being the first stereotyped book produced in the United States.[53] These associations looked to banks rather than churches for their organizational structure. Elias Boudinot credited the First Bank of the United States for inspiring the structure of the American Bible Society. "The Stockholders belonged to every State in the United States," he explained in appreciation of the bank's national focus. "They chose Managers, or rather Directors, in every part of the States. . . . They did not fail to have a quorum ever ready to transact the necessary business."[54] Leading businessmen served as the directors and managers of tract and Bible societies which, in turn, pioneered developments that transformed American business. These included nationally standardized pricing plans, distribution networks, business plans, marketing campaigns, and scales of operation, as well as innovations in corporate organization and accounting practices.[55]

Local societies consolidated to form national nondenominational organizations beginning in the second decade of the nineteenth century. In 1816, delegates from Bible societies across the United States, which now numbered more than one hundred, gathered in the Consistory Room of the Garden Street Church to create a single, national organization, the American Bible Society (ABS). These men represented a broad range of evangelical-leaning denominations and held a variety of theological beliefs. Despite their differences, they agreed on the value of distributing the Bible through a national network of auxiliaries and missionaries.[56] Evidence of their national aspirations, the president and vice presidents represented eleven states, stretching from Georgia to New Hampshire, and the District of Columbia.[57] The fact that two secretaries and ten of thirty-six managers had been managers of the NYBS speaks to evangelical New Yorkers' investment in this nationalizing program.[58] The nation's tract societies made a similar decision less than a decade later. In 1823, the New England Tract Society decided to rename itself the American Tract Society (ATS), having achieved the feat of publishing over four million copies of the eighty-six titles in its catalog in the nine years since its founding. Two years later, the NYTS merged with the ATS and convinced it to relocate to New York.[59]

In consolidating their publishing and distribution operations, both the ABS and the ATS needed to be headquartered in the nation's most convenient center. New York was the obvious choice. "The city of New-York, eminently distinguished by its natural and local advantages, its accumulating population, and its increasing commercial prosperity and influence, seems destined, in the wisdom of Divine Providence, to become the centre of these extended operations," the executive committee explained in the ABS's *First*

Annual Report. The report extolled the city's access to foreign and domestic shipping and communications networks. "When the canals which are now in progress shall be completed, there will be a direct inland water communication between this port and every village of note in the extended country west of the Alleghany Mountains," it enthusiastically reported. Bibles and tracts could be sent "at a very small expense, and very frequently at no expense at all, to the remotest part of the land."[60] New York proved such a hospitable location that both societies remained headquartered there well into the twentieth century.[61]

The ABS and ATS visibly marked the city's landscape with large, purpose-built structures that housed their printing, binding, bookselling, and editorial operations. These structures exhibited the latest innovations in internal organization and business efficiency by carefully sorting each aspect of publishing into its own specially designed and constructed space.[62] After several years of nomadic existence in rented rooms, the ABS opened a three-story structure at 115 Nassau Street, between Ann and Beekman, in 1823 (see fig. 0.1). The structure accommodated a meeting room for the society's managers, a depository that held one hundred thousand Bibles, space for eleven hand presses, a bindery, storage rooms for paper and printed sheets, and offices for the society's different committees.[63] The ATS built its first headquarters on the corner of Nassau and Spruce Streets in 1825 (fig. 4.1). The 80-by-48-foot brick building was four stories high with a garret. The first floor held a salesroom for society publications as well as retail space for rent. Upper floors contained the ATS's vast publishing operations: the second floor held administrative, editorial, meeting, and storage rooms; the third floor housed the folder, the binder, and the stereotype plate maker; and the fourth floor and garret were the domain of the printer. The ATS praised the liberality of New Yorkers in supporting the structure, noting that, "excepting the President and two other friends of the society, *all the donors to the Society's House reside in the city of New-York*."[64]

The ABS's new Bible House that arose at Astor Place in 1853 (fig. 4.2) illustrates the dramatic growth of these associations over the next generation. The six-story structure measured roughly 198 feet wide by 200 feet deep and occupied three-quarters of an acre of prime uptown real estate. Building for the future, the ABS rented some of the offices on the first, second, and third floors to other tenants until they might be needed. The rents covered the expenses of the structure, allowing the ABS to devote all donations to the printing of Bibles. At a cost of $250,000, the structure was no small investment for the society.[65]

FIGURE 4.1 An architect's rendition of the headquarters for the new American Tract Society. John McComb Jr., Tract House, 1825, from the John McComb Architectural Drawings Collection (PR040), box 12, number 212; neg. #67490, New-York Historical Society. Photography © New-York Historical Society.

BIBLE HOUSE (Astor Place), New York.

FIGURE 4.2 Bible House, Astor Place, New York, 1852, in Isaac Ferris, *Jubilee Memorial of the American Bible Society* (New York, 1867)

With national tract and Bible societies in place, American evangelicals began to create a distinctly American tract literature. In the late 1820s, the ATS began publishing tracts by New York authors, such as Rev. Elihu Baldwin's *Fashionable Amusements* and *On Universalism* as well as Rev. John Mitchell Mason's *Death of Hume and Finley Compared* and *Conversation with a Young Traveler*.[66] Hoping tracts written by American authors on American themes might appeal to a national audience, the ATS published *The Children of the Forest*, which it advertised as "an interesting and authentic narrative of the conversion of the two children, together with the father and mother, of a family in a new settlement," and *Eliza, The Chippeway Indian*. By the early 1830s, the presses of the ATS produced over five million tracts annually. Equally ambitious, the ABS produced more than three hundred thousand Bibles a year in the same period.

Having proven their ability to mass produce the gospel, these associations perfected models for mass distribution. In spring 1829, the ABS and ATS announced plans for the systematic national distribution of their publications. The ABS launched an initiative to distribute Bibles to every needy family in the country under the rather unassuming name of the "first general supply." Working through a network of local auxiliaries, it gave away over a half-million Bibles in a nation of three million families over the next two years. The ATS's "Systematic Monthly Distribution Plan" proposed to place the same tract each month into the hands of every family in the country, regardless of class or denomination. Choosing New York as its test field, it assigned evangelical volunteers to hand out tracts to 28,383 city families in March 1829. They reported back that only 388 families declined. Two years later, volunteers regularly visited 36,000 city families each month. The ATS expanded its distribution program to several leading American cities and over two hundred New England towns. Ultimately, though, both societies failed to achieve universal circulation. The primary obstacle lay not with production, as the New York presses proved immensely capable, but in distribution. Auxiliaries of voluntary distributors were unable to provide complete coverage and, even worse, often fell in arrears for pledges made to the national associations.[67]

Nevertheless, the massive production and distribution of evangelical print by nondenominational associations constituted the nation's first mass media.[68] It also manufactured distinct forms of nationalism that coalesced around a certain brand of Protestant Christianity. This "Protestant" nationalism sometimes successfully linked evangelical and American identities. In this formulation, other religions, especially Roman Catholicism, came to be seen as potentially dangerous to the state. One well-known result of this move was a string of Bible wars that rocked mid-nineteenth-century urban public schools.[69] This "Protestant" nationalism also represented competition between northeastern ministers and bourgeoisie and frontier revivalists for the souls of poor white settlers on the frontier. Religious nationalism did the work that the federal state was unable to do in the vast new western districts of the nation.[70] Both developments reflected important truths about urban evangelicals—they were fiercely anti-Catholic and thought expansively about the nation as a Christian one made in their image.

Nondenominational associations never enjoyed hegemonic power over the nation's rapidly growing denominational publishers. Some denominations saw the power of the nondenominational Bible and tract societies as a threat to their own structures, especially in their formulation of competing visions of the universal church. The initial announcement of the formation of the ABS, for example, elicited a quick denunciation from Bishop John Henry Hobart of the Protestant Episcopal Church, arguably New York's wealthiest and most powerful denomination. Representing the denomination's dominant high church faction, Hobart objected to the partnership of low church (evangelical) Episcopalians in the venture. A pamphlet war ensued in which Hobart decried the encroachment on his church and on the clergy's prerogative to distribute the Bible, which they had done through the Protestant Episcopalian Bible and Common Prayer Book Society since 1809.[71]

Denominational publishers stood at the forefront of the boom in religious magazine publishing in the city in the third decade of the nineteenth century.[72] The number of magazines, in general, rose from 35 in 1828 to 158 two decades later. By midcentury, New York publishers had nearly seventy million issues in annual circulation.[73] Some magazines, such as the *Christian Herald and Seaman's Magazine*, engaged with various reform associations but avoided appealing to any specific denomination. More were denominational organs addressed to national audiences and intended to keep their opinions on contentious doctrinal issues in the public sphere. By 1830, every major evangelical denomination had at least one newspaper or magazine published in New York. Churches that could not afford to support their own publications offered support to the efforts of sympathetic others. The African Methodist Episcopal Zion Church allowed Samuel Cornish, founder of the First Coloured Presbyterian Church, to use its basement for printing the pioneering black newspaper *Freedom's Journal* beginning in 1827. The magazine focused on two themes dear to the hearts of antebellum black Methodists: the importance of racial uplift and a need to counter the rising tide of white racism.[74]

Arguably the most successful national denominational periodicals published in New York were the *Methodist Magazine* and the *Christian Advocate and Journal*. In January 1816, Joshua Soule took charge of the heavily indebted Methodist Book Concern, the denomination's official publishing house.[75] Within two years, he launched a monthly miscellany, offering readers a range of material gathered under a variety of headings and used the well-established networks of circuit riders to get it into the hands of Methodists from Maine to Georgia. With a national circulation of 10,000, the *Methodist Magazine* was one of the first financially successful religious magazines. Soule's successor, Nathan Bangs, unveiled the *Christian Advocate*, a weekly magazine, in September 1826. Within months it had a subscription of over 20,000. After two years it had 25,000 (and added "and Journal" to its title), making it the most broadly circulated magazine in the entire country. The *Christian Advocate and Journal* became the denomination's primary organ for the remainder of the century.[76] Throughout that time, it remained tied to the New York community and a venue for local authors.

Denominational magazine publishing reinvigorated tract and book publishing. Nathan Bangs rented the basement of the ill-fated Wesleyan Seminary, over which Henry Chase had once been superintendent, and opened a bindery (fig. 4.3). In 1824, he orchestrated the purchase of the entire building and set up printing presses, ending the Book Concern's reliance on outsourcing to commercial publishers. Magazine publishing employed the presses much of the time, but so did the printing needs of the denomination's voluntary associations: the Methodist Episcopal Tract Society (1817), the Methodist Episcopal Sunday School Union (1827), and the Methodist Episcopal Bible Society (1828). In less than a decade their operations outgrew the three-and-a-half-story space on Crosby Street. A massive new five-and-a-half-story edifice that rivaled the operations of the ABS, the ATS, and commercial publishers arose on Mulberry Street in 1833.[77] By the 1830s, Methodists measured success not only in the millions of magazines and books they printed but also in their ability to inspire the founding of other denominational publishing houses.[78]

Evangelicalism's opponents also used periodicals to counter its arguments in the public sphere. The first Jewish periodical in the United States, the *Jew* (1823–1826), was launched in March 1823, three months after the American Society for the Melioration of the Condition of the Jews (ASMCJ) began its magazine, *Israel's Advocate* (1823–1825). Hebrew colonization had sparked the imagination of a handful of New York evangelicals, including Philip Milledoler and the converted Jew Samuel Frey, who founded the ASMCJ

HOMES OF THE METHODIST BOOK CONCERN IN NEW YORK, 1824–1915

(Center) The building at 150 Fifth Ave. (built 1889. Enlarged 1899) before the recent addition. (Below) Wesleyan Academy building, 1824–33. (Above, left) First Mulberry St. House, occupied 1833–36. (Top) Mulberry St. House, occupied 1836–1890. (Right) Store and office, 805 Broadway, 1869–89.

FIGURE 4.3 "Homes of the Methodist Book Concern in New York, 1824–1915," in James Richard Joy, *The Making of the Book Concern, 1789–1915* (New York, 1915)

in April 1820. Enthusiasm for the society's efforts to found and maintain a settlement for foreign Jews somewhere in the United States quickly waned and was only revived by a sizable bequest from Elias Boudinot, founder of the ABS. Solomon Jackson, editor of *Israel's Advocate,* refused to let the

ASMCJ's arguments about Jews' supposed desire for conversion go unchallenged.[79] While evangelicals never proposed a similar colonization effort for Roman Catholics, longstanding prejudices and slander led to the founding of the *Truth Teller* (1825–1855), the city's first Catholic periodical.[80]

All denominations valued periodicals for the unity they offered against the attacks of competing faiths, but in time they came to realize they were their own worst enemies. James O. Andrew, a young preacher in Georgia, remembered the excitement generated by the first issue of the *Methodist Magazine*. "Up to that time we had not even a thumb paper through which we might converse with one another from Maine to Georgia, or through whose columns we might be able to repel the numerous assaults which were constantly being made upon us," reflected Andrew. "We felt that we were rising in the world."[81] Yet in the process of coming together as a national community, evangelicals realized that they could, at times, hold fundamentally opposing views from their co-religionists. Many years later, Andrew, now a bishop of the church, stood at the center of a national crisis. Like the Presbyterians, Methodists allowed their once vocal stance against slavery to fall into silence. Rumor spread at the May 1844 General Conference that Andrew had come into possession of slaves through marriage, making him the first slaveholding American Methodist bishop. A bitter, month-long debate followed, ending with a vote along sectional lines for Andrew to desist from exercising the office of bishop. The following year, the Methodist Episcopal Church, South, held its first General Conference in Louisville, leaving the old conference to the antislavery northerners.[82] Presbyterians and Baptists experienced similar schisms.[83]

Secular newspapers gave close coverage to the disruptions within national denominations, wondering if they portended political division. "I will not say that such a separation would necessarily produce a dissolution of the political union of these States," Henry Clay wrote in a widely published opinion following the division of the Methodist Church, "but the example would be fraught with imminent danger, and, in co-operation with other causes unfortunately existing, its tendency on the stability of [the Union] would be perilous and alarming."[84] Rather than being an end unto themselves, denominational schisms proved the beginning of a conflicted and uncertain period leading up to the Civil War. In most white denominational newspapers and magazines the silence on antislavery was deafening.

Alongside nondenominational and denominational publishing houses, commercial publishers courted evangelical consumers. In the first quarter of the nineteenth century, printers like Jonathan Seymour on Nassau Street (see fig. 0.1) assumed job-printing works for churches and voluntary associations. Evangelical clients paid him for printing these works; he would not have personally taken on the risk involved in publishing them. That changed in the second quarter of the nineteenth century as each major trade house allied with one denomination or another. The most famous example of this was the relationship between Harper & Brothers and the Methodists. All four Harper brothers were devoted Methodists and conceived of their business as, in the words of one historian, "a priestly calling to sanctify the world of print." The firm participated in both the regular and religious book trades but resolved to print books that were "interesting, instructive, and moral." True to their evangelical faith, they refused to allow themselves or any of their employees to work on the Sabbath.[85]

Commercial publishers carved out their own niche in the market for evangelical print by expanding their range of genres and material forms. More fully immersed in the world of the secular book trades, they distributed their works in secular bookshops that would have turned a cold shoulder to nondenominational or denominational publishers. At the same time, their inclusion of a more catholic array of titles in their popular series, like *Harper's Family Library*, alongside religious classics opened the textual horizons for evangelical New Yorkers. Fears about the consequences of commercial publishers' worldly entanglements remained but did not prove insurmountable. In the end, commercial publishers sidestepped the efforts of nondenominational publishers to foster national unity and denominational publishers to create an imagined community. Instead, they made evangelical texts available and attractive to all, even those who did not identify as evangelical.[86]

Thus when Michael Floy sat down to write his account of the death of John Mather Jr., he lived in a city that offered incomparable resources for publishing it. Nondenominational, denominational, and denomination-associated commercial publishing houses all embraced and shared the newest technology, organizational infrastructure, and distribution strategies of the secular commercial publishing trade, many times operating at their forefront. The medium of the press proved both a powerful auxiliary and a weapon, although the mere presence of religious publishers was not enough to banish the "poisoned productions" of commercial publishers. If anything, the penny press with its lurid tales was on the rise in the 1830s.[87] To combat its supposedly destructive effects, evangelicals concentrated not only on making books and tracts more widely and cheaply available but also on crafting content and packaging that would warm the hearts of the fickle consumers who read them. Here Michael Floy made his contribution.

THE TEXTUAL FAITH OF MICHAEL FLOY

In the mid-1830s, the world of Michael Floy Jr. revolved around, in reverse order of importance, his family's nursery business, the Bowery Village Methodist Episcopal Church, and books. "I endeavor to employ my time in reading, and such is my thirst for knowledge, that I can truly say I esteem it above all earthly goods," he recorded in his diary. "I keep no money in my pocket for very long, for when I see a book that takes my fancy, have it I must." Over the three-year period covered by his extant diary, the young evangelical purchased, exchanged, and read more than 250 "useful" books, running the gamut from doctrinal treatises to biography, history to scientific dissertations. "I have never read a novel in my life and I do not think I ever will," he declared, although his insatiable thirst eventually got the better of him when he purchased *Gil Blas* and *The Castle of Otranto*.[88] So devoted was Floy to reading that he even daily outfitted himself to facilitate it. By his own account he wore a gray coat with three pockets, "one for a big pocket book containing maps, arithmetical & algebraical calculations, almanac, constitutions of the Bible & Sunday school societies, &c &c"; another for his pruning knife (for when he had to work in the nursery); and a third for the book he was currently reading.[89]

Michael Floy left a diary that richly details a life built around books. This was unusual, but his extensive engagement with sacred and secular texts was not. Texts permeated the lives of antebellum evangelical New Yorkers, mediating their understanding of evangelicalism, shaping their worldview, and informing their experience of life. Floy's example offers a corrective to top-down interpretations offered by historians of evangelical print culture that privilege the power of elites who ran tract and Bible societies to dictate evangelical reading. It also demonstrates that people actually engaged with the ideas in publications typically discounted as formulaic and sentimental. Rather than passively accept all he heard from the pulpit of the Bowery Village Methodist Episcopal Church, Floy actively synthesized his own beliefs and practices out of the books he read, shaping everything from the way he told his conversion narrative to how he proposed to his future wife. When a student in his Sunday school died, Floy made his own contribution to a body of literature that had meant so much to him.

From the start, evangelicalism established itself as a religious community that fundamentally functioned as a textual community. The Bible stood at the center of this community, offering the ultimate source of all spiritual truth. To aid men and women in understanding the scriptures, an informal evangelical canon appeared that was, as one scholar explains, "open, fluid, conditionally authoritative, and functionally sacred." New texts could be added, old ones modified or removed with ease. The primary criterion for inclusion was a work's usefulness in reinforcing the Word of the Bible. Through their intensive and extensive reading, evangelicals derived both an individual and group identity.[90] "My opinions of course are those of Wesley, as I am a Wesleyan Methodist," Floy wrote after finishing Wesley's *Journals*. Yet the sheer number of titles available to evangelicals and the diversity of theological ideas they contained typically precluded any slavish dependency on a single title. "If I disagreed ever so much from [Wesley's] opinions still I should say that he was a most extraordinary man," Floy respectfully qualified before critiquing the founder of Methodism's *Journals* as "often abrupt and carelessly written."[91] On other occasions, Floy found the ideas of British Calvinists more congenial.

New York Presbyterian minister George Prentiss powerfully captured this dynamic and fluid process of evangelical identity formation through textual engagement in the biography of his late wife Elizabeth Payson Prentiss. To understand Elizabeth, the daughter of an important evangelical minister, George explained, you had to appreciate six "elements" that shaped her religious life and thought. The foundation was provided by the "old Puritan element," which included the works of seventeenth-century Puritan divines—Baxter, Bunyan, Owen, and Flavel—and their early eighteenth-century heirs—Doddridge, Watts, and Edwards. These traditions were churned up and reinterpreted at the end of the eighteenth century by the "so-called Evangelical element"—Newton, More, and Wilberforce—who "helped in many ways to improve the general tone both of theological and devotional sentiment." In adulthood, three more elements modified those to which she had been exposed in her childhood: a "new evangelistic spirit," which inaugurated the great missionary movements of the nineteenth century; a "revival element," which placed renewed emphasis on special seasons of grace; and a "reform" element, which Prentiss noted to be the most disruptive but ultimately most powerful of the six. Contemporary British and American literary works provided the sixth and final element, testifying to evangelicalism's openness to secular as well as sacred influences. The poetry of Wordsworth, Tennyson, and Longfellow and the novels of Dickens took on special significance for Payson Prentiss, who, alongside Harriet Beecher Stowe and Susan Warner, emerged as a leading nineteenth-century evangelical woman writer.[92]

In New York, Prentiss and Floy had opportunities for acquiring texts, religious and secular, which evangelicals in other parts of the country could only dream about. Walking through the city, Floy remained on the lookout for new acquisitions. He bought books at auction, from the denominationally sanctioned catalog of the Methodist Book Concern where his brother worked, and from the stall of an itinerant Irishman near St. Thomas's church on Broadway who told his loyal customer that "his word was as good as his money." Occasionally he perceived the hand of Providence in these transactions. Trading a female canary and a cage for a stack of books, Floy debated whether a small title the bookseller threw in for free, the *Life of John Newton*, was worth carrying. He shoved it in his pocket only later to discover it to be a source of great spiritual enjoyment and instruction.[93] Floy's diary amply reveals that consumerism expanded the materials available for practicing his faith, rather than undercutting it. Every text provided a new opportunity to refine, modify, or adapt his understanding of evangelicalism.

The short conversion narrative Floy entered in his diary in November 1833 nicely illustrates the way in which commercially produced texts shaped his most intimate spiritual experiences. Floy's first serious awakening occurred in 1823 when the death of his mother made the fifteen-year-old resolve to seek out his salvation. Like so many before him, he turned to seventeenth-century steady sellers, Alleine's *Alarm to the Unconverted* and Baxter's *Call to the Unconverted*, conveniently repackaged for nineteenth-century evangelical audiences in one volume.[94] His convictions subsided when he entered Columbia College not long after, and five years passed before he again sought conversion. In the interim he hoped his strict morality might excuse his want of faith. "I used to think how very good I was, when my heart was 'deceitful & desperately wicked,'" he wrote in retrospect. Evangelicals knew from their Alleine and Baxter that passive adherence could never take the place of active, vital piety.[95]

Floy finally experienced conversion one Sunday when he attended the Allen Street Methodist Episcopal Church to impress a "very beautiful" Sunday school teacher. Sitting in the pews, a distracted Floy fantasized about becoming religious, not for the promise of salvation it offered, but so he could wear "a broad-brimmed hat so as to look solemn." Allen Street was in the midst of a massive revival at the time, and someone entreated him to stay after service to attend a prayer meeting. Reluctantly Floy agreed and soon experienced the kind of physically intense conversion experience for which Methodists were renowned (and in some circles reviled). "My very teeth chattered," he recalled; "sweat and tears completely drenched my handkerchief, and my cries could be heard all over the church."[96] He preferred the words of Isaac Watts to describe his feelings at that moment: "Oh, what immortal joys I felt, / And rapture all divine. / When Jesus told me I was his, / And my beloved mine!"[97] Floy carefully, and somewhat defensively, justified in his next diary entry the authenticity of his conversion, despite its emotionalism, a likely response to the dominant criticism in the press of Methodism's purported misleading enthusiasm. Or maybe Floy was trying to convince himself.[98]

After conversion, Floy threw himself into reading a range of religious writers popular among evangelicals. The standard texts of his denomination, namely the writings of John Wesley and John Fletcher, as well as other imprints of the Methodist Book Concern provided one source of inspiration. Connecting the Methodist Floy to the Congregationalist Prentiss was an affinity for another wellspring, seventeenth- and eighteenth-century British Nonconformist authors. Reprints of books by Alleine, Baxter, Bunyan, Doddridge, Flavel, and others were found in the ATS's fifteen-volume *Evangelical Family Library* (1832) as well as in individual copies from the city's denominational and nondenominational presses.[99] The timelessness of these books struck Floy. After reading Horneck's *Sermons on the Beatitudes*, he reflected: "I find that old divinity generally speaking is the best, more plain, simple and not so metaphysical as the modern; and I find ideas in the old writers which I thought were not known or imagined by them."[100]

Reading authors across the theological spectrum occasionally led to tensions between a strictly denominational understanding and a broader evangelical one. "Read today the life of Fletcher by Wesley; a man almost immaculate, but was Baxter not as pious?" Floy noted in his diary two years after his conversion. His reading inspired in him a heightened level of identification with its authors. "It is the opinion of many pious men that the souls of departed persons are often present with us in this world," Floy noted of a "strange conceit" he had indulged for some time. "I imagine Baxter always near and about me, and I feel comfort and pleasure in this thought, or whim if you please. But if he is not by me, I know One who is."[101] Why Floy fantasized about having Baxter, a Calvinist Independent, near him instead of Wesley or Fletcher, Arminian Methodists, raises important questions about the very nature of denominational identity during this period. This is especially important in light of arguments that one of the great transformations of the postrevolutionary era was the emergence of a new, hybridized theological center among American evangelicals.[102]

Floy's diary makes clear that his understanding of evangelicalism was less a matter of strict adherence to officially sanctioned denominational beliefs than an ongoing engagement with a larger body of ideas. He was surprised that a local Methodist preacher had not read works by influential Baptist

Robert Hall, whom he quite liked.[103] He expected not to enjoy Calvinist Rowland Hill's *Village Dialogues*, having heard that the author referred to one of Fletcher's writings as "filthy Antimonian expression," but found himself pleasantly surprised by Hill's take on sin.[104] Pascal's thoughts on religion also impressed him, to the point that he willingly absolved the great thinker of his Catholicism, calling it "a few errors of the head, errors in which he was brought up and educated."[105] Reading a text by eighteenth-century English scientist William Whewell helped him formulate one of his most telling admissions. "What I write is all in private and expresses my thoughts; and as I express my secret imaginations in this book, I will put down here one of them. . . . Here it is: I AM NOT A FREE MORAL AGENT, NOR DO I WISH TO BE ONE," an astonishing statement for a Methodist to make.[106]

The biographies of such popular Protestant missionaries as David Brainerd, Harriet Newell, and Henry Martyn strengthened Floy's interest in the missionary spirit and allowed him to vicariously experience the world beyond Manhattan. John Sargent's memoir of Martyn, in particular, afforded Floy "much profit and melancholy pleasure." Not much older than Floy when he embarked as a chaplain in the East India Company, Martyn's early death in 1812 made him a beloved figure among evangelical readers. Floy pulled out a map of Asia and put himself in Martyn's shoes, following his travels with his finger. "I found Tocat, where poor Henry expired after enduring incredible toils, anguish, and affliction of body and mind, vainly endeavoring to reach Constantinople, and then England; he died without the sight." Ultimately, Floy derived inspiration to spread the gospel from the seriousness and devotion of Martyn and others.[107]

Floy's Bowery Village was a far cry from Martyn's India, but it served as his missionary field. The Methodist community there had its origins in Mrs. Coutant's "upper room" prayer meeting. By 1795 the small congregation built a small two-story, gable-fronted building to serve as a combination schoolhouse and meetinghouse. Michael Floy Sr., a postrevolutionary emigrant from England, joined the congregation around this time and brought his children up in it. The War of 1812 proved particularly hard on the congregation, but by 1818 they built a dedicated meetinghouse next to the former building.[108] Floy's diary reveals the extent to which the people of Bowery Village perceived themselves, and were perceived by others, as a community apart.[109] Just as Floy assumed the overlapping identities of Wesleyan Methodist and evangelical, so, too, did he see himself as a Bowery Villager and a New Yorker.

Floy applied lessons derived from his reading to improve the spiritual and temporal lives of his neighbors. He worried when spiritual fervor within the church lagged, and to help revive it he organized a five-day outing to a camp meeting for twenty Bowery Villagers. The local singing association brought him delight. "I never enjoy myself more than when we are singing one of my favorite tunes at church in tune & time, and when our hearts are all in unison," he reflected. During the cold winter of 1834, he organized a local benevolent society to engage his neighbors in helping one another. From distributing wood to serving as one of two "lacquies" assisting local women in making clothes for the poor, Floy threw himself into helping others.[110]

Work as a teacher and superintendent of the local Sunday school immersed Floy in a thriving textual community. His position required him to purchase books for the library, discipline recalcitrant teachers, and plan exhibitions, but the most meaningful part of his labors was helping young children experience the joys of religion, often through texts. When Miss Ann Mather won a competition for committing Bible verses to heart by memorizing the whole gospel of St. Matthew, he grew uncharacteristically livid at the failure of her teacher, Mr. Post, to deliver the promised reward. He went out and bought her a new book himself to avoid disappointing or disillusioning the young girl or her classmates.[111] Later that year, Ann's brother John died, and Floy decided to preserve the young man's memory for the edification of his classmates through a published account of his final hours.

What is not included in Floy's *Memoir of John Mather* is as instructive as what is. No mention is made of the boy's conversion, if he even had one, and only a few specifics are given to establish his piety in life. In the latter half of the eighteenth century, evangelical writers increasingly extracted the deathbed scene from the broader life narrative, highlighting how the dying performed in these fleeting but crucial moments. An article in the British *Methodist Magazine* in 1800 justified the recording of deathbed narratives as not only a test of piety for the dying and "a display of power and grace of our Lord Jesus Christ," but also a reminder to the living to prepare to meet "the King of terrors without fear."[112] A good death was seen as the culmination of a lifelong spiritual journey, a moment of ultimate transition from one world to the next. Assurance and peace marked such a passing, although evangelicals frowned upon too much of the former as a sign that one might have been deceived in reading the Lord's intentions.[113]

Floy's deathbed interview with Mather follows the conventions of the genre. Traditionally such scenes involve a pious figure—such as a minister or patriarch—interrogating the dying on his or her readiness for transition. Floy placed himself in that role. Upon entering Mather's room, he perceived, though "the mortal paleness was on his cheeks," that "glory was in his soul." Wasting no time, he asked the young boy on what he placed his hopes for salvation. Laboring under great pain, Mather responded, "Jesus Christ," and soon after fell into convulsions, bringing the interview to an end. The genre promoted the idea that death could be instructive for the gathered, opening the way for the dying to interrogate the living. The painful side effects of tetanus made this hard for Mather, but Floy later learned the young boy had exhorted his parents to prepare to meet him in heaven.[114]

In describing the dying Mather, Floy combined the epistemologies of older devotional works with the conventions of more recent religious and secular biographies. Works of seventeenth- and eighteenth-century British divines, such as Philip Doddridge's *Rise and Progress of Religion in the Soul,* provided him with the contours of a pious life and death against which he would judge Mather's experience. Biography made him alert to questions of character. Floy had been reading steady sellers for years, but his interest, bordering on an obsession, in memoirs was a recent development. In November 1833, for example, he announced his intention to confine his future reading to biographies, beginning with his favorite, Doddridge's *Life of Colonel Gardiner.* His interest shifted from religious to secular figures over the coming years, but he continued to bring critical questions to bear on these texts, as he sought useful models of character and piety.[115] In *Colonel Gardiner,* he found not himself, but his older brother James, a Methodist preacher whom he admired (but also frequently critiqued).[116] The biographer's inability to convey the character of William Bramwell, another Methodist preacher, frustrated him. "We learn that he was very popular and useful," concluded Floy, "and do not know how to do to imitate him, and consequently not much practical benefit is to be derived from the book."[117] Floy even found spiritual instruction in Lockhart's *Life of Napoleon.* "Let me use as much exertion to secure a heavenly as Napoleon did to secure an earthly crown," he wrote. "I do admire an ardent soul."[118]

Running beneath the surface of *The Memoir of John Mather* is a fundamental question plaguing Sunday school literature: was John Mather old enough to have an authentic conversion experience? Floy took pains to establish his qualifications for judging, perhaps because teachers rarely assumed such roles within the genre.[119] But on the question of children's spirituality, he had expressed doubts in the past. A young boy from the Allen Street Church once caught him off guard with a request to attend an adult prayer meeting. "I was more surprised, for be it known that I had had much doubt concerning children becoming religious," he wrote at the time; "I thought it was sufficient to make religious impressions on their minds, and that when they grew up they would reflect on what they had been taught." Convinced after questioning the young boy of his sincerity, Floy found himself deeply moved when eight children kneeled at the altar rail. Three days later, however, Floy had to deal with a disapproving mother. The omission of Mather's conversion narrative is a nod to the uneasiness Floy felt, an issue that troubled other evangelicals as well.[120]

Floy's intention in writing his account initially appears to have been to use the example of Mather's deathbed to awaken the local community to their need for salvation. At the boy's funeral, the impression made on Mather's close friend Andrew Bridgman made Floy hopeful that a written account might similarly impress others. After composing the narrative, he read it to the Bowery Village Sunday School and "found they were all with their eyes at me; many of them were in tears." Even Floy could not escape the story's influence. "It seems as if I could not shake off the thoughts of the death of my Sunday scholar," he wrote the next day. "He is continually in my mind, and I feel a peculiar pleasure in contemplating him." Two weeks later, he found an opportunity to extend the usefulness of his narrative even further.[121]

Floy's residence and connections in New York created the conditions for expanding his narrative's influence nationally through publication. At a meeting of the Bowery Village Sunday School Association, Floy and his brother James were selected to form a committee to investigate publishing the account "for the use of the schools attached to this association," along with Mary Ann Farnam's account of the death of a scholar in the Adult African Sunday School. The "Brief Memoir of John Mather" appeared on June 20, 1834, under the "Children's Department" of the *Christian Advocate and Journal.* Later that summer, the Sunday School Union of the Methodist Episcopal Church added Floy's narrative, along with Farnam's account, to their standing catalog of tracts. Evangelicals across the country could now benefit from the dying experience of an eleven-year-old boy from Bowery Village.[122]

In the end, what did chronicling Mather's death mean to Floy? Undoubtedly some children's literature better revealed the worldview and intentions of authors.[123] On a superficial level, one detects a sense of flattery, that Floy felt touched to have made an impression on the boy. More significantly, he articulates the fear he had not done enough to secure the boy's salvation in life. Such guilt reflects the seriousness with which evangelicals took the mandate of the missionary spirit. Writing and publishing an account gave Floy another chance to prove his evangelical mettle; he might have failed Mather in life, but he could provide meaning to his death in awakening others. More than anything, writing gave Floy the chance to contribute to the evangelical textual community that had been instrumental in shaping his own beliefs, practices, and worldview.

Michael Floy Jr. never published another tract after the *Memoir of John Mather*, but he remained an active participant in evangelicalism's textual community. Setting up housekeeping in Harlem following his marriage in November 1836 forced him to make the difficult decision to sever his eight-year relationship with the Bowery Village Methodist Episcopal Sunday School. Marriage did not, however, impinge on his love of reading. If anything, he soon found new opportunities to test and develop his textually informed understanding of evangelicalism. A few months before his own death, Floy sat on the sickbed of his wife's aunt at a complete loss as to how he might console her. He immediately thought of a book he had recently read, Jacob Abbott's *The Way to Do Good*. "Where is the use in such avidity at reading books unless you derive some practical benefit from them?" he asked himself.[124] He already knew the answer. Floy turned to the dying woman and began to converse with her about the state of her soul.

BEYOND THE TEXT

At the annual meeting of the American Tract Society in New York in May 1836, Rev. James Milnor announced in the midst of updates about the previous year's publication and distribution achievements that the society had recently acquired a chair (fig. 4.4). This was not just any chair, however. It had belonged to Elizabeth Wallbridge, known to evangelical readers around the world as the subject of one of the nineteenth century's most popular tracts, Legh Richmond's *The Dairyman's Daughter*.[125] Purchased from the widow of Wallbridge's brother, the chair came to New York with a signed testimonial verifying its authenticity, which was reprinted alongside Milnor's address in that year's *Annual Report*. "To all who had read the Tract of the Dairyman's Daughter, or venerated the memory of its sainted author, and especially to those who had visited her tomb, and witnessed the beautiful scenery which the Tract so accurately delineates," Milnor explained, "the chair . . . would suggest the most solemn and interesting associations."[126] The presence of this relic in the lobby of the ATS on Nassau Street reveals as much about what evangelical print meant to converts as it does about their desire for validation beyond the text.

Evangelical authors and publishers hoped their publications would generate a dialogue on and off the printed page. The response of the Bowery Village Sunday School to Michael Floy's account of the last hours of John Mather Jr., for example, paved the way for its publication in a national religious magazine and as a stand-alone tract. But the reception of Floy's tract

FIGURE 4.4 The Dairyman's Daughter's Chair. American Tract Society Archives, Texas Baptist Historical Collection, Waco, TX

paled in comparison to the popularity of *The Dairyman's Daughter*, which appeared in scores of editions and in various textual, material, and linguistic forms. Readers' embrace of that tract catalyzed the production of supporting texts, such as published testimonials and even a history of her father, appropriately titled *The Dairyman*.[127] What is surprising is the extent to which evangelical readers wanted, demanded, and even needed something more than text. The anxieties of life's spiritual journey and a distrust of fiction, at a time when religious publishers began to experiment with the long-disparaged genre, made them sensitive to the truthfulness of the texts offered to them. Readers of Richmond's "authentic and interesting narrative" demanded authentication, validating the life of the subject and the efficacy of her narrative, in return for faith.[128]

Beginning in the early 1820s, tract societies bridged the gap between reader and subject through the creation of material relics. In a churchyard on the Isle of Wight, a gravestone was erected twenty years after Elizabeth Wallbridge's death for the benefit of large numbers of pilgrims who went to her last resting spot.[129] Evangelical New Yorkers who could not afford the passage to England could see her chair on display at the ATS's headquarters. The chair played no significant role in the story, but it provided a physical connection between subject and reader.[130] Wallbridge's grave and chair functioned in much the same way as the alleged grave of Charlotte Temple in New York's Trinity Church graveyard. These relics provided New Yorkers with sites for individual reflection and identification while simultaneously linking them to like-minded others through communal rituals of remembrance and pilgrimage. Located a few blocks from each other, Temple's gravestone and Wallbridge's chair were powerful reminders of the ways in which readers identified with and appropriated textual subjects to construct their own identities and to validate themselves as members of certain communities of faith.[131]

Michael Floy knew a great deal about constructing an individual and communal identity from textual sources. With the death of John Mather Jr. he saw an opportunity to make a contribution to the growing body of antebellum evangelical literature. His account is not known to have garnered as devoted a following as *The Dairyman's Daughter*, nor did it generate any interest in material relics of its subject. The more important lesson *The Memoir of John Mather, Jun.* has to offer is the one behind the published text: it is the story of the author himself. Floy concluded a diary entry recording his distribution of the tract to his Sunday school scholars with a scriptural paraphrase: "May our dear John being dead, yet speak." Through this tract and his highly detailed diary, it is Michael Floy who speaks, narrating a story of the evangelical impulse made possible by New York's emergence as a center for religious cultural production in the second quarter of the nineteenth century.

CHAPTER FIVE

Free Churches and the Limits of Reform

One Sabbath afternoon in late July 1828, a young evangelical merchant sat in the sanctuary of the Brick Presbyterian Church to hear the "celebrated Mr. Phinney" preach. In new canal towns and old coastal cities, Charles Grandison Finney repeatedly found himself before the same audiences: women and men who believed they could do nothing more than read the Bible, pray for a new heart, and wait for the Lord to convert them in his own time. The minister tried to shake the assembled from their complacency with a message of individual agency in a "pungent" hour-long extemporaneous sermon. He reminded them that their ministers have told the sinner "to do anything and everything but the very thing which God commanded him to do." What then would God have the sinner do? "God commanded him to repent *now*, to believe *now*, to make to him a new heart *now*." The young evangelical merchant in the pews found himself pleasantly surprised by this "man of great natural powers," who was by turns "effective, solemn & tender" and then "fearless & plain," but prone to "too many commonplace phrases." He appreciated how Finney linked a new evangelical emphasis on the free moral agency of the individual with the necessity of reform. The young man saw great potential and concluded that Finney was "a spiritual harrow."[1]

Through his liberating message and personal example, Finney appealed to middle-class evangelical businessmen like Lewis Tappan, the young merchant sitting in the Brick Church that day, and David Hale, a successful newspaper editor.[2] Finney's linkage of reform with new understandings of individualism provided the city's laity with a justification for their benevolent efforts, which had begun with the sponsorship of local urban missions and expanded into making New York a national center for a broad range of reforms. Finney, Tappan, and Hale were born in New England, converted to evangelicalism in adulthood, and held worldviews intricately shaped by their participation in the expanding market culture. This extensive experience informed (and funded) their efforts. Finney, in turn, relied on their financial, administrative, and organizational talents to ensure himself a venue. Together they would spread evangelicalism by reforming it. In the process, they learned the limits of what their fellow evangelicals and the larger city would accept.

LEWIS TAPPAN AND THE FREE CHURCH MOVEMENT

Two weeks after moving to New York in the winter of 1828, Lewis Tappan drafted a letter to Rev. Lyman Beecher on the propriety of founding a new evangelical church in the city. "From some observations already made," Tappan wrote, "I am led to believe that the evangelical churches in this city have no unity of action for the general cause of Xtianity." He went on to explain "that many of them are overgrown, & of course keep in obscurity many persons who might be highly useful; that the principal clergy are either timid or indecisive; [and] that a considerable number of laymen are in advance of their spiritual guides respecting the best means of extending religion." If other transplanted New Englanders—"Sons of Pilgrims," as he referred to them—would join him in forming a joint stock company of three hundred shares at $100 each, they could surely raise enough capital to build a new church. Then the only task left would be to select the right pastor. Perhaps Nathaniel William Taylor, a Yale professor and New England's leading theologian, might be convinced to relocate. Barely containing his enthusiasm, Tappan wanted to know, "What think you of a Pilgrim Church?"[3]

Regardless of what Lyman Beecher thought, Tappan's proposed "Pilgrim Church" never became a reality. Yet even in this early letter, Tappan displayed the organizational and financial talents that have led historians to laud him as a "great architect of valuable institutions."[4] Today he is remembered for putting those talents to work as an antislavery agitator and as a founder of the Mercantile Agency (the precursor to Dun & Bradstreet), but before either became his life's work, he concentrated his energy on devising new schemes for building up urban evangelical churches. With a devotion matched by few others, he studied and reflected upon efforts to convert the unconverted undertaken by evangelical New Yorkers. Distributing tracts for the New-York City Tract Society and collecting signatures for the General Union for Promoting the Observance of the Sabbath, he got to know his new neighbors, some of whom impressed him, and many more whom he found "dull & much, much below the spirit of the age."[5] Each Sabbath he attended different neighborhood churches on the northern edge of urban settlement and mission churches in the eastern part of the city. In his diary, he critiqued the sermons he heard, the ministers who preached them, and the congregations that sat in the pews around him. Some received only a single visit; others he returned to again and again.[6]

Early on, a little Presbyterian church on Allen Street particularly piqued Tappan's interest. The church originated in the efforts of missionaries Ward Stafford and Samuel Mills in the summer of 1816 in "a very forbidding district of the city." Over a decade later, the church continued to struggle. It lacked a settled minister and much of a congregation.[7] The arrival of Tappan's family in New York from Boston in November 1828 spelled the end of his involvement. "I have wished to attend Allen St. church, in order to assist in building up this poor, small & destitute church," he wrote in his diary, "but [it] is a mile & half from my house; my family cannot walk so far; & after mature deliberation it does not appear to be my duty to separate from them on the Sabbath."[8]

Tappan's observation of the Allen Street congregation convinced him that the voluntary association–sponsored missionary approach of the past decade was no longer working. "The almost total exclusion of the poor from the Presbyterian and Dutch churches; the great neglect of the careless and impenitent on the part of professing Christians; and the importance of more direct and faithful efforts for their conversion," he wrote, epitomized the problems of the city's spiritual marketplace.[9] A new plan was needed. Rather than putting the responsibility for the design and implementation of a new church in the hands of a missionary minister, as Allen Street had done, he believed concerned laity must take charge. He would make the conversion of others the primary responsibility of every member and embrace revivalism as the way to bring it about. The question remained, where to begin? Breaking once again with contemporary practice, Tappan decided against locating his new church on the expanding edge of urban settlement in favor of his own neighborhood in the First Ward. There he found plenty of women and men who felt shut out of the ward's nine churches. To compete for their attendance, the new church would offer them free seats.

In May 1830, Tappan gathered sympathetic evangelical friends to discuss the possibility of forming a church on this new plan. He proposed a "Free

Church" that abolished paid pews in preference of free seating, hoping to lure men and women who had otherwise escaped denominational efforts. Free seats were not an innovation in New York in 1830, but they did defy the conventional wisdom of financing a church. Since the seventeenth century, New York's churches capitalized the building of new meetinghouses by selling pews and charging holders an annual tax, or "rent," typically a percentage of the pew value, to cover the salary of the minister, upkeep of the structure, and other expenses.[10] Methodists had traditionally bucked this trend, opening up seating in their meetinghouses to all. They offset lost revenue by refusing to settle ministers, building plain and inexpensive meetinghouses, and centralizing ownership and control of all church property in a single board of trustees. Tappan openly admired their success and realized he needed to figure out how to make free seats financially viable.[11]

To devise a new model for funding evangelical churches, Lewis Tappan looked to the commercial marketplace. He found inspiration in the innovations of his older brother. Arthur Tappan entered the city's jobbing business in 1815. Having survived the depression following the War of 1812 and the Panic of 1819, he knew the vicissitudes of dealing in credit firsthand. He discovered that by breaking up large packages of imported British dry goods to sell by the piece for cash he could price his goods at only a small percentage over cost. "The low prices attracted the attention of purchasers," Lewis remembered, "and neighboring merchants predicted that this new kind of business would soon come to a termination." The opposite happened. Consumers hailed the democratization of access. Small, rural purchasers typically denied the best discounts especially appreciated it. Arthur more than made up in volume what he sacrificed in markup for credit-paying customers.[12] Selling to more for less, avoiding the pitfalls of encumbering credit, and keeping overhead costs low all struck Lewis as useful innovations that might be applied to the organizational model of urban churches.

Lewis also learned from Arthur the importance of linking commerce to Christian stewardship. As Arthur's business increased, so did his investment in charitable causes. "It was his prayerful inquiry: 'Lord, what wilt thou have me to do?'" Lewis remembered. "He resolved on consecrating a large portion of his gains to the cause of the Redeemer, by engaging, heart and purse, in the benevolent operations of the day."[13] Arthur also invested in business ventures with specifically evangelical objectives. In September 1827, he established a new daily paper, the *Journal of Commerce*, to exert "a wholesome moral influence" on fellow businessmen. The newspaper abstained from publishing "immoral advertisements" for liquor, circuses, and theaters and, unlike the other dailies in the city, refused to publish on

Sunday. Twelve months and a $30,000 loss later, Arthur signed the paper over to Lewis.[14] The latter ran it with an equal lack of financial success before selling it to David Hale and Gerard Hallock, the paper's editors and fellow evangelicals, who finally made a go of it.[15] The Tappans' experience with the *Journal of Commerce* suggested not only their commitment to innovate in order to further evangelical goals but also a willingness to cut their losses.

The key to a successful new urban church model, Lewis Tappan believed, came from a more efficient economy of scale. Where denominational churches were spending tens of thousands of dollars constructing elaborate new meetinghouses, Tappan's plan called for the use of rented commercial space. "It is a great mistake to suppose it requires wealth or large numbers, to maintain public worship," he reasoned, "for in a city like this, a few young Christians who can raise 1000 or 1500 dollars to begin with, hire a hall, and procure a preacher, can support public worship without difficulty, and make it instrumental of great good." Initial patronage by those whom the Lord had blessed, like the Tappans, would be offset in time by smaller contributions from a far greater volume of people.[16] Over time, one church might grow into many. "We think a church cannot act efficiently when it is composed of more than 200 or 300 members," Tappan explained. Once the maximum number of members was reached, a colony could be spun off to another neighborhood and a new church begun. "Such churches might be built up in every city, and in many villages," Tappan concluded. "Why should they not be extended throughout Christendom?"[17]

With a target audience identified and an organizational plan in place, Tappan needed one last component: a minister with a gospel message that would draw men and women in and, hopefully, lead to their conversion. He found his man not in the city's evangelical establishment, but in the Union Church, a little congregation on the northern edge of urban settlement. Eight months earlier, Anson G. Phelps Sr., an evangelical Presbyterian and wealthy metal importer and manufacturer, had lured Charles Grandison Finney back to New York. Phelps first leased a vacant meetinghouse on Vandewater Street and then purchased another on Prince Street for the revivalist.[18] There in the fall and winter of 1829–1830, Finney precipitated a revival that reportedly converted upward of two hundred.[19] Tappan knew he had found a man with a message that appealed to the urban masses.

Finney's popularity stemmed from his willingness to reduce impediments to individual conversion.[20] In one of his most influential and widely preached sermons, "Sinners Bound to Change Their Own Hearts," he rejected the Calvinist notion that man's sinfulness had been imputed to him through original sin and instead redefined sin as selfishness, placing the responsibility solely on the individual.[21] He argued that Christ died to make salvation possible for all, although he remained firmly Calvinist in his expectation that only the elect would embrace conversion. His passionately stated conviction that every man was a free moral agent endowed with the power to choose good or evil warmed the hearts of thousands and drew down the scorn of orthodox critics. Instead of waiting for the implantation of a new heart by the Holy Spirit, he exhorted, men and women possessed the natural ability to effect change themselves.[22] And when should they repent and make themselves new hearts? Immediately, he resoundingly answered. Inspired, Tappan determined to make new hearts through a new church structure.

Tappan's Free Church plan received its first test in late June 1830 when a small group gathered in an upper room in a hall at Nos. 1 and 3 Thames Street to form the First Free Presbyterian Church. The location seemed advantageous: the hall was just off Broadway, behind the well-known City Hotel (see map 5.1). True to Tappan's call for economic efficiency, it cost only $125 for the room to be "rudely fitted up as a place of worship."[23] The message of salvation emanating from the pulpit came not from Finney, however, who was off leading a revival in Rochester that would make his name, but from the next best thing, his young protégé, Rev. Joel Parker. Placards posted in the streets and advertisements in local newspapers alerted the public to the new church and its unconventional location. At the end of the summer, sixteen people came forward to officially organize the church. By January, the room's 350-person capacity no longer accommodated the throngs that came to hear Parker preach.[24]

The spaces First Free Presbyterian occupied in its early years demonstrate Tappan's willingness to occupy the landscape of secular New York. In February 1831, First Free Presbyterian moved a dozen blocks uptown to the Masonic Hall at 314 and 316 Broadway, the largest and most central auditorium in the city. Antebellum evangelicals more often fell on the side of anti-Masonry, yet the availability of the hall, their scanty budget, and a sense that they had embarked on something new overrode any potential objections to this symbolically charged space.[25] The gamble paid off. The increased foot traffic brought in strangers who sometimes left converts. By the end of the summer of 1831, the church had more than 200 members and far more in regular attendance. The church needed a permanent location but had insufficient financial resources to purchase land and build a meetinghouse. Tappan innovated once again. He orchestrated the purchase for $7,000 of four brick warehouses on the corner of Dey and Washington Streets farther

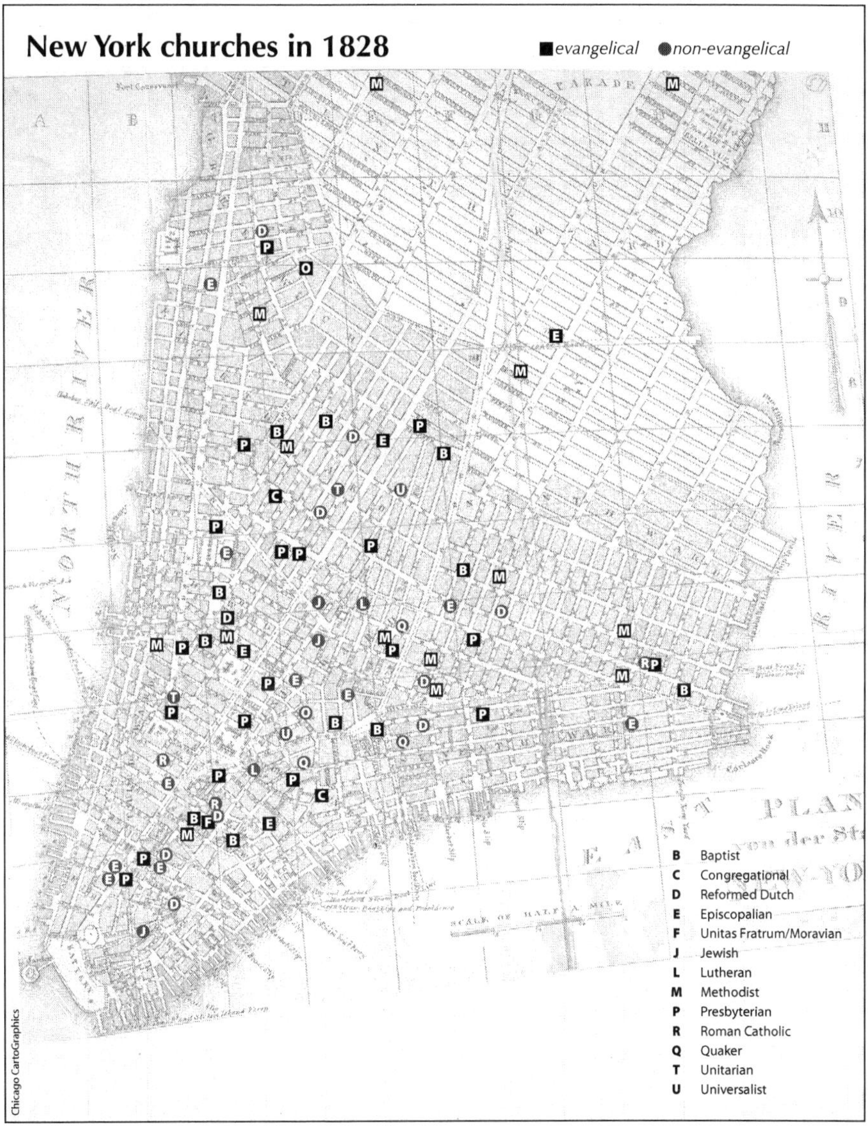

MAP 5.1 New York's religious landscape in 1828, by Dennis McClendon

FIGURE 5.1 Unknown artist, Chatham Theatre, ca. 1830. Lithograph from the collections of the Museum of the City of New York

downtown. The church transformed the upper lofts of this block into a 70-by-80 foot chapel that could accommodate 800 to 1,000, and enjoyed a steady income from the rents of ground-level shops. This mixing of sacred and secular surely turned a few heads. Yet in little over a year, First Free Presbyterian demonstrated beyond any measure of a doubt that churches could thrive in nonreligious spaces.[26]

Over the next four years, five more Free churches appeared in radically different spaces—secular halls, commercial buildings, even a theater—in settled parts of the city. Second Free Presbyterian began in February 1832 in Broadway Hall. It effected an even more dramatic rethinking of sacred space by transforming one of the most disreputable theaters in New York into an evangelical church. The Chatham Street Theater (fig. 5.1) stood in the heart of "the most irreligious population of New York" near Five Points, "a place of resort highly discreditable to the city."[27] For the same amount as it cost to purchase and fit up the brick warehouses on Dey Street, Tappan converted the theater's auditorium into a sanctuary and its barroom and saloons into prayer and lecture rooms (fig. 5.2).[28] Contributions from members of other urban evangelical churches offset half the expense on the condition that the space be made available for the city's major benevolent, missionary, and reform organizations' annual meetings held each year at the beginning of May. Third Free Presbyterian formed at the Masonic Hall by the end of 1832, and Fourth Free Presbyterian, in January 1834 in a hall in the Fourth Ward before moving to a converted brewery.[29] Two additional Free churches, including the Broadway Tabernacle, appeared soon after.[30] By the mid-1830s, most of the city's Free churches occupied distinctive structures around the core of downtown Manhattan.

Finney's distinctive rethinking of revivalism filled the Free churches. In the Rochester revival of 1830, Finney began to reject Edwards's notion of a

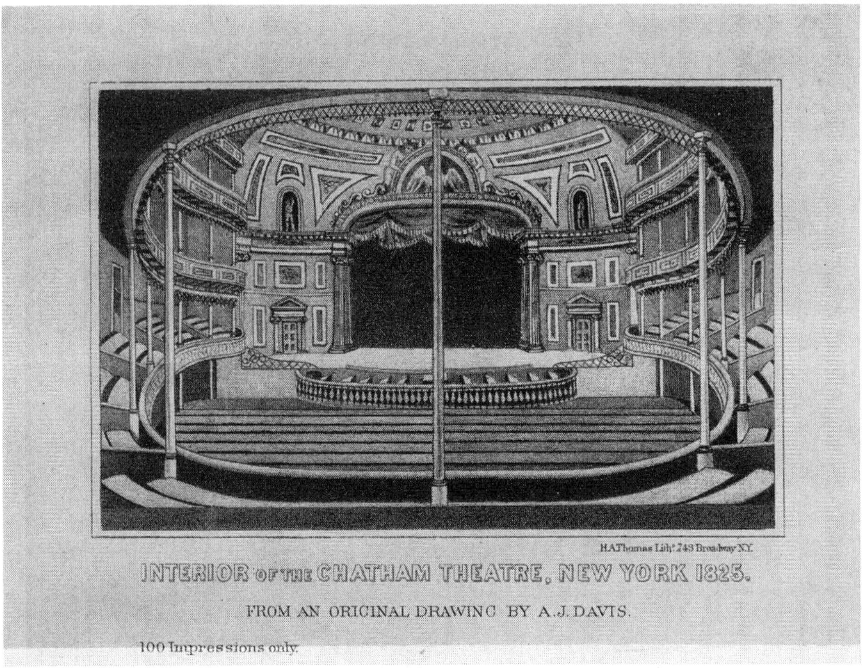

FIGURE 5.2 Interior of the Chatham Theatre before it was transformed into the Second Free Presbyterian Church, also known as the Chatham Chapel. From an original drawing by A. J. Davis, 1825, H. A. Thomas, litho, from PR020 (geographic file), box 83, f: Chatham Theatre; neg. #51371, New-York Historical Society. Photography © New-York Historical Society

revival as "a surprising work of God" and recast it as the "purely philosophical result of the right use of the constituted means." A revival is not a miracle, "something above the powers of nature," he famously explained, but the product of "the right exercise of the powers of nature."[31] Finney knew disruption of the status quo was key. Preaching and prayer could awaken sinners to repentance, but revivalists needed a few "new measures" to secure mass conversion. He found these means in the protracted meeting and the anxious bench. Protracted meetings forced the suspension of the quotidian lives of churchgoers for anywhere from a few days to a few weeks, compelling them to confront their lack of conversion. A pew at the front of the sanctuary for the unconverted, known as the anxious bench, goaded revival participants to publicly admit their struggle to find conversion in hopes of quick resolution.[32]

A minister's ability to promote revival often determined his success in the pulpit of a Free church. Joel Parker "entered the city with all the zeal and devotion of a missionary on heathen ground," one early convert remembered, and soon demonstrated his aptitude for "getting up" revivals at First Free Presbyterian.[33] Charles Finney assumed the pulpit of the Second Free Presbyterian in May 1832 and enjoyed even greater success. An extensive revival ensued, cut short only by an outbreak of cholera. Illness kept him from preaching until the following March. A protracted meeting upon his return converted five hundred in twenty days.[34] Third Free Presbyterian installed another Finney protégé, Dirck Lansing of Utica.[35] The departure of a minister, or the installation of the wrong minister, could have adverse effects. Returning from a voyage to the Mediterranean for his health in November 1834, Finney discovered that John Ingersoll, his associate pastor, had failed to retain most of the congregation of the Second Free Presbyterian in his absence. Some claimed that Ingersoll was abrasive, ineffective, and long-winded, but his greatest fault may simply have been that he was not Finney. Pews empty in Finney's absence tended to fill quickly in his presence.[36]

Free churches also benefited from an upswing in revivalism across the city. The Methodist church on Allen Street enjoyed far more success than its struggling Presbyterian sister down the street. An 1827 revival served as a premonition for a larger outpouring in late 1831 and early 1832 that converted between 700 and 800 and spread to other churches.[37] Overall, Methodists rose steadily from 2,623 members in 1825 to 5,433 in 1832 before hitting a plateau until the end of the decade (see the appendix). Many New School–leaning Presbyterian churches also benefited from revivals, while Old School congregations remained quiet. "The great features of the work were the same that appeared in

Apostolic times," one nineteenth-century historian remembered, "preaching in public and from house to house, united with prayer and a simple and faithful instruction from the Bible to the young."[38] Citywide revivalism primed the laity to play more involved roles in their churches.

Tappan insisted that bringing sinners to conversion was the work of all. "The minister, elders, teachers in the Bible classes and Sabbath school, and, in fact, every member of the church, considered it their duty to labour personally and unitedly for the *immediate* conversion of sinners," he remembered.[39] To this end, members of First Free Presbyterian hosted and participated in a full slate of meetings throughout the week.[40] Members served as "Visitors" to converse with, pray for, and ascertain the spiritual state of fellow congregants.[41] At Second Free Presbyterian, Finney specially instructed the laity on how to labor with those under conviction. "They were true to this teaching, and on the lookout at every meeting to see with whom the Word of God was taking effect," he recalled. "And they had faith enough to dismiss their fears, and to speak to any one before they retired, if possible, whom they saw to be affected by the Word."[42]

Their field extended beyond the sanctuary, often taking them deep into the city. "When I first went to Chatham St. Chapel, I informed the brethren that I did not wish to fill up the house with Christians from other churches, as my object was to gather from the world," Finney later wrote. "I wanted to secure the conversion of the ungodly to the utmost possible extent."[43] George Cragin found Finney's directive exhilarating. "Not a few," he remembered, followed the revivalist's advice to go "out into the streets and lanes of the city, and lay hold of every sinner we met and tell him he must repent and give his heart to God, or he would go to hell." Cragin later joined a group of thirty-four other unmarried young men and women, all Finney converts, who founded Third Free Presbyterian in hopes of being useful outside of the already established churches.[44] Tappan's plan for expansion had succeeded.

Free churches drew in disconnected men and women looking for community and meaning in the midst of an increasingly anonymous city. In Rochester, Finney hoped to convert the "great mass of the most influential people," but in Gotham he focused on Tappan's original stated mission to those underserved by the city's churches.[45] "They were not among the rich, although there were several men of property belonging to them," Finney later wrote. "In general they were gathered from among the middle and lower classes of New York citizens."[46] A listing of 325 church members in an early *Manual* of First Free Presbyterian confirms Finney's assessment.[47] As in most churches of the period, evangelical and otherwise, women outnumbered

Table 5.1. Aggregate membership statistics, Free Church Movement, New York, September 1830–February 1835

Church	*Members (M/F)*	*Professions of faith*	*Certificates*	*Baptisms*	*Prep for Ministry*
First	753 (301/452)	493	260	303	27
Second	426 (145/281)	302	104	106	9
Third	344 (115/229)	203	141		12
Fourth	64 (22/42)	26	38		3
Total	1,587 (583/1004)	1,024	543	409	51

Source: Lewis Tappan, "History of the Free Churches in the City of New York," in Andrew Reed and James Matheson, *A Narrative of the Visit to the American Churches by Deputation from the Congregational Union of England and Wales* (London, 1836), II: 375–76

men, on average, two to one. Uniting them, however, was their lack of connection to each other. Only one in five men who joined the church had a spouse who also joined. For women that number was closer to one in eight.[48] Historian Paul Johnson has argued in his analysis of Rochester that, among the married, women often converted and then brought their husbands into the church. Yet wives joined before their husbands in only four instances out of twenty-five couples in New York. Most joined simultaneously. In the absence of spousal ties, there is evidence of residential and occupational connections. Widow Sarah Ann Dubois, her daughter Elizabeth, and two women living with them at 46 Pearl Street all joined in the spring of 1831. Three of Arthur Tappan's clerks—Seth Bliss Hunt, Ebenezer Grosvenor Parker, and Marshall Bronson Blake—joined a little before them. None appear in the 1830 or 1831 city directories, and neither did most of their fellow congregants. They were too marginal, too unsettled, or too transitory to be recorded. Yet at First Free Presbyterian they found a community proud to print their names as members.

In early 1835, Lewis Tappan took stock of the spiritual ground he had helped cultivate over the previous five years. The results were impressive. More than fifteen hundred men and women had joined the first four Free churches, nearly twice as many by profession of faith as by certificate, and many of them as the result of revivals (table 5.1). An equal number experienced conversion but united with other churches. He had succeeded in creating a viable church for the city's underserved population, perfected an organizational model that allowed churches to efficiently and inexpensively reproduce themselves, and promoted a theology of evangelical individualism popular with the disconnected residents of the city. The idea even spread.

The city's Protestant Episcopal churches began to open free churches in the early 1830s.[49] Unfortunately, something else had begun to sprout alongside the gospel, which many considered a noxious weed threatening to choke the very health of the movement. The unwitting sower? Tappan himself.

REFORM AND THE LIMITS OF EVANGELICAL INDIVIDUALISM

Recently arrived from Vermont, Seth Bliss Hunt walked into Arthur Tappan's warehouse at 122 Pearl Street in June 1830 and asked for a clerkship, not knowing where his future might lead. After some wrangling, he secured a position. Tappan's influence soon began to rub off on the young clerk. By November, Hunt had joined the First Free Presbyterian Church, part of an innovative evangelical movement founded by his new employer's brother that coupled church membership with participation in reform. Like so many young men, Hunt had come to New York to make his fortune, not to reform the world. A little less than three years later, however, he found himself in the Chatham Street Chapel as a mob tried to disrupt an antislavery meeting. A more serious brush occurred the following July when he and his fellow clerks barricaded themselves in Tappan's store, guns in hand, ready to defend the premises (and potentially their lives) from another mob. Looking back forty years later, he wondered how it was that he had chosen to support abolition. He could not shake the feeling that abolition had chosen him. The day the Merchants' Hotel asked him to find alternative lodgings, he knew the die was cast. "I came, when a lad, from Vermont, thinking little, and at the time caring less, on the subject," Hunt remembered. "And yet here I was turned out of a hotel for being a clerk to an abolitionist!"[50]

Seth Hunt, the Tappan brothers, and thousands of other evangelical New Yorkers increasingly saw reform as integral to evangelicalism in the third decade of the nineteenth century as a result of their participation in the Free Church movement. As evangelical understandings of conversion shifted from an extended process to an immediate event, so, too, did the emphasis placed on involvement in social activism. Some reforms, like temperance, made sense within this individualistic framework, even if it meant asking people to give up an integral part of early American sociability.[51] Others, like abolition, seemed more of a stretch and proved uncomfortable to many in a city that had already "solved" its slavery problem with the Gradual Emancipation Law of 1799, which made provision for the freedom of all New York slaves by 1827. Free churches took the lead in linking church membership and reform participation, only to be subjected, in time, to increasing distrust and hostility from nonevangelicals and evangelicals alike.

Charles Grandison Finney preached that an individual's duty to participate in reform sprang from the same obligations owed the Lord for his or her conversion. Influenced by the New Divinity movement, he defined sin as selfishness and godliness as a state of "disinterested benevolence." Conversion effected a change from selfishness to benevolence; the converted naturally desired to devote themselves to doing good for the sake of God's glory. "As saints supremely value the highest good of being, they will, and must, take a deep interest in whatever is promotive of that end," he wrote later in life. "Hence, their spirit is necessarily that of the reformer. To the universal reformation of the world they stand committed."[52] Wedding the right reform movement to a revival could create a dynamic synergy, channeling the spiritual zeal of new converts into reforming themselves and their communities. The challenge was finding the right reform given local social, economic, and political conditions.[53]

Evangelical New Yorkers had many reforms to choose from in the early 1830s. Free churches initially sought to engage congregants' energies across a broad range of them. "Common benevolence requires that those who can enjoy a blessing which is capable of being diffused, should impart it to others," First Free Presbyterian's 1832 *Manual* explained, ". . . as the very *spirit* and *design* of Christianity are benevolent, and a profession of religion is equivalent to enrolling [one's] name as a *promoter of all good objects*."[54] Anyone seeking admission had to agree to abstain from distilled spirits, for example.[55] Even grocers renting space on the ground level assented to this temperance pledge, although this requirement reduced the rent the church could collect. Within the churches, committees of three to five laymen informed the congregation each month about particular reform efforts and solicited donations. They generally advocated reforms popular and broadly accepted by evangelicals: tract and Bible distribution, foreign and home missions, Sunday schools, and temperance. Noticeably absent was antislavery, a reform many deemed overly divisive. That soon changed.[56]

The landscape of antislavery activism shifted from gradual to immediate emancipation just as the Free Church movement emerged. Creating colonies of freed slaves in Africa dominated white antislavery activism in the 1820s until African American abolitionists, many of them evangelical, vociferously rejected the movement as an effort to rid the United States of its free black population. In its place, they issued a radical call for the immediate end of slavery and the granting of equal rights.[57] Before long, Lewis and

Arthur Tappan and other white middle-class evangelicals dropped their support for colonization. They devoted their organizational energies and growing mercantile wealth to support local and national organizations that took an immediatist stance.[58] Evangelicalism had led them to see that sin was disobedience to God. What greater sin plagued the nation than slavery, they asked? Just as conversion could be the immediate decision of the sinner, so, too, was the renunciation of sin. To them, the sin of slavery fell no more on slaveholders than on those made complicit by failing to denounce it.[59]

As African American and white evangelicals embraced immediate abolition, Finney began to "arouse public attention to the subject" and received a mixed reception. His arousal of New Yorkers did not always play out in the ways he anticipated. In October 1833, a mob stormed the Chatham Street Chapel during a meeting of the New York Anti-Slavery Society, forcing Arthur Tappan, Seth Hunt, and others to escape out a back door. Not to be deterred, Finney stood in the same place two months later and informed the congregation that he would no longer serve communion to slaveholders. Finney's linkage of Free churches with immediate abolition made them some of the most symbolically charged spaces in the city.[60]

Many New Yorkers felt that evangelicals had foisted abolition on them. Rumors of amalgamation, the contemporary term for racial mixing, circulated throughout Gotham in the spring of 1834, thanks in part to the rhetoric of the partisan press. Individual evangelicals and whole churches were accused of challenging traditional social and spatial distinctions that New Yorkers wanted left alone. One stated that Arthur Tappan left his wife to marry a "Negress." Another accused Henry Ludlow of the Spring Street Presbyterian Church of performing interracial marriages. The breaking point came when Tappan invited Samuel Cornish, Presbyterian minister and publisher of the pioneering African American newspaper *Freedom's Journal,* to sit in his pew one Sabbath at the Laight Street Presbyterian Church. White evangelicals took offense and some threatened to leave the church. Laight Street's minister, Rev. Samuel Hanson Cox, also an abolitionist firebrand, attempted to relieve tensions with a midweek lecture that asked his flock to consider whether they would treat Christ, who "was probably a dark Syrian hue," as they did Cornish. The strategy backfired. Cox successfully offended much of the white population inside and outside of the church. One merchant responded, "And would you believe it? he called my Saviour a nigger! God damn him!"[61]

Anti-abolition riots in July 1834 revealed the extent to which evangelical churches, especially the Free churches, were linked to antislavery in the eyes of New Yorkers. Over the course of three nights in early July, the city erupted in rioting. An evangelical topography of salvation and reform was replaced by one of racial hatred and terror, as mobs attempted to eviscerate leading evangelicals through symbolic attacks on their property. Evangelical churches and black neighborhoods bore the brunt of the mob's anger (see map 5.2). The first riot began July 9 at the Chatham Street Chapel when a reported crowd of two thousand gathered to shut down an abolitionist meeting rumored to be taking place.[62] Another group assembled on Rose Street and trashed Lewis Tappan's house. Contingents from each group then descended on the Bowery Theater, where a performer was accused of making anti-American comments. The following evening, the mob broadened its scope, threatening, but not harming, the homes of Cox, Ludlow, and William Green Jr., another leading lay participant in the Free Church movement.

The greatest anti-evangelical destruction occurred on the third and final evening of the riot. Two waves of mobs attacked the homes and churches of white evangelical laity, including an attempted assault on Arthur Tappan's store, bravely defended by Seth Hunt and fellow clerks, and the trashing of Cox's and Ludlow's private residences and of churches.[63] A third, and most destructive, wave attacked homes, churches, and bodies in a predominantly black neighborhood in the Five Points.[64] By Saturday, the mayor had compiled a list of "contemplated attacks" from requests for protection from nervous residents. Whereas the attacks of the previous days had been contained in localized areas, the new list included the homes and institutions of leading evangelicals and black entrepreneurs scattered across the city. Members of both groups clearly saw the pattern in the previous nights' actions and assumed they were next.[65] Historians often credit the enlistment of a large militia with preventing more destruction, but the fact that the mobs had already compromised much of the offending evangelical landscape suggests that their work was largely done.

In the aftermath of the riots, evangelical New Yorkers—black and white—questioned the linkage between evangelicalism and reform. Some white evangelicals, like William Green Jr., saw the riots as a blessing. "I believe the Lord means to bless the Free Churches," he wrote to an absent Finney, "*because* of the stand they have taken in defense of the rights of man, and for raising their voice against the oppressor."[66] He, however, was in the minority. The reaction of the members of the Laight Street Church was more representative. A statement in the *Courier and Enquirer*, the same paper accused of fomenting the mobs, distanced them from Samuel Hanson Cox, the minister of their now demolished church. It stated that "of the nine trustees who

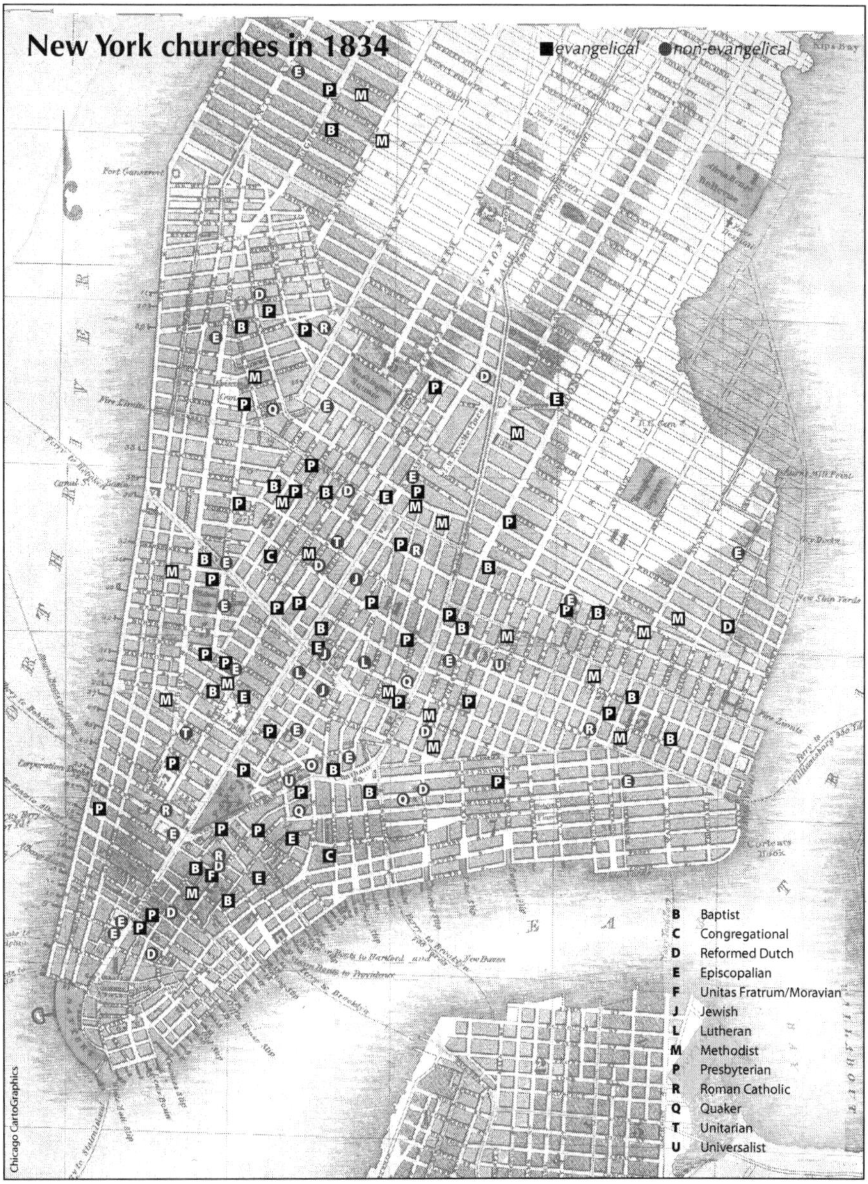

MAP 5.2 New York's religious landscape in 1834, by Dennis McClendon

represent the congregation only *one* approves of the doctrines and opinions of Dr. Cox, and not one-fortieth of his congregation coincide with him on the subject of immediate abolition."[67] Black evangelicals shifted their focus to the reform of their communities through occupational, intellectual, and moral education. They distanced themselves from abolition and white evangelicals even more than they had before the riots.[68]

Startled like many of his followers, Finney recognized the threat antislavery posed to revivalism and began to publicly distance himself from abolition. Out of the country when the riots occurred, he debated whether to return to Chatham Street at all. "Some think the church would scatter in every direction," he wrote his wife, "as soon as it was known that I was going on account of the abolition movements."[69] The only way to restore the church, he decided, was to uncouple revivalism from reform. To that end, he poured himself into his famous "Lectures on Revivals" in December 1834 and January 1835.[70] Later published as a best-selling book, they signaled a theological return to evangelical individualism and a backing away from antislavery reform.[71] The move worked. The lectures revived the Chatham Street Chapel. Ever mindful of the importance of public opinion, Finney vigilantly guarded his success and made sure that the thousands who attended his lectures saw African Americans safely contained in a segregated gallery. His personal commitment to abolition would have to wait for the safer venue of Oberlin, Ohio, where he moved the following May.

As Finney breathed new life into the Free Church movement, he began to butt heads with Lewis Tappan, who did not take kindly to the marginalization of abolition. At a trustees' meeting to discuss the formation of a fifth Free church, Tappan challenged Finney's new stance. His motion to treat all men in the new church equally, irrespective of color, provoked Finney to reply adamantly, "40 of the best men in the city could not force the practice of associating in churches with people of color." The evangelist went on to criticize the recent election of Thomas Van Renssellaer, a black abolitionist, to the church's board of trustees, warning them it would be the end of the enterprise. "I fear we must [remove Van Renssellaer from the board]," Tappan sniped back in his diary, "because there does not appear high religious principle enough to carry out the principles adopted." Mocking Finney, he concluded, "It is not *expedient* forsooth!"[72]

Black and white evangelicals were equally wary of Tappan in the aftermath of the 1834 riots. Having lost interest in the Fifth Free church, Tappan investigated the possibility of joining the Colored Presbyterian Church.[73] One of the church's clergymen attempted to dissuade him, explaining that a heavy debt lay on their church and that his presence might impede the giving of "some persons now friendly."[74] Leading members of Chatham Street Chapel approached him about returning, desirous of his annual contribution of $500 to the church he joined. When asked if mixed seating was a condition of his return, Tappan characteristically replied that while he would never force any such condition on a church, he also could never imagine himself belonging to a church that did not hold such a view.[75] Finally he decided to return to First Free Presbyterian, where his wife and family worshipped. Rev. Elijah Barrows was rightfully hesitant; he told Tappan flat out of his fear that the reformer's "peculiar views on slavery" would cause trouble. Tappan assured Barrows that he would not force his ideas on the church, but he would also not silence himself.[76] Perhaps the promise of a sizable annual contribution made Barrows forget his fears, as Tappan joined the church in May.

The Panic of 1837 dealt as great, if not a greater, blow to the Free churches than the 1834 riots. The failure of J. L. and S. I. Joseph and Company in March 1837 set off a domino effect that overwhelmed the city's overextended business community. Nearly one month later, 128 firms had gone under.[77] Wealthy evangelicals, including Arthur Tappan, watched helplessly as their fortunes disappeared.[78] On May 1, to the shock of many (and the glee of anti-abolitionists), Tappan & Co. suspended payment. Lewis Tappan's diaries offer little insight into either brother's reaction to the devastating downturn that left the firm a staggering $1.1 million in debt.[79] His biography of Arthur, written thirty years later, presents a picture of Christian resignation clearly softened by time. "He bore the disappointment like a man who had done all he could to avert a calamity," Lewis wrote, "and when it came, resigned himself to the will of God." No amount of humility, however, changed the fact that the wealth so crucial to supporting the city's reform movements had evaporated.[80]

Repercussions of the panic resonated throughout secular and sacred New York. Massive losses meant massive layoffs. The construction trade nearly dried up. Imports dropped from $118 million in 1836 to $79 million in 1837 and fell even lower the following year.[81] Evangelical voluntary organizations tried to relieve the newly destitute masses but labored under the burden of decreasing donations. "I have been astonished to find that the pecuniary embarrassments of the few past years have so far crippled the movements of the great benevolent societies for want of funds," wrote Finney.[82] These developments confirmed what many suspected: "as the fervor of Christians in the work of saving souls abated, the expenses of public worship, which

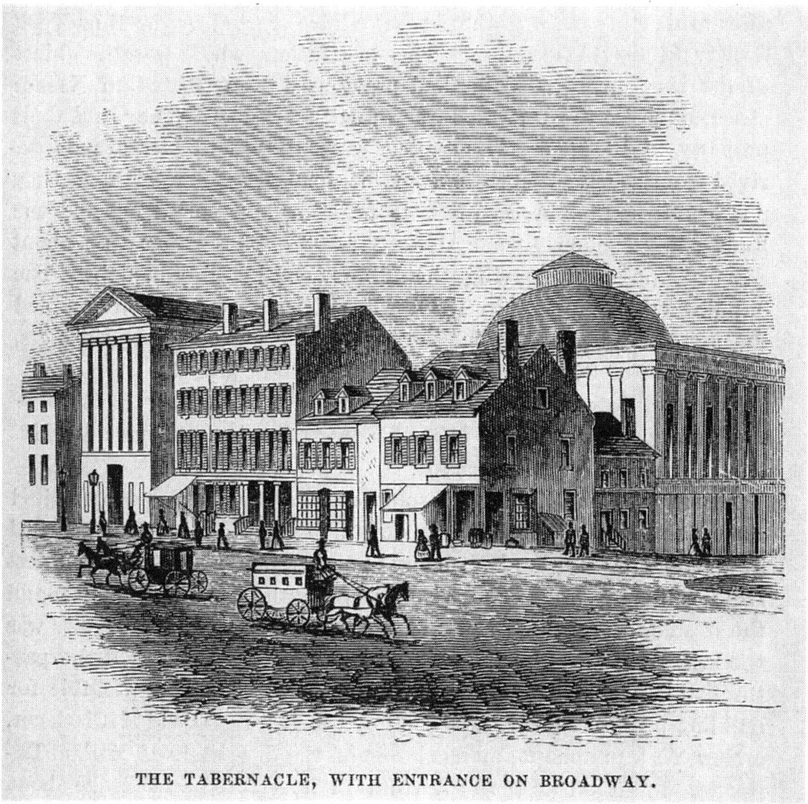

FIGURE 5.3 Exterior of the Broadway Tabernacle Church in *Manual of the Corporation of New York for the Year* (New York, 1865)

were not thought of in the zeal of a revival, began to be felt as a heavy burden."[83]

As the panic wore on, the financially strapped First Free Presbyterian was forced to merge with the Broadway Tabernacle, the sixth of the Free churches (fig. 5.3).[84] Built at the behest of Finney, the Tabernacle represented the culmination of the movement. The four previous Free churches were neighborhood based and formed a ring around the city, while the Tabernacle, begun in 1835 and dedicated in April 1836, stood in the city's commercial and geographical center. It challenged the supremacy of Protestant Episcopal churches that traditionally dominated the city's main thoroughfare and made a bold statement of achievement for an upstart evangelical movement dedicated to reinserting religion into the urban secular landscape.[85] The structure went against Tappan's economically efficient retrofit model, being built new at a cost of $66,500.[86] An acoustically and aesthetically concerned Finney, not a purse-pinching Tappan, wanted a grand stage on which to perform and insisted on the design's dramatic departure in scale and plan. The central auditorium sat twenty-five hundred in circular seating under a large rotunda pierced by a skylight (fig. 5.4). Joseph Ditto, a Free church member and contractor for the previous churches, told Finney he "feared that it would injure his reputation to build a church with such an interior," but built it just the same.[87]

The Broadway Tabernacle departed from the earlier Free Church model in two important additional ways. First, it made no commitment to temperance

FIGURE 5.4 Fanny Palmer's lithograph of the interior of the Broadway Tabernacle Church, 1850. Courtesy, American Antiquarian Society

or antislavery in its articles, a traditional component of admission to a Free church.[88] This reticence is understandable given that New Yorkers had already burned the unfinished building as an "Amalgamation Church" in July 1835, exactly a year after the disastrous riots.[89] Second, it called a potentially proslavery minister. Abolitionists suspected that the antislavery sentiments of Joel Parker, original minister of First Free Presbyterian, had softened as he ministered to evangelical slaveholders in New Orleans in the mid-1830s.[90] Tappan presented a lengthy series of objections to what he deemed Parker's inconsistent stances on the Sabbath and slavery when the congregation met to consider the propriety of issuing a call.[91] Tappan likened Parker to "a vane on the top of a sanctuary," whose antislavery sentiments blew whichever way the wind did.[92] Much of the congregation did not take kindly to Parker being called a "weather cock" and voted nearly four to one to issue a call.[93]

Disappointed but undaunted, Tappan decided that if he could not control what was preached from the pulpit, he could at least work on his own initiative. He gathered signatures for a Broadway Tabernacle Anti-Slavery Society, knowing full well that Parker and others would be unsupportive. "It was thought that the formation of an Anti-Slavery Society would serve as a bond of union to the aggrieved members and prevent them from leaving the church," Tappan explained in justification of his actions. In mid-December 1838, he submitted an official request to form a society. Soon after, Parker explained to the congregation in a Sunday morning sermon that he and the session disapproved and would not let it go forward. Tappan's published account of the day presented his response as the very model of civility, pointing out to Parker that "the measure was a peaceful and Christian one" and that the signers only meant to exercise their "Christian liberty." His private diary preserved a more contemptuous, and likely more accurate, scene in which he told Parker, "I should do all I could to form such a society in every church in the city." Three days later, Tappan received a summons to appear before the session on the charge of disorderly and unchristian conduct.[94]

Tappan took the trial and ensuing events as vindication of his right to pursue reform through the church. The session summoned him in early January 1839 on charges of slandering Parker. After three tension-filled days in which Tappan complained of every action of the session and they, understandably, grew weary of his obvious contempt for them, he was found guilty of contumacy and excluded.[95] The Presbytery of New York refused to overturn his conviction in March, but the General Assembly sustained his appeal in May. Happy with his victory, Tappan shared his experience with the world by publishing a copy of the trial proceedings a little more than a week later. "I have felt grieved at publishing the faults of old friends & of occasioning reproach to professors of religion," Tappan wrote in his diary, "but it seemed a paramount duty to publish . . . for the protection of those who may be exposed to tyrannical acts, & to guard those who have power from abusing it."[96]

Tappan's insistence on his own right to reform tolled the death knell of the Broadway Tabernacle. As New York newspapers reported the bickering between Tappan, Parker, and the session, rank and file members lost confidence and transferred to other churches. Many African American members left when the trustees tightened strictures on segregated seating.[97] The Sunday school dwindled. Tappan did not even remain at the Tabernacle after his exoneration, leaving it for the New York Congregational church. Returning to an evening lecture in July, he seemed surprised that the audience had so decreased but thought it might be owing to the warm weather. "A moral apathy appears to have gathered over the churches," Tappan judged, refusing to acknowledge his own complicity in the church's downfall.[98] A little more than a year later the church was foreclosed upon, and Parker resigned his pulpit.[99]

Lewis Tappan's dedication to reform played as much of a role in the demise of the Free Church movement as it did in its spectacular growth. By the end of the 1830s, Free churches thrived in other East Coast cities but were largely defunct in New York. In June 1839, just as Tappan received word of his vindication, the *New York Evangelist* printed what amounted to the Free churches' obituary. All had resorted to renting their pews, with the exception of the Chatham Street Chapel.[100] The failure of Tappan's movement lay in what Seth Hunt unwittingly discovered and the mobs of 1834 rejected. Reform and evangelicalism had come to be seen as integrally connected, thanks in no small part to Finney's preaching and Tappan's organizational efforts. Within the Free churches, disinterested benevolence was not a voluntary condition. Evangelicals, especially in the aftermath of the 1834 riots, realized that their attendance made them complicit in the glare of a hostile world. In the end, Tappan achieved his intention of exposing evangelical New Yorkers to reform movements that shaped the city and the nation for the next generation. An unintended result, however, was the emergence of a new vision for Free churches dedicated not to defending the place of reform as a community-centered activity within the church, but to protecting the individual congregant's right of private judgment. Within the same walls where Lewis Tappan's vision unraveled arose a new conception of an urban free church through the efforts (and wallet) of Tappan's former employee, David Hale.

A "NEW ENGLAND CONGREGATIONAL CHURCH" IN NEW YORK

"This is the Broadway Tabernacle Church of Jesus Christ, not of Anti-Slavery; and it must always be dangerous for a church as such to depart from the single design of its formation," David Hale explained to his fellow congregants two weeks after Lewis Tappan's trial. "We have Whigs and Van Buren men, tariff and free trade men, abolitionists and colonizationists," he continued. "We differ about all these things and many more, yet there is one thing about which we all agree, and on this we unite." What was it upon which they agreed? An individual's right of private judgment. Questions of reform must be decided by—not for—congregants. This and a long list of ecclesiastical and civil liberties denied Tappan during his trial by the session and minister of the Tabernacle made Hale realize their rights as congregants were in jeopardy. "We cannot afford to have the active love and youthful vigor of the Tabernacle Church fall into such decrepitude, nor to have any part of so deadly a process pass upon us," he declared.[101] Hale blended elements from his own romanticized understanding of the New England Congregational Church model, his admiration for Finney's evangelical individualism, and his extensive business experience. Under his guiding hand, the Free Church movement of the 1830s was reborn as the Congregational Church movement of the 1840s.

Tappan and Hale must have struck evangelical New Yorkers as unlikely allies in the winter of 1839, although the latter's interest in the former's trial was based more on principle than personal affection. Both grew up and began their careers in New England before moving to New York.[102] Tappan served as Hale's boss at the *Journal of Commerce* for a short time, before selling the paper to him and his partner, Gerard Hallock, in 1828. Over the next decade, Hale displayed little sympathy for the antislavery movement in the pages of the *Journal*.[103] Attracted by Finney's preaching, he joined the Broadway Tabernacle on his own in 1836, his wife and daughter preferring the community of First Baptist church instead.[104] The Tabernacle first exposed him to the Free Church movement, and he liked what he saw. When First Free Presbyterian merged with the Tabernacle in February 1838, Tappan and Hale found themselves once again thrown together.

Hale appreciated the Free Church's efforts to promote the free moral agency and right of private judgment of individual congregants. Previously, as a member of the Brick Presbyterian church, he keenly felt the sting of the loss of that liberty. "Having on one occasion indulged in a freedom of remark about the state of the church, which gave offense to some present," his biographer recalled, "he was thereafter doomed to silence by the most pointed neglect."[105] Finney's move following the 1834 riots to de-emphasize the link between the church and specific reforms appealed to Hale, even if it angered Tappan. Antislavery had turned more people off than on to evangelicalism by mid-decade. Hale knew there existed only a fine line between protecting the rights of zealous congregants and shielding their fellow congregants from them. Tappan's trial made him believe that the core principles that attracted him to the Tabernacle, "liberty of thought and speech, and above all, liberty of Christian action," were imperiled.[106]

The problem at the Broadway Tabernacle, Hale realized, lay not in the injustice of an isolated incident but in a corrupt leadership structure. The same ruling body that denied Tappan the basic rights of the secular courtroom—to call witnesses to testify on his behalf, to have a stenographer record testimony, to be judged by a jury of impartial peers—could do the same to others. When deprived of the opportunity to discuss these issues at the church's annual meeting, Hale felt aggrieved and pushed into action. "The noise and confusion of our April meeting was not made to keep me down particularly, but to keep *you* down, or rather to keep us all in a state of subjection together," he printed in a broadside distributed to fellow congregants a few days later. "It will depend on the lifting of our hands, whether we are thus subjugated, for whatever the eldership may arrogate, they know the fact, that the whole control over them *is* in the members of the church, and cannot possibly be taken away."[107] He proceeded to compare the relationship between the congregation and the session to "that between Luther and the Pope; the Puritans and the Hierarchy; the revolutionary patriots of '76 and Lord North."[108] When William Green Jr. foreclosed on the church in 1840, Hale saw his chance to wipe the slate clean.

Hale bought the foreclosed building outright on July 2, 1840, and invited the congregation to unite with him in forming a Congregational church, "on the pattern of the primitive churches and the churches of New England" that very evening. Rumors had circulated of Catholic and Universalist interest in the meetinghouse, which Hale capitalized on to present himself as a defender of evangelicalism in the heart of the city.[109] The congregation's response, however, was lukewarm. Of several hundred present, only thirty or forty expressed interest. Some must have been suspicious of what it meant for a wealthy layman to own a church. (Privately Gerard Hallock warned him that he might appear to be "speculating in churches.")[110] Others displayed justifiable wariness of Congregational churches, as the handful of earlier ones in the city had proven short-lived.[111] Structured denominations provided a sense of membership in a national, even international church, as well as more pragmatic functions such as sharing ministers, raising funds, and discussing matters of discipline. Back in 1830, Tappan appreciated this climate and jettisoned his plan for a Congregational Pilgrim Church in favor of his Presbyterian-sponsored Free Church movement. "Not ten respectable families in New York would attend a Congregational Church," one critic told Hale. Undeterred, Hale signed up fifteen by the end of the summer.[112]

Hale learned early in his business career to reconcile the demands of the market and the meetinghouse. "Bargains filled my heart," he wrote after one Lord's Supper at the Park Street Church in Boston, "and left the dying Savior too little room." Resolution came by eliding the two. "With him religion was not occasional, but habitual," his biographer remembered. "As he himself expressed it, it was a 'heart-business' and a 'life-business.'"[113] Hale sought employment both remunerative and devotional, and along the way developed a knack for improving on the innovations of others. The *Journal of Commerce*, which pleased the orthodox with its refusal to print on Sunday but failed to impress the business community, provided his first challenge. Early, credible information proved key in the speculative market of the 1830s, so he established a semaphore signal service to secure the latest news from incoming ships and instituted a regularly scheduled relay of horses from Washington, DC.[114] His guarantee of first access offset the inconvenience occasioned by no Sabbath publication. The Tabernacle proved another challenge.

Hale began by rethinking the Tabernacle's polity, which he deemed its most offensive element. A "New England Congregational Church" needed a proper set of organizational principles. Inspiration came from that most "New England" of "New England Congregational Churches," the Park Street Church of Boston. Founded in 1809 in reaction to surging interest in Unitarianism, Park Street quickly emerged as a center of evangelical activity and a symbol of defensive orthodoxy. The Tabernacle also saw itself on the defensive, not against Unitarianism, which made few inroads in New York, but against corrupt denominations. Hale "substantially" copied Park Street's articles of faith, form of admission, and covenant and then convened an ecclesiastical council to publicly and legally install the new church under these articles. The hand-selected guest list of leading pastors from New York, Philadelphia, New Haven, Hartford, and Providence put a Congregational seal of approval on the endeavor.[115] Only William Patton of the Spring Street Church represented the city's formidable Presbyterian establishment at the ceremony.

The Tabernacle's new organizational structure vested decision making in the congregation, although in practice Hale retained the de facto power to decide important issues. The offices of deacons and trustees continued to administer temporal and financial concerns, but Hale reconfigured the office of elders under the more innocuous and vaguely corporate-sounding title of "committeemen." This position existed, Hale stressed, "to fix responsibility, and not to have the power of final decision, because that rested solely with the Church in its business meetings."[116] Committeemen quickly learned the value of responding favorably to the will of the church's "proprietor," as Hale was called.[117] When the congregation elected Hale's first choice for minister, the young E. W. Andrews of Hartford, he saw it as a vindication of his New England project.[118]

The interior of the Tabernacle was also reimagined through a New England lens. The board of trustees, on which Hale sat as chairman, retained a system of pew rentals and drew up a map of the sanctuary. Schematized on paper, Finney's radical innovation in sacred space suddenly looked like that most traditional of plans, the New England long-form meetinghouse. New Englanders had long abandoned placing the pulpit on the long wall of the church in favor of the longitudinal plan, yet here it was in the heart of New York.[119] Those nostalgic for the old New England Way could once again choose, for a price, where to situate themselves within the larger community. (They also chose to limit the place of others, such as African American worshippers, who were relegated to the southeast corner of sanctuary.)[120] It soon became clear that those willing to purchase pews numbered far fewer than the seating available. No problem, thought Hale and the trustees. They desired to retain the Free Church movement's commitment to providing seats for those not served by other city churches.[121] Their hybrid plan of rented pews and free seats, they thought, might foster a traditional sense of community while serving the needs of a growing metropolis.

Unlike a true New England Congregational church, the Tabernacle's congregation did not own its meetinghouse. Instead it leased carefully spelled-out parts of it from its generous proprietor for less than what covered the mortgage payments.[122] Hale the businessman could not deny the financial potential of such a large meeting space in the heart of a rapidly growing city. What he envisioned as a New England meetinghouse he also saw as a premier public speaking venue. Its exterior form and style resonated more with leading civic structures like the Third Exchange (1836–1842) than with contemporary evangelical churches. Tappan's willingness to rent the ground floors of the First and Fourth Free Presbyterian churches to retailers and to allow benevolent and reform societies use of the Chatham Street Chapel for meetings provided a precedent for financing churches through mixed use. Would Tappan have ever let the sanctuary to the Odd Fellows, the Millerites,

A CASE OF HATS.

DEAR MR. GREELEY, will you have the kindness to get your Items man "who runs with 45," to pass "that" hat over to the Reverend DAVID HALE? The following paragraph from Monday's *Journal of Commerce* shall be your receipt for the same:

"He [the Reverend DAVID HALE aforesaid] has never put a cent of the earnings of the Tabernacle into his own pocket, beyond the simple interest of the money paid out, nor taken the least compensation for his services."

P. S. For the truth of the above, the Reverend gentleman begs to refer to Signor SIVORI, Prince LEOPOLD DE MEYER, Baron HERZ, and the New York Sacred Music Society.

FIGURE 5.5 David Hale came under criticism from the New York press for renting out the Broadway Tabernacle during the week, as seen in this notice in *Yankee Doodle,* November 7, 1846. Courtesy, American Antiquarian Society

or an "Exhibition of Laughing Gas"? Probably not, but Hale saw no problem with secular audiences helping to fund his spiritual vision.[123]

Critics jumped at the chance to accuse "Reverend Hale" of lining his pockets and desecrating sacred space "to purposes but little removed from the theater" (fig. 5.5).[124] Hale defended his actions by explaining that he had "been accustomed in my native land of New England, to see dedicated meeting houses used for town meetings, political discussions, and a great many other purposes, whenever a large house was required by the people." Besides, "it is only among Catholics and Episcopalians that the worship of God is thought to be so much a matter of *place*, that a building used for worship, can be for nothing else."[125] All proceeds, he assured his detractors, went toward repairs and a sinking fund to pay down the mortgage and interest.

Evangelicals also expressed reservations about this blending of sacred and secular uses. Some pewholders openly complained about being displaced by strangers unaware of, unaccustomed to, or unconcerned about seating policies in this hybrid space. Andrews also strongly expressed his "discomfort . . . from not seeing his parishioners regularly in their wonted places, their seats preoccupied by strangers." The trustees worked with Hale to mitigate these concerns, but problems persisted.[126] At the annual meeting of the church in 1841, Hale attempted to divert blame, prodding the trustees to "take effectual measures for protecting pews proprietors in the use of their pews on the Sabbath, at least during the daytime." The ensuing discussion laid bare the reality of the Tabernacle. It was big, crowded, anonymous—everything that a New England Congregational church was not.[127]

On the question of the place of reform within the church, Hale intended to avoid a situation like the one that had brought down the previous one. The very first article of the new constitution defined the church in such a way as to exclude reform from its central mission: "The design of a Christian Church we understand to be the enjoyment of Christian ordinances, and the maintenance of the worship of God."[128] On the question of whether the church could collect for specific charities, Hale articulated his opposition:

> Whereas a Congregational Church professes no power to compel a member to engage in any particular department of Christian labour; And whereas there are now societies to which Christians may unite themselves for the furtherance of all works of Christian benevolence if they believe that their usefulness will be thereby promoted; And whereas we have in this church members who are connected with almost all the great religious charitable societies, who may see to the interest of those societies; and whereas there is great diversity of opinion among us in reference to the various charitable movements of the day, but great harmony in regard to the peculiar and special designs of the Church, which harmony might be interrupted as it has been in other churches, by any effort to cooperate in our organized capacity with other societies . . . it is inexpedient that public contributions should be taken up on the Sabbath for any other purpose than the support of public worship and Christian ordinances in this Church and congregation.[129]

A decade earlier, First Free Presbyterian saw its role as encouraging congregants to embrace reform and providing opportunities for their involvement. A destructive set of riots and several foreclosures later, the Tabernacle encouraged its members to look outside the church for those opportunities.[130]

Membership records reveal that rather than capturing new converts, the church at first attracted those who had already been saved. The ratio of people joining by certificate to those by profession, two to one, was the exact inverse of First Free Presbyterian. A journal kept by the committee with notes on the 160 men and women who put themselves forward for membership from March 1843 through September 1845 reveals that women outnumbered men, but by a narrower margin (60/40) than at most evangelical churches (see the appendix, table A.6).[131] Familial ties played an important role, nearly half identifying another family member as their reason for joining. One in three men joined with a spouse. When Mrs. Isabella Menair joined in April 1843, so did her three sisters, her husband, and her sister-in-law.[132] Many were former members of the now defunct Free churches, like Miss Angeline White, who first joined First Free Presbyterian and came to the Broadway Tabernacle at its merger, or William Manwaring, a printer, who united under Joel Parker but soon after "wandered away."[133] The Tabernacle appealed as much, if not more, to Tappan's Free Church community as it did to Hale's New Englanders.

Beyond the walls of the Tabernacle, Hale extended his vision by encouraging and providing seed money for the founding of new Congregational churches throughout the city.[134] With names like the Church of the Pilgrims (1844) and the Church of the Puritans (1846), the nostalgic appeal of Hale's "New England Congregational Church" lingered, yet each employed an organizational model better suited for a large urban church. "In the midst of our rejoicing at the success of what has been denominated an experiment," a clerk recorded in a guardedly optimistic note, "let us ever remember, that we are a spectacle for all to gaze at & according[ly] as we demean ourselves, so will the peculiar principles by which we are governed, be honored or disgraced."[135] In the end, however, new Congregational churches were only a blip in a vast field of new evangelical churches that arose in the city in the 1840s (see map 5.3).

The departure of the Tabernacle's first minister, E. W. Andrews, revealed the latent anticlericalism that critics justly identified at the heart of Hale's model. "A Congregational Church formed at the Broadway Tabernacle would become a home for dissatisfied, restless, ungovernable spirits from other churches," one newspaper editor predicted, "and would soon develop into a hornet's nest, involved in civil war, and sting itself to death."[136] Congregational autonomy came at the expense of ministerial authority. Andrews simply grew tired of competing with Hale. Few traces of Andrews's opinions appear in the official minutes of the church, while Hale's run throughout. Hale wanted a revivalist; Andrews wanted a pulpit around which he could gather a devoted following. Neither got his wish.[137] After three and a half years, Andrews tendered his resignation. Several members pushed for an open discussion of Andrews's reasons for leaving to lay bare some of these internal tensions. Hale saw the divisive potential and quashed the conversation.[138] In seeking to protect the autonomy of the individual, Hale sometimes failed to realize the

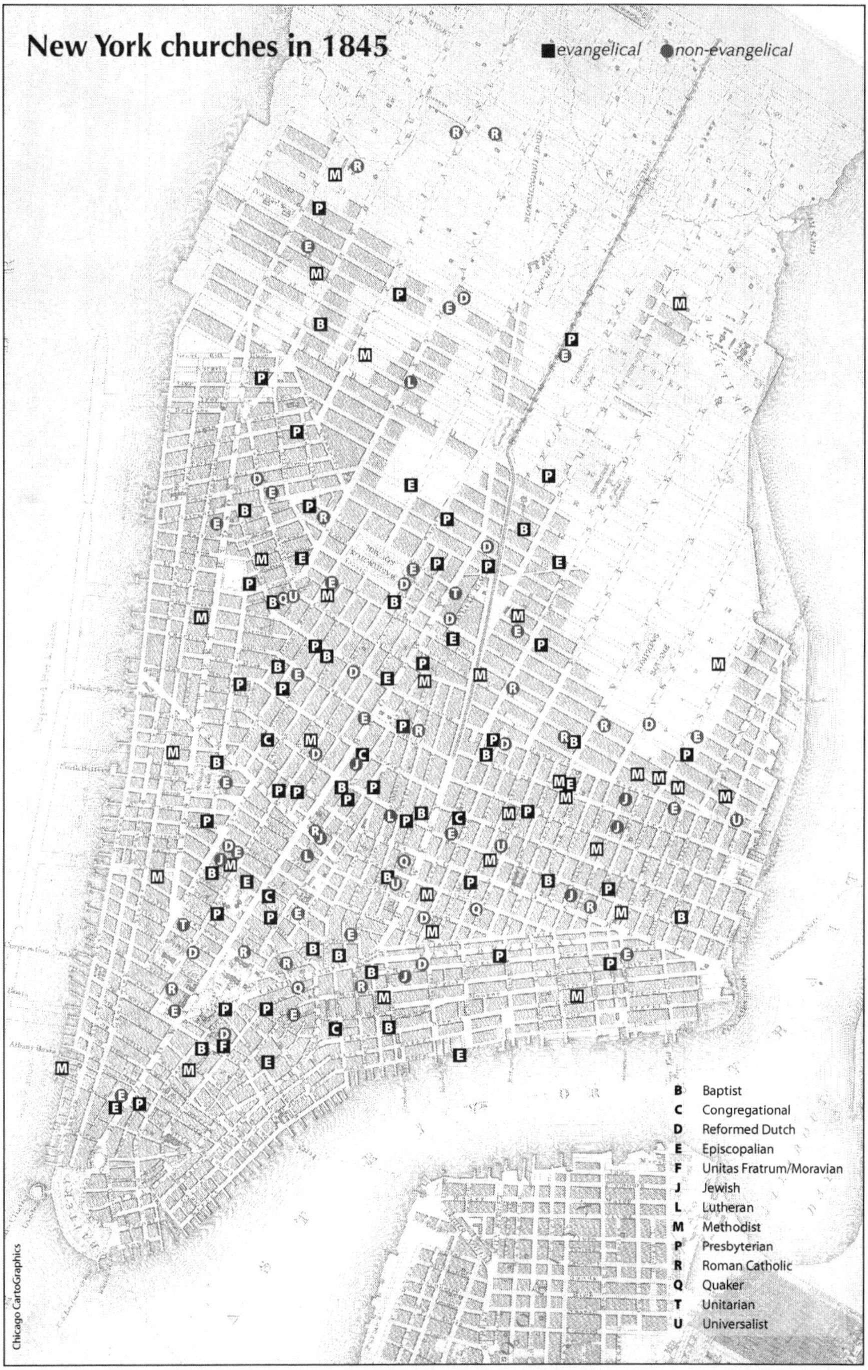

MAP 5.3 New York's religious landscape in 1845, by Dennis McClendon

extent to which acting on his own individual impulses imposed on the desires of others.

The Tabernacle's second minister, Joseph Thompson, made an adjustment of Hale's power a condition of accepting the position. In New York, the loss of a minister traditionally spelled the end of a Congregational church. Yet the Tabernacle had already proven itself unlike its predecessors. An influential evangelical layman with deep pockets and a vision, not a charismatic preacher, had been the church's pied piper. Thompson, the church's unanimous choice for its second minister, had all the hallmarks of a great pastor. He was young, a Yale graduate sympathetic to Finney and Taylor, and an urbanite who knew the opportunities and pitfalls of a city pulpit.[139] As it turned out, he also knew about Hale. His initial decline of the church's call is a masterful example of passive aggression. Not "having any *personal* objections to the uses of the building weighed with me against accepting the call," he wrote to Hale, in reference to one of Andrews's chief complaints. "I approve & commend the course of the proprietor in relation to it." Yet, he continued, he had to acknowledge "that a prejudice against the Tabernacle *exists* in the community" and "in the nature of the case, must prevent the growth of the congregation in the most desirable form."[140] Hale felt the sting of Thompson's critique but tried to set him at ease. "If you come to be my pastor you may defeat my plans and get me voted down as often as you please, by fair discussion, and you shall never lose my affectionate regard on that account," he pleaded.[141]

To secure Thompson, and in so doing the future of the Broadway Tabernacle, Hale knew he had to cease being the "proprietor" and become like every other member of the church. Within two weeks of Thompson's decline of the call, Hale granted what some church members had desired for five years: he allowed the church to purchase its meetinghouse. In half an hour, the congregation raised nearly $12,000 by selling pews. Hale agreed to accept this as a down payment and let them draw a mortgage on him for the remainder of the amount. At its 1845 annual meeting, an excited congregation voted thanks "to the proprietor for the magnanimous liberality which has been exercised by him toward the church, to this auspicious consummation." Whether cynically or sincerely, one member even put forward Hale's name at a special meeting two weeks later in a vote for a new pastor; sixty-three others chose to reissue a call to Joseph Thompson. The young minister accepted, and once again the leading Congregational ministers of New England, New York, and New Jersey descended to confer their approval.[142]

The pastorate of Joseph Thompson marked a new chapter in the history of the Broadway Tabernacle. Control of the church's future direction shifted back into the hands of the clergy, while retaining its founding objective to protect the rights of the individual congregant. Thompson worked quickly to solidify his power by initiating a revision of the church's articles of faith, form of admission, and covenant. He wisely placed Hale on the committee, although divested of controlling power. The original Park Street–inspired documents gave the church a measure of legitimacy when it most needed it, but their "stern orthodoxy" and failure to recognize "that there is ample provision for the salvation of all men, on condition of their repentance and faith" would no longer do. Thompson and the committee scrapped them and began anew.[143] The time was right for transition. Hale exceeded many in his zealous championing of individual evangelicals' free moral agency and right of private judgment through his design and implementation of a lay-centered organizational plan, his willingness to take financial risks, and his readiness to limit potentially divisive elements, such as reform, even if they were seen as integral to evangelicalism. Over time, "New England" proved more symbolic referent than reality, but the Congregational model breathed new life into the Free Church movement. Along the way Hale encountered the limits of his own evangelical agency but stopped short of destroying the church in the name of that right. Thompson could now restore the role of minister to where it traditionally belonged in a "New England Congregational Church."

CONCLUSION

Evangelicalism inspired New Yorkers like Lewis Tappan and David Hale to use their organizational talents to push the boundaries of lay agency in spreading the gospel in the 1830s and '40s. Charles G. Finney's theology of evangelical individualism, with its emphasis on the free moral agency of the individual, and his call for disinterested benevolence influenced them both, even if they disagreed about how to create a church that furthered these ideals. (It also set the stage for showdowns with ministers whose authority they minimized, if not completely discounted.) Their experience as successful New York City businessmen proved an inspiration, not an impediment, to their efforts. Both found a calling in creating spaces especially suited for urban evangelicals of all ranks to gather freely to hear the gospel.

Along the way, Tappan and Hale confronted the limits of evangelicalism. Both learned that the exertion of one's spiritual prerogative, regardless of the sincerity of one's disinterestedness, at times collided with that of the urban community. Within the walls of the meetinghouse, this confrontation manifested itself as internal tensions and the occasional church trial; outside, the reaction could be far more violent, as they discovered in the riotous summer of 1834. Tappan's refusal to curtail his own individual commitment to reform at the insistence of the minister and a majority of the congregation unraveled a once successful movement. Having lost his church's first minister, Hale was given the chance in settling the second to realize the extent to which he had unwittingly stymied his own project. In the end, Lewis Tappan found himself persona non grata in most of the city's evangelical churches and poured more energy into abolitionism than evangelicalism later in life.[144] Hale, on the other hand, spent the remainder of his days as a much loved and symbolic, if no longer actual, patriarch of a successful urban church in the commercial heart of New York City.

The experiences of Lewis Tappan and David Hale are part and parcel of the efforts of a much greater number of antebellum women and men inspired by evangelicalism and reform. They embraced the age's ethos of individualism and democratic progress, while often vehemently disagreeing with the policies of Andrew Jackson, the period's symbol.[145] Over the course of the 1830s, thousands of evangelical New Yorkers pushed the limits of their lay agency within their households and their neighborhoods, even if not on the same scale as Tappan and Hale. Clerks became abolitionists, mothers canvassed disagreeable neighborhoods distributing tracts, Sunday school converts exhorted their parents to holy living, and the disenfranchised dared to challenge their second-class status. Along the way many ran up against the limits of what their churches and the larger world would accept.

PART III

1840–1860

CHAPTER SIX

Perfection and the Antebellum Urban Evangelical Woman

At a large social gathering at midcentury, a respectable evangelical lady rose and did what many antebellum New Yorkers considered to be unrespectable: she addressed a mixed crowd of clergy and laity. Many in the room knew her to be "of strong and influential piety" and "of more than ordinary mental and cultivated ability." She knew them to be an audience to whom she could safely "open her lips in testimony for Jesus." Having recently achieved sanctification and obtained the gift of holy speech, which "promised tongue of fire," she felt herself under the same obligations to use it as the women who received it on the Day of Pentecost. Despite the supportive environment, the weight of the conflict between "the will of the church and the will of Christ" had lain too long on her shoulders. She broke down in tears. The gathered were sympathetic but not surprised. "We knew that not only the church to which this lady belonged," lamented Phoebe Worrall Palmer, "but many other churches, in like manner would withstand the utterance of a Spirit-baptized Mary in the church assembly."[1] Palmer knew this woman's experience all too well.

In the middle of the nineteenth century, Phoebe Worrall Palmer (fig. 6.1) ranked alongside Henry Ward Beecher as one of Evangelical Gotham's most influential theologians, writers, and revivalists. But Palmer was everything Beecher was not. She was studiously plain in all aspects of appearance and life; he was famously flamboyant. She was quiet and reserved; he was boisterous. She proffered a rational and biblical theology of perfection; he appealed to the emotions with a gospel of love. She advocated reform as an instrument for the betterment of the self; he preferred it to transform society. She

FIGURE 6.1 Phoebe Worrall Palmer, from Richard Wheatley, ed., *The Life and Letters of Mrs. Phoebe Palmer* (New York, 1881)

crafted a ministry in response to the conventions, currents, and institutions of antebellum urban evangelicalism; he (and his famous Congregationalist family) helped bring those mores into being.[2] Today Beecher is celebrated while Palmer has been largely forgotten. Yet her theology of perfection, intimately shaped by her experience of antebellum New York, shifted urban evangelicals' focus from their communities back to their individual spiritual selves. Her ideas changed the tide of evangelicalism in the tumultuous years between the recovery from the Panic of 1837 and the onset of the Civil War.[3]

GROWING UP EVANGELICAL IN GOTHAM

Dorothea and Henry Worrall welcomed Phoebe, their fourth child, into the world on December 18, 1807. Like so many of the founding generation, Henry was born elsewhere and made his way to New York in adulthood. Phoebe never knew the dislocations of migration nor the challenges of building a community out of wartime destruction. She grew up amid a vibrant and expanding urban evangelical community structured around home, church, and city. Her father's generation understood that all three had to work together to bring a rising generation to early conversion, to sustain the converted, and to remake the world in their image. They modified old rituals, practices, and institutions and developed new ones to impart crucial cultural competencies necessary to sustain and, in time, expand, the evangelical community locally, nationally, and internationally. The stress they placed on youthful conversion was not without its complications. It ultimately caused more anxiety than comfort. Phoebe spent much of her early adulthood mired in spiritual crisis.

The home served as the first place where a young child learned about evangelical belief and practice. Through family worship—structured around Bible reading, religious instruction, hymn singing, and prayer—parents sought to train their children in the ways of their faith. Henry Worrall took seriously his duty to oversee an observant household. He provided each of his children with a hymnbook and tolerated no absences at the family worship that opened and closed each day. Success hinged on repetition and strict observance. "Even the infant seemed to know that quietness was the order of the hour," Palmer's biographer noted. "Thus were the members of that family taught to reverence all the institutions of piety, to honor and obey their parents, to revere the Sabbath, to love the means of grace, and to seek first the kingdom of God, and His righteousness."[4] Many elements of Phoebe's childhood family worship—its structure, domestic setting, and the central role of the Bible—later reappeared in her ministry.

Changes within urban domestic space facilitated and reinforced the rituals and practices of evangelical family worship. Beginning in the 1810s, townhouses went up in new neighborhoods across the city at a distance from workshops and countinghouses. No longer were work and domestic functions combined in the lives of middling and upper-class families, as they had been a generation before. (An unintended consequence of this move was the unleashing of unattached workers into homosocial boardinghouse communities, where they often engaged in activities that evangelicals frowned on.) Women exerted their influence through homemaking and childrearing in these new gender-segregated domestic settings. The parlor gained new importance to the life of the family. The Worralls possessed the necessary means to participate in this cultural trend: they moved the family residence to Duane Street, several blocks from Henry's iron foundry on Elm Street.[5] Their new residence provided not only a respite from the heat and smell of industrial operations but also proximity to the Duane Street Methodist Episcopal Church, where the family regularly worshipped.[6]

Churches served as a second place where children learned about evangelicalism. Most evangelical houses of worship held morning, afternoon, and evening Sabbath services. Audiences included those who had been born again, like Henry and Dorothea; those who still sought the experience, like the Worrall children; and those who simply came out of curiosity—to hear the preacher, to see the pretty young women, or to be seen. (Occasionally some came to be openly hostile.) The rituals and practices of sanctuary worship were built around the leadership of male ministers, although the women who made up a majority of those sitting in the pews exerted an equally important influence. Methodists often varied their preachers to maximize effect. On a Sunday in May 1825, for example, seventeen-year-old Phoebe noted hearing sermons by three different ministers on the importance of conversion, the necessity of doing the best you can for others, and the danger of worldly temptation—salient messages for a young resident of Gotham.[7]

Sunday schools emerged as an integral aspect of the organizational and educational apparatus within antebellum evangelical churches. New York's earliest Sunday schools derived from British antecedents pioneered at the end of the eighteenth century in industrializing urban centers, where growing numbers of working children were feared to be falling through the cracks. Individual New Yorkers initiated informal Sunday schools to combine religious teaching with basic literacy education beginning in the 1790s.[8] By the time Phoebe came of age in the second decade of the nineteenth century, they had lost their missionary edge and become a mainstay of most congregations.[9] Literacy was no longer an end unto itself but a means to bring children to conversion. Some denominations, such as the Methodists, created their own Sunday school structures, while others, such as the Presbyterians and Protestant Episcopalians, banded together to form nondenominational organizations like the New-York Sunday School Union.[10]

Evangelical churches offered formal and informal opportunities throughout the week for more specialized modes of community support and engagement. Methodists created class meetings to bring together same- and mixed-sex groups of ten to twenty-five adults for weekly prayer, testimony, and instruction under the guidance of an experienced, typically male, class leader. These meetings provided emotional support and instilled strict self-control that helped participants avoid evil, do good, and observe the sacraments of the church. (It also offered a useful means of surveillance in a large city where a lone minister could not singlehandedly shepherd hundreds of scattered congregants.)[11] Congregations also frequently hosted prayer meetings, lectures, trustee and deacon's meetings, and other events.

Urban revivals, camp meetings, and love feasts (gatherings where church members shared their religious experience) occurred sporadically throughout the year and offered moments of emotional release, escape, and connection. They could be annual fixtures on the calendar, like the August camp meeting at Sing Sing and the New Year's love feast, or spontaneous events, such as urban revivals, which occurred when a minister touched a chord within the community or brought in a semiprofessional or professional revivalist. All incorporated hymn singing, allowing for a more stirring and expressive performance of evangelical religion; preaching, aimed at persuading auditors of the essential elements of doctrine; and prayer and exhortation, encouraging participants to communicate directly with Christ and the Holy Spirit. The last was often accompanied by such ecstatic elements as fainting, trances, involuntary cries and shouts, and even speaking in tongues. These occurred to the delight of those seeking conversion and to the (occasional) consternation of ministers and respectable church members who feared enthusiasm. Testimonies capped the experience and demonstrated the efficacy of what had just transpired. Yet the energy needed to sustain a revival or camp meeting diminished its longevity. New Yorkers could only disrupt their lives for so long before returning to their jobs and families.[12]

While evangelical ministers frequently preached against the danger of worldliness, it would be a mistake to discount the formative role the city played in the lives of young evangelicals. New York was a city of wonder and vice. Each walk along the wharves, pass through the marketplace, and errand around the corner held the potential of an encounter with someone new, someone whose beliefs, practices, and worldview might call one's own religious identity into question, whether intentionally or not. Living in a city meant constantly defending the parameters of inclusion, of determining who did and did not belong. Urban residents confronted daily challenges unlike they faced in the homogenous communities from which many hailed. The city expanded the materials available for fashioning individual identities, but it also introduced doubt and temptation.

As much as the city acted upon evangelical belief and practice, urban evangelicals acted upon the city. Phoebe grew up in the great age of social activism. Reform was the buzzword on every urban evangelical's lips, even if little agreement existed on which reforms were the most important. Children and adolescents participated in a range of benevolent activities: they taught in Sunday schools, distributed Bibles and tracts, petitioned against slavery and other societal evils, and signed (and got others to sign) temperance pledges.[13] Participation in community-focused activism allowed young evangelicals to feel as if they were defending the world their parents had built while contributing to its betterment.[14]

Antebellum evangelical New Yorkers promoted conversion as both an essential resource and important cultural capital for their children and used their homes, churches, and the city to achieve it. Those who came to New York following the American Revolution, such as Henry Worrall, often experienced conversion in adulthood.[15] Yet they purposely encouraged conversion in their children at younger and younger ages. They did this for multiple reasons. First, they sought to provide their children with opportunities they themselves had not enjoyed. Second, conversion offered a line of defense against the temptation (and manifold opportunities) to sin in the city's taverns, brothels, gambling dens, and dance halls. Third, and most important, conversion was not only crucial for the salvation of the individual but also key social capital. Achieving conversion could influence one's social relations, marriage prospects, and business opportunities. Parents understood conversion as a form of endowment that benefited their children in this world and the next. Children appreciated that these competencies allowed them to do things impossible in other times and places.[16]

Children of evangelicals frequently responded in kind to their parents' designs. Phoebe's sister Sarah experienced conversion at the age of thirteen while attending a camp meeting. Convinced she had sinned against God by failing to honor her mother, she grew distraught and threw herself on the altar within the revival tent, begging God's forgiveness. Before long she felt the soothing words of Christ fill her heart and overwhelm her. "Totally unconscious of earthly surroundings, for some time I was permitted to luxuriate with the angelic choir," she recalled at the end of her life. Carried in her mother's arms out of the revival tent, Sarah had reconciled herself to her earthly and heavenly parents through conversion.[17]

Not everyone agreed with this new focus. Evangelicals had long been suspicious of childhood piety. They feared the young had neither the maturity nor the experience to discern a true work of the Lord in their soul. Criticism often played out along generational lines. Phoebe explored these issues in *Mary; or, The Young Christian*, a memoir she edited based on the life of a childhood friend. In the story, the mother encourages the ten-year-old protagonist to consider her soul as they enter the sanctuary for a Sabbath evening revival meeting. "Mary, there are so many getting religion now, I think it is high time for you to begin in earnest to seek it," she prods. Her words had their intended effect. Mary at first failed to obtain "the desire of her heart" but succeeded three days later at another evening meeting.[18] Mary's grandmother did not share her enthusiasm. "I am sure there can be nothing real or lasting in it," she complained. "I suppose her childish feelings have been wrought up to a high state of excitement at those noisy meetings, and she was persuaded that she had religion; but who could think that a child of her age could know what true religion is?"[19]

Phoebe Worrall's conversion experience validated the grandmother's doubts. Like her sister, Phoebe "gave herself to the Saviour in childhood." But this is all she ever really recorded about her experience. "So early in life was the love of God shed abroad in her heart, that occasionally it was a subject of perplexity with her, that she could not so distinctly trace the hour of her conversion, as many others," explained her biographer.[20] An anxious uncertainty about conversion became the formative factor in shaping Palmer's adult life. Everything that came after—her search for sanctification; theology of perfection; ministry; and use of print, prayer meetings, and revivalism—can be traced back to this fundamental concern.

Courtship and marriage provided a momentary distraction. Nineteen-year-old Phoebe met twenty-three-year-old Walter Clarke Palmer, a recent graduate of the Rutgers Medical College of Physicians, in summer 1826.[21] He also grew up in New York's evangelical community and experienced conversion at a young age but shared none of Phoebe's doubts about the authenticity of his experience. The two married in September 1827, and Phoebe traded the household (and oversight) of her father for that of her new husband. They moved multiple times before settling for over three decades at 54 Rivington Street.[22] The Worralls lived on the other side of town but were never far away.

But Palmer's shadow of doubt about her salvation continued to grow after her marriage. Every day she interacted with a husband and sister more confident in their spiritual experiences. A major revival at the Methodist meetinghouse on Allen Street in spring 1832 seemed to offer an opportunity to allay her anxiety. When the pastor invited those who "desired a deeper work of grace" to approach the altar, Phoebe was among the first to step forward (although in her account she deferred to Walter to lead). The revival "quickened" her, but it was Walter who turned out to be "greatly blessed." Phoebe did "not doubt but scores have been brought to the Lord through his agency" as a revival leader, although she did worry that his excessive labors might kill him. "I am getting on feebly in the divine life:—not so much lacking in good purposes, as in carrying out my ever earnest resolve," the defeated wife concluded. "I ought to be more openly active. I lack faith and courage."[23]

Palmer's experience of motherhood only amplified her sense of spiritual inadequacy. Three of her first four children died in infancy. "I will not attempt to describe the pressure of the last crushing trial," she wrote after the death of the second. "Surely I needed it, or it would not have been given." She told herself that a jealous God would brook no others before him. "I saw that I had concentrated my time and attentions far too exclusively, to the neglect of religious activities demanded." She resolved to make amends. The survival of her third child past infancy gave her confidence that she might be right with God, but all that vanished when her fourth child perished in a tragic accident.[24] Palmer fell into a deep depression. Pacing the floorboards of her room and crying out in anguish, she recorded that "a gentle whisper" suggested this reflected the actions of a loving, rather than a jealous, God. "He doth not willingly grieve or afflict the children of men," this voice comforted. "If not *willingly*, then he has some specific design, in this, the greatest of all the trials you have been called to endure."[25] What that specific design was, however, Phoebe had yet to discern.

The Way of Holiness

"Is there not a shorter way?" The provocative question confronted readers in the lead article of the last number of the *Christian Advocate and Journal* for 1842. Subscribers were more accustomed to doctrinal and polemical writings by ministers than to a narrative written by a housewife about the spiritual journey of a female protagonist toward sanctification. The article commenced a series that offered a novel roadmap to gaining the "second blessing," the state of growing in divine grace after conversion and living without sin. There is an urgency in the work that spoke to those raised in a culture of youthful conversion and anxious about the authenticity of their early impressions. The author's privileging of sanctification over conversion, the Bible over personal experience, reason over emotion, and the individual over community spoke as much to the realities of the antebellum urban condition as to contemporary developments within evangelicalism. Readers might not at first have known the author, who modestly signed the series "P," but in time they did. Evangelical embrace of *The Way of Holiness* made it one of the most popular devotional works of the nineteenth century and launched Phoebe Worrall Palmer's ministry.[26]

In the mid-1830s, evangelicals began to rediscover John Wesley's writings on sanctification. Wesley believed the process of cleansing man from sin began at the moment of conversion and continued, through grace, over the life of the believer. Conversion thus marked a stage, not the culmination, of the spiritual journey. He argued that a second work of grace—a "second blessing"—should occur at a later point and cleanse the converted of sin entirely and imbue her or him with perfect love. This second blessing initiated a stage in an "ongoing, dynamic process of grace that engenders a Christlike and socially responsible nature in the believer." He rejected Calvinist understandings of sin as a component of the passions or the emotions and believed that it was instead a derivative of man's will. His emphasis on man's perfectibility led followers to refer to the state of sanctification as holiness or perfectionism, even though Wesley never believed that anyone could become completely perfect.[27]

Perfectionism appealed to antebellum urban evangelicals. Focus on individual conversion among the postrevolutionary generation and on community-centered social activism by their children overshadowed eighteenth-century ideas about sanctification. Yet evangelicals unsatisfied with their conversion experience increasingly sought something more; they desired for God to free them from their inner disposition to sin and to fill them with divine love. Just how to do this became a matter of considerable, and occasionally contentious, dispute. Denominational papers, such as the Methodist *Christian Advocate and Journal*, and nondenominational journals, such as Timothy Merritt's *Guide to Christian Perfection*, provided forums for discussion. Palmer actively contributed to these publications, engaged in public debates with other advocates, and eventually edited her own holiness periodical.[28]

Palmer came to understand sanctification firsthand through the experience of her sister Sarah. A class leader at the Duane Street Church first introduced Sarah to the concept soon after her conversion. Over the next fifteen years, Sarah wrestled with how she would achieve the second blessing. Some urged her to accept the necessity of faith alone; others insisted the experience had to have an emotional component. Moments of hopefulness gave way to long periods of discouragement. "I will give up this intense anxiety about the witness of the Spirit as to holiness," she exclaimed in a moment of frustration. "My class-leader and other good people live without it. I must have allowed my mind to be unnecessarily absorbed on this subject."[29] Eventually the writings of eighteenth-century British Methodist Hester Ann Rogers helped her overcome the impasse. "I waited speechless and motionless, expecting an instantaneous baptism," she later recalled of the moment at half-past two in the afternoon of May 21, 1835, when she finally achieved sanctification, "but felt no emotion except a sacred stillness."[30]

Longstanding doubts about whether Palmer had actually experienced conversion threatened to derail her search even before it began. Evangelicals agreed that conversion was a necessary prerequisite to sanctification. "Whenever my soul had reached out most ardently for the witness of holiness, the adversary has suggested most persistently the question of my justification," she confided. "When I let the subject of entire sanctification alone, and do not reach out after higher attainments," she confessed, "then I seem to have rest in the assurance of my adoption." Palmer had seen firsthand Sarah's struggle with her heart and her head and put her faith in the latter. Through an exploration of the scripture and a consecration of self, Palmer eventually convinced herself, once and for all, that she had been converted and was indeed "a Child of God."[31]

Out of this period came a cornerstone of Palmer's future ministry, her insistence on reliance on the Word of the Bible rather than the experience of man. Evangelicals had long looked to personal narratives of exemplary women and men as guides to the spiritual journey. But these narratives often took circuitous paths rife with detours and blind alleys. Palmer had experienced enough distractions and dead ends; she needed a surer guide. By adopting the Bible as her "rule of life," she covenanted with God to be a "Bible Christian." When "I have *believed God's* WORD, I have felt happy and assured," she reflected. "But I now see that the error of my religious life had been a desire for signs and wonders. . . . I have wanted some great thing, unwilling to rely unwaveringly on the still small voice of the Spirit." She swore to "most carefully seek to know the mind of the spirit, as recorded in the WRITTEN WORD, though it might lead to an experience unlike all the world beside."[32]

Palmer's emphasis on the Bible as the ultimate source of knowledge mirrored the centrality it assumed within American evangelical culture by midcentury. Organizations like the American Bible Society and the American Tract Society played an important role in this development by making the Bible cheaply available to the masses. Evangelicals advocated reason as the preferred means to understand it. Rather than being antagonistic to evangelicalism, the ideas associated with the Enlightenment profoundly shaped the new popular religious movement. Instinctive deference to inherited confessions gave way to more self-evident propositions organized by scientific method. Embrace of Scottish Commonsense moral reasoning allowed evangelicals to ratify what their consciousnesses perceived to be true. Evangelical confidence in their ability to read and interpret the Bible for themselves shaped their response to everything from mundane local experiences to contentious national political issues like slavery.[33]

Yet as Palmer took control of the process of sanctification and drew nearer to God, she encountered an unexpected final hurdle. Before she could achieve sanctification, she had to "give up" the "one with which every fibre of [her] being seemed interwoven": her husband. The required sacrifice at first took Palmer aback. "With amazement, I asked, can it be that the Lord requires that this one beloved object, dearer to me than life itself, be bound to the altar? What shall I have to live for if I give up this object?"[34] By all accounts, Walter Palmer was an unlikely stumbling block. Antebellum evangelical tracts are full of sinning husbands—slaves to drink, gambling, and even violence—but Walter possessed none of these vices. "Why this last sacrifice was required, I then knew not," Palmer recalled, "nor was it for me to question."[35] The cost felt high, but the potential reward was great. Undeterred in her desire to die unto sin and already conditioned to loss, she severed her last tie to this world. (Palmer interpreted this as a spiritual, not a literal separation.) Henceforth Palmer commemorated the date of her sanctification—July 26, 1837—as "the day of days" for the remainder of her life.

This experience informed another cornerstone of her ministry, the idea of the altar sacrifice. Palmer fervently advocated that the believer, through faith, must present body and soul to God as a living sacrifice. She derived her understanding from a phrase in Matthew 23:19—"the altar sanctifieth the gift"—which she interpreted to mean that whatever is laid on the altar becomes the Lord's property. "Holiness is an entire salvation from sin; a redemption from *all* iniquity," she explained. "The soul through faith being laid upon that altar that sanctifieth the gift, experiences *continually* the all-cleansing efficacy of the blood of Jesus; and through this it knows the blessedness of being presented faultless before the throne."[36] An individual must also be prepared to sacrifice any impediments to that connection with God. Relinquishing her reliance on Walter rewarded Phoebe with peace of mind and confidence that her "consecration was absolute and universal, and in view of all coming time."[37]

Palmer's altar sacrifice amounted to nothing less than a declaration of spiritual independence within an antebellum urban culture that emphasized women's dependence. Prescriptions of middle-class domesticity relegated women to the household, bearing children, managing domestic servants, and fulfilling the needs of their husbands.[38] Contemporary religious ideologies justified and reinforced these prescriptions. As antebellum evangelicals succeeded in the urban economy—Henry Worrall owned a successful iron foundry, Walter Palmer was a physician, Sarah's husband Thomas Lankford was an architect—they became increasingly entrenched in a middle-class culture that reinforced gendered ideas about dependence. They lost sight of eighteenth-century evangelicalism's radical embrace of the equality of all souls before God. Palmer's insistence on the altar sacrifice signaled a shift back to the individual that had profound implications.

Like so many urban evangelicals, Palmer turned to the medium of print to share her experience. In the six years following her "day of days," she wrote about sanctification in a variety of genres. Between December 1839 and March 1840, the monthly *Guide to Christian Perfection* serialized an account of her experience in the form of a letter to a female friend.[39] A more systematic exposition followed in the October and November 1841 issues of the weekly *Christian Advocate and Journal*.[40] But it was her third published series, "The Way of Holiness," that sealed her reputation. "The Way" told the story of a female protagonist's search for sanctification. It was originally published in the *Christian Advocate and Journal* in December 1842 and January 1843 and soon after reprinted in the *Guide to Christian Perfection*.[41] New York commercial publishers Piercy and Reed packaged the installments as a stand-alone book later in 1843. *The Way of Holiness* sold more than 24,000 copies in the United States over the next eight years and was published in thirty-six editions before the Civil War. English, Canadian, French, and German reprints followed, numbering upward of 100,000 copies.[42] *The Way* became an instant classic of holiness literature.

Palmer used *The Way of Holiness* to reimagine Bunyan's beloved *Pilgrim's Progress*. The narrative opens with a conundrum and a sense of urgency. A couple journeying toward the heavenly city have already achieved conversion but face the daunting challenge of achieving sanctification. When the male companion inquires as to how they might get on the path to the city, the female protagonist affirms with more confidence than knowledge, "THERE IS A SHORTER WAY! O! I am sure this long waiting and struggling with the power of darkness is not necessary."[43] Palmer proceeds to invert Bunyan's narrative by making the woman the guide. Over the following pages, she proceeds to show the shorter way and rewrites the entire process of achieving sanctification.

The Way presents a model of the religious life rooted in Palmer's personal experience. The Bible, rather than the "opinions and experiences of professors," provides the true "rule of life" for her protagonist. *The Way* calls on readers to stop seeking holiness and to start living it.[44] To that end, it offers concrete steps by which sanctification can be achieved. Assurance ultimately comes from faith, not feeling. Undergirding this journey is a belief in the agency of man to achieve sanctification. The female protagonist's agency is exemplified by her decision "to sacrifice what was of all earthly objects surpassingly dear," by placing God before her spouse, as Palmer had done a few years earlier.[45] In so doing, she can present herself as a living sacrifice to the Lord.

Palmer concludes *The Way of Holiness* with a justification for the ministry of print, prayer, and revivalism that consumed her next thirty years. Assured of the blessedness of the "shorter way," her protagonist burns to communicate what she has learned. "Her now newly-inspired spirit could scarcely conceive of a higher ambition, in the present state of existence," Palmer explained, than "to say to every lover of Jesus, 'This is the will of God, even *your* sanctification.'"[46] In fact, she had no choice in the matter. "*If* it is a *gift from God,* God is not exclusive in the impartation . . . you will be required to declare it."[47] The implications of this mandate were significant in a society where exhorting and preaching by women flew in the face of long-established conventions. But her justification was clear. "The church is represented as Christ's body," her protagonist explained. "I am one of the members of that body. If I, by testifying of the Spirit's operation on my heart, am individually benefitted, the whole body is advantaged . . . while if I neglect to testify, and, in consequence, suffer loss, my relation to the body will of necessity cause it to participate in that loss."[48] Palmer followed her own advice: the health of her soul and the church depended on it.

PALMER'S MINISTRY

After achieving sanctification, Palmer privately counseled other women but felt destined for something more. Her calling was revealed one day in 1840. "The Spirit told of things to come," she remembered after opening her Bible and her eyes fell on Haggai 2:23. The passage lifted her from the mire of a spiritual struggle and convinced her that she, like its subject, Zerubbabel, had been chosen by God to be his servant. "Perceptions of the great blessedness of the work to which the Lord might call me in identification with the great fundamental truth of Christianity '*Holiness to the Lord*,' were granted" and confirmed her hopes. At the same time, she recalled, "A view was also given of the trials I should be called to endure, in connection with my open identification with Truth."[49]

For Palmer to act on her calling required challenging entrenched societal and religious norms. A fine line existed between what constituted informal, private sharing and formal, public speaking. Traditionalists long pointed to biblical injunctions against women's speaking in church, most famously articulated in Paul's letter to the Corinthians (I Cor. 14:34–35b). They contended women were biologically unsuited to the task; that they were emotional, illogical, and prone to hysteria; and that the stability of society and the welfare of the family depended on their resignation to the domestic sphere.[50] A "Cult of True Womanhood" within antebellum prescriptive literature reinforced the notion that womanly virtue resided in purity, piety, submissiveness, and domesticity.[51] To speak before a public forum—courthouse, lecture room, or church—was assumed to require masculine qualities of strength, competitiveness, and combativeness. The True Woman would naturally shy away from such public activity.

Yet antebellum New York was home to a number of ambitious women who felt called, whether by God or their own sense of self-worth, to enter the public sphere to communicate their experience to others.[52] Women like Margaret Fuller, Fanny Wright, and Dorothy Ripley employed multiple rationales to counter arguments used to silence them. If women and men were created with different natures and talents, then it stood to reason there would be times when their voices might be needed in the public sphere. Women's spiritual superiority and role as nurturing mothers or Mothers-in-Israel, some contended, made them better suited than men to speak on certain topics. Others derived their arguments from natural law. Proponents of universal personhood stressed that women and men were ultimately the same and shared a common humanity. The rights of men extended to women, they claimed.[53]

Palmer tended to be more sympathetic to arguments based on difference than on sameness but ultimately believed her authority owed less to the inherent characteristics of her sex and more to gifts proffered by the Holy Ghost. She believed individuals touched by the Holy Spirit—regardless of sex—were obligated to share their experience, privately and publicly. Their authority was derived from God, not nature, and limited to those who had

had a saving experience. Conversion and sanctification imparted an irresistible urge and power to serve as God's mouthpieces. The Day of Pentecost carried more authority for her than the writings of Montesquieu.[54]

Palmer's launching of a public ministry happened at a propitious time and place. Her experience of sanctification preceded the Panic of 1837 by only a few months. Publication of *The Way of Holiness* in 1843 coincided with the end of the recession that followed the panic and the beginning of fourteen years of optimistic and unprecedented expansion, locally and nationally. Her childhood in New York's urban evangelical community had given her the competencies necessary for utilizing the strategies for public activity—publishing, prayer meetings, and revivalism—common among antebellum evangelicals. Her centrally located townhouse on Rivington Street gave her access to the city's leading evangelical clergy, churches, and benevolent organizations.

Publishing allowed Palmer to disseminate her theology of perfection not only to Methodist audiences but also to evangelicals more broadly. She grew up in a burgeoning world of evangelical print and would, in time, avail herself of the city's nondenominational, denominational, and commercial publishers. The volume of her output before the Civil War alone—seven books and numerous essays, letters, and articles—marked her as a prolific author; her diverse use of genres distinguished her as an unusual one. Like many antebellum women, she began by writing occasional poetry.[55] Beginning in the 1840s, she experimented with editing the biographies of pious women, using them to engage with specific spiritual issues she was then grappling with. *Mary; or, The Young Christian* (1841), as we saw, helped her address the authenticity of childhood conversion. Biographies of Lydia Noyes Cox (1845) and Mary Gardner (1851) offered model evangelical women who experienced sanctification, lived holy lives, and sought to be useful to God and their fellow man in the larger world.[56]

Publication of *The Way of Holiness* in 1843 marked an important shift in Palmer's writing toward devotional and polemical theology, terrain more commonly left to men in this period. Three works over the next twelve years sought to clarify arguments in *The Way* in particular and about sanctification more broadly. A *Present to My Christian Friend on Entire Devotion to God* (1845) elaborated on the core of her theology and offered examples of those who had received sanctifying grace. *Faith and Its Effects* (1848) and *Incidental Illustrations of the Economy of Salvation, Its Doctrines and Duties* (1855) brought together excerpts from her correspondence with real people attempting to achieve sanctification or lead sanctified lives. Each evidences Palmer's embrace of her role as a spiritual counselor.

The changing credit line on Palmer's publications reveals her increasing confidence in her authority as a public religious figure. She—or her editors—signed her earliest articles with the initial "P," if any acknowledgment of her authorship appeared at all. Similarly, the first edition of *The Way of Holiness* did not have her name on the title page. An experience in her urban milieu, however, soon changed her mind. Passing one day the Bowery Theater, a few blocks from her home, she noticed a "flaming" placard announcing the names of the play's actors, male and female. "Here are the servants of Satan who are not afraid or ashamed to let their names appear," she reacted, according to her biographer. "Shall the servants of the Heavenly King be less bold?"[57] Thenceforth her publications identified "Mrs. Phoebe Palmer" as their author.

Palmer even founded her own publishing firm. When Foster & Palmer, Jr. began in 1855, Elon Foster had just received his doctorate from the General Theological Seminary and married Palmer's eldest daughter Sarah. Palmer's son Walter—the Palmer, Jr. of the firm's title—remained Foster's partner until 1868 when he became sole proprietor. During those thirteen years, Foster & Palmer, Jr. emerged as important publishers of *The Way of Holiness* and other works by holiness authors. In 1864 they purchased a magazine, the *Guide to Holiness,* and installed Phoebe as assistant editor. Under her tenure, the periodical peaked with 37,000 subscribers at the end of her life.[58] By putting the firm in the hands of her son-in-law and son, Palmer ostensibly conformed to contemporary business conventions; that Walter Jr. was only thirteen years old when the firm was founded reinforces the controlling stake she enjoyed in the venture.[59]

By midcentury, Palmer was known across the city, and around the nation, as the host of the Tuesday Meeting for the Promotion of Holiness. Her sister Sarah founded the Tuesday Meeting following her sanctification experience in 1835 by merging the female prayer meetings of the Allen Street and Mulberry Street Methodist Episcopal churches.[60] Beginning at half-past two every Tuesday afternoon, seekers and converts gathered in the parlor at 54 Rivington Street.[61] After an introductory reading of the scriptures, singing, and prayer, those in attendance testified to the personal experience of sanctification. "Testimony follows testimony in quick succession," Palmer recorded. "The testimony of the seeker of salvation, or of the timid, lisping babe in Zion, is listened to with as much interest as that of the most deeply experienced."[62] Over the course of the afternoon, attendees learned more about holiness and supported others going through the process.

The Tuesday Meeting challenged contemporary practice by relaxing prohibitions against women's speaking on religious topics in mixed gatherings.

Locating it in the private space of the parlor rather than in the public space of the church empowered its participants to speak on topics usually denied to them. In late 1839, the Tuesday Meeting evolved into a mixed-sex meeting after an out-of-town visitor asked to bring her husband. Sarah had been open to his attendance, but it was the instrumental role Phoebe played in bringing him to sanctification following a private dinner at their house that convinced them it was acceptable.[63] Henceforth, men participated alongside women. Phoebe and Sarah's insistence that the meeting function as a social rather than a formal gathering helped assuage concerns about this departure from evangelical practice. Palmer came to realize how the private space of the parlor allowed her to model changes that she wanted to implement in the public spaces of the church, camp meeting, and world.

For more than thirty-four years the Tuesday Meeting thrived under Palmer's leadership. It became an important Manhattan institution that encouraged active participation by laity and clergy, regardless of denomination.[64] Evangelicals from around the corner and across the country made their way to the Tuesday Meeting. Much like evangelicalism, holiness appealed across traditional lines of division because it was rooted in the Bible instead of doctrine. Any Bible Christian—"irrespective of name and party"—could understand its major principles, Palmer believed, if they applied themselves to the scriptures. At one meeting Palmer noted seeing "a Presbyterian minister at the head of the room, a Methodist minister next, a Baptist student of theology next, and a Moravian next; and this was not in any degree by special design." The Tuesday Meeting mirrored the diversity, and crowdedness, of the urban spiritual marketplace.[65] Over the 1840s and '50s, upward of 150 turned out each week. Visitors regularly spilled out of the parlors into the hallway and stairs, prompting the Palmers to add a sizable addition to their home in 1857 to accommodate the crowds.[66]

The Tuesday Meeting allowed urban evangelicals to reconcile contemporary social demands of respectability with the rigors of individual piety. As the city rebounded from recession, middle- and upper-class New Yorkers increasingly embraced comfort, gentility, taste, and manners in their surroundings and behavior. More exclusive Renaissance-style townhouses in new northern residential neighborhoods, with comfortable parlors and servants' quarters, replaced the more democratic Greek Revival homes in mixed-use neighborhoods of the previous generation. Some began to attach religious significance to these markers of status, while others worried they constituted distracting worldly temptations. Palmer crafted a middle way. She insisted on a spiritual, rather than a literal, separation from the things of the world in favor of love for God. But even as she rejected the trappings of "gay fashionable society," she accepted evangelicals' embrace of wealth, education, taste, and manners as long as they were consecrated to God.[67]

In gender relations, however, the Tuesday Meeting represented an important rethinking of what constituted sacred space and women's religious authority. In a telling 1838 diary entry, Palmer refers to the Tuesday Meeting as "this church in the house" and trusts that "through the blessing of God" it "has been one of the nurseries of the general church."[68] The notion of a woman-led meeting as a nursery for believers was a conservative one, but the possibility that the house could supplant the church had a radical edge. The role Palmer created for herself and other women within the Tuesday Meeting also contradicted expectations of the time. "You may wonder why I should regard it so needful, that a special person should be present to take charge of the meeting, when there are generally three or four ministers, and several leaders, etc., present," she wrote to a friend. "The reason is . . . that it is a *peculiar* meeting, and needs that peculiar management, which [is] very *childlike*—simple piety, exhibits, and it is not every day that you can meet with those who know just how to come *down* to the *simplicity* of the gospel."[69] Palmer's concern reflects as much a desire to bolster women's religious authority as a fear of male usurpation.

The Tuesday Meeting emerged as a locally and nationally recognized institution that provided evangelical women with access to new forms of religious authority. Followers established Tuesday Meetings in other cities to promote holiness, to support its adherents, and to extend religious authority to women.[70] Much about the actual structure of the Tuesday Meeting ostensibly sought to reinforce gendered societal conventions, but none could deny the power it invested in women. By encouraging women's participation, deemphasizing the distance between the clergy and the laity, and creating an evangelical, rather than denominational, environment, the Tuesday Meeting came to resemble camp meetings, another phenomenon of the period in which Palmer actively participated.[71]

Camp meetings emerged as a common feature of middle-class evangelical life, urban and rural, over the early nineteenth century. Multiday affairs, they combined the fervor of revivalism with the sociability that arises when a large number of like-minded individuals gather in isolated environs. They occurred primarily in the summer months at locations just outside the city when the heat (and outbreak of disease) made urban life unbearable. The Sing Sing camp meeting (fig. 6.2) was a pleasant two-hour boat trip up the Hudson accessible by steamers that departed from the foot of Harrison Street

FIGURE 6.2 Joseph Beekman Smith, Sing-Sing Camp-Meeting, 1838, lithograph, hand-colored, Museum of Fine Arts, Boston, Gift of Maxim Karolik for the M. and M. Karolik Collection of American Watercolors and Drawings, 1800–1875, 62.99. Photography © 2016 Museum of Fine Arts

twice daily.[72] Multiple camp meetings on Long Island catered to those looking for an experience closer to home. All manner of activity, sacred and secular, took place in these temporary communities. Most important for Palmer, camp meetings emerged as one of the first places that women took up public speaking.[73]

Invitations for Palmer to speak at camp meetings came as early as 1839, following her holiness series in the *Christian Advocate and Journal*. Her first engagements took her to Long Island and up the Hudson, but later she traveled further afield. On these trips she spoke freely one-on-one, in prayer meetings, and even in larger assemblies after male ministers and exhorters had finished. Her hosts saw her presence as integral to their work and sometimes fought over her presence. "I cannot describe to you the weight of responsibility I, at times, feel to be resting upon me, in view of these various calls, as they seem to be accumulating," Palmer explained to a friend. "By the manner in which I am sustained, I have no reason to think otherwise than that the invitations I receive, and the providential openings which seem to say, 'Go forward,' should be regarded as the voice of God."[74]

By midcentury, Palmer emerged as an effective and popular revivalist. The number of invitations received from ministers seeking to promote revivals in their churches began to rival those from camp meeting organizers. She regularly found herself on the road for months at a time. In 1851, for example, she helped the minister of Ithaca's Methodist Episcopal Church in January, labored with religious leaders in Philadelphia in February, rushed to Albany for a revival that had spontaneously erupted in April, all before kicking off the beginning of the camp meeting season from June to August. "Never, I think, on any camp ground, have I witnessed such a general work," Palmer wrote with gratitude about the last camp meeting of the 1851 season, in Spafford, New York, where 150 experienced conversion and a comparable number sanctification.[75] Palmer's extensive traveling became a topic of conversation among friends. "You look at my address, and perhaps you exclaim, 'Where will our sister next alight?'" she joked in fall 1855.[76] Before the decade was out, Palmer crossed the Atlantic for four years of evangelistic travels.

As Palmer came into her own as a speaker, she faced the challenge of distinguishing between her own and the Holy Spirit's desires. "The Spirit's process is not quite as rapid, (though always equally sure) under some circumstances, as others," she explained to her husband. "At some places where I go, I find a people prepared of the Lord, and I only seem required to gather the harvest. At others, the fallow ground is to be broken up, and then the seed is to be sown, and the fruit, of course, cannot be so quickly gathered."[77] Different destinations presented different challenges but also manifested different expectations for the role Palmer would play. On the rare occasion when she recoiled from taking a public role, she believed the Holy Spirit reproved her for withholding her talents.[78]

In the end, Palmer's ministry represents a paradox of antebellum evangelical womanhood. As she appeared to reinforce dominant structures, she simultaneously subverted them. She fervently believed that women had distinct roles to play within the family and society. But she also believed that authority bestowed from on high, as it had been on the Day of Pentecost, came regardless of gender and had to be honored, no matter how far from home it took her. She traced her privation from her family back to the seminal moment in her sanctification experience, the altar sacrifice of her husband, her one last idol. That decision brought her spiritual reward and a public career, but it also necessitated a certain alienation from her family.[79] She often headed out on the road with other female companions, leaving her husband behind in Manhattan to watch his practice and their children for long periods of time. In an ironic inversion, Phoebe owed her independence to Walter's economic dependence on his urban medical practice, which consumed eleven out of twelve months of his time a year.[80] To do all this, she drew on strategies familiar to young women growing up in an antebellum urban evangelical community—publishing, prayer groups, and camp meetings—to disseminate her ideas to local, national, and international audiences.

INTO THE FIVE POINTS

When in New York, Phoebe Palmer participated in the forms of benevolence and reform popular among urban evangelicals for more than a generation. Early in her marriage she wondered if her and Walter's true calling might be as foreign missionaries, like the courageous ministers and their devoted wives in popular biographies who burned to convert the heathen in Serampore and Tahiti, and often paid with their lives. Ultimately she opted for the less romantic, but more pressing, field of domestic missions. "I thought of the absorption I should feel, in the work of saving souls, if thus wholly given up," she confided in her journal, "and I resolved to make the work of the Lord as absorbing here, as though I were on missionary ground, and my career has ever since been influenced by these resolves."[81] She distributed tracts across the city to an all-too-familiar cast of sick widows, abandoned women, and intemperate men; visited New York's infamous Tombs Prison in the hope of convincing prisoners to embrace Jesus before it was too late; and helped found a mission in the city's most notorious neighborhood, Five Points. She even adopted an immigrant Jewish boy, until his family came back for him.

Historians have argued that important shifts in audience and strategy occurred in mid-nineteenth-century urban benevolence and reform. Where Isabella Graham, Ezra Stiles Ely, Ward Stafford, and Henry Chase focused their energies on fallen adults, Palmer's generation pursued poor children. This change arose from a broader reaction by Protestant reformers to the emergence, in the words of one historian, of "hordes of rootless tenement-bred children" across the city. Expanding opportunities for citizenship, rising rates of infant mortality, and the spread of slums made saving urban children increasingly desirable. Evidence of the shift can be seen in the opening of the Colored Orphan Asylum (1836), the formation of the Association for Improving the Condition of the Poor (1843), the creation of the Home for the Friendless and the House of Industry by the American Female Guardian Society (1848), and the founding of the Children's Aid Society (1853). As reformers embraced more melioristic, pragmatic strategies focused on "secular" salvation, they left behind older, conversion-focused strategies. The temporal won out over the spiritual, so the argument goes.[82]

What these theories of the "secularization" of reform miss, and Palmer's experience convincingly illustrates, is the simultaneous refocusing within evangelical culture on the spiritual lives of children. The rise of Sunday schools, the emphasis placed on domestic devotional life, and the increasing acceptance of youthful conversion all occurred prior to, and independently of, these new developments within benevolence and reform. Evangelicals refused to see an either-or situation; they attended to both spiritual and temporal needs. Targeting children had other benefits. "We plead for the children—for we commence with the Sabbath school . . . because through them we hope to reach the parents," wrote one reformer.[83] Annual reports and the well-known volume *The Old Brewery, and the New Mission House at Five Points* (1854) are filled with examples of evangelical efforts to gather young children into Sunday and day schools that yielded access to, and sometimes the conversion of, their parents.

Irish and German immigrants also emerged as an audience for reformers' efforts at midcentury, although more the result of demography than ideological choice. New York's population grew dramatically between 1840 and 1860. Many of the half-million new residents had fled famine in Ireland and political upheaval in the German states.[84] They often had a difficult time escaping poverty, hamstrung by the conditions under which they arrived, the Protestant nature of the city's power structures, boom and bust economic cycles, and the expense of urban real estate. Packed into tenements, they lived cheek by jowl with native-born Protestants, including a disproportionate number of the city's dwindling African American population.[85] Evangelical reformers went after all of them. Ancient Protestant animosities toward Roman Catholics and Jews undeniably informed evangelical efforts, but their faith was a contributing, not a primary, factor in this focus.[86] Evangelicals quickly realized the unlikelihood of large-scale conversion of either.

Phoebe Palmer engaged with these new audiences institutionally through her involvement with the Ladies' Home Missionary Society of the Methodist Episcopal Church (LHMS). The society was founded in April 1844 in response to a perceived lack of "efficient means . . . to improve the moral and spiritual condition of the poor and destitute in this city." The LHMS raised funds to support urban missionaries, appointed by the New York Annual Conference. These Methodist ministers spread the gospel in parts of the city destitute of preaching; visited the poor, sick, and needy; established Sunday schools and encouraged children to attend them; and promoted the temperance cause. Members generally limited their involvement to raising money, retreating from the intensity of lay-driven tract and Bible distribution and home visitations that characterized the 1830s.[87]

The first, and more successful, of the two distinct forms of urban missions the LHMS supported was the creation of congregations in neighborhoods distant from established Methodist Episcopal churches with growing populations of poor, typically native-born Protestants. This approach differed little from the efforts of the Presbyterians twenty years earlier. Missionaries rented spaces (often in former commercial structures), preached and established Sunday schools, and eventually gathered members into established churches. Ezra Withey's mission on the west side of the city became the Jane Street Methodist Episcopal Church; the Dry Dock Mission became the Ninth Street ME Church; the Fiftieth Street Mission became the Lexington Avenue ME Church; and the Hedding Mission became Seventeenth Street ME Church.[88] Palmer took a special interest in the last. When the New York Conference failed to appoint a missionary for it in 1852, she invited her own candidate to dinner at her house with two visiting bishops of the national church. An appointment was made soon after.[89]

The second, and less successful, approach was to send missionaries to work with specific immigrant populations in the hope of making conversions. John M. Hartmann, a German-speaking missionary hired soon after the founding of the LHMS, opened a mission station at Bloomingdale, a favorite site of the German population for Sabbath respites of drinking, gambling, and "all sorts of pleasure-taking." Hartmann greeted German leisure seekers with evangelical preaching and song. He also opened a Sunday school conducted in German and English. Of all the LHMS missionaries, Hartmann was the most blatant about his intention to convert Catholics; he was also among the less successful. The German Mission did not secure its own church until 1849, when it purchased an old frame meetinghouse on West 36th Street near Ninth Avenue. Not until 1864 did the congregation have the wherewithal to build a new church.[90] Even less successful LHMS-sponsored missions to Germans included the German bethel ship in 1849 and the Lower German Mission on Washington Street in 1850.[91]

In 1848, the LHMS turned its attention to the Five Points neighborhood. Old-time New Yorkers knew Five Points as the intersection of Little Water, Cross, Anthony, Orange, and Mulberry Streets, near the former site of the Collect Pond. African American and immigrant New Yorkers knew Five Points as home, an assemblage of rickety tenements that overshadowed storefronts and cellars that doubled as dance halls, bars, and brothels. White evangelical New Yorkers thought of Five Points as a place where angels feared to tread. After 1842, the rest of the world knew Five Points through Charles Dickens's vivid (and lurid) descriptions in his *American Notes*. For the LHMS, Five Points was nothing less than a "synonym for ignorance the most entire, for misery the most abject, for crime of the darkest dye, for degradation so deep that human nature cannot sink below it."[92] In other words, it was a perfect venue for an urban mission.[93]

Launching a mission in Five Points was easier said than done. At first the LHMS could not secure suitable rooms and believed a school run by the Union Mission, already in operation, adequately covered the ground.[94] Behind the scenes, members questioned the mission's likelihood of success. "I will give ten dollars toward the sustainment of another German mission, but not one dollar will I give toward the sustainment of one at Five Points, for it will be money thrown away," Palmer remembered a fellow board member saying. Others agreed.[95] Two years after the mission was first proposed, the Methodist Conference finally appointed Louis Pease. An advisory board "of gentlemen of the highest respectability and standing" worked with Pease to secure a twenty-by-forty-foot storefront at the corner of Little Water and Cross Streets that could accommodate as many as 200 in evening meetings, a Sunday school, and a day school. "We believe the time for action, the most wise, the most earnest, the most rigorously sustained, is fully come," Imogen Mercein, corresponding secretary of the LHMS, exclaimed in the national Methodist newspaper.[96] The Five Points Mission combined the hallmarks of their previous missions: it served a specific neighborhood but focused on making conversions rather than gathering a formal congregation.

Louis Pease had a different vision for the Five Points Mission than his sponsors, an issue that created significant tension over the coming years. The LHMS wanted him to attend to the spiritual needs of the neighborhood, but Pease identified intemperance and unemployment as pressing temporal impediments that needed to be addressed first. "Want of proper employment is the greatest occasion of vice and crime here," he reflected in early 1851, "and the greatest obstacle in the reformation of this people."[97] As a remedy, he rented a house adjacent to the mission room on Little Water Street, opened a workroom with paid employment, relocated his family, and offered the remainder of the rooms to needy men and women.[98] On top of this, he oversaw a day school with two hundred children, a Sunday school with even more, an evening school, a forty-person class meeting, and a Temperance Society with seven hundred pledged members. Pease quickly became overwhelmed; the LHMS equally quickly became dissatisfied.[99] A major reorganization at

FIGURE 6.3 "Old Brewery," in *The Old Brewery, and the New Mission House at the Five Points* (New York, 1854)

the next annual Methodist Conference saw Pease, his workshop, and his home released to the patronage of the National Temperance Society and a new missionary appointed to oversee the LHMS mission.

In 1852 the LHMS decided to make a material transformation in order to effect a spiritual one in the hearts of Five Points' residents. It set its sights on a derelict structure at the heart of Five Points. Erected as Coulter's Brewery in 1792 and converted into a tenement in 1837, the Old Brewery (fig. 6.3) housed newly arrived immigrants, African Americans, and the "vicious poor." Crime and misery proliferated in its dark and dirty rooms and cellar. The LHMS purchased and demolished the structure in 1852 and erected the New Mission House (fig 6.4) early the next year.[100] The purpose-built brick building was five stories high and included a chapel that sat five hundred, two schoolrooms, an apartment for the missionary and his family, and twenty additional apartments for the missionary to dispense to "poor and deserving" families.[101] The New Mission House more closely resembled the new middle-class townhouses

FIGURE 6.4 "The New Mission House at the Five Points," in *The Old Brewery, and the New Mission House at the Five Points* (New York, 1854)

like the one in which the Palmers lived than it did the surrounding tenements. It served as a center for the activities of the appointed missionaries and the ladies who supported their efforts through active neighborhood visitation. Most important, it was a visible symbol of change.

Efforts of the LHMS in Five Points did not go without notice. Much to its surprise, the society soon found itself on the defensive against two very different camps: the city's Roman Catholic clergy and other Protestant reformers. Relations between evangelical and Roman Catholic New Yorkers frayed at midcentury. Public battles erupted in the early 1840s between Bishop John Hughes and the Public School Society, a private organization that supported an extensive network of city schools, over how taxpayer money should be apportioned. The Public School Society was not an evangelical organization and, in fact, had been instrumental in the passage of an 1825 ordinance that denied public funds to any religious society after a request by the evangelical Bethel Baptist Church for its schools. (Seven years later Roman Catholics were actually successful in getting around the ordinance for their Orphan Asylum.) Yet the battles awakened longstanding animosities between Protestants and Catholics and unleashed destructive waves of cultural and political nativism to which evangelicals would have been sympathetic.[102]

The conversion of Roman Catholics to Protestantism was not an explicit objective of the LHMS, but the writings of its members make clear that this group composed a significant portion of the audience for their efforts. Conversion stories published in religious and secular newspapers and gathered in *The Old Brewery, and the New Mission House* amply document the presence of Catholics in the neighborhood. In "Triumphant Death," two visiting ladies of the LHMS found an "ignorant Catholic" dying of consumption in a tenement in Cow Bay, nursed him in his final days, and buried him, at his request, in a Protestant cemetery.[103] In another story, a young child in the Five Points Mission School led the ladies to his parents, "industrious, but poor Roman Catholics." His mother entrusted the care of the children to one of the ladies after her passing. "You are aware that I am a Protestant, are you not?" the cautious visitor asked the dying mother. "And in giving me your children I must do what I should conceive to be my duty toward them. Their education must be such as is directed by the word of God."[104] The dying mother had no issue with Methodist attention on her deathbed or care for her children, but many Catholic clergy did.

Roman Catholics turned to the pulpit and the press to denounce the society's efforts. Bishop John Hughes's emphasis on Tridentine Catholicism reinforced the hierarchy and power of the clergy over the laity. He personally had little patience for Protestant meddling with two of the most important rituals of Catholic life: the raising of children and the passage to the world to come.[105] Catholic priests went from house to house in the neighborhood warning people not to attend the preaching of the mission or allow their children to attend the Sunday school. They reportedly threatened excommunication and the withholding of the sacraments of the church, even in death, for those who did not.

At first taken aback, the LHMS countered that the Catholic Church had largely ignored Five Points. "We had not supposed that the Romish Church were very much concerned about the people of the Five Points," it wrote. "We did not even know that any considerable portion of them were claimed as Catholics, until the Catholic priests took the alarm."[106] It published stories about the failings of priests to care for residents. In one story, a priest huffily rebuked a sickly woman who thought she was dying but who recovered by the time he arrived. "This troubled her, and she did not dare again to send for him," it reported.[107] In another story, a poor Catholic woman was given permission to bury her dead child in Calvary, the Catholic cemetery, but not enough money to pay for the expense. The LHMS missionary gave her the balance.[108] Such stories are clearly self-serving but reveal a Catholic Church overwhelmed by the massive waves of immigration. They also suggest the conditions under which lay Catholics might have been attracted to the Methodist mission.[109]

The LHMS found just as formidable a rival in their former missionary, Louis Pease, and his supporters. Pease continued to work in Five Points after his dismissal from the mission. In 1854 he officially opened the Five Points House of Industry with a three-fold goal: to aid the destitute in their search for employment, to care for needy children and others, and "to imbue the objects of its care with pure principles of Christianity."[110] That care differed significantly from what the LHMS offered. History had already shown that when evangelical reformers focused their efforts in the same neighborhood, competition for resources and audience invariably ensued. Both sides availed themselves of the religious and secular press in airing their grievances. The LHMS publicly suspected Pease of trying to divert contributions for its mission and for stirring the pot of public opinion against it.[111]

The main issue between Pease and the LHMS reflected a larger ideological battle waged in the 1850s over whether the proper means of charitable support should be primarily temporal or spiritual. Historians have argued that supplying spiritual aid in the hope of effecting conversion, which marked efforts of the 1820s and '30s, gave way to what has been characterized as a more "secular" and pragmatic approach of providing temporal aid—employment, housing, food, clothing—to effect a moral transformation in the 1840s and '50s.[112] Most midcentury urban reform organizations followed this lead, but the LHMS stood steadfast in its emphasis on the importance of both. "Its object was not to supply merely temporal wants," Rev. James Floy, Michael Floy's brother, offered in a stinging rejoinder in 1853. "It had a holier end in view . . . for at this very period there was a widely diffused kind of infidelity that would place the temporal benefits of the poor above their spiritual wants, and inculcated as the paramount duty, that to clothe the naked and feed the hungry were the first labours of charity." Had not the Redeemer, Floy asked, "laboured more to supply the necessities of the immortal soul, than those of the frail mortal body?"[113] Pease and other reformers leapt on statements like this to accuse the LHMS of being "a sectarian, fanatical enterprise, which proposed to reform the Five Points, exclusively by spiritual means."[114] For them, such an approach was backward and inadequate.

The LHMS responded in kind. It reminded fellow New Yorkers that it also provided temporal aid. Missionaries and visitors distributed food, clothing, and shelter alongside spiritual advice because they learned early on "that if this course is not pursued, the people of this locality will not listen carefully to what you say about their spiritual interests."[115] Regular requests for, and acknowledgments of, donations of clothing and food to the mission in city newspapers reinforced this. Stories in *The Old Brewery, and the New Mission House* amply documented the LHMS's contribution of both temporal and spiritual aid. Some even took swipes at Pease, downgrading his contributions to local benevolence and occasionally painting him in a negative light.[116] In city papers the LHMS's supporters questioned the motives of Pease and his fellow reformers in running a "secular institution" that functioned primarily as "a clothing establishment . . . to employ men and women to work for him, and to see his wares to the best profit." They also smeared him as a Fourierite, socialist, materialist, and communist.[117]

Phoebe Palmer reflected on the contributions of the Five Points Mission on a Sunday afternoon visit in mid-January 1858. By then public rancor between the LHMS and Pease's House of Industry had subsided. Both had large, purpose-built structures that changed the face of the neighborhood, supplied day schools, and provided material aid.[118] While the mission has been judged a failure for not achieving "an appreciable number of converts," supporters measured success in other ways.[119] Palmer personally derived gratification from "the improvement of scores of children rescued from the haunts of crime and degradation," especially in contrast to what she had encountered six years earlier.[120]

Palmer also engaged with the city's new immigrant audiences through personal efforts to convert Jewish immigrants. References to Jews are scarce in LHMS writings, despite the large numbers of them arriving in the city at this time. An exception is a story told by one of the missionaries about a "poor-looking Jew, with the longest possible face, and the most wo-begone expression," who came into the mission one day and asked if the missionary could do "something for him." Over the coming weeks, the man, who initially declared, "I am pantheist and don't believe noting [*sic*]," slowly grew interested in Christianity and finally confessed his love for Christ and his belief that his sins had been forgiven.[121] While no other Jews make an appearance in the volume, the missionary's story represents a pervasive fantasy held by evangelical New Yorkers.

The conversion of Jews had a different appeal than the conversion of Roman Catholics. Evangelical desire for the latter was rooted in an argument about the true nature of the Christian faith, but their desire for the former reflected a long-held belief that it was a prerequisite to the Christian millennium. Palmer had great hopes for ushering in the end times; she even wrote a short tract about it.[122] Several Protestant societies based in New York made the conversion of the Jews their mission in the 1840s. The American Society for Meliorating the Condition of the Jews, the city's longest lasting Jewish missionary society, shifted its focus at that time from founding a rural colony for Hebrew converts to sponsoring urban domestic missions aimed at conversion. New York Baptists, Presbyterians, and Protestant Episcopalians all formed short-lived societies or sponsored missions to a similar end; the New York City Mission joined their efforts a decade later. Palmer helped found the Ladies' Jewish Association and Industrial Tea Meeting in 1854 to hire a Hebrew Christian missionary and secure a place of worship for converts. By August 1855, the association had decided against renting a place and instead met weekly in Palmer's townhouse. Like so many other efforts, it did not last long.[123]

The culmination of Palmer's interest came with her adoption of a young Jewish boy named Leopold Solomon. In April 1855, the Palmers opened their home to Solomon after his parents had him thrown in a city prison for expressing a desire to convert to Christianity. Few Jews in New York displayed a genuine interest in the gospel, making Solomon all the more attractive to the Palmers. They convinced city authorities to indenture the boy to their care with the intention of training him for the ministry. "We already take much comfort in him," Phoebe wrote to a close friend, "and expect that he will be a blessing to thousands of the house of Israel." The following summer, the Palmers sent Solomon off to the Charlotteville Seminary to train for the ministry. He begged to return to the city at the close of the term. Once back, Palmer recorded, "His relatives began to lurk around our premises and obtained occasional interviews with him." Before long Solomon's family had gotten him "in their cruel grasp." An August 1856 letter from Palmer sounds a note of finality on her efforts. "We did it for Christ's sake," she wrote without regret, "and feel thankful that we were thus permitted to show our love for His precious cause, by making efforts to rescue one of His persecuted members."[124]

In the end, the *idea* of the conversion of Roman Catholics and Jews to Protestantism influenced antebellum urban evangelicals more than any actual *success* in their endeavors. Palmer accurately read the interest of fellow evangelical New Yorkers when she wrote to a friend in 1855 that, despite having 40,000 Jews in the city, "very few Christians seem to be interested in making efforts for their salvation."[125] That sentiment applied equally to converting the much greater number of Roman Catholics. By the mid-1850s, many evangelicals had withdrawn from activism, more content to let professional missionaries do the work, and focused instead on their own search for sanctification. Ironically it was Phoebe Palmer who was at the forefront of that shift.

"A LAITY FOR THE TIMES"

In the midst of the uncommonly cold winter of 1857, Phoebe Palmer issued a challenge to the readers of the *Christian Advocate and Journal.* After recounting the abysmal reports of new accessions to the Methodist Episcopal Church over the previous year, she called them to arms. "What say you, brethren of the ministry and laity, to the accession of hundreds of thousands to our ranks the coming year? What say you, daughters of Zion? Shall we have the greatest revival that has ever been witnessed, during the coming year?" Some readers might have paused and pondered; others likely just scanned the page to find another article. Yet within a year, Manhattan witnessed one of the greatest urban revivals in a generation. It did so in the grips of a devastating economic panic and a divisive political climate that tore the nation apart over the place of slavery in a land of freedom. Even though Palmer is frequently missing from histories of the ensuing revival, her series, entitled "A Laity for the Times," paved the way for it.

Methodists were accustomed to posting sizable annual membership gains. Barely present in North America before the American Revolution, Methodism emerged by the middle of the nineteenth century as the nation's largest Protestant denomination. An extensive system of circuits ensured that no corner of the nation escaped the regular visit of an itinerating Methodist preacher. Even the 1844 division of the national denomination into the Methodist Episcopal Church and the Methodist Episcopal Church, South had not slowed its growth.[126] That is, until 1856. Instead of adding the usual tens of thousands of new members, the northern church added only 896.[127] As if to heighten their alarm, a concurrent series in the *Christian Advocate and Journal* revealed whom they were slipping behind in the spiritual marketplace.[128]

Palmer could have used her series "A Laity for the Times" to plumb the reasons for the decline but instead argued it was more profitable "to go devoutly to work, with our well recognized means to make a better year of the ensuing one."[129] Revivalism was the most important of these means. She shared the view of fellow Methodist James V. Watson, author of *Helps to the Promotion of Revivals* (1856), that revivals were not miracles but the result of "natural causes," of man's use of appropriate means to quicken the Church's interest in the subject of religion.[130] "If we consider them as miracles—as occurring arbitrarily—as being confined to particular seasons of the year,"

Watson explained, "we are in great danger of losing sight of our responsibility in the case; of *waiting* for a revival instead of *working* for it."[131] Watson and Palmer's view reflects Methodism's long embrace of Arminian notions of the free agency of man. (It took Calvinist Baptists, Presbyterians, and Congregationalists longer to get to that point, although Charles Grandison Finney paved the way in his New York revivals in the 1830s.) Just as *The Way of Holiness* provided a practical guide to sanctification, "A Laity for the Times" provided a concrete plan for growth in grace through revivalism.

Palmer wrote her series to make Methodists "earnestly and intelligently aware of the great work they are called to do."[132] She put her rationale in terms any city dweller could understand. "The necessity of individual effort in enlisting partisans in politics, temperance, or any other important movement is ever being kept before the public," she noted. "Supineness is deemed disloyalty, and is often pronounced treachery to the cause." If so much energy could be exerted in political matters of the day, why then was there such apathy toward spiritual matters? Certainly it was not for lack of an audience. In New York City, "souls condemned *already*" were not hard to find. "There are those *among* us, those who are eating at our own table, sitting by our fireside, members of our household, neighbors dwelling near us, persons frequenting the same sanctuary, perhaps sitting beside us, who are already sentenced to everlasting burnings," she reminded readers. The souls of the perishing were on their hands.[133]

For those not convinced by a call to duty, Palmer appealed to self-interest. "The bestowments of grace do not begin to multiply until the intrusted gifts are actually brought into use," she explained, "and then they multiply in the hands of the recipient as rapidly as did the loaves and fishes in the hands of Christ's early disciples." Palmer centered her argument on individual rewards in language that made sense to men and women accustomed to a booming, market-driven economy. Few of Palmer's urban middle-class followers could deny that God had been generous in endowing his faithful with gifts of "time, talent, and tithes" in postrecession New York. She reminded them of their obligation to consecrate those gifts for the benefit of the church but also promised a return on their investment. "How soon would the man with one talent be rejoicing in the possession of five, and the man of five talents be exulting in more than tenfold returns?"[134] After twenty years of ministering to evangelical New Yorkers, Phoebe Palmer knew how they thought.

"A Laity for the Times" is a resolutely optimistic work. Focusing on what was to come, rather than what had been, made sense from the perspective of February and March 1857. Palmer intimately knew the gloomy relentlessness of bitter days and ice-covered streets, as she spent her winter in the city leading the Tuesday Meeting, catching up on her correspondence, and pursuing writing projects. From her parlor on Rivington Street, she dreamed of greener pastures as she received invitations to speak during the upcoming summer camp-meeting season. She turned fifty that year, and with her surviving children reaching adulthood and Walter's business requiring less and less of his time, she knew she could enjoy more time on the road. While "A Laity for the Times" did not enjoy the broad circulation of *The Way of Holiness*, it had a significant impact. Seeds sown in wintertime germinated and blossomed over the coming year.

Lower Canada, not New York City, provided the first setting for testing Palmer's ideas. Leaving the city in late June, she traveled among the towns on the northern shore of Lake Ontario. Bowing to local practice, she allowed husband Walter to speak first to the hundreds that gathered at these camp meetings before she addressed the crowd.[135] Letters back to friends reveal how the revivals cut across denominational boundaries and even once, she rather gleefully reported, made incursion into Catholic territory (although she beat a quick retreat).[136] At Prescott, she asked attendees to go home and make efforts for the conversion of their friends, the central message from "A Laity for the Times." But a chance overnight in Hamilton, at the far western shore of Lake Ontario, provided that season's greatest success. Over the course of a few days in October, Palmer was convinced that God "stamp[ed] our ideas of a 'laity for the times' with signal success" and claimed as many as two thousand converts as evidence.[137] Evangelical New Yorkers read of Palmer's achievements in the first November issue of the *Christian Advocate and Journal*, although by that time they had their own stirrings of revival.

Revival arrived in New York in the fall of 1857 alongside financial panic, economic depression, and escalating political tensions. Past and present narratives of the revival typically begin with the efforts of missionary Jeremiah Lanphier, not with "A Laity for the Times."[138] Lanphier served as an urban missionary in the rapidly changing downtown and waterfront districts. Sensing an uptick in interest in late September, he began to hold weekly prayer meetings at the North Dutch Church on the corner of William and Fulton Streets. The crowds that turned out looked different than those who went to Palmer's Canadian revivals. Businessmen and their clerks packed into the few remaining downtown meetinghouses. The day before Palmer's revival in Hamilton launched, Lanphier decided that enough interest existed to justify running daily prayer meetings, except on Sundays. Five days later, on October 13, a massive run on New York City banks began. In retaliation, the banks suspended specie payments and began calling in loans. The worst financial panic in a generation had begun.[139]

The revival gained steam and spread to other cities as the panic worsened over the winter months of 1857–58.[140] Palmer remained in the city during the late fall and early winter, leading the Tuesday Meeting and counseling friends and followers. Revival activity peaked in March and April when James Bennett of the *New York Herald* and Horace Greeley of the *New York Daily Tribune* decided it merited coverage alongside debates in Washington over the Lecompton Constitution and the great "Mormon War" in the Utah Territory. These secular newspaper editors had long taken opposing sides on political issues of the day but agreed on the newsworthiness of the conversions of the city's suffering businessmen, a segment of the population that typically shied away from evangelical conversion.[141] The star of their accounts was not Phoebe Palmer but Henry Ward Beecher. No stranger to questions of faith and wealth, Beecher initially intended to sit the revival out, but historians have suggested he needed a distraction from his most recent accusation of marital infidelity.[142] From the pulpit of Plymouth Church, Beecher packed in the crowds each week.

As the revival gained traction, evangelical New Yorkers disagreed as to whether its energies should be promoting conversionist or reformist ends. Evangelical New Yorkers had experienced revivals for well over a century and had seen the energy released by them channeled in a variety of ways. For Palmer, active involvement of the sanctified in the conversion of others mattered far more than the accomplishment of specific societal reforms. In her thinking, the former would naturally benefit the latter. When she does identify a specific end in "A Laity for the Times," it initially seems rather boosterish and parochial: that the Methodist Church "would be known as a living Church of the living God, and stand forth as an example to all evangelical Churches in the land." Further on readers discovered a more catholic, but also more imperial, vision: "The design of God in raising [the Church] up would speedily be met," Palmer explained. "The continent would be reformed, and Scriptural holiness spread over these lands."[143]

Not everyone agreed with Palmer's desire for conversionist ends. They hoped to draw on the long tradition of linking revivalism to community reform. George Barrell Cheever, abolitionist and evangelical minister of the uptown Congregational Church of the Puritans, published a much different call to arms in March 1858. Cheever's "The Two Revivals" appeared in the pages of the *Independent*, a newspaper produced by New York's evangelical Congregationalist community.[144] A contemporary of Palmer and Beecher, Cheever's vocal antislavery convictions meant he had more in common with the latter than the former. Cheever, in fact, continued to hold those convictions and refused to mute his opposition to slavery when so many other urban evangelical ministers dropped theirs.[145] By the late 1850s, Cheever emerged as one of the most vocal opponents to the "peculiar institution" in the city, a tenuous position given New York's longstanding connection to Southern cotton.

In "The Two Revivals," Cheever called his readers' attention to the fact that "side by side with the wondrous revival of religion now going forward in our country" there was "a revival of the most damning and atrocious wickedness that ever was endured in any Christian or civilized Society." Cheever sounded the alarm against "avarice, cruelty, injustice, and inhumanity" and offered a stinging critique of recent political events. He warned that Christians caught up in the revival had been blindsided. They "are too much occupied with the revivals of religion in their own congregations to pay any attention to the morals of the government or country, or to remember the claims of oppressed and enslaved humanity, or to raise any outcry from the Word of God against the perpetuation of such vast political and social crimes." The charge was harsh. He believed evangelical New Yorkers were just as complicit as the city's "millionaires, mammon-worshippers, and respectable and Christian cotton-conservatives" who supported slavery as "essential to the existence and supremacy of their interests." Cheever ended with a blatant slam against Palmer's approach to revival: "A revival that shows its faith by its works will always gain the victory, in the end, over that which is satisfied with the mere theory of conversion and of righteousness."[146]

Cheever's reformist and Palmer's conversionist approaches represent vibrant but opposing revival strategies that stood in tension throughout the nineteenth century. Antislavery stood as a flashpoint between them. Cheever was not alone in his hope that the revival might catalyze broader societal change. "Instead of the *great revival* of 1858, we should be happy to read the *great reformation* of 1858," Harriet Beecher Stowe wrote a week after Cheever's article came out, although in the coming weeks she considerably muted her call.[147] For Cheever and other antislavery evangelicals, many of them Congregationalists with New England roots, revival provided an opportunity for an engaged community of Christians to remake the social order and restore the nation as a virtuous Christian republic through direct religious action. Bleeding Kansas, the Dred Scott Decision, and the election of James Buchanan all served as harbingers of moral failure that might be countered by the mobilization of evangelicals willing to take a stand against slavery.

For Palmer and more socially conservative evangelicals, those issues were cause for different alarm. Over the past few decades they had witnessed the progressive fragmentation of evangelical America over the issue of antislavery and abolition—locally, in the race riots of 1834; nationally, in the division of the Baptist, Methodist, and Presbyterian denominations into northern and southern bodies in 1844 and 1845—and hoped that revival might heal those wounds. Palmer wanted the revival to foster social harmony. Her theology of perfection resolutely focused on the revival as a means to foster individual conversion and sanctification. Converted, reformed individuals gathered into revitalized churches would also have a shaping influence on a virtuous, Christian republic, but it would be indirect.[148]

No evangelical New Yorker reading "A Laity for the Times" would have mistaken it as a call to arms against slavery. Palmer's focus on individual conversion came at the expense of broader societal change. In a city dependent on Southern cotton, her theology of perfection allowed those caught up in the revival to sidestep taking a stand on slavery, the issue wrenching the nation apart. One needed to focus first and foremost on the self; after that came the issues of the world. Such a stance proved appealing to many. Antislavery proponents like Cheever stood at the margins of urban evangelical society by the late 1850s. He and a diminishing number of publicly like-minded ministers risked alienating their congregations with their stances. And some did. A few weeks after the appearance of "The Two Revivals," Cheever faced a major revolt within his congregation, and a large number of members demanded letters of dismissal so that they could join other churches.[149] As tensions over evangelical antislavery sentiments increased, Beecher, always attuned to the winds of popular sentiment, backed off his antislavery activism.[150] Evangelical laity knew they had just as much to lose.

In the end, Phoebe Palmer proved more representative of the mainstream urban evangelical response to antislavery in waning years of the tumultuous 1850s than Cheever or Beecher. For someone who took very public stands in her career as a theologian, author, and revivalist, the absence of public activism or pronouncements against slavery speaks volumes. As Oberlin Perfectionists Asa Mahan and Charles Grandison Finney loudly expressed their opposition, Palmer and other New York City Perfectionists matched them with silence. One historian even labels Palmer and her circle as "the architects of the policy of silence which later became the regret of Northern Methodism."[151] While that is a hefty charge, her conversionist focus in "A Laity for the Times" and silence on antislavery and abolition is all the more deafening in light of the critique she soon made of the longstanding suppression of women's spiritual gifts.

Promise of the Father

As the flames of revival cooled in the autumn of 1858, leading evangelical New Yorkers quickly sought to set its meaning and memory in print. Samuel I. Prime's *The Power of Prayer* and Talbot W. Chambers's *The Noon Prayer Meeting of the North Dutch Church* followed the lead of the secular newspapers and told the history of the revival through the stories of white middle-class business men. In so doing, they sought to erase the participation and contributions of women and African Americans, even though they composed the majority of members of urban evangelical churches throughout the period.[152] Palmer knew firsthand of the efforts of social and religious conservatives across the city and around the nation to curtail the public activities of women. She responded, in kind, with the publication of the *Promise of the Father* (1859), a passionate plea for women's religious authority.

"Do not be startled, dear reader. We do not intend to discuss the question of 'Women's Rights' or of 'Women's Preaching,'" begins Palmer with an admonition meant to appease middle-class audiences. "We leave this for those whose ability and tastes may better fit them for discussions of this sort."[153] In the four hundred plus pages that follow, however, Palmer is anything but apologetic. She acknowledges that woman has "her legitimate sphere of action, which differs in most cases materially from that of man" but offers a blistering critique of the unfairness and negative consequences of denying "a gift of power, delegated to the church on the day of Pentecost," to half the population. That gift to speak—the titular *promise of the father*—had been granted equally by the Holy Spirit to women and men of the early church. Palmer argues the problem lay not with women who wanted to exercise this gift but with men who denied them this right. "So long has this endowment of power been withheld from use by the dissuasive sentiments of the pulpit, press, and church officials," she argues, "that it will now need the combined aid of these to give the public mind a proper direction, and undo a wrong introduced by the man of sin centuries ago."[154]

In chapter after chapter, Palmer skillfully dismantles arguments against female preaching and marshals examples of women from the primitive church, eighteenth-century Methodism, and the current day blessed with the gift of prophecy and preaching. In a thinly veiled swipe at Prime and Chambers, she scathingly characterizes the typical businessman as being of "ordinary intellectual ability" and so engrossed in "the ever-varying whirl" of business that he has little time to read the Bible or to reflect on his spiritual existence. Such men could not possibly develop "a state of spirituality that would particularly fit [them] for close and effectual communion with

God in leading the devotions of others, either in prayer or speaking." A focus on these men came at the expense of devoted women, who "were not regarded any more than if they had been infants or heathen women."[155] Such was a huge mistake. Pressures of worldly cares for these women "are made subservient to greater spirituality of mind, by pressing them more closely to the heart of Christ, as their almighty Friend, and the compassionate bearer of all their burdens."[156] They are the ones to be celebrated and promoted.

As copies of *The Promise of the Father* appeared on city booksellers' shelves, Phoebe Worrall Palmer sailed out of New York Harbor on a steamer bound for Liverpool in June 1859, leaving a complex legacy for her fellow evangelical New Yorkers in her wake. She had spent her entire life shaping and being shaped by the city's evangelical community. Feelings of spiritual inadequacy over her youthful conversion experience haunted her in adulthood before giving way to the joys of an individually directed and biblically grounded approach to sanctification. By introducing *The Way of Holiness* into mainstream evangelical practice she provided women and men with a rationale for taking charge of their own spiritual development. Instructing them to separate themselves spiritually from all that they held dear—even their spouses, if need be—amounted to a radical call for individualism. She spread her message through the strategies familiar to her from her youth—publishing, prayer meetings, and revivalism—and pushed the boundaries of acceptable practice.

While Phoebe Palmer's efforts to create a "laity for the times" inspired women and men to assume religious authority long denied them through revivalism, it also had unsettling repercussions. It allowed those who preferred her conversionist vision to the reformist vision of antislavery ministers to remain silent on issues tearing the nation apart. Palmer's three-and-a-half year evangelical campaign around Great Britain allowed her to spread her ideas about perfectionism, honed over the previous decades, to a transatlantic audience. It also only confirmed her ambivalence about reformist outcomes of revival. The trip allowed Palmer to convert thousands; it also allowed her to sit out escalating tensions over slavery and the outbreak of the Civil War back home.

CHAPTER SEVEN

Moving Uptown

"Great Excitement in John Street. Trouble among the Methodists." "A Muss among the Methodists—The John Street Difficulty." "The John Street Methodist Church. The Fight Gets into the Streets." Over the last weekend of July 1856, curious headlines confronted New Yorkers in their favorite secular newspapers about a Friday night riot at the downtown John Street Methodist Episcopal Church.[1] The *New York Dispatch* offered the most colorful account (and the only one written in rhyming couplets). It tells of a competition between two factions for possession of the church: the "up-towners," who having "tasted air up town, . . . wished to tear the old church down," and the "down-towners," remnants of that "congregation tried and true," who desired to continue worshipping there. Tensions came to a head when the uptowners resorted to street justice—"vagram men"—after legal justice failed to dislodge the downtowners. A punch was thrown, the police rushed in, and "the fun grew fast and furious." The riot proved short lived. "In less time than it takes to tell," the uptowners and their hired thugs "fled the exciting scene pell-mell," conceding the meetinghouse to the downtowners. The *Dispatch* concluded, "'Tis a painful sight when godly men fall out and fight." It was also an increasingly common one at midcentury as downtown evangelical congregations debated whether or not to move uptown.[2]

John Street Methodists were not alone in wrestling with the developments reshaping New York in the 1840s and '50s. Developers who sat anxiously on the sidelines during the recession that followed the Panic of 1837 exploded in a frenzy of residential building that charged up the island from 14th to 50th Streets between 1843 and 1857, when another panic struck. They found willing partners in evangelical denominations that had long favored the forward edge of urban settlement. At the same time, an expansive commercial economy fueled the redevelopment of lower Manhattan's previously mixed residential and artisanal neighborhoods into commercial districts. It provided some with the financial resources that allowed them to move north, while it trapped others in the older part of the city. Denominations that had seen their financial resources dwindle in the panic accepted generous bounties for their sparsely attended and often indebted downtown locations. Add to all this an unprecedented influx of non-Protestant immigrants who piled into tenements and slums in once "respectable" neighborhoods surrounding these churches. Few congregations resisted the temptation to cash in and follow their congregants uptown. In July 1856, John Street was one of the last holdouts.

Downtown evangelical congregations were never passive victims of these developments. The actions of Baptists, Methodists, Presbyterians, and a handful of other denominations since the end of the American Revolution helped put them in motion. Evangelical competition in a dynamic and expansive spiritual marketplace, aggressive church-building strategies, and an embrace of a new rhetoric of domesticity contributed to the growth of the city and the experience of life within it. In turn, the city provided the financial, social, and organizational resources that allowed evangelical congregations to thrive and expand their reach locally, nationally, and globally. Over the first half of the nineteenth century, evangelical denominations dominated the urban spiritual marketplace. But by the eve of the Civil War, they saw signs of the erosion of their hard-earned position. Longstanding tensions between egalitarian ideologies and inegalitarian power structures resulted in factionalism that pitted congregants against one another. Downtown churches like John Street that wished to remain in situ had to reinvent themselves for post–Civil War urban society. John Street accepted the challenge.

The John Street Methodist Episcopal Church provides a useful lens for exploring the ways in which evangelicalism's efforts to transform the city allowed the city ultimately to transform evangelicalism. To understand the riot in 1856 requires revisiting John Street at different points in its nearly ninety-year history on the same lot in lower Manhattan.

INDEPENDENCE, 1783

Seven years of British wartime occupation had not been kind to many of the city's houses of worship, especially those known for the patriotic lean-

FIGURE 7.1 First John Street Methodist Episcopal Church (opened 1768) from Joseph Beekman Smith, *The Three Buildings of the John Street Methodist Church, NYC (Buildings Erected 1768–1841), Study for a Lithograph*, 1841–44, watercolor, ink, and graphite on paper, 14½ × 38⅞ in.; obj. #X.387, New-York Historical Society. Photography © New-York Historical Society

ings of their congregations. Thanks to Methodists' adherence to British founder John Wesley's loyalism, the John Street meetinghouse (fig. 7.1) emerged largely unscathed. Evacuation of the British in late November 1783 created a greater problem than their occupying presence. As congregations of other churches returned to rebuild, many of John Street's members departed with the British. John Street weathered the exodus and patriotic backlash to evolve over the following decades from the city's only Methodist church to the mother church of one of the nation's most popular evangelical denominations.

As Methodists reinvented themselves for the republican city and nation, they drew on the hallmarks that distinguished them in the colonial period. Unlike many of the city's colonial churches, Methodists offered a faith based on voluntary choice rather than ethnic ties.[3] A community of

Palatines, converted under the preaching of John Wesley during their time in Ireland, had transplanted Methodism to New York in the decade prior to the American Revolution. According to a narrative retold by nineteenth-century Methodists, the exiled community grew lax in its devotions until one day Barbara Heck (right foreground in fig. 7.1) caught some young men playing cards. She threw their cards into the fire and immediately set off to command Philip Embury, who had been a local preacher back in Ireland (to whom she speaks in fig. 7.1), to begin preaching. Embury objected, saying he had neither meetinghouse nor congregation; Heck assured him if he preached in his own house to his own people, others would follow. Embury found support from another displaced Methodist preacher, Captain Thomas Webb, a former British army officer known for his eye patch and for preaching in his regimentals (center foreground of fig. 7.1). As Heck predicted, people soon flocked. African slaves and British soldiers, Dutch housewives and Scottish artisans came to Embury's parlor to learn what they must do to achieve salvation.[4]

Methodists retained their willingness to rethink sacred space to suit the urban context. Before the war they had made two important contributions that became central to the postwar spiritual marketplace. First, they occupied the Rigging Loft as the city's first storefront church.[5] As the nascent congregation outgrew Embury's house, it rented a larger room before settling into the loft on Horse-and-Cart Street in 1767 (see fig. 1.4). The upper floor of the long and narrow (60-by-18-foot) structure was a sail loft, which allowed women and men to worship in an unencumbered space.[6] English Methodists had already radically stripped the requirements of religious space down to the bare essentials needed to preach the Word, which meant little more than a desk for the preacher and benches for the congregation. (The colonial John Street meetinghouse had no altar because Methodists during Wesley's life considered their worship to be auxiliary to the Church of England and took communion at nearby Trinity or St. Paul's Anglican churches.)[7] Unable to build a church, New York Methodists popularized building reuse, a form that became the primary incubator for new evangelical congregations in the nineteenth century and remains a hallmark of urban religion today.

Once able to build, prewar Methodists created a meetinghouse prototype, which become a pervasive urban vernacular form. In 1768, the congregation purchased two adjacent lots on John Street and erected the first purpose-built Methodist meetinghouse in North America (see fig. 7.1). It was small (42 by 60 feet), three bays wide, and two and a half stories high, with restrained Georgian details. Its gable end faced the street, and it had no steeple. Its builders used the cheapest materials around—ballast stone from the hulls of ships—and rejected much of the ornament of other churches as the trappings of the world and distractions from the gospel. (The meetinghouse's bright blue plastered exterior was apparently an exception.) The interior remained unfinished for many years, mirroring the plainness of its exterior.[8] Later Methodists credited the meetinghouse's design to a vision of Barbara Heck, but what she claimed to have seen bore a strong resemblance to the Methodist meetinghouses in which she had worshipped back in Ireland.[9] The first meetinghouse was well suited to the exigencies of a tight urban real estate market: it was economical, could be built as large or as small as the lot allowed, and best of all, offered a recognizable brand within the urban spiritual marketplace. It remained the standard urban evangelical meetinghouse form up to the Civil War.

Finally, Methodists maintained their enthusiasm for competing in the city's spiritual marketplace with an egalitarian promise of salvation. Methodist itinerants preached the necessity of conversion to anyone who would listen, regardless of race, class, gender, or age. Advocating the equality of the believer's soul before God posed a radical challenge to colonial conceptions of the church as rooted in a strict social hierarchy. Methodists matched their manner to their message. They preached plainly and deliberately to people outside in market squares and fields. Inside the meetinghouse, worshippers sat not by family groups in pews but on movable benches separated by gender, women to the right and men to the left.[10] Publications available for free or minimal cost outlined a simple "method" that anyone could follow in daily life. Books and community sustained the faithful after itinerant ministers left town. "For the plain and simple gospel suits best for any people; for the unlearned can understand, and the learned are sure to understand," explained Philadelphia Methodist Richard Allen. No doubt he spoke for many of his New York sisters and brothers.[11]

But the egalitarian message preached in the John Street meetinghouse was promoted and sustained by an inegalitarian institution that alienated segments of its congregation over time. American Methodists deviated little from Wesley's hierarchical and patriarchal structure of bishops, presiding elders, and traveling preachers. The appeal of Methodism to African Americans and women is something of a paradox. Historian David Hempton points out that both groups "comprehensively shaped" Methodism but never received "immediate release from entrenched positions of subordination" to white male control. Instead, each developed strategies—separation for blacks, pious

FIGURE 7.2 Peter Williams Sr. (1750–1823), by unidentified artist, ca. 1810; oil on canvas, 25 × 24¼ inches; negative #1305; obj. #X.173, New-York Historical Society. Photography © New-York Historical Society

domesticity for women—that allowed them to carve out their own realms of power.[12] Not all white men agreed either. Vigorous debates arose on both sides of the Atlantic following Wesley's death in 1791 over questions of power, authority, and representation. Many came to question the church's place in a democratic society. Bishop Francis Asbury defended the necessity of the Episcopal structure, not on the grounds of hierarchical privilege but because it offered the best form of government for achieving missionary objectives. Such a rationale rang hollow for some.[13]

Few appreciated that tension better than Peter Williams Sr. (fig. 7.2). Like many urban slaves, Williams had the opportunity to sample the different faiths in the city's spiritual marketplace and found Methodism's message of spiritual liberation through individual conversion particularly compelling.

When his loyalist owner fled the city, Williams, rather than leaving with him for the uncertain promise of freedom in Canada, was able to remain in New York, having discovered that the John Street church also offered a key to his legal liberation. (He likely also hoped the republican state would follow, but that took much longer.) The church's trustees purchased Williams with the understanding that he would pay them back. Thus for nearly thirteen years, an American Methodist corporation whose British founder passionately rejected slavery as sinful owned a slave. Williams served as the church's sexton (as represented in fig. 7.1, where he holds the door of the church open), while his wife, Molly, like so many Mothers-in-Israel, catered to the needs of white male itinerant preachers who stayed in the small parsonage in front of the church.[14]

Every Sunday when Molly and Peter Williams looked up at the John Street meetinghouse's "negro pews," they must have been struck with an uneasy feeling about their place within the community. How did they square the disjuncture between Methodism's message of the spiritual equality of individuals before God with the reality of their spatial segregation before man? The American Revolution provided the opportunity and justification to throw off social, economic, and legal distinctions, but those empowered to form the new American republic interpreted the Declaration of Independence's promise "all men are created equal" far more narrowly than many hoped. It seems an unlikely coincidence that the same year Williams finally achieved legal freedom he and several other African American Methodists rented a secular space—a stable several blocks to the north—in which to form a spiritual community of their own design. Within a few years, they built a new meetinghouse and formed an all-black congregation, the African Methodist Episcopal Zion (AMEZ) Church. The church elected to remain, however, under the authority of the white Methodist Conference for two more decades. For reasons conjectured but never recorded, Williams did not formally join the new AMEZ Church, opting to remain within the fold of the congregation responsible for his spiritual and legal liberation.[15]

The primitive first John Street meetinghouse stood at the end of the eighteenth century as an evangelical outpost in a chaotic Atlantic port, a beacon for those who sought a community defined not by ethnicity but by the shared experience of evangelical rebirth. Methodist experience in the colonial city had given them the chance to develop strategies that brought success in the urban spiritual marketplace. Yet from the vantage of 1783, it stood poised for an uncertain future. How a single meetinghouse would become the mother of dozens in the city and thousands across the nation was a story that remained to be told. Some were bound not to be happy with how it played out.

RESPECTABILITY, 1818

New Yorkers celebrated the return of peace and commercial prosperity following the War of 1812. With the Treaty of Ghent, the British threat to American sovereignty on the continent was repulsed once and for all, and the trade lanes of the Atlantic reopened. The city resumed its quest to be the commercial, rather than political, center for the nation. Newcomers flooded in from around the Atlantic World in search of opportunities, and optimism spread into every corner of the city. John Street Methodists demonstrated the success they had achieved by tearing down their colonial meetinghouse and rebuilding it as one of the finest (and most expensive) houses of worship in the city (fig. 7.3). The second meetinghouse stood at the center of an expanding network of churches, missionary organizations, benevolent institutions, and reform movements then shaping the city, nation, and world.

When dedicated in January 1818, the second meetinghouse reflected the accomplishments of the Methodist community over the previous generation. That year the city was home to 3,158 Methodists (2,195 white and 963 "colored"), spread out across eight churches. This was a substantial increase from the 60 members reported back in 1784 at the first meeting of the New York Conference. Methodists had one of the most highly centralized power structures among the city's denominations. All eight Methodist churches were grouped into a single circuit served by an annually appointed council of ministers, who rotated among them in their preaching duties. A board of trustees, drawn from leading laity and elected annually by the male membership, oversaw temporal issues, especially related to property and money. As early as 1810 Francis Asbury noted that the first meetinghouse was showing its age and suggested that "something larger and better occupy its place." Seven years passed before the frugal trustees gave conditional assent to the project. When Rev. W. Thacher raised a subscription of $5,000 in five days, testament to the booming economy, the trustees relented and gave their permission.[16]

If the first meetinghouse "bore upon the whole, an appearance as plain and simple as the lives of its projectors," then the second one presented a far more respectable face to the world.[17] Built on the same site, the new structure proudly fronted the busy street, rather than hiding at the back of the lot. It was twice as large (62 by 87 feet) and built of costlier materials but stylistically paid homage to the evangelical vernacular of its predecessor. The

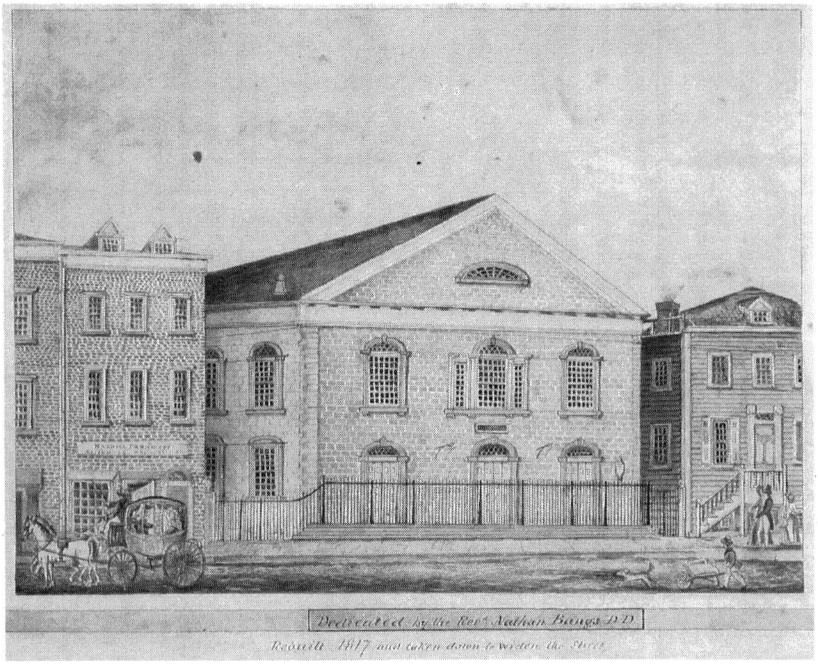

FIGURE 7.3 Second John Street Methodist Episcopal Church (opened 1818), from Joseph Beekman Smith, *The Three Buildings of the John Street Methodist Church, NYC (Buildings Erected 1768–1841), Study for a Lithograph*, 1841–44, watercolor, ink, and graphite on paper, 14½ × 38⅞ in.; obj. #X.387, New-York Historical Society. Photography © New-York Historical Society

exterior reflected the street's changing profile: it looked to the new three-story brick storefronts more than the older one- and two-story wooden shops and houses of artisans. Refined interior furnishings reflected changing standards of middle-class domestic comfort and included fixed pews, a paneled pulpit, and a carpeted altar. An innovative spatial arrangement placed the pulpit on the wall fronting the street with a sloped floor ascending to the back of the auditorium. Methodists now faced the world head on rather than turning their backs to it. An exterior tablet over the center door reinforced their accomplishments to passersby. It stated, in gilt letters on a black ground, "According to this time it shall be said, What hath God Wrought?"[18]

Denominations invested primarily in building new meetinghouses rather than rebuilding older ones in the generation following the American Revolution. By 1820 the number of houses of worship in the city's spiritual marketplace had tripled, even with the disruptions of the intervening war (see table A.2 in the appendix). Meetinghouses stretched as far north as Greenwich Village and the Bowery but had the greatest concentration on the west side, a few streets back from the North River, and up the center of the city, between Broadway and Bowery (see map 3.1). The city's population also tripled during this period, so the ratio of meetinghouses to people remained constant (see table A.3 in the appendix). Evangelical denominations that embraced voluntary choice over ethnic ties as the basis for membership—Baptists, Methodists, and Presbyterians—enjoyed the greatest growth and largely displaced the colonial-era dominance of ethnic Protestant churches. Non-Protestant faiths saw few gains in the marketplace. Their time would come later.

The second meetinghouse anchored an expanding network of churches across the northern edge of the city, systematically reaching out to laboring and middling folk. Historians have noted that economic advocates believed the grid facilitated "an all-encompassing, impersonal, systematic exchange of commodities" and that political advocates appreciated how transparent order, or the idea of it at least, opened the way for the smoother functioning of the city.[19] Fewer have noted how the city's denominations, especially evangelical ones, saw the grid as opening the way for the conversion of the city through organized and systematic settlement. The New York Conference eagerly sent out itinerants to gather new congregations, while lay trustees provided funding (and on one occasion a wooden frame) to construct new meetinghouses.[20] The names of these new churches—Forsyth Street (1789), Duane Street (1797), Bedford Street (1810), Allen Street (1811), and Bowery Village (1818)—mapped their spread and allowed potential worshippers to locate them more readily. All replicated the architectural form and style of the evangelical vernacular and extended the Methodist brand.[21] By the early 1820s, expansion had become so standardized that a contemporary history referred to their church building as "a business of ordinary consideration" rather than the "momentous undertaking" it once had been.[22]

Expansion, however, came at a price. In mid-October 1813, the leaders' meeting took up a letter submitted by a Brother Munson that included several questions about the allocation of monthly lay contributions. Of particular concern was whether they were being applied to the debt accumulated in building new meetinghouses. As the rate of construction accelerated, so had the cost. Nearly a decade elapsed between the construction of the city's second Methodist meetinghouse (1789) and its third (1797), but construction of the fourth and fifth—Bedford Street and Allen Street—occurred in the same year (1810), inflicting a heavy burden. Methodists tried to offset the expense by renting meetinghouse basements for secular purposes, like bottling ale and cider under Duane Street or the storage of cider and malt liquor under Bedford Street and Allen Street.[23] Church leaders made no promises to Munson but agreed to annually report the sums collected.[24] The debt issue was resurrected later that decade when the $30,000 price tag of the second John Street meetinghouse coupled with the construction of a church at Bowery Village pushed the conference's debt up to $17,000 in March 1818 (and then up to $32,500 in April 1820).[25]

The tension between Methodism's traditional egalitarian message and its inegalitarian power structure grew more fraught after the opening of the second John Street meetinghouse. A growing number disagreed with the direction the denomination appeared to be heading. "O! how much is ease, honour and the applause or the respect of the rich and great sought after by some," lamented minister William Stilwell. "And is not the discipline of the church oftentimes enforced upon the poor, whilst the rich trample it under foot?"[26] Stilwell had joined the Methodists as an itinerant six years earlier but over time had grown concerned about the autocratic decision making of the church's trustees and the heavy debt incurred in building new meetinghouses. His concerns were as much cultural as economic.[27] Fearful that Methodism was becoming too entranced by the lure of respectability, Stilwell and his uncle Samuel, a prominent layman, led more than 350 of the "prudent, plain part of the society" out of John Street and other city Methodist churches in July 1820 to form the independent Methodist Society.[28] His appointment the year before to minister to the AMEZ churches brought him in contact with African American leaders who shared his concerns and joined him.

There was more than a kernel of truth to leading Methodist minister Nathan Bangs's reference to the dissidents as an "uptown faction." Many who joined Stilwell's Methodist Society came from the northern artisan neighborhoods. They recoiled at the expense of a meetinghouse too far away for them to attend comfortably; its ostentation, reflected Methodist historian Samuel Seaman, seemed "a serious departure from the primitive simplicity of Methodism."[29] The Methodist Society demonstrated its commitment to a plainer and more authentic worship experience in the meetinghouse it constructed about a half-mile to the north on Chrystie Street. The "intensely democratic" Methodist Society had no bishops or presiding elders, and every member, male and female, had a vote on issues facing the church.[30] More than eight hundred members of the AMEZ congregations followed the Stilwellites' lead. They asked Stilwell to ordain their elders so that they might become independent congregations. As their names suggest, they still considered themselves Methodist and heirs of Wesley, even if they severed any formal connection with the city's Methodist Conference.

As New York's Methodists celebrated their newfound respectability with the opening of the second meetinghouse on John Street in 1818, minister Joshua Soule spoke with optimism for the future. "Let every Christian rejoice that this religion is destined to cover the whole earth," he exhorted. "We live at an eventful period—The time, yea, the set time to favour Zion is come—Thousands are engaged for her prosperity—the prophecies are fulfilling—Jesus shall have the heathen for his inheritance, and the uttermost parts of the earth for a possession."[31] The next two decades bore out Soule's predictions. But Nathan Bangs, on his way to becoming one of the city and nation's most powerful Methodist ministers, concluded with a more restrained tone in his sermon earlier in the day, reminding the gathered to cleave to the "old paths" instead of just running out into the new ways.[32] As the next two decades revealed, that was easier said than done.

"THAT SACRED SPOT," 1841

The Panic of 1837 caught New Yorkers, pious and profane, off guard. The city had thrived as a national commercial center by looking east across the Atlantic and west to the nation's expanding hinterland. Rapid growth fostered an unbridled optimism as the swelling population followed the grid north to new neighborhoods. None anticipated that such a collapse lay on the horizon. The John Street Methodists were caught off guard again two years later when the Common Council decided to widen John Street. The new street, as projected, fell eight feet within the sanctuary of the 1818 meetinghouse. In deciding whether or not to rebuild in 1839, the trustees had to consider traditional Methodist strategies for church building alongside a shifting landscape, a diversifying marketplace, a fragmenting denomination, and a new imperative within antebellum evangelicalism to reach underserved audiences. Their decision to rebuild a third time on the same spot flew in the face of conventional wisdom. It also required a novel justification, which they found by looking backward.

The opening of the Erie Canal in 1825 secured New York's position as the nation's preeminent seaport, emporium, and financial center. The canal connected New York with the Great Lakes, ensuring access for city merchants to the vast markets of the west. Commercial success brought profound changes in the scale, organization, and rhythms of the city's economy.[33] New Yorkers also learned that national prominence made them more susceptible to misfortune elsewhere. When New Orleans merchants defaulted on vast sums owed to a New York firm because of a drop in the price of cotton, the loss triggered a chain reaction that caused the worst financial panic and recession that New Yorkers had yet witnessed.[34]

The booming commercial economy before the panic attracted women and men from places familiar and new. The population grew steadily from just over 120,000 inhabitants in 1820 to more than 312,000 by 1840.[35] Foreign immigration through New York rose from 3,800 in 1820 to 30,000 in 1832 to 60,000 in 1837, the last being 75 percent of the national total of new immigrants that year. Most continued on their journeys, but enough stayed behind, either in search of new opportunities or because they could not afford to move elsewhere. High mortality rates, declining economic opportunities, and periodic outbreaks of violence kept the city's African American population from experiencing similar success. While their overall number increased, their percentage within the population eroded from 8.7 percent in 1820 to 5.2 percent in 1840.[36]

To make room for this expanding population, New Yorkers enthusiastically extended the systematic landscape of the grid. They followed the Commissioners' Plan as they opened new districts across the northern edge of the city. Outward development followed three thrusts: one following the line of Greenwich Street along the Hudson River, a second along the East River waterfront, and a third up the center of the island between Bowery and Broadway (see map 5.3).[37] Speculative building ventures, such as those by Clement Moore in Chelsea and John Jacob Astor in Bloomingdale, drew middling and elite New Yorkers northward out of the settled city. New forms of transportation—omnibuses and railroads—brought them there.[38] By the time the panic struck, settlement extended as far north as 22nd Street on the city's west side, 14th Street in the center of the island, and 5th Street along the East River.

Despite its promise of transparency, the systematic landscape masked important distinctions that gave rise, in time, to yet another model of urban spatial organization. As the city expanded, New Yorkers increasingly sorted themselves into districts based on class.[39] The desirability of uptown and downtown flipped beginning in the 1830s as wealthy and middling New Yorkers commenced a steady exodus to the gridded neighborhoods around Washington and Tompkins Squares and, the following decade, Gramercy Park and Union Square. Five Points, Chatham Square, and the slums of the Fourth Ward became the domain of those on the other end of the economic spectrum.[40] Residential redistricting worked in collaboration with commercial and industrial expansion. A massive fire in the heart of the city on a cold December night in 1835 destroyed 674 buildings. The affected area was rebuilt as an almost exclusively commercial district, pushing out the remaining vestiges of residences.[41] By the end of the decade, the systematic landscape of the grid had inadvertently paved the way for a landscape segmented by class and function.

All this was on the minds of the trustees when they learned in 1839 about the proposed widening of John Street. The city's Common Council pursued the project to impose the grid's regularity on an irregular section of the city and to make it more functional as a commercial district. Three- and four-story brick countinghouses had already replaced much of the earlier mixed-residential fabric on the street. The trustees identified three options. The first two—modify the second meetinghouse by moving the front wall back to accommodate the expansion of the street, or tear down the whole structure and rebuild it to fit the modified lot—were within the realm of what had been done before. The third option—tear the meetinghouse down, sell the land, and relocate to a neighborhood uptown—was new, but one simultaneously contemplated by other downtown evangelical churches. The trustees' decision had important ramifications not only for the John Street congregation but also for the city's Methodist and evangelical communities.[42]

In making their decision, the trustees had to take into account John Street's dwindling congregation. What was once the city's premier congregation had only a little more than a quarter of the membership of the city's largest Methodist churches in 1839. Of the fourteen churches that reported membership numbers to the New York Conference that year, just three were smaller.[43] John Street was no longer home to the same congregation that rebuilt it twenty years earlier as one of the most respectable in the city. If a house of worship reflected those who worshipped inside, a new meetinghouse would have a very different face to present to the world.

The dwindling of the John Street congregation was not indicative of the health of the larger urban spiritual marketplace. The number of houses of worship increased from 68 in 1820 to 165 in 1840 (see table A.3 in the appendix). Protestant faiths continued to dominate the marketplace with evangelical denominations accounting for more than half of the city's churches. (Evangelical congregations within traditionally nonevangelical denominations, such as the Protestant Episcopalians and the Reformed Dutch, raise that number even higher.) Non-Protestant churches also increased. A second Jewish congregation—B'Nai Jeshurum—opened in 1825 when thirty-two

Ashkenazic members broke away from Shearith Israel.[44] Roman Catholics experienced more substantial growth, adding two churches in the 1820s and four in the 1830s. The expanding presence of Catholics and Jews foreshadowed important changes, but for now New York remained a Protestant town.

Methodism also thrived at this time, but in meetinghouses to the north of John Street. Methodists continued to rely on the systematic grid to plant new neighborhood congregations on the edges of urban settlement. Efforts begun in the homes of local converts and rented commercial spaces bloomed into the Willett Street (1826) and 2nd Street (1832) churches on the east side and Greene Street (1832) and 18th Street (1836) on the west side (see map 5.3). Builders drew on the form and style of the evangelical vernacular, carefully signaling to passersby the experience offered within. Methodists also planted congregations in Manhattan's outlying hamlets at Rose Hill (27th Street and Lexington Avenue, 1827), Yorkville (86th Street and Third Avenue, 1830), Harlem (1836), and Bloomingdale (41st Street and Eighth Avenue, 1840). Within a few years the rapidly growing city subsumed these rural communities into its northward rolling expanse.[45]

Questions of placement, authority, and respectability remained contentious. The founding of the Vestry Street (1833) and Mulberry Street (1834) churches went against the grain not only by opening in the heart of the settled city instead of on the edge of settlement but also by being organized by elite and middle-class laity instead of by clergy and trustees. These churches' exteriors echoed the evangelical vernacular, but their interiors departed from longstanding practice by installing family-oriented pews for sale.[46] As early as 1830, Methodist ministers had floated the idea of selling pews to fund the construction of new meetinghouses instead of increasing the New York Conference's onerous debt. A committee considered the idea but rejected it as "not lawful or expedient." Three years later, the laity of the Vestry and Mulberry Street churches formed joint-stock companies and did it anyway. In so doing, they bypassed the Methodist Conference altogether.

In the wake of the Stilwellite schism, other congregations that understood themselves in the tradition of eighteenth-century Wesleyan Methodism but had grown disillusioned with Methodism's authoritarian nature broke away. Methodist Protestants, Welsh Methodists, Primitive Methodists, and Wesleyan Methodists had precarious existences in the city. They rarely lasted long in the same location, some never acquired an actual house of worship, and others flipped from one denominational membership to another. With the exception of the African Methodist Union, which opened on 15th Street and Seventh Avenue in 1836, these congregations set up shop in the settled part of the city between Canal and Houston Streets. They mirrored the segregation pervasive within local and national Methodism. White congregations settled on the west and east edges of the city in the Ninth, Eleventh, and Thirteenth Wards, while black congregations clustered in the center around Five Points. Despite their fragility, these churches epitomized the vitality of a dynamic urban spiritual marketplace where most faiths could find an audience, for a short period at least. In all, Methodists initiated ten new congregations, and schismatic groups another nine, between 1818 and 1841 (see table A.2 in the appendix).[47]

Methodists' competitors followed similar strategies. Presbyterians, Baptists, and Protestant Episcopalians built new neighborhood churches in the central and northern districts of the city, especially between Canal Street and Washington Square Park to the west of Bowery. Each major denomination rushed to position themselves in up-and-coming neighborhoods. When Chelsea opened up for settlement in the late 1820s, Methodists got there early, and within a few years each major denomination had a church around Eighth Avenue between 16th and 20th Streets in the 1830s.[48] Episcopalians shared Methodist interest in looking to the northern hamlets.[49] Among all the Protestant denominations, only Baptists focused energy on establishing new neighborhood churches in the southern, settled part of the city. They did so by opportunistically taking over several houses of worship vacated by other congregations.[50]

Finally, the trustees had to acknowledge the larger evangelical interest in the establishment of missionary churches for nontraditional audiences in overlooked parts of the city. Presbyterians, as we have seen, responded early and enthusiastically. Energetic missionaries sponsored by voluntary lay associations founded five different churches on the East River waterfront (today's Lower East Side) in the late 1810s and 1820s. Engaged members of the laity ushered in the Free Church movement along the axes of Broadway and Bowery a decade later. Finally, the Presbytery launched efforts to convert Germans in the mid-1830s.[51] Evangelical Protestant Episcopalians also joined in the effort, to a lesser extent, opening up missionary churches in eastern parts of the city where they had not previously made efforts to plant congregations.[52] While Methodist Henry Chase labored at the Mariner's Church for more than thirty years, Methodists did not found explicitly mission-oriented churches before 1840.

In March 1840, the trustees contemplated purchasing the former brick church of the Society of Christian Friends at the intersection of Duane

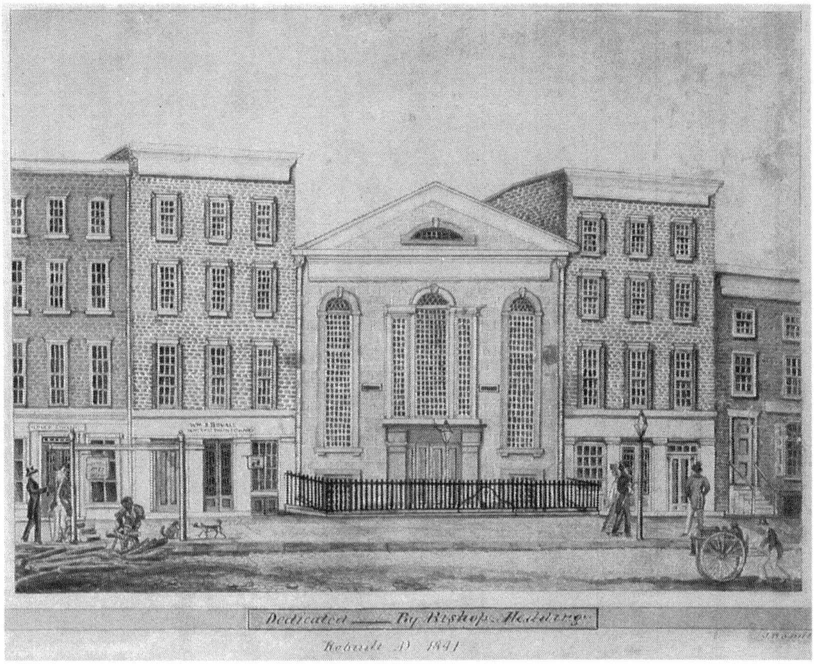

FIGURE 7.4 Third John Street Methodist Episcopal Church (opened 1841), from Joseph Beekman Smith, *The Three Buildings of the John Street Methodist Church, NYC (Buildings Erected 1768–1841), Study for a Lithograph*, 1841–44, watercolor, ink, and graphite on paper, 14½ × 38⅞ in.; obj. #X.387, New-York Historical Society. Photography © New-York Historical Society

Street and City Hall Place, a structure still downtown but in an area less encroached on than John Street. That month they went even further by proposing to sell the meetinghouse to the Methodist Missionary Society and thus replace the neighborhood church with a mission station. (The proceeds would be used to build a new church uptown.) Neither of these plans came to pass.[53] Instead, the trustees agreed to take their chances and rebuild on the same spot.

In rebuilding a third time, the trustees innovatively adapted to the current and future reality of the neighborhood. The third meetinghouse (fig. 7.4) echoed the form and function of its predecessor but possessed only a fraction of its capacity. It was built in the evangelical vernacular but of cheaper materials. A narrower structure (40 by 80 feet) allowed the trustees to use the remainder of the valuable lot to erect flanking four-story brick countinghouses.

Built on granite piers to accommodate ground level shops, the structures combined retail and commercial space. These commercial properties were intended to provide the church with a valuable source of rental income, especially as wealthier congregants moved north.[54] In all, the structures that arose on John Street reflected a creative response to the realities of their location.

Before 1838 the decision about John Street's future would have been the prerogative of a single board of trustees for the entire city. But a wave of democratization swept over Methodist power structures in the decades following the Stilwellite schism. In 1832, the New York Conference divided into two charges, East and West, with separate preachers and stewards for each but retaining a single board of trustees. The proliferation of splinter sects, the establishment of the Vestry Street and Mulberry Street churches on their own foundations, and lay concern about rising indebtedness exerted pressure for further change.[55] By March 1835 permission had been granted to elect a board of trustees for each charge. But authority continued to unravel, and within three years each congregation had been put on its own foundation. John Street, where New York Methodism began, was one of the last to eschew Wesley's preferred structure. In 1838, it incorporated as an independent congregation and turned direction of temporal matters over to a board of trustees elected by the congregation.[56]

The trustees' decision to rebuild flew in the face of conventional wisdom. Eighteenth- and early nineteenth-century evangelicals valued meetinghouses only as long as they fit the needs of their congregations. John Street no longer had a full congregation. Thus a novel rationale was utilized to justify rebuilding: to "secure to the *Methodist Episcopal Church forever* that sacred spot, toward which converge all pleasing recollections of early Methodism."[57]

New Yorkers increasingly remembered their past in the second quarter of the nineteenth century as urban development erased the city's older fabric. The series "Antiquities of New York" in the *New-York Mirror* (1827) regaled readers with stories about New Amsterdam and original Dutch buildings standing in the city.[58] *A Familiar Conversational History of the Evangelical Churches of New-York* used the loss of several churches in the December 1835 fire as an occasion to narrate a history of New York's Protestant churches. The book's narrator pitted himself against "the spirit of enterprise and innovation," which "utterly regardless of the veneration with which they used to be looked upon, with a ruthless hand, has swept away all traces of many of these buildings."[59] In a similar vein, the John Street meetinghouse came to be venerated not simply as a physical place but as a "sacred spot," the birthplace of North American Methodism. It was a memory constructed around "ordinary" women and men, like Barbara Heck, Philip Embury, Captain Webb, and Peter Williams Sr. "Its first disciples had no name, no rank, no means, no scholarship, no power, no human credentials," one historian concluded in 1858. "It was introduced by a few poor, unknown, and unnoticed emigrants."[60]

Joseph Beekman Smith did more than any of his contemporaries to shape the memory of New York Methodism. Born in New York City in 1796, Smith grew up in a pious family that worshipped at John Street. His father was a class leader, local preacher, and longtime member of the board of trustees who played a key role in the decision to rebuild the second and third meetinghouses. His brothers William and Peter published one of the first histories of New York Methodism, to which Joseph contributed an image of

FIGURE 7.5 Self-portrait of Joseph Beekman Smith, reproduced from John Kouwenhoven, *The Columbia Historical Portrait of New York City* (Doubleday, 1953), 62

the original meetinghouse.[61] Better known today for his marine paintings, Smith created iconic images of the three John Street meetinghouses (figs. 7.1, 7.3, and 7.4) and several other sites related to Methodism's past.[62] They provide some of the best-documented, if heavily romanticized, images we have of these early structures. His paintings, perhaps the most famous being a large canvas of the original meetinghouse on display in the church's museum today, gloss over tensions within the meetinghouse and denomination in order to construct a usable, harmonious past for nineteenth-century Methodists.[63] That said, Smith likely believed in some sense in the "truthfulness" of his representations. His undated self-portrait (fig. 7.5) reveals just how integral Methodism in general and John Street in particular were to his identity. He filled the image with symbols of his craft, his political leanings, and his religious identity. On an easel to his left, in the center of the room, is one of his paintings of the original meetinghouse, for the world to see.

As the third meetinghouse opened in late April 1841, the congregation faced the future with guarded optimism, but few underlying issues had actually been resolved. The shifting residential landscape of the city continued to lure audiences traditionally attracted to Methodism northward, commercial expansion gladly snapped up their properties, and those who lived in the neighborhood were not, by and large, interested in the version of the gospel John Street had to offer. Even more painfully, Methodists realized that their whittling away at Methodism's hierarchical structures of authority offered no guarantee of harmony. In fact, they might have made things worse.

THE RIOT, JULY 25, 1856

Pressure to sell the third John Street meetinghouse intensified over the 1850s and finally came to a head a late July evening in 1856. Moving uptown had become a common occurrence for downtown evangelical congregations by this point; rioting over that decision, less so. The preceding fifteen years had seen New York's economy come roaring back and its population swell, but at John Street, membership numbers dwindled, flanking rental properties provided more headaches than income, and the surrounding neighborhood population exhibited little interest in its message. In resolving what to do next, the church was in no better position to effect consensus than ever before, despite having spent the past ninety years addressing questions of authority and power within the denomination. When negotiations broke down, the congregation, uncharacteristically, resorted to violence.

Once the recession following the Panic of 1837 lifted, the city's commercial trade, banking, and industrial sectors moved quickly to reclaim national dominance. By 1849, more than three thousand ships annually sailed or steamed into New York harbor from 150 different foreign ports, three times the number that arrived before the panic. The waterfront was segmented—the East River for Liverpool packets and clipper ships, the North River for deeper-draw coastal and transatlantic steamships—to accommodate this vast commerce. The California Gold Rush propelled the city to become a national banking center that provided depositories for six hundred of the nation's seven hundred commercial banks. It also became the nation's manufacturing center through the massing of small firms (employing under one hundred people) rather than by investing in large mills, as was done in Lowell and Manchester. The outcome of these developments was mixed: they brought vast wealth to the city but also exacerbated the social divide. Occasionally the economy trembled, as it did in 1853, but New Yorkers' faith in the market kept them from anticipating the massive collapse that came the year after the John Street riot.[64]

The scale and scope of immigration changed dramatically in the 1840s and '50s. New York had nearly 630,000 residents in 1855, twice as many as in 1840, solidifying its place as the most populous city in the United States. (Five years later it reached 813,000 inhabitants.) Foreign immigration, driven by famine in Ireland and the failure of political revolution in Germany, accounted primarily for this massive growth. The city's Irish population grew from an estimated 70,000 in 1845 to 204,000 in 1860—one-quarter of the entire city's population. The city's German population grew by an even greater margin, from 24,416 in 1845 to 118,292 in 1860.[65] Significant numbers of native-born immigrants moved to the city each year as well, but the pull of opportunities elsewhere, especially in the West, diminished their overall gains. The only group not growing was African Americans. That community declined from 5.2 percent to 1.5 percent of the population and fell, in real numbers, from 16,358 to 12,574.[66]

As the economy boomed and the population increased, New Yorkers rushed up the island from 14th to 50th Streets to settle in new neighborhoods that church builders and residential developers laid out for them. Railroad lines proliferated, connecting downtown and uptown, as well as the city with Long Island, New Jersey, and upstate.[67] The midcentury urban landscape was increasingly segmented by class and function. Nathaniel Parker Willis reflected in 1852 that Bleecker Street had become a line of social division. Above Bleecker emerged a primarily residential zone for middle- and upper-class families.[68] Below Bleecker, once mixed-use neighborhoods gave way to either commercial or industrial interests. Genteel mansions and townhouses devolved into ramshackle and dangerous tenements as more prosperous inhabitants moved north. New York writers gave this class segmentation a moral valence. In works with titles like *Sunshine and Shadow in New York*, they referred to the city as being actually two cities or, with decidedly ethnic and religious overtones, two nations. In their telling, the sun typically shined down on middle-class Protestant neighborhoods to the north, while shadows disproportionately fell over Roman Catholic and Jewish neighborhoods to the south.[69]

The John Street congregation felt these economic, demographic, and geographic developments acutely. The booming economy accelerated the encroachment of commercial properties. An 1857 insurance map reveals nearly every structure on the block other than the church had been rebuilt as either a brick or a stone store. (The one exception is identified as a "second-class industrial structure" that most likely housed a printer or bookbinder.)[70] In contrast, residential housing surrounded one of the city's newest Methodist meetinghouses, Trinity Methodist Episcopal Church (1856) on West 34th Street near Eighth Avenue.[71] The flanking commercial rental properties from the 1841 rebuilding did not prove as profitable as hoped. Within less than a decade the trustees tried to sell them, with the church even serving as the mortgager for one of the purchasers. Regrettably, he soon defaulted.[72]

Even with the massive population influx of the time, John Street could not find sufficient numbers of new members to replace those who moved away. The decision to rebuild and a revival in 1841 revitalized the congregation, which grew from 260 in 1839 to 419 in 1843, but the gains proved temporary.[73] The congregation settled into decline over the next fifteen years. The number of class meetings—weekly gatherings for prayer, exhortation, and the sharing of testimonials for members of the church in good standing—decreased from fourteen in 1848 to eight in 1854.[74] By 1856, John Street reported only 134 members to the New York Conference, half the number it had when the trustees decided to rebuild in 1839.[75]

New residents of the district displayed little interest in taking the place of the departed. Most were recently landed Catholic and Jewish immigrants, two communities who were never much of a target audience for Methodists.[76] The trustees of John Street acknowledged this reality. A petition submitted to the State Supreme Court in May 1855 by a faction in favor of selling the meetinghouse argued that the neighborhood was now "in the proportion of 150 Catholic families to 10 of all other sects."[77] An article in the *New York Herald* a year later lamented the upcoming sale of the nearby Brick Presbyterian Church and echoed the sentiment about the changing neighborhood. Much of the area had turned commercial it argued, but "here and there, in cellars and garrets, there remains a pretty considerable sprinkling of Irish, French, Spanish, Italian and Dutch tenants, shoeless, perhaps, but with souls to be saved."[78] To minister to these new non-Protestant neighbors required the John Street Methodists to change their approach, message, and strategy from that of a neighborhood church to an urban mission.

Ongoing segmentation and diversification of the city's spiritual marketplace also worked against John Street. The city added more than 110 new houses of worship between 1840 and 1855, a rate of increase still strong but slower than the previous period (see table A.2 in the appendix). Every year the number of attractive new uptown churches increased, providing plenty of destinations for the remaining congregants. Twelve out of eighteen new Methodist congregations initiated between 1840 and 1860 were uptown (see map 7.1). Methodists relied on established strategies to found new churches: they focused on areas recently opened for settlement, started out in domestic and commercial rental properties, and built meetinghouses as the nucleus of new neighborhoods. The location of new churches can be used to track the northern edge of settlement. By the middle of the 1850s, they could be found on 34th Street and Eighth Avenue (Trinity Methodist Episcopal Church, 1856) and 37th Street between Second and Third Avenues (Thirty-Seventh Street Methodist Episcopal Church, 1854). By the end of the decade, they hosted a class meeting in the old Beekman Mansion on 51st Street (later the 50th Street Church), supported a minister who preached on the second floor of a frame building at the corner of 58th and Eighth Avenue (later St. John's), and had a frame church on 50th Street just west of Third Avenue (the Lexington Avenue Church).[79] The pace of urban growth stymied Methodist desire for systematic coverage, but by 1860, they had planted at least one and typically two congregations in each of the wards north of 14th Street.[80]

Other Protestant denominations shared the Methodists' uptown strategy. Equally overwhelmed, evangelical denominations concentrated their energies on the west side from Washington Square to 57th Street. Baptists opened twice as many, and Presbyterian six times as many, new churches on the west side as they did on the east. While Methodists and Baptists shied away from Fifth Avenue, Presbyterians did not.[81] By the late 1850s, a traveler moving northward up the elite thoroughfare would have passed First Presbyterian (1846) on the corner of 12th Street, Fifth Avenue Presbyterian (1852) on the corner of 19th Street, Madison Square Presbyterian (1855) on the corner of 24th Street, and Brick Presbyterian (1858) on the corner of 37th Street.[82] Episcopalians, who added more churches than any other

MAP 7.1 Map of the city's different houses of worship, 1856, by Dennis McClendon

denomination between 1840 and 1860, opened three on Fifth Avenue during this time. They focused their efforts, however, on the east side of the city between 20th and 40th Streets.[83] By 1860, there were more than one hundred Protestant churches north of 10th Street, where there had been less than a dozen before 1840.

The number of downtown churches focused entirely on mission work to nontraditional audiences also increased, reminding John Street Methodists of the future reality in that part of the city. In 1841, Methodists opened a German mission in a hired house on the corner of Essex and Stanton Streets and received sufficient encouragement to build a church on East 2nd Street the following year. In 1844, they opened the Mariner's Methodist Episcopal Church on Cherry Street near Rutgers Place. Efforts at converting sailors and members of the maritime community expanded the following year with two more initiatives: an old packet ship was purchased, fitted up as a place of worship, named the Bethel Ship John Wesley, and moored at the foot of Rector Street; and a Sunday school was opened over a lager-beer saloon on 10th Street between Avenues B and C in the Dry Dock neighborhood.[84] The Second German Methodist Episcopal Mission on Eighth Avenue and 38th Street opened in 1843, but it proved the exception to the locative strategies for this cohort of missions. By the 1850s, the New York Conference minutes reported other missions, but they did not result in the building of meetinghouses.[85] The initiative for most of these missions came from lay organizations, like the Asbury Society and the Ladies' Home Missionary Society, rather than from the conference or individual congregations.

Methodists entered an already crowded missionary field. The Reformed Dutch and, to a lesser extent, Presbyterians and Protestant Episcopalians, initiated missions to German immigrants beginning in the mid-1830s.[86] Organized attempts to convert sailors dated back even earlier to Henry Chase's nondenominational Mariner's Church (1819), but after 1840 all evangelical denominations scrambled to set up their own missions. This included two floating mission chapels for sailors, docked on either side of the island, as well as open-air preaching at Coenties Slip and a land-based mission on Pearl Street initiated by low church Episcopalian missionary societies.[87] While Presbyterians were the most active workers in the mission field in the 1820s and '30s, that honor went to Protestant Episcopalians in the 1840s. Under the auspices of their City Mission Society and subsidiary groups, they founded missions aimed at not only Germans and sailors but also French, British, and Jewish residents; inaugurated urban missions at Forsyth Street,

Astor Place, and Madison Street, as the Methodists had done in Five Points; and even opened free churches, returning to a form widely experimented with in the 1830s.[88]

Finally, for the first time, Methodists had strong competition from non-Protestant quarters. The number of Catholic churches rose from 10 to 24 and Jewish synagogues from 3 to 17 between 1840 and 1860. Even more alarming for evangelicals was the number of women and men who reported worshipping "on a regular basis" in these churches. According to the 1855 state census, more than 100,000 New Yorkers identified as attending the city's Catholic churches as opposed to 64,835 attending evangelical ones. That left, roughly, one house of worship for every 450 evangelicals as opposed to one for every 4,000 Catholics. Even accounting for the potential problems with these numbers, Catholic churches were bursting at the seams while evangelical churches had plenty of space in the pews.[89]

The trustees and congregation of John Street knew their future in that location bore more resemblance to a downtown mission than an uptown neighborhood church, even if they chose not to admit it. Scores of other downtown churches similarly faced commercial encroachment, declining membership, and a segmented landscape. Beginning in the early 1840s, the John Street trustees opted to sell off their properties and relocate to residential districts uptown. By the mid-1850s, what began as a trickle turned into a flood, leaving few Protestant churches—evangelical or otherwise—south of Chambers Street. Some congregations abandoned locations they had occupied for more than a century and a half.[90] Others sold off expensive houses of worship less than two decades old.[91] The prices offered were tempting. The City Intelligence column in the April 29, 1856, edition of the *New York Herald* announced that the Brick Presbyterian Church, in a desirable location fronting City Hall Park, would be auctioned off with a starting bid of $225,000. "The property is now likely to be more available for commercial uses than (owing to the disappearance of dwellings in that once aristocratic neighborhood) it has been for religious purposes for ten years past," the article noted. The *New York Times* purchased and razed the structure to erect its new headquarters.[92]

Typically the movement uptown was enacted not only through a spatial relocation but also a stylistic reinvention. Evangelical churches shed the vernacular of the earlier period and built in styles that a previous generation would have found anathema for their worldly (or worse yet, "popish") overtones.[93] The Mulberry Street Church, for example, accepted an offer from St. Phillip's Protestant Episcopal Church to purchase its meetinghouse in October 1856. The Methodist congregation, which had always prided itself on its respect-

FIGURE 7.6 St. Paul's Methodist Episcopal Church, corner of Fourth Avenue and 22nd Street (opened 1857), in Matthew Simpson, ed., *Cyclopaedia of Methodism* (Philadelphia, 1878)

ability, purchased land on the corner of Fourth Avenue and 22nd Street in 1857 and erected a Methodist meetinghouse unlike anything previously seen in the city (fig. 7.6). While the structure's three-bay, two-and-a-half story form echoed the evangelical vernacular, its massive steeple was a stunning departure. In this structure the congregation not only abandoned the traditional Methodist brand but also renamed themselves St. Paul's, the first time a New York City Methodist church bore the name of a saint.[94]

Churches that held out the longest downtown found themselves required to defend their decision to move uptown. Once one of the city's largest and most important evangelical congregations, the Broadway Tabernacle Church, on the corner of Broadway and Worth, finally relented, sold its premises, and prepared to move up to 34th Street and Sixth Avenue in the spring of 1857. Joseph Thompson, the church's minister, justified the decision in his last sermon at the Tabernacle. Taking as his text Genesis 12:7–8, he explained that like Abraham they must worship God with a movable, not a fixed, altar. The Tabernacle had pitched its tent on Broadway in the 1830s, but now was the time to move to a more eligible site. He pointed to the loss of more than six hundred congregants by dismissal to other churches since 1840 and the decisions of the "more than twenty churches, of various denominations, [that] have within a few years removed from below the Tabernacle to points higher up town."[95] To drive the point home, he listed them in a footnote. Thompson did not think much of John Street's long-term chances, noting "the attempt to remove the John st Methodist Church, has been *temporarily* over-ruled by the Court" [emphasis added].[96]

By the mid-1850s, whether or not to move uptown remained an unsettled and highly contentious question at John Street. Neither the decision to rebuild in 1841 nor the shift in oversight from the New York Conference to its own board of trustees had made decision making any easier. Issues of authority continued to plague the church despite its having grown more democratic in response to challenges from below. Instead, one form of power struggle replaced another. Where Methodists once bristled at the authoritarian decision making of a centralized board of trustees, their concern shifted in the 1850s to the board of trustees elected by their own male members. The trustees' journal reveals that the board actively considered selling the church and purchasing land uptown for a new structure several times over these two decades. Each time, they failed to reach consensus.[97]

Tensions came to a head in May 1855 when a faction of the board of trustees submitted to the State Supreme Court a petition asking for permission to sell the church property and move uptown.[98] As the petition wended its way through the courts, congregants who favored remaining in situ forced a showdown at the August election of new trustees. "After the meeting had been organized for about twenty minutes, and no manifestation of opposition being obvious during that short period," an article in the *New York Daily Times* reported, "the Trustees who were in favor of *moving up town* split off from the meeting and organized another in the same room, producing some confusion." The regular meeting continued, and trustees were elected. But the uptown faction elected its own set of trustees. "There are, therefore, two distinct sets of Trustees." With more than a hint of understatement, the article concluded, "The Church is not through its troubles yet."[99]

The State Supreme Court initially ruled in favor of the uptown contingent, but the downtown faction successfully secured an injunction that restrained sale of the church property, so the court sent the case to arbitration.[100] In an ironic move, the court referred the local church matter back to the authority of the national denomination's highest body. Matthew Simpson, one of the bishops of the Methodist Episcopal General Conference was asked to arbitrate.[101] By April 1856, Simpson reaffirmed the original petition that granted the uptown faction the right to sell the church. The court upheld Simpson's judgment the same month.[102] Throughout, the board of trustees who wanted to stay downtown entrenched themselves even more.

In a last-ditch effort to save the meetinghouse, female congregants, a segment excluded from the church's formal power structures, turned their exclusion into an advantage. On the Monday before the Friday riot, several women members took possession of the church. Among them was Mary McPherson, a fifty-six-year-old widow who had been a member of John Street for "a great many years." Unlike their husbands, brothers, and sons, McPherson and the congregation's other female members had not been served with the recent injunction that allowed the board of trustees to close the church.[103] In a month's time a new election of trustees was scheduled to take place. The downtown faction hoped to muster enough votes to outnumber the uptown faction, but that election would not take place if the uptown faction successfully closed the church.[104] With the goal of keeping the church open, no matter what, McPherson and several unlikely activists occupied the structure. She was a formidable opponent. "Strong in her convictions and very decided in her preferences, it was not easy for her to yield to the wishes of others," her obituary recalled.[105] Before long, the secular press caught wind of the downtown contingent's action. "These women have accordingly remained in the church night and day since the commencement of the serious difficulty—keeping the doors and windows secured against any ordinary means of ingress," the *New York Daily Tribune* reported.[106] Soon, however, McPherson and the other occupiers found themselves in the middle of a serious confrontation.

Throughout the standoff, the willingness of uptown and downtown factions to resort to the court of public opinion in secular newspapers to make their cases circumvented a more traditional reliance on denominational and religious publications. New York City dailies assiduously documented the details of the tensions at John Street and provide much of what we know about the incident. Details of these tensions made good fodder for sensational news stories, but in many ways they reflected the painful shortcomings of the empire of evangelical print launched over the previous half-century. Religious newspapers, by and large, chose not to air the grievances of these two factions. Such squabbling within the "birthplace of Methodism" in America was embarrassing for the nation's largest evangelical denomination. Religious newspapers sought to instill confidence in their national audiences, not introduce doubt. And to that point, the national evangelical press at midcentury favored silence on contentious topics, such as slavery, in the name of community cohesion and peace. As the religious press grew more concerned about preserving a specific image of evangelicalism, the secular press gladly documented all the messy details.

The riot turned out to be a single-day event, to everyone's relief, but the occupation and the litigation continued for years. Only in early 1858 was the issue of the rightful possessor of the third meetinghouse finally decided, much in reverse of the drift of earlier litigation. In an agreement worked out between representatives of the uptown and downtown factions, the John Street meetinghouse was preserved in its original location. It was to be sold to the Local Preachers Association of the Methodist Episcopal Church of New York and Brooklyn, a move that acknowledged the future function of the meetinghouse not as the home to a settled neighborhood congregation but as a preaching station serving varied audiences. Those in search of a congregation in keeping with John Street's original purpose were invited to join a proposed new church up on 24th Street. Much of the agreement involved dismissing the flurry of suits and countersuits that each side had instituted over the previous few years and settling on who would be responsible for the substantial legal bills the fight had incurred.[107] Ninety years after the Methodists built their first meetinghouse in North America on John Street, they had (once again) committed to remaining on that site in perpetuity, even if they were unclear if they would have a congregation to serve.

LOOKING BACKWARD, LOOKING FORWARD

"Old John Street Church is a hallowed place," Methodist historian J. B. Wakeley wrote in 1858, echoing sentiments expressed by the church's trustees two decades earlier; "It bears the same relation to American Methodism that Plymouth Rock, Faneuil Hall, and Independence Hall do to this country. . . . We venerate John-street Church as the *mother of us all*, the mother of numerous and thrifty children."[108] But children do not always get along with their mothers, as the previous ninety years demonstrated. While the writer covering the 1856 riot for the *New York Dispatch* believed that tensions within the congregation were of recent origin—"a congregation true and tried, whom Belzebub could not divide, / till some of them o'er wealthy grew and moved up on Fifth Avenue"—the opposite was the case. The egalitarian message of Methodism, which caused it to be such a vibrant urban faith and had made it attractive to so many New Yorkers—regardless of division of gender, race, and class—was perpetuated by an inegalitarian leadership structure. Peter Williams Sr., William Stilwell, and Mary McPherson knew well the gap between Methodism's promise and reality. But at the end of the 1850s, John Street Methodist Episcopal Church remained on the same plot of downtown land Methodists had purchased ninety years earlier.

All of the city's denominations, evangelical and otherwise, looked away from John Street toward the northern edge of urban settlement on the eve of the Civil War. The announcement in 1857 of the opening of a new Central Park only confirmed their long-held strategies. Church builders and residential developers rushed to place themselves near this new landmark. On the west side stood the North West Presbyterian Church (1855), the Central Park Baptist Church (1857), and St. Timothy's Protestant Episcopal Church (1860). On the east side, New Yorkers found the Lexington Avenue Methodist Episcopal Church (1846) and a Methodist class meeting that began in the Beekman Mansion in 1860. Right in the center, taking up a whole block on the east side of Fifth Avenue between 50th and 51st Streets, arose a new St. Patrick's Roman Catholic Cathedral. Formerly located downtown near Five Points, St. Patrick's uptown location announced that the city's Irish Catholic population had arrived just as much as their Protestant competitors. The structure took twelve years to finish (1858–1870); upon completion it overshadowed all the others.

In the midst of all of this, the John Street meetinghouse found itself a shrine, a landlord, a church without a congregation, and a mission station among non-English speaking and largely non-Protestant immigrant populations. Each role reflected a different deal made to keep open that "sacred spot" in lower Manhattan. Methodists could not complain about the circumstances that landed them in this situation because they were complicit in them. Evangelical engagement with the modernizing city played a direct role in the development of the city. As challengers to establishment faiths, evangelicals laid the groundwork for a rich and competitive spiritual marketplace and then faced the challenge of competing with other faiths in that marketplace. As builders of churches and communities, they provided an important engine of urban expansion that saw hundreds of churches slowly advance northward up a systematic and later segmented landscape. Finally, and perhaps most important, as purveyors of a popular religious movement that privileged both the individual, through the creation of a personal relationship with God through conversion, and the community, by championing social activism, evangelicals helped thousands of New Yorkers mediate the often overwhelming experience of being Christian in a modernizing city. Moving north came to be a significant component of that experience at midcentury.

Refusing to cede the field, Methodists adapted, as evangelicals had always done, and developed new strategies for their lone downtown congregation. Within a month of the announcement of the settlement, city newspapers buzzed about a revival that brought an often absent demographic—businessmen—into the church in droves. During what came to be known as the Revival of 1857–58, John Street happily opened its doors to these new worshippers for midday prayer meetings.[109] But on the Sabbath, these men worshipped back uptown near their residences. Realizing these businessmen were not enough to sustain the church permanently, the trustees eventually hired professional missionaries. In 1863, Brother Joiner served as colporteur, an evangelical term for a professional tract distributor and missionary, to the local neighborhood. A few years later, Sister Cornelia Hill, one of the first paid professional female Protestant missionaries in New York, replaced Joiner. Hill tended to be more direct in her estimations of her prospects. "As a general rule," she reported, "I have passed by the Irish Catholics whom there are very many in my district," noting that she could not "command the time to visit them without neglecting others who are far more likely to be influenced by my efforts." Hill was more realist than pessimist. In words that could have been uttered by Barbara Heck a century earlier, Hill reminded John Street's leadership in 1866 that "the Harvest-time, though certain, is yet a long way off."[110] The John Street Methodists continue to strive for that harvest today.

CONCLUSION

What Hath God Wrought?

Bird's-eye views of New York, like John Bornet's *Panorama of Manhattan Island* (fig. C.1), first appeared in the middle decades of the nineteenth century at a point when the city could no longer be comprehended from the vantage of a ship in the harbor or the banks of Brooklyn or Hoboken. New artistic genres, like new cities, require new conventions of representation.[1] Bornet embraced a totalizing view, assuming an all-encompassing eye to see as only God could. A forest of impossibly tall church steeples serve as markers of religious achievement and reminders of the spiritual marketplace's northward advance alongside residential and commercial development. With a more subtle hand, Bornet depicted sunshine shimmering over some parts of the city while shadows fall heavily over others. The heaviest shadows are reserved for Five Points and the tenement districts of the East and Hudson River waterfronts, areas of longstanding missionary concern. It is unknown whether John Bornet identified as evangelical, but his *Panorama* certainly evokes the question asked by John Street Methodists over the mantle of their second meetinghouse, merchant Divie Bethune in his private diary, minister and inventor Samuel F. B. Morse on discovering the secret to modern communication, and countless other awe-inspired nineteenth-century evangelical New Yorkers: "What hath God wrought?"[2]

Any assessment of the achievements of God's urban mortal intermediaries at midcentury must begin with the acknowledgment that they occurred over eight decades in a city with a greater reputation for sin than piety. Evangelical Gotham emerged with the arrival of women and men from around the Atlantic World in the postrevolutionary city. A spiritual marketplace formed

FIGURE C.1 John Bornet, *Panorama of Manhattan Island, City of New York and Environs*, 1854, lithograph, 25¼ × 38¼ inches, neg. #51371, New-York Historical Society. Photography © New-York Historical Society

on a novel set of rules awaited them. They created communities around a burgeoning number of Baptist, Methodist, Presbyterian, and other denominations' meetinghouses before turning, with halting, tentative steps, into the city to help the needy in their midst. Brimming with confidence after the War of 1812, benevolent voluntary associations initiated urban missions, Sunday schools, seamen's bethels, Free churches, and other innovative ventures to share the gospel with overlooked audiences. National organizations printed tracts, Bibles, and denominational newspapers and distributed them across the city, throughout the country, and around the world. The turbulent 1830s tested the limits of their acceptance of reform and saw a financial panic wipe away their most engaged supporters' resources. Many found themselves increasingly torn between the inward needs and outward demands of their faith. Yet evangelical New Yorkers remained unwavering in their desire to foster a vibrant religious community in the heart of the city, even in the face of a tidal wave of non-Protestant immigration, an exodus of native-born

Protestants up the island, and the election of a Republican president whose abhorrence of slavery threatened to tear the nation asunder.

New York continued its unprecedented growth between 1860 and 1900, a cataclysmic civil war notwithstanding. The outbreak of hostilities in 1861 exacerbated economic, political, and cultural tensions simmering for decades as a result of the city's extensive commercial, social, and cultural ties to the South. Initial fervor for the war quickly cooled, even as the city's industries profited. When the nation's new draft law went into effect in mid-July 1863, the city's long-maligned African American community once again bore the brunt of hostility over four days of riots. Relentless expansion resumed after the war. It was facilitated by the lure of Central Park and the lurch of an elevated mass-transit system. Spectacular new bridges spanned the waters to Brooklyn, the Bronx, and Queens, hastening the development of suburbs. Cast-iron "cathedrals of commerce" competed with the steeples of the few remaining downtown churches.[3] Women and men flowed into the city from Ireland, Germany, and, after 1880, southern and eastern Europe. Too poor to keep moving, they piled into tenements that neither state legislation nor reform movements could curtail. And then, in 1898, New York became the second largest city in the world, just after London, when it incorporated the five surrounding boroughs. New York greeted the twentieth century with 3.4 million residents, 1.85 million of them on the island of Manhattan. Chicago and St. Louis might have grown at a faster rate during this period, but they could not challenge New York's economic, commercial, and cultural supremacy.[4]

Evangelical Gotham continued to grow and develop alongside the city, although it did so in a far more crowded spiritual marketplace. Evangelical church building followed the systematic grid as residential development rolled northward from the base of Central Park. Downtown locations were shuttered and turned over to missions or, more likely, non-Protestant congregations. John Street had saved itself by appealing to its past as a rationale for its future; few others opted to do the same. Evangelical New Yorkers had more churches to choose from in terms of absolute numbers and denominational variety by the turn of the twentieth century than ever before, but their share of the marketplace shrank. Baptist, Congregational, Methodist, and Presbyterian churches accounted for only 27 percent of the houses of worship listed in a 1901 city directory. Congregations of Roman Catholics (14 percent of the marketplace) and Jews (a staggering 28 percent) staked their competing claims.[5] Rather than retreating, evangelical New Yorkers were reinvigorated by this profusion of faiths. Variety stimulated growth rather than turning people away.[6]

In the face of change, evangelicals innovated, as they had always done. To give but three examples: When uniformed members of the Salvation Army marched down the gangplank of the steamer *Australia* at Castle Garden in mid-March 1880, they prepared to do battle with the forces of evil in the city. Few could miss the stirring brass, drums, and tambourines or the catchy hymns of the martial organization, no matter how hard they tried. A generation later, the Abyssinian Baptist Church, which had long struggled in dilapidated downtown structures, opened a massive new Gothic- and Tudor-style church in Harlem that could accommodate and serve thousands. Not only had the city's African American evangelicals finally arrived socially and financially but also politically when they sent their pastor, Adam Clayton Powell Jr., off to the US House of Representatives in 1945, the first person of African American descent from New York to be elected to Congress. And between mid-May and September 1957, Billy Graham filled Madison Square Garden for an urban revival in which nearly two million took part. Graham might have publicly castigated New York City as "Sodom on the Subway," but he owed his success to the social, organizational, and commercial persistence of Evangelical Gotham.[7]

Throughout, evangelical New Yorkers navigated Gotham with a genuinely popular and fundamentally modern urban religion. Individual feelings of isolation and anomie remained a constant for those who crossed into New York, but so, too, was the web of evangelical meetinghouses, missions, voluntary associations, asylums, and orphanages waiting to offer support. As denominational and sectarian choices proliferated, evangelicalism's appeal lay in the ease with which its small core of common principles could be incorporated into the matrix of beliefs and practices provided by them. Theologians as diverse as Ward Stafford, Charles Grandison Finney, and Phoebe Palmer offered important interventions that empowered women and men to engage actively with their surroundings rather than depend on an all-powerful God. Urban evangelicalism was formed, adapted, and negotiated just as much in the city's streets, parlors, and countinghouses as in its churches. In time, New York became more religiously plural, rabidly democratic, commercially oriented, ethnically diverse, and technologically advanced; in other words, it became more *modern*. Evangelical clergy and laity embraced this world, even as Roman Catholic clergy, under the powerful Bishop John Hughes and his successors, turned the tide of American Catholicism toward a more hierarchical, autocratic, and reflexive faith.[8] Evangelical New Yorkers were active improvisers, not passive receivers of the Word.

New Yorkers built Evangelical Gotham by putting the economic, social, and technological resources of the city to work for them. They dispensed with long-held notions of sacred space, freeing them up to utilize such diverse places as storefronts, stables, and ships' decks for worship. They designed their meetinghouses in a distinctive vernacular, alerting the city's perpetually transient population to their presence through an innovative form of branding. Commercial organizational models helped them rethink the age-old problem of funding their distribution of the Word, whether through preaching from the pulpits of Free churches or supplying tract and Bible society colporteurs with free publications. Armed with Bibles, empowered by conviction, and marshaled by voluntary associations, men and, more often, women spread out across the city. At the height of their power they achieved universal access to the urban population. Early adoption of the newest technologies of production and distribution gave them an edge in their goals.

As evangelical New Yorkers remade their own lives, they sought to remake the lives of their neighbors. They ventured into dark alleys, cramped garrets, and damp basements in search of the unconverted. They preached and visited in public institutions and later founded their own institutions to support those buffeted by the city's commercial and moral economies. Following the War of 1812, a plethora of reforms—temperance, Sunday schools, colonization, antislavery, and more—were acted upon by an expanding number of voluntary associations. New audiences—such as prostitutes and sailors—were sought out and met on their own turf. But at the height of their effort to reform the city, evangelicals confronted their limits. Urban reform required confidence and money, both of which were in shortened supply after the Panic of 1837. National organizations remained, although increasingly battered by sectional disagreement over antislavery. Many fell silent on the issue altogether. The face of reform changed as professional missionaries assumed work once undertaken by the laity. Rhetoric often outpaced reality: Protestants tended to focus on those with whom they felt the greatest chance for success.

Evangelical New Yorkers did nothing less than make the city between the American Revolution and the Civil War. Their systematic strategy of aggressively building in newly opening neighborhoods put them on the forward edge of urban development. (That willingness to expand to new neighborhoods also led them to abandon entire areas of the city, something the shrinking congregation at John Street knew all too well.) Asylums, bethels, book concerns, missions, and orphanages supported by lay voluntary associations and denominations expanded that presence. In time, immigrant Roman Catholics and Jews proved more formidable opponents than High Church Protestant Episcopalians, but a community is more than its churches and societies; it is, fundamentally, its people. Fifteen percent of the city's adult population identified as evangelical and joined a city church by the middle of the nineteenth century. That might not sound like much, but it was five times what it had been at the close of the American Revolution. Given the high bar evangelical churches set by making conversion a criteria for membership, the number of spouses, children, cousins, and neighbors still hopefully waiting for conversion was undoubtedly much higher.

This massive emotional, financial, and spiritual investment in the city came at a cost. The principles at the core of evangelical belief and practice—individual conversion and community-focused social activism—exist in continual tension. They provided the rationale for aggressive interventions in the city, hope to the hopeless, friends for the friendless, and homes for the homeless, but just as easily supplied an excuse for withdrawal, into meetinghouses, parlors, and even their own spiritual selves at moments when their presence was most needed. Ezra Stiles Ely introduced a generation of New Yorkers to the needs of the poor and downtrodden in their midst through the published journals of his two years' residency in the almshouse and hospital, but he spent the remainder of his life in one of the plushest urban evangelical pulpits in Philadelphia. Lewis Tappan allowed his dedication to one of his great individual commitments—antislavery—to cause the downfall of his great social creation, the Free Church system. Phoebe Palmer called on her fellow New Yorkers to come to revival even as she provided them with the most persuasive rationale for focusing on their individual spiritual well-being. And every worshipper at the John Street church had to decide for her or himself whether to join the exodus of middle-class Protestants up the island or to stay put, even as nearly every other evangelical meetinghouse shuttered. These choices were not limited to the antebellum period; Evangelical Gotham always had been and always would be a profoundly ambivalent place.

Acknowledgments

My journey to Evangelical Gotham began more than a decade ago. The way was paved by caring mentors—Christine MacPherson, Ann Noyes, Susan Wood, Mary Ciccarelli, Carolyn Schindler, Charlie Gofen, Patricia Tracy, Regina Kunzel, and Jane Anderson Szele—who kindled in me the curiosity, confidence, and skills I needed to get there. In the ensuing years I have walked New York's streets, read its tracts, sat in its churches, and found myself in more than a few of its blind alleys. My journey has never been solitary, and I am profoundly grateful for that.

The journey began in Philadelphia, where I could not have asked for a more supportive set of guides than Robert Blair St. George, Daniel Richter, Michael Zuckerman, and Peter Stallybrass. Simultaneously traveling to other places and times were Rene Alvarez, Francesca Bregoli, Anne Casey, Tanya Gentic, Andrew Heath, Vanessa Mongey, Justine Murison, Katie Paugh, Sarah Klimenko Riedl, Brian Rouleau, Jennifer Schaaf, Laura Keenan Spero, Patrick Spero, and Sarah Van Beurden. I would never have gotten out of the gate without the support of Joan Plonski and the late Deborah Broadnax.

My search for the papers and material remains of evangelical New Yorkers took me to Gotham's leading repositories, as well as to others farther afield. I am especially indebted to Ted O'Reilly at the New-York Historical Society, Jason Radmacher at the John Street Methodist Episcopal Church, and Thomas Lannon at the New-York Public Library. I would not have been able to utilize these and other archives without the financial assistance of several grants and fellowships, including the Reese Fellowship from the American Antiquarian Society; a Short-Term Fellowship from the Gilder Lehrman

Institute of American History; an Andrew W. Mellon Foundation Fellowship from the Library Company; a Winterthur Fellowship from the Winterthur Museum, Garden & Library; a Research Fellowship from the Presbyterian Historical Society; and a Jacob Price Research Fellowship from the William L. Clements Library. For access to the reading room of Widener Library, where I wrote much of the first draft of this book, I thank Cheryl Souza, Kristen Blake, and the late Karl Liem.

I returned to the American Antiquarian Society for the 2007–2008 year as the Hench Fellow. Few institutions can rival the AAS for richness of its collections, staff, and community. Every curator and staff member at AAS has in some way shaped this work. Special thanks go to Caroline Sloat, Paul Erickson, Joanne Chaison, Laura Wasowicz, Vincent Golden, David Whitesell, Gigi Barnhill, Lauren Hewes, Ellen Dunlap, John Hench, Jaclyn Penny, Meg Bocian-Pellicane, and Nigel Gully. A New England ice storm could not keep Amanda Porterfield, Jon Butler, Randy Balmer, Robert Gross, and Margaretta Lovell from offering valuable advice on an early draft. Under the generous dome and within the Goddard Daniels House began what I expect to be lifelong friendships with Ted Andrews, Jeanne DeLombard, Stephen Marini, Marina Moskowitz, Simon Newman, Stacey Robertson, and Lily Santoro-Williams.

Journeys rarely follow the path we initially envision for them. A year at Georgetown University and two years at Dr. Williams's Centre for Dissenting Studies, a joint venture between Dr. Williams's Library and Queen Mary, University of London, introduced me to the urban religion of two new cities as I taught and pursued other projects. Tuesday evenings at the Auld Shillelagh with Ben Bankhurst, Sunday mornings at Wesley's City Road Chapel with Leslie Griffiths, and most days in between at the British Library with Rose Dixon gave my life structure, meaning, and enjoyment during my time in London. A series of workshops led by John Corrigan, David Bodenhamer, and Trevor Harris gave me new tools for digitally mapping the world I had uncovered.

In Chicago this journey came to completion. The Newberry Library has provided me with a research home for the past several years. The support and friendship of Christopher Cantwell, Diane Dillon, Kristin Emery, and Danny Greene have been much appreciated.

Colleagues and students at Loyola University Chicago—Robert Bucholz, John Donoghue, Timothy Gilfoyle, Jeffrey Glover, Elliott Gorn, Nathan Jeremie-Brink, Suzanne Kaufman, Nathan Matten, Patricia Mooney-Melvin, Prue Moylan, Michelle Nickerson, John Pincince, Stephen Schloesser, and

Elizabeth Tandy Shermer—have supported me in ways both large and small. Some ensured I had research money for final archival trips, others read drafts and offered valuable feedback, and a few have been constant companions at our weekly happy hour, where moral support flows as freely as the Berghoff's lager.

Throughout, I could always depend on my family back in the Boston area. My parents, Clayton and Barbara Roberts, have well fulfilled their role by posing the obligatory question at family dinners: "Is it done yet?" They are my best publicists and have even read some of the earlier drafts. A. J. and Megan Belisle and Logan and Nathan Scoponi have not, but the distraction they provide has been just as valuable.

Finally, I have had three steadfast companions without whom I could not have completed this book. From the back ell of the Allen house in Historic Deerfield to the front porch of a charming Dutch colonial in Columbus, Margaret Sumner has indulged my need to talk about what it meant to be religious in early America for over two decades. Nicole Maurantonio has read drafts of this book more times and more closely than anyone else, and somehow managed to muster enthusiasm for it even when I could not. And no matter how far afield I ventured, Crisostomo Gouveia has always been there, quietly supporting my work, resolving my computer crises, and enabling me not to have to learn how to drive a car with a manual transmission. Crossing and dwelling in Evangelical Gotham has been his lot as much as it has been mine, and somehow he's never complained. For these blessings and many more, I am eternally grateful.

Appendix

Historians of early American religion have long sought to quantify their subject matter. In 1846, a contemporary reviewer lauded Jonathan Greenleaf's *A History of the Churches, of All Denominations, in the City of New York* as a "statistical book" that "diligently" and "scrupulously" documented 217 extant, and 60 extinct, city churches (see table A.1). Greenleaf's efforts, the reviewer favorably commented, led to the recovery of the founding date of the city's first house of worship (1642) and to the revelation (to Protestant and Catholic readers at least) that New York was home to nine synagogues. Greenleaf went to great lengths to assure readers of the accuracy of his account, even including testimonials from leading clergymen representing fifteen different denominations. Presenting an objective history of New York's many faiths poses a challenge at any time, but especially so in the competitive antebellum spiritual marketplace.[1]

Historians of religion today continue to put their confidence in numbers. They seek proxies for abstract concepts like piety and power in numbers of congregations, communicants, and clergy. Finke and Stark's *The Churching of America* (1992; 2005) and Gaustad and Barlow's *New Historical Atlas of Religion in America* (2000) collect and analyze a monumental amount of data to explain why Americans have flocked to institutional religions as their cousins across the Atlantic have steadily fallen away.[2] Terry Bilhartz's pioneering study, *Urban Religion and the Second Great Awakening: Church and Society in Early National Baltimore* (1986), takes a similar approach on a local level. Bilhartz painstakingly gathers rarely used data from scores of church registers to create a demographic profile of Baltimore's churchgoers and clergy. From

TABLE A.1. Snapshot of New York's churches in June 1845

	No. of communicants	No. of active churches	No. of extinct churches
		Evangelical Protestant	
Baptist	8,744	31	15
Congregational	1,027	8	9
Methodist Episcopal	9,595	25	
Methodist Society	300	1	
African Methodist	2,445	7	
Methodist Protestant	220	2	
Primitive Methodist	n.d.	1	
Wesleyan Methodist	120	2	
German Evangelical Mission	60	1	
Welsh Methodist	105	1	
Moravian	120	1	
Presbyterian	11,428	28	21
Associate Reformed	430	5	
Associate	785	3	
Reformed	835	3	
Mariner's Church	n.d.		
Total	36,214	119	45
		Mixed Evangelical	
Protestant Episcopal	6,476	41	9
Reformed Dutch	4,773	16	3
Total	11,249	57	12
		Non-Evangelical Protestant	
Christian Church	n.d.	2	
Lutheran	n.d.	6	
Mormon	n.d.		
New Jerusalem	n.d.	2	
Quaker	n.d.	4	1
Second Adventist	n.d.		
Unitarian	n.d.	2	
Universalist	n.d.	4	2
Total		20	3
		Non-Protestant	
Roman Catholic	n.d.	16	
Jewish	n.d.	9	
Total		25	
		Total	
	47,463	221	60

Source: Jonathan Greenleaf, *A History of all the Churches of All Denominations, in the City of New York, from the First Settlement to the Year 1846* (New York: E. French, 1846)

Note: n.d. = no data

these numbers, he concludes that Baltimore might have had the highest percentage of church adherents of any antebellum American city.[3]

The fragmentary nature of surviving data presents a primary challenge to historians seeking to recover the empirical underpinnings of antebellum urban religion. Bilhartz likens the task to "piecing together a puzzle with two-thirds of the pieces marred and the remainder missing."[4] New York is no exception. Records of New Yorkers' religious activity survive in a variety of published and manuscript sources, but none are complete. Citywide and denominational histories provide valuable information but are susceptible to the biases of their authors.[5] City directories, published annually from the late eighteenth century onward, reveal the diversity of the urban spiritual landscape over time and space but are not always accurate. Manuscript and published denominational minutes preserve annual membership numbers, but not every congregation submitted data. State and federal censuses collect information on houses of worship and worshippers, but only toward the end of the period of this study.[6] Some churches published manuals or anniversary volumes, and all utilized manuscript ledgers for trustees, elders, deacons, and membership records. Locating those records today for the sixty congregations that Greenleaf reported extinct by 1846 is well nigh impossible. But for congregations that survived into the late nineteenth or early twentieth century, many can be found in national repositories or in the vaults and cupboards of churches.[7] Despite the odds, a surprising amount of material exists today.

What follows is an attempt to provide a broad outline of the data available for quantifying the experience of evangelicals specifically, and the religious more generally, in New York City between 1783 and 1860. More work remains to be done, but this is meant to be suggestive of what might be gleaned from such an approach.

CONGREGATIONS

New York City was home to one of early America's most plural spiritual marketplaces. Nineteenth-century historians liked to trace the city's embrace of pluralism back to Peter Stuyvesant's 1664 articles of capitulation, which secured liberty of conscience in divine worship and church discipline for Dutch residents who remained in the conquered city.[8] Religious freedom proved more symbolic than actual for some groups in the colonial city. Pluralism usually meant Protestant pluralism, and established Anglican and Reformed Dutch churches occasionally stymied the efforts of upstart

Presbyterians, Baptists, and Methodists. The American Revolution changed all this. The State Constitution of 1777 formalized pluralism in law when it granted all religious bodies—Protestant, Catholic, Jewish, and other—"a perfect parity of rights" and refused to "lay doctrinal restrictions upon civil freedoms, as did many other states." Additional legislation in 1784 allowed congregations to apply for incorporation. Rather than pragmatically accede to a new political reality, New Yorkers enthusiastically embraced pluralism, both intellectually and theologically. They believed that religion, across denominations, undergirded traditional morality and promoted the virtuous citizenry the new nation so desperately needed.[9] The diversity of the city's antebellum congregations spoke to their broad investment in this project.

Table A.2 reconstructs the number of congregations in New York City by denomination over five-year increments between 1785 and 1860. The nineteenth century saw the great rise of institutional religion as individual eighteenth-century churches and sects coalesced into national denominations.[10] Grouping into evangelical, mixed-evangelical, nonevangelical, and non-Protestant categories reflects each denomination's varying degrees of openness to the hallmarks of evangelicalism—conversion and social activism.[11]

The data reveals that evangelical congregations emerged from the margins to the center of the urban spiritual marketplace in the generation following the American Revolution. By 1815 they accounted for half of the city's congregations. Baptists, Methodists, and Presbyterians all witnessed dramatic growth in this period. The city's former established churches, the Reformed Dutch and the newly christened Protestant Episcopalians, remained steady with about a third of the churches in the marketplace. They had the advantage of greater wealth, larger structures, and more visible and accessible locations within the growing city. On the margins of the marketplace remained the city's handful of nonevangelical Protestant and non-Protestant faiths. In all, the number of houses of worship in the city nearly tripled. This is impressive given that the War of 1812 brought growth to a standstill and forced several congregations to close their doors.

With peace came the return of temporal and spiritual prosperity, ushering in twenty-five years (1815–1840) of evangelical supremacy. Evangelicals peaked in 1835 with 59 percent of the overall market share. Presbyterians enjoyed the greatest growth, increasing the number of their meetinghouses five-fold through aggressive and innovative proselytizing. Baptists and Methodists had slightly less impressive growth, with the latter splintering into a range of factions. Roman Catholics and Jews also greatly expanded the number of their congregations, but their share of the overall market remained

TABLE A.2. Number of congregations by denomination, New York City, 1785–1860

	1785	1790	1795	1800	1805	1810	1815	1820	1825	1830	1835	1840	1845	1850	1855	1860
	Evangelical Protestant															
Baptist	1	2	3	4	4	7	6	6	11	15	21	21	26	33	33	35
Congregational		1	1	1	2	4	1	3	3	2	1	5	8	9	9	4
Methodist Episcopal	1	2	2	4	4	6	6	7	7	10	16	16	27	29	33	32
Methodist Society								1	3	1	1	1	1	1	1	
African Methodist				1	1	1	2	3	3	4	4	4	4	3	5	5
Methodist Protestant										2	2	2	1	2	2	1
Primitive Methodist										1	3	3	1			
Wesleyan Methodist													2	1	1	4
Welsh Methodist					1					1	1	1	1	1	1	1
German Methodist																
Calvinistic Methodist																
Moravian	1	1	1	1	1	1	1	1	1	1	1	1	1	1	1	1
Presbyterian	2	2	2	3	3	5	6	10	20	21	32	30	33	35	39	43
Associate Reformed	1	1	1	2	2	2	3	3			1	2	2	2	5	1
Associate	1	1	1	1	1	1	1	1	1	2	2	3	2	4	4	6
Reformed				1	1	1	1	1	1	2	3	3	3	4	5	5
Mariner's Church								1	1	1	1	1	1		3	
Total	7	10	11	18	20	28	27	37	51	63	89	93	113	125	142	138
Percentage of whole	35%	43%	44%	51%	51%	51%	50%	54%	54%	54%	59%	56%	52%	53%	52%	49%
	Mixed Evangelical Protestant															
Protestant Episcopal	3	3	4	5	7	12	12	14	19	21	28	29	37	46	53	53
Reformed Dutch	5	5	5	5	5	7	7	8	11	13	13	16	17	17	22	23
Total	8	8	9	10	12	19	19	22	30	34	41	45	54	63	75	76
Percentage of whole	40%	35%	36%	29%	31%	35%	35%	32%	32%	29%	27%	27%	25%	27%	27%	27%

(continued)

TABLE A.2. *(continued)*

	1785	1790	1795	1800	1805	1810	1815	1820	1825	1830	1835	1840	1845	1850	1855	1860
	Non-Evangelical Protestant															
Christian Church										1	1	1	1	1	1	
Lutheran	1	1	1	2	2	2	1	1	2	2	2	2	3	3	3	5
Mormon													1			
New Jerusalem						1	1	1	1	1	1	1	2			
Quaker	2	2	2	2	2	2	2	2	2	3	4	4	4	4	4	3
Second Adventists													2		2	
Unitarian								1	1	2	2	2	2	2	2	3
Universalist				1	1	1	1	1	2	2	2	4	4	4	4	5
Total	3	3	3	5	5	6	5	6	8	11	12	14	19	14	16	16
Percentage of whole	15%	13%	12%	14%	13%	11%	9%	9%	9%	9%	8%	8%	9%	6%	6%	6%
	Non-Protestant															
Roman Catholic	1	1	1	1	1	1	2	2	3	5	7	10	17	19	24	32
Jewish	1	1	1	1	1	1	1	1	2	3	3	3	9	10	17	17
Total	2	2	2	2	2	2	3	3	5	8	10	13	26	29	41	49
Percentage of whole	10%	9%	8%	6%	5%	4%	6%	4%	5%	7%	7%	8%	12%	12%	15%	17%
	Other															
													4	6	1	2
	Totals															
Total no. of congregations in the city	20	23	25	35	39	55	54	68	94	116	152	165	216	237	275	281
Increase over previous five years		15%	9%	40%	11%	41%	−2%	26%	38%	23%	31%	9%	31%	10%	16%	2%

TABLE A.3. Congregation and population growth in New York City, 1785–1860

	1785	*1790*	*1795*	*1800*	*1805*	*1810*	*1815*	*1820*	*1825*	*1830*	*1835*	*1840*	*1845*	*1850*	*1855*	*1860*
Evangelical Protestant	7	10	11	18	20	28	27	37	51	63	89	93	113	125	142	138
Mixed Evangelical Protestant	8	8	9	10	12	19	19	22	30	34	41	45	54	63	75	76
Non-Evangelical Protestant	3	3	3	5	5	6	5	6	8	11	12	14	19	14	16	16
Roman Catholic	1	1	1	1	1	1	2	2	3	5	7	10	17	19	24	32
Jewish	1	1	1	1	1	1	1	1	2	3	3	3	9	10	17	17
Other													4	6	1	2
Total	20	23	25	35	39	55	54	68	94	116	152	165	216	237	275	281
Change		15%	9%	40%	11%	41%	–2%	26%	38%	23%	31%	9%	31%	10%	16%	2%
City population	23,610	33,131	n.d.	60,515	75,770	96,373	100,233	123,706	166,086	202,589	270,089	311,660	378,013	515,547	629,904	813,669
Change		40%		83%	25%	27%	4%	23%	34%	22%	33%	15%	21%	36%	22%	29%
Ratio of churches to people	1:1,181	1:1,441		1:1,729	1:1,943	1:1,752	1:1,856	1:1,819	1:1,767	1:1,746	1:1,777	1:1,889	1:1,750	1:2,175	1:2,290	1:2,895

miniscule at 8 percent. These years saw a proliferation of new religious groups as New York developed into what Jon Butler has described as an "antebellum spiritual hothouse."[12] Even more numerous were the spiritual figures, like the Prophet Matthias, who blew through town, never gathering a stable, permanent congregation.[13] The Panic of 1837 curtailed growth and forced a handful of churches, many of them Presbyterian, to close their doors. Despite this, the number of houses of worship in the city more than tripled during this time.

Over the two decades leading up to the Civil War (1840–1860), evangelicals saw their position within the city erode. By 1860, evangelical meetinghouses accounted for just under half of the spiritual marketplace. Methodists had doubled their number of houses of worship, but Baptists and Presbyterians grew at slower rates. Mixed-evangelical and nonevangelical faiths also lost ground. The real winners in the marketplace were Roman Catholics and Jews. European immigration changed the face of New York at midcentury. The number of Jewish synagogues grew almost six-fold while the number of Catholic churches more than tripled. In all, the non-Protestant market share increased to 17 percent. On the eve of the Civil War, New York's spiritual landscape looked much different than it did following the Revolution.

Correlating population and congregation growth reveals that only for the first four decades of the nineteenth century did the latter keep pace with the former (see table A.3). Immediately after the Revolution the ratio of meetinghouses to city residents rose from 1:1,181 (1785) to 1:1,729 (1800). The ratio hit a plateau between 1:1,750 and 1:1,900 for four decades before increasingly considerably from 1:2,175 (1850) to 1:2,895 (1860). By midcentury, the number of new arrivals simply overwhelmed the ability of denominations to keep up.[14] Even factoring in a general increase in meetinghouse size, and hence seating capacity, the city could not accommodate all its residents in available meetinghouses by 1860.[15]

MEMBERS

Ascertaining the number of men and women who joined these churches is complicated by the fact that eighteenth- and nineteenth-century denominations displayed little consensus over what constituted a church member. Protestant Episcopalians counted as communicants those who subscribed to the rite of confirmation, open to anyone baptized in the church and ready to join the body of believers.[16] Evangelical denominations, by and large, expected members to have and be willing to share, publicly or in private, their experience of conversion. For most Protestant denominations, church membership was typically for life and ended only with dismissal to another church or excommunication, a relatively uncommon practice. Methodists, however, calculated membership from weekly attendance in class meetings.[17] As a result, Methodist numbers show the greatest fluctuation over time but serve as the best indicator of the waxing and waning of devotion.

Scholars agree there were more nonmembers than members sitting in the pews each Sunday. "To classify as churched only those who were communicants or formal members, however defined, would eliminate many whom the clergy themselves counted as faithful adherents," argue Patricia Bonomi and Peter Eisenstadt.[18] Regular attendance, they propose, is a better indicator of adherence than application for membership. Typically, individuals attended worship with their families. Evidence that Reformed Dutch clergy saw families as the foundation of their congregations can be seen in published annual reports from the late 1810s. These reports list the number of families, total size of congregation, number in communion, as well as statistics on accessions and removals.[19] The number in communion in a particular congregation ranged anywhere from 10 to 78 percent of the reported number of congregants. While that percentage varied widely from church to church, it remained relatively stable within those churches over time.[20] Bilhartz seeks an even broader understanding of adherence and calculates churchgoing on the basis of "all individuals willing to allow one particular denomination to baptize, marry, or bury their immediate family members." Bilhartz's definition leads him to conclude that Baltimore's religious adherence approached 50 percent of the population by 1830.[21]

For the purposes of this study, I prefer a more conservative approach that focuses on the men and women who experienced conversion and formally joined churches. Recovering that number is at once an easy and a difficult task. New York's three leading evangelical denominations annually published statistics of their members (see table A.4). Vagaries of reporting within denominations and preservation within the archive make these numbers incomplete, but they do provide a sense of general trends.[22]

Membership activity in Baptist, Methodist, and Presbyterian congregations followed the same basic cycles of expansion and contraction as church building did between 1785 and 1860. Each denomination enjoyed a period of rapid growth immediately following the American Revolution that lasted through the War of 1812. Between 1815 and 1840, the number of members tripled as the number of congregations did. Fluctuations occurred within denominations as specific groups broke away from leading denominations.[23] Denominational data for the final period (1840–1860) is the most fragmentary,

TABLE A.4. Total number of reported members in New York's leading evangelical denominations, 1786–1860

	1786	*1790*	*1796*	*1800*	*1805*	*1810*	*1816*	*1820*
	Baptists							
Total	170	223	320	370	481	1,107	1,373	1,972[a]
Change		31%	43%	16%	30%	130%	24%	44%
	Methodists							
New York Conference (East and West after 1831)	203	624	786	776	940	2,200	2,572	2,528
Zion and Asbury (African Methodist Episcopal)								690
Harlem Churches								
Pewed Churches (Vestry St and Mulberry St)								
Total	203	624	786	776	940	2,200	2,572	3,218
Change		207%	26%	–1%	21%	134%	17%	25%
	Presbyterians							
First Presbytery					470	1,129	1,986	2,495
Second Presbytery								
Third Presbytery								
Total	n.d.	n.d.	n.d.	n.d.	470	1,129	1,986	2,495
Change						140%	76%	26%
	Other (Congregational, Moravian, Bethels)							
Total								
	Baptists, Methodists, and Presbyterians combined							
Total	373	847	1,106	1,146	1,891	4,436	5,931	7,685
Change		127%	31%	4%	65%	135%	34%	30%
	Roman Catholics							
Total								
	As compared to total population of New York							
Total adult population[b]		20,970		37,624		58,540		75,610
Evangelicals		4%		3%		8%		10%
Total population		[33,131]		[60,515]		[96,373]		[123,706]
Roman Catholics								

Sources: Baptist: *Minutes of the Philadelphia Baptist Association* (1784–1790), *New York Baptist Association* (1791–1819), *Warwick Baptist Association* (1791–1805), *Hudson River Baptist Association* (1816–1819); Methodist: *Minutes of the Annual Conferences of the Methodist Episcopal Church*, vols. 1–3 (New York: T. Mason and G. Lane, for the Methodist Episcopal Church, at the Conference Office, 200 Mulberry-Street, 1840–1845); Presbyterian: "Records of the Presbytery of New York, so far as they are extant, prior to the year 1810. Copied from the originals, in the possession of the Presbytery of Newark. By Order of the Presbytery of New York, October 1, 1847," "The Record," 1845 numbers from Jonathan Greenleaf, *A History of all the Churches of all Denominations, in the City of New York, from the First Settlement to the Year 1846* (New York: E. French, 1846)

Note: n.d. = no data; i.d. = incomplete data

[a] I have yet to locate any extant copies of the New York or Hudson River Baptist Association for 1820 or after. This number is for 1819.

[b] in five year increments beginning in 1785

1825	*1830*	*1836*	*1840*	*1845*	*1850*	*1855*	*Attending According to Census*	*1860*
n.d.	n.d.	n.d.	n.d.	8,744	n.d.	7,276	12,440	n.d.
2,623	3,955	5,128	5,772	8,973				
		109	238	105				
		156	403	493				
2,623	3,955	5,393	6,413	9,571	8,580	13,676	22,645	i.d.
−18%	51%	36%	19%	49%				
3,772	5,331	1,354	2,418					
680	927	887	740					
		4,624	5,567					
4,452	6,258	6,865	8,725	11,428	10,822	14,247	24,725	14,153
78%	41%	10%	27%	31%				
						1,550	5,025	
7,075	10,213	12,258	15,138	29,743	19,402	36,749	64,835	
−8%	44%	20%	23%	96%				
						78,488	100,500	
	127,928		206,450			425,694		
	8%		7%			9%	15%	
	[202,589]		[311,660]	[371,223]	[515,547]	[629,904]		[805,658]
						18%	24%	

owing to reporting failure in the nineteenth century and preservation issues in the twentieth.[24] That said, the reporting of religious attendance in the 1855 state census provides a valuable snapshot. This census is remembered more for reporting that the city's 24 Catholic churches had nearly as large a usual attendance (100,500) as the city's 218 Protestant churches (118,225). The Catholic number is almost certainly inflated, and too little attention is paid to the 64,835 reported evangelicals.[25]

Even using a conservative method of reckoning, it appears that the percentage of New Yorkers who had a conversion experience and joined an evangelical church increased steadily from 4 percent of the city's adult population in 1790 to 15 percent in 1855. Three factors increase the number who would have identified as evangelical. First, this count does not include members of to the city's evangelical Protestant Episcopal and Reformed Dutch congregations. Evidence from an 1857 debate suggests that at least eleven Episcopalian churches in the city, with over 6,300 members, were low church (evangelical leaning).[26] Second, a significant portion of urban evangelicals chose not to join a church. New Yorkers were transient people, unsure how long they might remain in the city. Many hesitated to formally join a church—or had a hard time finding one to their liking. Their number is difficult to recover, but likely sizable.

Finally, this number does not include those who lived in evangelical households, participated in evangelical-sponsored social activism, or read evangelical tracts but for whom a conversion experience was elusive. Spouses, children, parents, brothers, and sisters of church members might well have identified as evangelical while waiting for their stony hearts to be melted.

RACE AND GENDER

Historians have long acknowledged the appeal of evangelicalism to African American women and men and white women. Quantitative records provide valuable insight into broader trends among these important segments of the evangelical population.

African American New Yorkers embraced church building with a zeal that exceeded that of their white counterparts. Evangelical denominations had a conflicted legacy when it came to race. Segregated congregations formed as early as the first decade of the nineteenth century. African Americans sought their own worship space apart from white congregants who consigned them to the galleries of urban meetinghouses. The names they chose for their churches—Abyssinian Baptist (1809), African Methodist Episcopal Zion (1820), and First Colored Presbyterian (1822)—expressed pride in their race and their autonomy, if not complete independence from national denominations. For congregations less clearly denoted—St. Philip's (1809), Asbury (1813), or Zion (1832)—editors of city directories made sure to identify them as "(colored)" after their listings.[27] By midcentury, every major Protestant denomination had an African American congregation; many had more than one. At least twenty black churches and missions—eighteen of them evangelical—were founded before the Civil War.[28]

The number of congregants in those churches over time is more difficult to recover. Methodists were the only evangelical denomination to report membership numbers by race. In 1816, nearly a third of all New York Methodists were African American.[29] Five years later the AME Zion and Asbury congregations withdrew from the New York Conference and the percentage plummeted, rarely reaching above 1 to 2 percent over the next four decades.[30] Presbyterian and Baptist membership numbers are even more difficult to reconstruct. Greenleaf's *History* provides the best surviving snapshot of church membership (see table A.5). By his count, New York had eleven evangelical and two nonevangelical black congregations in June 1845. Membership in the evangelical churches totaled 3,780, 29 percent of the city's African American population. Adjusting that for the estimated number over the age of ten raises the percentage to 36 percent.[31] This represents a rate of evangelical church membership three to four times that of their white counterparts. Factoring in the two nonevangelical congregations reveals that almost 40 percent belonged to a church. These astonishing numbers confirm the overwhelming interest of antebellum urban African Americans in religious life in general and evangelicalism in particular.[32]

No denomination publicly reported its membership numbers by sex. Uncovering the extent of black and white women's presence in New York's churches requires looking at the records of individual congregations. Table A.6 illustrates the sex ratio of new members in a few congregations over the span of this study. The results are, of course, more suggestive than definitive, but they reveal the overwhelming numerical dominance of women within the membership of evangelical congregations: they consistently composed between 60 and 70 percent of church members.

Evangelicalism disproportionately appealed to women for a range of reasons. Religion offered a measure of autonomy to those normally disempowered in postrevolutionary society. Evangelicalism often functioned as a household-centered religion, the result of a conscientious decision by ministers and the networks of women who sustained them. For some women, conversion amounted to an act of rebellion that effectively challenged the patriarchal household.[33] In fact, evangelicalism had become so associated with women by

TABLE A.5. Snapshot of members in New York's African American churches in June 1845

	No. of Communicants	Percentage of African Americans in 1845 state census (n = 12,913)	Percentage of African Americans over age 10 (estimated n = 10,589)[a]
		Evangelical Protestant	
Baptist			
Abyssinian	451		
Zion	446		
Congregational			
Colored Congregational	25		
Methodist			
AME Zion	1,196		
Little Zion (AMEZ)	66		
Twenty-Second Street (AMEZ)	14		
Asbury	70		
Bethel (AME)	736		
Harlem Branch of Bethel (AME)	13		
African Union	350		
Presbyterian			
Colored Presbyterian	413		
Total	3,780	29%	36%
		Non-Evangelical Protestant	
Protestant Episcopal			
St Philip's	300		
Church of the Messiah[b]	20		
Total	320	2%	3%
		Total Churched	
	4,100	32%	39%

Source: Jonathan Greenleaf, *A History of all the Churches of all Denominations, in the City of New York, from the First Settlement to the Year 1846* (New York: E. French, 1846)

Note: Extinct in June 1845: Protestant Episcopal (St Matthew's Church) and Reformed Dutch (Colored Reformed Dutch)

[a]Calculated based on the assumption that the percentage over age 10 reported in the 1840 Federal Census is consistent

[b]Greenleaf reports that "a congregation of between one and two hundred is assembled here" but does not count among communicants (p. 98).

TABLE A.6. New members of various churches by sex, 1784–1845

	First Baptist Church, 1784–1790																	
	1784		*1785*		*1786*		*1787*		*1788*		*1789*		*1790 (partial)*				*Total*	
	No.	%	*No.*	%	*No.*	%	*No.*	%	*No.*	%	*No.*	%	*No.*	%			*No.*	%
Male	7	50%	28	44%	10	33%	18	49%	3	30%	8	32%	5	26%			79	40%
Female	7	50%	36	56%	20	67%	19	51%	7	70%	16	64%	14	74%			119	60%
	Rutgers Street Presbyterian Church by Sex, 1805–1811																	
	Dec. 1805		*1806*		*1807*		*1808*		*1809*		*1810*		*March 1811*				*Total*	
	No.	%	*No.*	%	*No.*	%	*No.*	%	*No.*	%	*No.*	%	*No.*	%			*No.*	%
Male	5	45%	21	33%	35	32%	15	21%	16	28%	31	30%	12	35%			135	30%
Female	6	55%	42	67%	73	68%	57	79%	42	72%	73	70%	22	65%			315	70%
	Brick Presbyterian Church by Sex, 1809–1816																	
	1809		*1810*		*1811*		*1812*		*1813*		*1814*		*1815*		*1816*		*Total*	
	No.	%	*No.*	%	*No.*	%	*No.*	%	*No.*	%	*No.*	%	*No.*	%	*No.*	%	*No.*	%
Male	3	18%	12	30%	13	34%	10	21%	11	26%	13	31%	15	31%	31	26%	108	27%
Female	14	82%	28	70%	25	66%	37	79%	32	74%	29	69%	34	69%	88	74%	287	73%

(continued)

TABLE A.6. (*continued*)

Seventh Presbyterian Church, 1818–1836

	1818	1819	1820	1821	1822	1823	1824	1825	1826	1827	1828	1829	1830	1831	1832	1833	1834	1835	1836	Total	
																				No.	%
Male	9	8	8	11	12	10	7	10	4	11	15	6	10	34	48	23	16	19	96	357	29%
Female	31	29	24	20	26	33	16	18	10	35	38	18	30	65	122	46	45	86	180	872	71%

Broadway Tabernacle Church by Sex, 1840–1845

	1840		1841		1842		1843		1844		1845		Total	
	No.	%	No.	%	No.	%	No.	%	No.	%	No.	%	No.	%
Male	41	55%	39	35%	58	45%	35	40%	21	41%	21	46%	215	43%
Female	33	45%	72	65%	72	55%	53	60%	30	59%	25	54%	285	57%

Sources: First Baptist Church (New York, NY) "Record Book A (1762–)," Collection of the First Baptist Church, New York City; Philip Milledoler Papers, New York Historical Society; "Records of the Doings of the Session of the Brick Church Commencing May 1809 [to 1827]," Collection of the Presbyterian Historical Society, Philadelphia (Vault BX 9211.N70028 B71 v.1); Seventh Presbyterian Church, "Record Book," Collection of the Presbyterian Historical Society, Philadelphia, PA; "Chronological List of Members," in Susan Hayes Ward, *The History of the Broadway Tabernacle, from Its Organization in 1840 to the Close of 1900 . . .* (NY, 1901), 257–66

the early nineteenth century in some parts of the nation that denominations made a concerted effort to shift their message or ideology to attract more men.[34] Yet as historian Ann Braude reminds us, the story of American religion is, ultimately, a story of women.[35]

New York witnessed dramatic demographic and geographic expansion between the end of the American Revolution and the Civil War. The city's spiritual marketplace grew alongside at an impressive, if not always consistent, rate. By 1860, New York had a greater number of churches in a wider variety of denominations than eighty years earlier. This diversity was readily apparent to anyone walking the streets of the city. Those willing to venture inside urban meetinghouses would have found, at least among the evangelicals, increasing numbers of members. Much like the rest of the country, New Yorkers were more fully churched on the eve of the Civil War than they were on the eve of the American Revolution.

Abbreviations

AAS: American Antiquarian Society, Worcester, MA.
ABS: American Bible Society
ATS: American Tract Society
BTC NYHS: Broadway Tabernacle Church Collection, New York Historical Society, New York, NY
CAJ: *Christian Advocate and Journal*
CHSM: *Christian Herald and Seaman's Magazine*
JSMEC: John Street Methodist Episcopal Church, New York, NY
LOC: Library of Congress, Washington, DC
MER NYPL: Methodist Episcopal Records, New York Public Library, New York, NY
NYHS: New-York Historical Society, New York, NY
NYPL: New York Public Library, New York, NY
PHS: Presbyterian Historical Society, Philadelphia, PA
WCL: William Clements Library, University of Michigan, Ann Arbor, MI

Notes

INTRODUCTION

1. James Fenimore Cooper, *New York, Being an Introduction to an Unpublished Manuscript, by the Author, Entitled, "The Towns of Manhattan"* (New York: S. A. Jacobs for W. F. Payson, 1930), 5.

2. Edwin G. Burrows and Mike Wallace, *Gotham: A History of New York City to 1898* (New York: Oxford University Press, 1999), xvi.

3. The literature is vast and well summarized in Burrows and Wallace, *Gotham*. Important works include the following: on the importance of real estate development, see Elizabeth Blackmar, *Manhattan for Rent, 1785–1850* (Ithaca, NY: Cornell University Press, 1989), and David Scobey, *Empire City: The Making and Meaning of the New York City Landscape* (Philadelphia: Temple University Press, 2002); on immigration, see Robert Ernst, *Immigrant Life in New York City, 1825–1863* (New York: Octagon Books, 1979); and on commerce, see Edward K. Spann, *The New Metropolis: New York City, 1840–1857* (New York: Columbia University Press, 1981).

4. See Nathan O. Hatch, *The Democratization of American Religion* (New Haven, CT: Yale University Press, 1989); Christine Leigh Heyrman, *Southern Cross: The Beginnings of the Bible Belt* (Chapel Hill, NC: University of North Carolina Press, 1997); and John Wigger, *Taking Heaven by Storm: Methodism and the Rise of Popular Christianity in America* (New York: Oxford University Press, 1998).

5. See Dee Andrews, *The Methodists and Revolutionary America, 1760–1800: The Shaping of an Evangelical Culture* (Princeton, NJ: Princeton University Press, 2000); Kyle Bulthius, *Four Steeples over the City Streets: Religion and Society in New York's Early Republic Congregations* (New York: New York University Press, 2014); Craig D. Townsend, *Faith in Their Own Color: Black Episcopalians in Antebellum New York City* (New York: Columbia University Press, 2005); Firth Haring Fabend, *Zion on the Hudson: Dutch New York and New Jersey in the Age of Revivals* (New Brunswick, NJ: Rutgers University Press, 2000); Paul Johnson and Sean Wilentz, *Kingdom of Matthias: A Story of Sex and Salvation in Nineteenth-Century America* (New York: Oxford University Press, 1994); Kathryn T. Long, *The Revival of 1857–1858: Interpreting an American Religious Awakening* (New York: Oxford University Press, 1998); Carroll Smith-Rosenberg, *Religion and the Rise of the American City: The New York City Mission Movement, 1812–1870* (Ithaca, NY: Cornell University Press, 1971); and Timothy L. Smith, *Revivalism and Social Reform in Mid-Nineteenth-Century America* (New York: Abingdon Press, 1957).

6. See Ray Allen Billington, *The Protestant Crusade, 1800–1860* (New York: Macmillan and Company, 1938); Mark Noll, *The Rise of Evangelicalism: The Age of Edwards, Whitefield, and the Wesleys* (Downers Grove, IL: InterVarsity Press, 2003), 16–17.

7. Inspired by Donald Mathew's influential essay, *Religion in the Old South* (Chicago: University of Chicago Press, 1977), historians have understood evangelicalism as a social process more than

a religious perception. See Rhys Isaac, *The Transformation of Virginia, 1740–1790* (Chapel Hill, NC: University of North Carolina Press, 1982); Susan Juster, *Disorderly Women: Sexual Politics & Evangelicalism in Revolutionary New England* (Ithaca, NY: Cornell University Press, 1994); Paul Johnson, *A Shopkeeper's Millennium: Society and Revivals in Rochester, New York, 1815–1837* (New York: Hill and Wang, 1978); and Stephanie McCurry, *Masters of Small Worlds: Yeoman Households, Gender Relations, and the Political Culture of the Antebellum South Carolina Low Country* (New York: Oxford University Press, 1995). Works that take religious experience seriously include Heyrman, *Southern Cross*; Jon Sensbach, *Rebecca's Revival: Creating Black Christianity in the Atlantic World* (Cambridge, MA: Harvard University Press, 2005); and Catherine Brekus, *Sarah Osborn's World: The Rise of Evangelical Christianity in Early America* (New Haven, CT: Yale University Press, 2012).

8. David Bebbington has identified four of these principles—conversion, activism, biblicism, and crucicentrism—to which I add a fifth, revivalism. See D. W. Bebbington, *Evangelicalism in Modern Britain: A History from the 1730s to the 1980s* (London: Unwin Hyman, 1989), 2–17.

9. The role and consequences of conversion differed between puritanism and evangelicalism. English Puritans hoped that conversion would transform the church and nation, while in New England it formed the bedrock on which church and state rested. The focus shifted to the individual within eighteenth-century evangelicalism. Bruce Hindmarsh, *The Evangelical Conversion Narrative: Spiritual Autobiography in Early Modern England* (New York: Oxford University Press, 2005), 74.

10. Ibid., 79.

11. Brekus, *Sarah Osborn's World*, 8. Brekus riffs off Hindmarsh, *Conversion Narrative*, 77.

12. On modernization within the North American context, see Jon Butler, *Becoming America: The Revolution before 1776* (Cambridge, MA: Harvard University Press, 2000), and Richard D. Brown, *Modernization: The Transformation of American Life, 1600–1865* (New York: Hill and Wang, 1976).

13. Kyle Bulthius argues for the disappearance (and elusive search to recover) "organic unity" in *Four Steeples*, chap. 1.

14. Early scholars reified popular religion as something approaching a distinct system of religious phenomena and movement that existed outside of organized or formal religion. But in time, scholars shifted their focus to uncover the mechanics of adoption, adaptation, and negotiation of beliefs and practices within religion more broadly. For the former, see Peter Williams, *Popular Religion in America: Symbolic Change and the Modernization Process in Historical Perspective* (Englewood Cliffs, NJ: Prentice Hall, 1980), 3–13. For the latter, see Robert Orsi, *The Madonna of 115th Street: Faith and Community in Italian Harlem, 1880–1950* (New Haven, CT: Yale University Press, 1985), and David Hall, *Worlds of Wonder, Days of Judgment: Popular Religious Belief in Early New England* (Cambridge, MA: Harvard University Press, 1989).

15. Charles Lippy, *Being Religious, American Style: A History of Popular Religiosity in the United States* (Westport, CT: Greenwood Press, 1994), 10. See also David Hall, ed., *Lived Religion in America: Towards a History of Practice* (Princeton, NJ: Princeton University Press, 1997).

16. Robert A. Orsi, "Everyday Miracles: The Study of Lived Religion," in Hall, ed., *Lived Religion*, 8.

17. Robert A. Orsi, "Introduction: Crossing the City Line," in *Gods of the City: Religion and the American Urban Landscape*, ed. Robert A. Orsi (Bloomington: Indiana University Press, 1999), 43.

18. For more on emplacement in environments built by others, see Orsi, *Madonna*, and Thomas Tweed, *Our Lady of Exile: Diasporic Religion at a Catholic Cuban Shrine in Miami* (Oxford: Oxford University Press, 1997).

19. See Stephen A. Marini, "Religious Change in Revolutionary Society, 1750–1790: Historiography, Contexts, Processes, Patterns." Paper delivered before the Boston Area Early American Studies Seminar, April 5, 2007.

20. My interpretation of the spiritual marketplace is strongly shaped by the work of Peter Berger, "A Market Model for the Analysis of Ecumenicity," *Social Research* 30 (1963): 77–93.

CHAPTER ONE

1. Charles Lahatt, "Personal Account," in "Misc. Mss. Lahatt, Charles," NYHS.

2. The Trans-Atlantic Slave Trade Database documents 1,872,124 slaves embarked from African ports between 1775 and 1800. Of that number, 21,171 disembarked in North America. http://www.slavevoyages.org/tast/database/search.faces, accessed October 3, 2014.

3. Ira Rosenwaike, *Population History of New York City* (Syracuse, NY: Syracuse University Press, 1972), 16–17.

4. John Bunyan, *The Pilgrim's Progress* (Philadelphia: John C Winston, 1909), Project Gutenberg, http://www.gutenberg.org/files/39452/39452-h/39452-h.htm, 13. Originally published in London in 1678, *Pilgrim's Progress* went through hundreds of editions over the seventeenth, eighteenth, and nineteenth centuries, making it one of the most reprinted texts of the period. For more on the publishing history of the text, see Isabel Hofmeyr, *The Portable Bunyan: A Transnational History of "The Pilgrim's Progress"* (Princeton, NJ: Princeton University Press, 2004).

5. Lahatt, "Personal Account," 3.

6. For more on the centrality of Bunyan's narrative to American evangelicals, see Candy Gunther Brown, *The Word in the World: Evangelical Writing, Publishing, and Reading in America, 1789–1880* (Chapel Hill, NC: University of North Carolina Press, 2004), 8–9. See also David E. Smith, *John Bunyan in America* (Bloomington: Indiana University Press, [1966]).

7. Lahatt, "Personal Account," [9–10].

8. [Divie Bethune], *The Power of Faith, Exemplified in the Life and Writings of the Late Mrs. Isabella Graham* (New-York, [1843]), 24, 28–41.

9. Grant Thorburn, *Forty Years' Residence in America; or, The Doctrine of a Particular Providence Exemplified in the Life of Grant Thorburn, Seedsman, New York* (Boston, 1834), 18–19.

10. *Consecrated Talents; or, The Life of Mrs. Mary W. Mason* (New York, 1870), 35–36.

11. New York's conservative Gradual Emancipation Act of 1799 meant others had to wait longer for theirs. George White, *A Brief Account of the Life, Experience, Travels, and Gospel Labours of George White, an African; Written by Himself and Revised by a Friend* (New York, 1810), reprinted in *Black Itinerants of the Gospel: The Narratives of John Jea and George White*, ed. Graham Russell Hodges (Madison, WI: Madison House, 1993), 53.

12. An understanding of religion predicated on movement serves as an important corrective to older studies that have postulated that religion functions as a rigid, static system. Movement pervades all aspects of religion, from the formation of an individual's basic beliefs, a process, as I explored in the introduction, shaped by the flowing together of different beliefs and practices from a range of sources, to the ways in which people mark and cross the ultimate horizon of human life. See Thomas A. Tweed, *Crossing and Dwelling: A Theory of Religion* (Cambridge, MA: Harvard University Press, 2006), 73–79. The quote is from Charles H. Long, *Significations: Signs, Symbols, and Images in the Interpretation of Religion* (Aurora, CO: Davies Group, 1995), 7, as quoted in Tweed, *Crossing and Dwelling*, 74.

13. Frank Lambert, *"Pedlar in Divinity": George Whitefield and the Transatlantic Revivals* (Princeton, NJ: Princeton University Press, 1994), 75–84.

14. Catherine Brekus, *Sarah Osborn's World: The Rise of Evangelical Christianity in Early America* (New Haven, CT: Yale University Press, 2012), 7. On modernization within the North American context, see Jon Butler, *Becoming America: The Revolution before 1776* (Cambridge, MA: Harvard University Press, 2000) and Richard D. Brown, *Modernization: The Transformation of American Life, 1600–1865* (New York: Hill and Wang, 1976).

15. Bruce Hindmarsh, *The Evangelical Conversion Narrative* (Oxford: Oxford University Press, 2005). Other important works on Anglo-American spiritual autobiographies include Jerrald C. Brauer, "Conversion: From Puritanism to Revivalism," *Journal of Religion* 58 (1978): 227–43;

Daniel B. Shea Jr., *Spiritual Autobiography in America* (Princeton, NJ: Princeton University Press, 1968) and "The Art and Instruction of Jonathan Edwards's Personal Narrative," *American Literature* 37 (1965): 17–32; and Amanda Porterfield, *Feminine Spirituality in America: From Sarah Edwards to Martha Graham* (Philadelphia: Temple University Press, 1980).

16. Several scholars have explored the intersection of evangelicalism and the Enlightenment in the eighteenth century. See Catherine A. Brekus, "Sarah Osborn's Enlightenment: Reimagining Eighteenth-Century Intellectual History," in *Reimaging the Past: The Religious History of American Women*, ed. Catharine A. Brekus (Chapel Hill: University of North Carolina Press, 2007), 114; Brekus, *Sarah Osborn's World*; D. W. Bebbington, *Evangelicalism in Modern Britain: A History from the 1730s to the 1980s* (Boston: Unwin Hyman, 1989); Mark A. Noll, *The Rise of Evangelicalism: The Age of Edwards, Whitefield, and the Wesleys* (Downers Grove, IL: InterVarsity Press, 2003); and Hindmarsh, *Evangelical Conversion Narrative*, 73 (quote).

17. Sarah Sergeant Miller, "Memoir," reprinted in Samuel Miller, *The Life of Samuel Miller, DD, LLD* (Philadelphia, 1869), 148–49.

18. See, for example, Lahatt, "Personal Account," [16] which has reworkings of two earlier passages from the narrative. At the end of his narrative he dated the work "August 5, 1848, Portland, Chautaqua County, New York," at which time he was 84 years old.

19. Divie Bethune, Diary (February 21, 1796—February 5, 1797), WCL.

20. John Stanford, *The Goodness of God in the Conversion of Youth: A Sermon on the Death of Charles I. S. Hazzard* (New York, 1799), 11.

21. John Wesley's account of his heart being "strangely warmed" in 1738 at Aldersgate was one of the most famous of such experiences. See Henry D. Rack, "John Wesley," *Oxford Dictionary of National Biography* 58 (Oxford: Oxford University Press, 2004), 185. The centrality of the heart in evangelical culture has deep antecedents in western European culture. See Eric Jager, *The Book of the Heart* (Chicago: University of Chicago Press, 2000).

22. For more on steady sellers, see David Hall, *Worlds of Wonder, Days of Judgment: Popular Religious Belief in Early New England* (Cambridge, MA: Harvard University Press, 1989), 48–52.

23. Philip Doddridge's *Rise and Progress of Religion in the Soul* (1745) went through multiple editions and was a staple of the American Tract Society's antebellum distribution.

24. George W. Bethune, *Memoirs of Mrs. Joanna Bethune* (New York, 1863), 64.

25. White, *Brief Account*, 53.

26. At just under a million, the city's population was twice that of the next largest European city, Paris, and thirty times that of New York. "Population," in *The London Encyclopedia*, ed. Ben Weinreb and Christopher Hibbert (London: PaperMac, 1983), 630–32.

27. George Whitefield, *Watching, the Peculiar Duty of a Christian: A Sermon Preached at Mary-le-Bone, Moorfields, and Kennington-Common* (London, 1739), 5.

28. Hindmarsh, *Evangelical Conversion Narrative*, 69.

29. Lahatt, "Personal Account," 3. For more on this phenomenon, see Hindmarsh, *Evangelical Conversion Narrative*, 69.

30. Daniel De Vinné, *Recollections of Fifty Years in the Ministry* (New York, 1869), 11.

31. Lahatt, "Personal Account," 3.

32. De Vinné, *Recollections*, 11.

33. Jonathan Greenleaf, *A History of the Churches, of All Denominations, in the City of New York, from the First Settlement to the Year 1846* (New York, 1846), 24–26.

34. Philip Milledoler, "Memoirs of an Outline of the Life of Philip Milledoler of New York," box 3, Philip Milledoler Collection, NYHS, 5–6.

35. Milledoler, "Memoirs," 6–6a.

36. John Stanford, *The Conversion of Juvenis, A Series of Letters between a Young Man and a Minister* (New York, 1794), 5–6.

37. Ibid., 7–18.

38. Hill maintained a more liberal policy toward distributing the sacrament than most, evidence

of his belief in its efficacy to bring men and women closer to the Lord. Edwin Sidney, *The Life of the Rev. Rowland Hill* (New York, 1834), 146. Lahatt, "Personal Memoir," 4.

39. Bethune, *Memoirs*, 70–71; This is a direct reference to Bunyan's story: *Pilgrim's Progress*, 50.

40. Milledoler, "Memoirs," 6–6a.

41. *Life of Samuel Miller*, 160–61.

42. Lahatt, "Personal Memoir," 4.

43. Compare Bunyan's colorful telling in *Pilgrim's Progress*, 47–48, with White's description. *Brief Account*, 54–55.

44. Bunyan, *Pilgrim's Progress*, 87. See Bethune's brief spiritual autobiography in Diary (January 10, 1819–October 10, 1819), WCL, entry for February 21, 1819. See also "Obituary: Divie Bethune, Esq.," *Christian Herald and Seaman's Magazine* IX (October 1824): 626–32.

45. Lahatt, "Personal Account," [3].

46. Stanford, *Conversion*, 7.

47. Reconciliation, Whitefield preached again and again, could only be achieved through a forsaking of the world through a spiritual rebirth in Jesus Christ. George Whitefield, *The Serpent's Beguiling Eve Explained, Considered, and Applied to All under Temptation* (London, [1741]), 5–10.

48. Joanna Graham Bethune, *The Unpublished Letters and Correspondence of Mrs. Isabella Graham, from the Year 1767 to 1814* (New York, 1838), 144–45.

49. Some read persecution as a test. See [Bethune], *Power of Faith*, 311, and Bethune, *Unpublished Letters*, 238.

50. See Peter Linebaugh and Marcus Rediker, *The Many-Headed Hydra: Sailors, Slaves, Commoners, and the Hidden History of the Revolutionary Atlantic* (Boston: Beacon Press, 2000).

51. Thorburn, *Forty Years' Residence*, 23.

52. See "An Account of the Death of Captain Swinburn, Late of This Port, in an Extract of a Letter from the Rev. Mr. Hallet, to Mrs. Swinburn, Dated Grenada, April 19th, 1796," *Experienced Christian's Magazine* 1 (September 1796): 151.

53. "To open their eyes, that they may turn from darkness to light, and from the power of Satan to God; that they may receive through faith which is in me, forgiveness of sins, and an inheritance among them that are sanctified" (Acts 26:18, KJV).

54. For an evangelical interpretation of this passage, see John Wesley, *Explanatory Notes on the New Testament* (London, 1755), 370.

55. Lahatt, "Personal Account," 10.

56. John H. Moss, "A Short Account of the Life and Experience of John H. Moss, Written by Himself," *Experienced Christian's Magazine* II (September 1805): 153–57, quotes 153.

57. Tweed, *Crossing and Dwelling*, 74.

58. "[A]s clusters of dwelling practices," argues Thomas Tweed, "religions orient individuals and groups in time and space, transform the natural environment, and allow devotees to inhabit the worlds they construct." *Crossing and Dwelling*, 82.

59. John Gano, *Biographical Memoirs of the Late Rev. John Gano, of Frankfort, (Kentucky) Formerly of the City of New-York* (New York, 1806), 116–17.

60. Quoted in Thomas E. V. Smith, *The City of New York in the Year of Washington's Inauguration, 1789* (New York, 1889), 5–6.

61. Edwin G. Burrows and Mike Wallace, *Gotham: A History of New York City to 1898* (Oxford: Oxford University Press, 1999), chap. 20; and Smith, *The City of New York*, chap. 7. An overview of this period can also be found in Sidney I. Pomerantz, *New York: An American City, 1783–1803* (New York: Columbia University Press, 1938).

62. For more on the power of established colonial churches, see Burrows and Wallace, *Gotham*, 103–5.

63. Chappel's paintings are memory maps, illustrations of the city of his youth executed much later in life. Most of Chappel's paintings are now in the collection of the Metropolitan Museum of Art. For more on Chappel, see John Caldwell, Kathleen Luhrs, and Oswaldo Rodriquez Roque, eds.,

American Paintings in the Metropolitan Museum of Art, Volume 1: A Catalogue of Works by Artists Born by 1815 (New York: Metropolitan Museum of Art, 1994), 439–49.

64. See Article XXXVIII of the Constitution of New York, 1777, http://www.nhumanities.org/ccs/docs/ny-1777.htm, accessed March 18, 2015.

65. Richard Pointer, *Protestant Pluralism and the New York Experience: A Study of Eighteenth-Century Religious Diversity* (Bloomington: Indiana University Press, 1988), 104–5.

66. Lahatt, "Personal Account," [11].

67. Christopher Rush, *A Short Account of the Rise and Progress of the African M.E. Church in America* (New York, 1843; republished in 1866), 9–12.

68. Lahatt, "Personal Account," [11].

69. Christians have long held linked the idea of the "upper room" with a space of heightened spiritual significance. See Paul J. Achtemeier, ed., *The HarperCollins Bible Dictionary* (San Francisco: HarperSanFrancisco, 1996), 1185.

70. As early as 1784, Brooklyn had a small community of Methodists served by the occasional itinerant preacher. A decade later the nascent congregation formed themselves into the Sands Street Methodist Episcopal Church and built a meetinghouse. See Henry Isham Hazelton, *The Boroughs of Brooklyn and Queens, Counties of Nassau and Suffolk, Long Island, New York, 1609–1924* (New York, 1925), 1253–79.

71. F. Bottome, *Bowery Village Methodist Episcopal Church. A Discourse* (New York, 1864), 6–20.

72. *A Familiar Conversational History of the Evangelical Churches of New-York* (New York, 1839), 196–97. For the reference to the possible occupation of the space by a schismatic Anglican group in 1774, see Morgan A. Dix, *A History of the Parish of Trinity Church in the City of New York* (New York, 1898), 356.

73. [Bethune], *Power of Faith*, 124. The emphasis is Graham's.

74. George W. Dolbey, *The Architectural Expression of Methodism: The First Hundred Years* (London: Epworth, 1964).

75. The Anglican chapel openly declared its allegiance to colonial power and metropolitan culture through its adoption of stylistic elements favored by Sir Christopher Wren and his student James Gibbs, the architects responsible for the rebuilding of London's spiritual landscape after the Great Fire of 1666. Thomas McBean, a pupil of James Gibbs, designed St. Paul's. See E. Clowes Chorley, *Quarter of a Millennium: Trinity Church in the City of New York, 1697–1947* (Philadelphia: Church Historical Society, 1947), 61.

76. See Noll, *Rise of Evangelicalism*, 15.

77. Stanford, *Conversion*, 40–45.

78. From the *New York Observer of the 4th of July* (1867), 213, reprinted in *Life of Samuel Miller*, 89n2.

79. See "Baptism," in J. Gordon Melton, *Encyclopedia of Protestantism* (New York: Facts on File, 1995), 66–69; and "Baptism," in Randall Balmer, *Encyclopedia of Evangelicalism*, rev. ed. (Waco, TX: Baylor University Press, 2005), 54.

80. Mark S. Schantz, *Piety in Providence: Class Dimensions of Religious Experience in Antebellum Rhode Island* (Ithaca, NY: Cornell University Press, 2000), chap. 1.

81. For examples of these tickets, see J. B. Wakeley, *Lost Chapters Recovered from the Early History of American Methodism* (New York, 1858), 412–25.

82. Bethune, Diary, (October 9, 1803–January 6, 1805), WCL, entry for July 29, 1804. Bethune's frustration with Graham and Mason returned in June 1807 when he found himself suspended from Communion, pending investigation. See the June 28, 1807 entry in Diary (March 1, 1807–December 6, 1807), WCL.

83. By 1804, the issue had become so fractious that the General Conference of the Methodist Episcopal Church ended up printing two *Disciplines*, one for northern states and Virginia, and another for southern states. Dee Andrews, *The Methodists and Revolutionary America, 1760–1800:*

The Shaping of An Evangelical Culture (Princeton, NJ: Princeton University Press, 2000), 125–26, 310n12.

84. The act granted freedom only to those born to slaves after July 4, 1799, while requiring them to be bound in indentures to the owners of their parents until age 25 for women and age 28 for men. Slaves born before July 4, 1799, would have to wait until 1817 for the state to free them. Patrick Rael, "The Long Death of Slavery," in *Slavery in New York*, ed. Ira Berlin and Leslie M. Harris (New York: New Press, 2005), 114; Shane White, *Stories of Freedom in Black New York* (Cambridge, MA: Harvard University Press, 2002), chap. 1; Leslie Harris, *In the Shadow of Slavery: African Americans in New York City, 1626–1863* (Chicago: University of Chicago Press, 2003), 72.

85. Scholars have offered a range of interpretations for why black Methodists sought to separate themselves from the white Methodists in the John Street meetinghouse. See Christopher Rush, *A Short Account of the Rise and Progress of the African M.E. Church in America* (New York, 1866), chap. 1; William Jacob Walls, *The African Methodist Episcopal Zion Church* (Charlotte, NC: A.M.E. Zion [1974]), chaps. 6–7; Andrews, *Methodists*, 151; Harris, *Shadow*, 83–84; Kyle Bulthius, *Four Steeples over the City: Religion and Society in New York's Early Republic Congregations* (New York: New York University Press, 2014), 82–90.

86. Robert A. Orsi, "Introduction: Crossing the City Line," in *Gods of the City: Religion and the American Urban Landscape*, ed. Robert A. Orsi (Bloomington: Indiana University Press, 1999), 55.

87. Bethune, *Memoirs*, 58.

88. Robert Bruce Mullin, ed., *Moneygripe's Apprentice: The Personal Narrative of Samuel Seabury III* (New Haven, CT: Yale University Press, 1989), 70.

89. There is a rich literature on labor in Early Republic New York. See, for example, Sean Wilentz, *Chants Democratic: New York City and the Rise of the American Working Class, 1788–1850* (New York: Oxford University Press, 1984), 77–86; Howard Rock, *Artisans of the New Republic: The Tradesmen of New York City in the Age of Jefferson* (New York: New York University Press, 1979), 304–12; and Christine Stansell, *City of Women: Sex and Class in New York, 1789–1860* (New York: Knopf, 1986).

90. Mullin, *Moneygripe's Apprentice*, 70–74.

91. Burrows and Wallace, *Gotham*, 387.

92. Andrews, *Methodists*, 167.

93. Sam Bass Warner Jr., *Streetcar Suburbs: The Process of Growth in Boston, 1870–1900*, 2nd ed. (Cambridge, MA: Harvard University Press, 1978).

94. Eric Homberger, *The Historical Atlas of New York City* (New York, 1994), 69.

95. Samuel A. Seaman, *Annals of New York Methodism, Being a History of the Methodist Episcopal Church in the City of New York, from A.D. 1766 to A.D. 1890* (New York, 1892), 103, 105, 110–13. On the strong presence of the laboring classes in New York Methodism see Andrews, *Methodists*, chap. 6; and Bulthius, *Four Steeples*, 73–77.

96. Thomas Morrell's appointment to this position in order to build the Forsyth Street Methodist Episcopal Church is preserved in Seaman, *Annals*, 105.

97. In 1810, a frame Methodist meetinghouse arose on Bedford Street in the northwest corner of the city, almost in Greenwich Village, and a stone meetinghouse was built on Allen Street in the northeast section of the city. Both congregations had begun years earlier as prayer meetings. Seaman, *Annals*, 179–81 (Bedford Street), 181–82 (Allen Street). On the area, see Guernsey, *New York City and Vicinity during the War of 1812–15*, vol. 1 (New York, 1889), 33.

98. Baptists' tradition of congregational autonomy also worked against their efforts for large-scale systematic planning.

99. Greenleaf, *History of the Churches*, 240–41; Bob Gore, *We've Come This Far: The Abyssinian Baptist Church, A Photographic Journal* (New York: Stewart, Tabori & Chang, 2001), 24–30; Genna Rae McNeil, Houston Bryan Roberson, Quinton Hosford Dixie, and Kevin McGruder, *Witness: Two Hundred Years of African-American Faith and Practice at the Abyssinian Baptist Church of Harlem, New*

York (Grand Rapids, MI: Eerdmans, 2014), chap. 1. Record Book A of the First Baptist Church has the 1809 petition for separation from the black congregants, which was granted, but no record on an 1807 request. See Record Book A, Collection of the First Baptist Church, New York City.

100. Greenleaf, *History of the Churches*, 242–43.

101. Stephen N Rowan, *Jacob's Address to Laban: A Sermon, Preached in the Reformed Dutch Church at Greenwich, in the City of New York, August 9, 1818, on Occasion of Announcing to the Congregation the Resignation of His Call* (New York, 1818), 12. Definition of "ordinary hearers" drawn from Samuel Rutherford, *The Due Right of Presbyteries; or, A Peaceable Plea for the Government of the Church of Scotland* (London, 1644), 268. Residents of Greenwich Village successfully petitioned the Classis of the Reformed Dutch Church, the equivalent of the Methodist Conference or Presbyterian Synod, to build a church for them so that they would not have to walk all the way down to lower Manhattan for services. Greenleaf, *History of the Churches*, 29–31.

102. The total number who had joined as full members was even higher at 229, but the high rate of transience in the city—and competition within the spiritual marketplace—had drawn away 74, and 22 had died.

103. Rowan, *Jacob's Address*, 13. The church's Consistory responded to Rowan's narrative of progress with a narrative of declining membership. *Reply to the Sermon of the Rev Stephen N. Rowan, Delivered at Greenwich, in the City of New-York, August 9, 1818* (New York, 1818), 8.

104. Greenleaf, *History of the Churches*, 158–61.

105. See the appendix for more on this issue.

106. Burrows and Wallace, *Gotham*, chap. 26.

107. Calculation based on the population for the city in 1800 (60,515) and in 1816 (93,634) as reported in Rosenwaike, *Population History*, 17.

108. Gardiner Spring, *Something Must be Done: A New Year's Sermon, Preached on the Last Day of the Old Year* (New York, 1816), 5.

109. Highlights of this rich literature include Whitney Cross, *The Burned-Over District: The Social and Intellectual History of Enthusiastic Religion in Western New York, 1800–1850* (Ithaca, NY: Cornell University Press, 1950); Bernard Weisberger, *They Gathered at the River: The Story of the Great Revivalists and Their Impact upon Religion in America* (Boston: Little, Brown, 1958); Curtis Johnson, *Islands of Holiness: Rural Religion in Upstate New York, 1790–1860* (Ithaca, NY: Cornell University Press, 1989); and Nathan Hatch, *The Democratization of American Christianity* (New Haven: Yale University Press, 1989). An important opposing view on revivalism can be seen in Jon Butler, "Enthusiasm Described and Decried: The Great Awakening as Interpretive Fiction," *Journal of American History* 69 (September 1982): 305–25.

110. Timothy Smith tries to push back our understanding of the origins of urban revivalism in New York City to 1839 in *Revivalism and Social Reform*, while Kathryn Long focuses on the Revival of 1857–58 as the first great urban revival. See Timothy L Smith, *Revivalism and Social Reform: American Protestantism on the Eve of the Civil War* (Nashville: Abingdon Press, 1957), chap. 4; and Kathryn Long, "The Power of Interpretation: The Revival of 1857–58 and the Historiography of Revivalism in America," *Religion and American Culture* 4 (Winter 1994): 77–105, and *The Revival of 1857–58: Interpreting an American Religious Awakening* (New York: Oxford University Press, 1998). Paul Johnson famously explores urban revivalism in Rochester, New York, in 1832. See *A Shopkeeper's Millennium: Society and Revivals in Rochester, New York, 1815–1837* (New York: Hill and Wang, 1978).

111. Wakeley, *Lost Chapters*, 356, 358; Seaman, *Annals*, 79, 90, 103, 113, 141, 168, 175, 181, 214, 247–57.

112. Milledoler, "Memoirs", 38; Greenleaf, *History of the Churches*, 132–35. For a brief biography of Henry Rutgers and a discussion of his philanthropy, see Guernsey, *New York City*, Vol. 1, 14–15.

113. Milledoler oversaw revivals in the springs of 1806, 1807, 1810, and 1811, reminding us of the seasonality of revival activity as well. See Philip Milledoler, "[A]n account of members rec'd into

full communion of the Church in Rutgers St. New York from August 5th 1805 to May 2d 1813 including the time of my ministry in that Church" in "Records of Sermons, 1801–1805," box 3, Philip Milledoler Collection, NYHS.

114. John Lambert, *Travels through Lower Canada and the United States in 1806, 1807, and 1808*, vol. 2 (London, 1810), 155–58.

115. Milledoler, "Account."

116. Henry Rutgers had previously erected a small wooden meetinghouse that sat 250–300 people across the street from the site of the Rutgers meetinghouse for a Welsh congregation. Milledoler, "Memoirs," 39–41.

117. Philip Milledoler, Diary, 1807–1811, box 5, Philip Milledoler Collection, NYHS, entry for February 4, 1808.

118. Between December 1805 and March 1811, Milledoler reported that 218 women (72%) entered the church on examination, as compared to 85 men (28%). Milledoler, "Account."

119. Milledoler, Diary, entry for March 1808.

120. Record Book A, First Baptist Church of New York City, entries for November 14 and 28, 1809.

121. Paul Gilje, *The Road to Mobocracy: Popular Disorder in New York City, 1763–1834* (Chapel Hill: University of North Carolina Press, 1987), 212–13.

122. On Broad's trial for abusing his slave and her daughter, see [Henry C. Southwick], *The Trial of Amos Broad and His Wife* (New York, 1809). Broad experienced conversion soon after his release from his sixty-day sentence and purchased the Rose Street meetinghouse. On Broad's effort to attain licensing as a Baptist minister, see Record Book A, First Baptist Church of New York City, entry for May 27, 1810. See also Gilje, *Mobocracy*, 214–20; and Harris, *Shadow*, 106–7.

123. Hindmarsh, *Evangelical Conversion Narrative*, 73.

124. Those challenges would continue after the publication of his *Life* in 1810. He applied to be appointed as a deacon in the AMEZ Church three times, beginning in 1811, before he was finally accepted in 1816. In 1820 he left the AMEZ for Richard Allen's AME Church, where he was ordained a deacon in June 1822. His duties placed him on preaching tours for the next six years before he retired to New York and to shoemaking. See Hodges, ed., *Black Itinerants of the Gospel*, 16–17.

125. Bethune retold this narrative, refining it as he went, in response to different crises he faced. When life went smoothly, Bethune did not write about it, a possible insight into the writing habits of other spiritual autobiographers. Divie Bethune, Diary (February 21, 1796–February 5, 1797), WCL, September 18, 1796.

126. The impious husband was apprehended and brought back by the neighbors. White, *Brief Account*, 73–76, 82.

127. Lahatt, "Personal Account," [26].

CHAPTER TWO

1. Ezra Stiles Ely, *A Sermon for the Rich to Buy, That They May Benefit Themselves and the Poor* (New York, 1810), quotes 21, 23, 19. For the background on Ely's decision to preach the initial sermon, see Ely, *Visits of Mercy; or, The Journals of the Rev. Ezra Stiles Ely, D.D.*, vol. 1 (Philadelphia, 1829), x–xi.

2. Conrad Edick Wright, *The Transformation of Charity in Postrevolutionary New England* (Boston: Northeastern University Press, 1992), part 1.

3. On Wesley's efforts, see Richard P. Heitzenrater, *Wesley and the People Called Methodists* (Nashville, TN: Abingdon Press, 1995). On Whitefield, especially the orphanage that he founded in Georgia, see Frank Lambert, *"Pedlar in Divinity": George Whitefield and the Transatlantic Revivals* (Princeton, NJ: Princeton University Press, 1994).

4. On the history of New York's almshouse, see Raymond A. Mohl, *Poverty in New York, 1783–1825* (New York: Oxford University Press, 1971), chap. 6. For more on state-sponsored poor relief see David M. Schneider, *The History of Public Welfare in New York State, 1609–1866* (Chicago: University of Chicago Press, 1938), and Robert E. Cray Jr., *Paupers and Poor Relief in New York City and Its Rural Environs, 1700–1830* (Philadelphia: Temple University Press, 1988). Historians have made much of the increasing institutionalization of municipal relief in the early nineteenth century. They have argued that, like the penitentiary and the insane asylum, the almshouse used a distinctive external architecture to make it foreboding, a crossing of the "quasi-military tone of the penitentiary or the less coercive but still regulatory quality of the insane asylum." See David J. Rothman, *The Discovery of the Asylum: Social Order and Disorder in the New Republic* (1971; Boston: Little, Brown, 1990), chap. 8, quote 191.

5. Although overseen by a private board of twenty-six governors, the New York Hospital, which opened in 1791, benefited from a municipal annuity for much of the late eighteenth and early nineteenth centuries. Henry J. Cammann and Hugh N. Camp, *The Charities of New York, Brooklyn, and Staten Island* (New York, 1868), 111–20.

6. John Lambert, *Travels through Lower Canada and the United States in 1806, 1807, and 1808*, vol. 2 (London, 1810), 177.

7. Edmund M. Blunt, *Blunt's Stranger's Guide to the City of New-York* (New York, 1817), 179, 185.

8. Examples of private associations based on ethnicity include the German Society (1784), St. Andrew's Society (for Scottish immigrants), St. Patrick's Society (for Irish immigrants), St. George's Society (for English immigrants), and the Frenchmen's Benevolent Society (1808); on political affiliation, the Tammany Society (1805) and the Society of Cincinnati; on vocation, the Marine Society (1770) and the Society of Mechanics and Tradesmen (1792); on shared ideology, the Humane Society (1787) and the Manumission Society (1785). Lambert, *Travels*, 176–77. The strength of these associations, argues one historian, played a part in determining whether member of these groups ended up in the almshouse. See Cray, *Paupers*, 178.

9. Lambert, *Travels*, 177; and Blunt, *Stranger's Guide*, 184.

10. "Assistance Society Minutes," vol. 82A, MR NYPL.

11. John Street Methodist Episcopal Church, "Poor Fund Treasurer Accounts (1790–1820)," vol. 94, MR NYPL. See Dee Andrew's analysis of these records in *The Methodists and Revolutionary America, 1760–1800: The Shaping of an Evangelical Culture* (Princeton, NJ: Princeton University Press, 2000), 117.

12. Previous studies that have touched on the Ladies' Society include Carroll Smith-Rosenberg, *Religion and the Rise of the American City: The New York City Mission Movement, 1812–1870* (Ithaca, NY: Cornell University Press, 1971), 26–27; Christine Stansell, *City of Women: Sex and Class in New York, 1789–1860* (New York: Knopf, 1986),14–16. For the most extensive treatment of Graham's life, see Anne M. Boylan, *On the Origins of Women's Activism: New York and Boston, 1797–1840* (Chapel Hill: University of North Carolina Press, 2002), 96–118.

13. "I cannot say it is my daily companion," she wrote to her mother in Scotland about Doddridge, "but I can with truth say, it is often so." [Divie Bethune], *The Power of Faith, Exemplified in the Life and Writings of the Late Mrs. Isabella Graham* (New York, [1843]), 10–11.

14. Joanna Graham Bethune, ed., *The Unpublished Letters and Correspondence of Mrs. Isabella Graham, from the Year 1767 to 1814* (New York, 1838), 32–33. On Graham's life and experience during this period, see [Bethune], *Power of Faith* (1843), 24, 28–41.

15. [Bethune], *Power of Faith* (1843), 41–46, 56–64, 60, 82.

16. At one point she demanded that her husband's coffin be exhumed so that she could confirm that he was, in fact, dead. Ibid., 41.

17. Ibid., 171–77. For a letter from a friend, and watcher at her husband's last illness, in Antigua encouraging Graham to see her loss as the positive work of the Lord, see Bethune, *Unpublished Letters*, 125–29.

18. Bethune, *Unpublished Letters*, 209–12.

19. Ibid., 222.

20. Ibid., 180.

21. Mohl, *Poverty*, 105–6.

22. Bethune, *Unpublished Letters*, 198.

23. [Bethune], *Power of Faith* (1843), 143–44.

24. Boylan, *Origins*, 228.

25. Comparing the list of officers and managers of the society in 1798 with *Longsworth's Almanac*, the leading New York directory of the period, reveals that seven were married to merchants, one, to a shopkeeper, and one, a mason; two were independent widows and three were unmarried women (one the daughter of the city's postmaster); for two, it is unclear whether they were wives or widows. Boylan, *Origins*, 236.

26. John Stanford, *Composure in Death. A Discourse, Delivered in the Orphan Asylum, New-York, on the Death of Mrs. Sarah Hoffman* (New York, [1821?]), 26.

27. *Constitution of the Ladies Society, Established in New-York, for the Relief of Poor Widows with Small Children* (New York, 1799), 7.

28. In 1799, for example, the managers purchased "linen, checks, &c" and distributed them among the widows to be made into shirts. They were sold at Divie Bethune's store on the corner of South-Street and Murray's wharf. Ibid., 13.

29. [Bethune], *Power of Faith*, 395–98.

30. Philip Milledoler, *A Discourse Delivered in the Presbyterian Church in Wall-Street, March 23, 1806, for a Society of Ladies, Instituted for the Relief of Poor Widows with Small Children* (New York, 1806), 22.

31. Stanford, *Composure*, 29–30.

32. In 1806, the society had spent $2,458.30 on relieving widows, "besides very much for the sick from their own pantries, having it cooked in their own kitchens, and in many instances, giving daily personal attendance." [Bethune], *Power of Faith* (1816), 399. See also *Constitution of the Ladies' Society, Established in New York, for the Relief of Poor Widows with Small Children*, 2nd ed. (New York, 1800), 17.

33. *Constitution* (1800), 18.

34. *Constitution* (1799), 9, 12; and *Constitution* (1800), 17.

35. [Bethune], *Power of Faith* (1843), 197.

36. Milledoler, *Discourse*, 4.

37. Samuel Miller, *A Sermon, Preached March 13th, 1808, for the Benefit of the Society Instituted in the City of New York, for the Relief of Poor Widows with Small Children* (New York, 1808), 31.

38. Gardiner Spring, *A Sermon, Preached April 21, 1811, for the Benefit of a Society of Ladies, Instituted for the Relief of Poor Widows with Small Children* (New York, 1811), 4.

39. Stanford, *Composure*, 17.

40. [Bethune] *Power of Faith* (1843), 308, 355.

41. These tensions boiled over in an 1804 controversy over the placement of a new meetinghouse. Ezra Stiles Ely, *Memoirs of the Rev. Zebulon Ely, A.M., of Lebanon, Connecticut* (Philadelphia, 1825), 37–38, 53. On Lebanon, see George McLean Milne, *Lebanon: Three Centuries in a Connecticut Hill Town* (Canaan, NH: Published for the Lebanon Historical Society, 1985). On the political tensions, see John W. Ifkovic, *Connecticut's Nationalist Revolutionary: Jonathan Trumbull, Jr.* (Hartford, CT: American Revolution Bicentennial Commission of Connecticut, 1977), 77–80.

42. Ironically, the previous president and Ely's namesake, Ezra Stiles, hated Dwight. See Edmund S. Morgan, "Ezra Stiles and Timothy Dwight," *Proceedings of the Massachusetts Historical Society* 72 (1963): 101–17.

43. Colin Wells, *The Devil and Doctor Dwight: Satire and Theology in the Early American Republic* (Chapel Hill: University of North Carolina Press, 2002).

44. John R. Fitzmier, *New England's Moral Legislator: Timothy Dwight, 1752–1817* (Bloomington: Indiana University Press, 1998), 53–59.

45. Samuel Miller, minister of the city's First Presbyterian Church, preserved two different takes on what came to be known as the Hopkinsian Controversy. He supported Spring in the controversy not because he held similar views but because he felt he should have a right to his own thoughts. Miller also reprints an account from Philip Milledoler, who articulated his fear of the insidious aims of New Divinity preachers. Miller admits he suggested Ely write *A Contrast* but did not like it when it was written. Samuel Miller, *The Life of Samuel Miller, D.D. L.L.D.* (Philadelphia, 1869), 288, 297–304. On the anger directed toward Ely, see Whelpley, *Triangle*, 71–75.

46. Whelpley, *Triangle*, 72.

47. [Ezra Stiles Ely], *William and Ellen: A Poem in Three Cantos; With Other Poetical Works of an American* (New York, 1811), vii, x.

48. In addition to the hospital and almshouse, Stanford preached in the state prison. Charles G. Sommers, *Memoir of the Rev. John Stanford, D.D. Late Chaplain to the Humane and Criminal Institutions in the City of New-York* (New York, 1835), 111–13. See also Mohl, *Poverty*, 98–99.

49. Ely, *Journal*, 68.

50. See Ezra Stiles Ely, *The Journal of the Stated Preacher to the Hospital and Almshouse, in the City of New-York, for the Year of our Lord 1811* (New York, 1812), and Ely, *The Second Journal of the Stated Preacher to the Hospital and Almshouse, in the City of New-York, for a Part of the Year of our Lord, 1813* (Philadelphia, 1815).

51. Only the Methodists among the city's evangelical population eschewed seating by pews, although they instituted a rigid system of class meetings that ensured people felt their place within the congregation. See Philip F. Hardt, *The Soul of Methodism: The Class Meeting in Early New York City Methodism* (Lanham, MD: University Press of America, 2000).

52. Ely, *Journal*, 30–31.

53. John Williams and Roswell Graves, "Christian Salutation," *Massachusetts Baptist Missionary Magazine* 2 (September 1802), 329.

54. Ely, *Journal*, 77.

55. Ibid., 87.

56. Ely commented in early 1811 that it was "a singular fact, that all my public preaching hitherto has been in the rooms of the female paupers." Ibid., 57. Ely records conversations with more men than women in his first *Journal* (57 to 44), but few developed into the long-term relationships that characterized his interaction with African American men and white women. See the appendix.

57. Ely, *Journal*, 80.

58. Jonathan Edwards spent upward of thirteen hours writing each day. See Jon Butler, *Becoming America: The Revolution before 1776* (Cambridge, MA: Harvard University Press, 2000), 133.

59. Historians have long assumed the motivations behind this shift from community to individual to be primarily about social control. I share Conrad Wright's reservations about such an interpretation. While reformers hoped to exert some influence, reducing their primary motivations such fails to acknowledge their genuine belief that what they had to offer was a good thing. See Wright, *The Transformation of Charity*, appendix 1. The most influential presentations of the social control thesis include Clifford S. Griffin, "Religious Benevolence as Social Control, 1815–1860," *Mississippi Valley Historical Review* 44, no. 3 (1957): 423–44; Lois W. Banner, "Religious Benevolence as Social Control: A Critique of an Interpretation," *Journal of American History* 60, no. 1 (1973): 23–41; Paul Boyer, *Urban Masses and Moral Order in America, 1820–1920* (Cambridge, MA: Harvard University Press, 1978); and Paul E. Johnson, *A Shopkeeper's Millennium: Society and Revivals in Rochester, New York, 1815–1837* (New York: Hill & Wang, 1978).

60. Ely, *Journal*, 136.

61. The most influential missionary tracts include John Eliot's *New England's First Fruits* (1643), Experience Mayhew's *Indian Converts* (1727), and Jonathan Edwards, ed., *An Account of the Life of the Late Reverend David Brainerd* (1749).

62. David Fairer and Christine Gerrard, *Eighteenth-Century Poetry: An Annotated Anthology*, 2nd ed. (Malden, MA: Blackwell, 2004), 470.

63. See Rowland Hill, *Village Dialogues* (1801); Hannah More, *The Shepherd of Salisbury Plain* (1795–1797); and Legh Richmond, *The Annals of the Poor* (1814).

64. Ely, *Journal*, 56.

65. "Counts and clergymen, lawyers, physicians, sailors, and harlots, meet here," Ely reflected after a year and a half in the almshouse and hospital, "as the fable states them to have done, in the ferry house at the River Styx." Ely, *Second Journal*, 78.

66. Scholars seeking to recover indigenous voices have increasingly read missionary-penned texts across the grain, attuning themselves to the model encounters those missionaries desired and looking for fissures within them as evidence of what the indigenous really believed. Hilary Wyss refers to these narratives as autoethnographies, stories in which "colonized people actively engage with the language of the colonizer as a means of establishing a place for themselves in the colonial order." Similar questions of engagement, language, and power persist in Ely's accounts. See Wyss, *Writing Indians: Literacy, Christianity, and Native Community in Early America* (Amherst: University of Massachusetts Press, 2000), 62.

67. Ely, *Journal*, 161. In this view, Ely distinguished himself from his two primary evangelical competitors for urban souls: Arminians, found among the Methodists and Low Church Protestant Episcopalians, and New Divinity, against whom Ely had already railed. See Fitzmier, *Moral Legislator*, 110–17.

68. Ely, *Journal*, 144.

69. Ibid., 115, 164, 51, 161, respectively.

70. Ibid., 14, 182–84, 203.

71. Ibid., 141, 226.

72. Ibid., 36, 165–66.

73. Ely, *Second Journal*, 94.

74. "My heart is good by nature," the woman told Ely; "I never saw a distressed person but I wished to help them, and did all in my power. I've done all I could, and behaved as well as I know how, and therefore expect that God won't be very strict with me." Ibid., 44.

75. "The doctrine of the sinner's being declared legally just, while in himself unjust, and accepted as pure, on account of the obedience and sufferings of Christ, while in himself impure, was a new doctrine to her, which she has yet to learn." Ely, *Journal*, 29–30.

76. Ely, *Journal*, 101–2. On the syncretic nature of black Christianity, see Mechal Sobel, *Trabelin On': The Slave Journey to an Afro-Baptist Faith* (Princeton, NJ: Princeton University Press, 1988); and Sylvia R. Frey and Betty Wood, *Come Shouting to Zion: African American Protestantism in the American South and British Caribbean to 1830* (Chapel Hill: University of North Carolina Press, 1999).

77. Leslie Harris, *In the Shadow of Slavery: African Americans in New York City, 1626–1863* (Chicago: University of Chicago Press, 2003), 3, 76.

78. Ely, *Second Journal*, 89–90, 168.

79. Ely, *Journal*, 19–20, 33–34; 79–80.

80. Ibid., 161, 176. For a description of Caroline and her backstory, pp. 154–56. On her repentance and Ely's quote about her potential art, see p. 167.

81. Ibid., 213–14.

82. Ely, *Journal* , 220–24; and *Second Journal*, 220.

83. Ely, *Second Journal*, 223–36.

84. Susanna Rowson, *Charlotte. A Tale of Truth* ([Philadelphia], 1794). Other examples of this genre in popular New York magazines and newspapers include "Angelina: A Tale," *Weekly Museum*, September 6, 1800, and "Emma, or a Tale of Woe. Founded on Fact," *Weekly Museum*, July 27, 1805.

85. Both were reprints of stories that first appeared in London papers. See "Caroline; or, the Seduced American," *Philadelphia Minerva*, January 14 and 21, 1797; and "From the London Oracle of Nov. 1: Seduction, and Its Effects," *The Daily Advertiser*, January 29, 1801.

86. See Cathy N. Davidson, *Revolution and the Word: The Rise of the Novel in America* (New York: Oxford University Press, 1986), 105, 135; Clare A. Lyons, *Sex among the Rabble: An Intimate History of Gender and Power in the Age of Revolution, Philadelphia, 1730–1830* (Chapel Hill: University of North Carolina Press, 2006), 316–18; and Marion Rust, "What's Wrong with Charlotte Temple?" *William and Mary Quarterly* 60 (January 2003): 99–118.

87. Stansell, *City of Women*, 11–18. See Timothy Gilfoyle, *City of Eros: New York City, Prostitution, and the Commercialization of Sex, 1790–1820* (New York: Norton, 1992) and Patricia Cline Cohen, *The Murder of Helen Jewett: The Life and Death of a Prostitute in Nineteenth-Century New York* (New York: Knopf, 1998).

88. Lyons, *Sex*, chap. 6.

89. London had established a Magdalen society as early as 1758. In 1800 a group of concerned white men founded a Magdalen society in Philadelphia and opened a Magdalen house by 1807. New York did not found a Magdalen society until late 1811. See Lyons, *Sex*, 324–25.

90. Ely, *Journal*, 60, 91.

91. Rust, "What's Wrong with Charlotte Temple?," 111.

92. Ely, *Journal*, 195–96. Ely's critics, ever ready to impugn him, insinuated that he frequently visited "Ladies of pleasure." See John Steele, *A History of Ecclesiastical Proceedings Relative to the Third Presbyterian Church in Philadelphia, the Rev. Ezra Stiles Ely, and Several of the Judicatories of the Church with Which They Are Connected* (Philadelphia, 1814), 64. On the popular misogyny that the ideological climate of postrevolutionary society reinvigorated, see Stansell, *City of Women*, 21–30.

93. [Ely], *William and Ellen*, 131–34.

94. Lyons, *Sex*, 328–31.

95. Ely, *Journal*, 11.

96. Here I follow Laura M. Stevens, who argues that Protestant British missionaries tried to craft an imperial identity out of a colonial encounter in their publications. See *British Missionaries, Native Americans, and Colonial Sensibility* (Philadelphia: University of Pennsylvania Press, 2004), 4.

97. On Ely's desire for state support, see *A Sermon for the Rich to Buy*, 20; on Milledoler's skepticism of such support, see Ely, *Journal*, 10.

98. Ely, *Journal*, 6.

99. See the character letter written by evangelical New York layman John E. Caldwell on Ely's behalf, February 23, 1813, reprinted in Steele, *History of Ecclesiastical Proceedings*, 25.

100. Ely, *Second Journal*, 27.

101. Ibid., ix, 81.

102. Ely cataloged some of the most common sources of mental disorder, which included love of money, love of country, vicious company, avarice, disappointments, intemperance, novel reading, slavery, and adultery. See Ely, *Journal*, 235, 236–58.

103. Ely, *Second Journal*, 84–85.

104. Frederick R. Karl, *A Reader's Guide to the Development of the English Novel in the Eighteenth Century* (London: Thames and Hudson, 1975), chapter 6, esp. 220–21.

105. Ely, *Journal*, 32–33.

106. I am indebted to Laura Stevens's discussion of the difference between sympathy and pity in *British Missionaries*, 9–12.

107. Ely, *Second Journal*, iii. The first London edition of the first *Journal* appeared before the first American edition of the *Second Journal* (1815).

108. Stevens, *British Missionaries*, 142.

109. Ely, *Journal*, 103, 156, 211; *Second Journal*, 13.

110. Amanda Porterfield, *Conceived in Doubt: Religion and Politics in the New American Nation* (Chicago: University of Chicago Press, 2012).

111. Ely, *Journal*, 174, 184.

112. Jay P. Dolan, *The Immigrant Church: New York's Irish and German Catholics, 1815–1865* (Baltimore, MD: Johns Hopkins University Press, 1975), chapter 1.

113. In one episode Ely antagonized an "old, deformed" Irish Roman Catholic woman who told him she loved Christ because "he died to help us do good works, to be shaure; and charity, you know, covers a multitude of sins. You can't deny that!" Ely could and did deny that, turning to the bed of another and praying out loud "that our good works could not save us, and entreated God that no one might be left to trust in outward ceremonies." Not to be denied, the enraged old woman cried out, "Christ died to help us do good works, I say; he died for the holy Catholic Church." Previous to this another woman who heard the conversation got her dig in at the Catholic woman, asking her, "But do you confess your sins to Christ?" To this, the other woman snapped back, "What is that to you? Are you my Father confessor?" Ely, *Second Journal*, 45–47; see also, 75–76. *Journal*, 129–30, 105.

114. Bleecker had a long history of individual action during periods of hardship. These included forming a Samaritan Society in January 1805 and a Fuel Association in December 1813. Mohl, *Poverty*, 138–39, 142. See Ely, *Second Journal*, 32.

115. For more on "Blind George," see Ely, *Journal*, 27, 38, 57, 67, 103–4, 131.

116. Ely, *Journal*, 52–53. Bleecker had a reputation as a troublemaker in the city's Baptist churches as well. See Edward Probyn Memorandum Book, 1812–1820, BV Probyn, NYHS.

117. Ely, *Journal*, 137–39.

118. Ely, *Sermon for the Rich to Buy*, 18.

119. Circulation number is from Ely, *Visits of Mercy*, vol. 1 (Philadelphia, 1829), x.

120. Ely's departure proved even more contentious than his entry into New York. See Steele, *A History of Ecclesiastical Proceedings*.

121. Ezra Stiles Ely, *Duty of Christian Freemen to Elect Christian Rulers* (Philadelphia, 1828). For more on Ely's efforts, see Eric R. Schlereth, "Fits of Political Religion: Stalking Infidelity and the Politics of Moral Reform in Antebellum America," *Early American Studies: An Interdisciplinary Journal* 5 (2007): 288–323.

122. See letter from Rev. John Romeyn, New York, to John Steele, Philadelphia, dated January 7, 1813, in the midst of Ely's trial before the Presbytery of New York. Reprinted in Steele, *History of the Ecclesiastical Proceedings*, 16.

123. Ely, *Second Journal*, 14.

124. *Report of a Committee on the Subject of Pauperism* (New York, 1818).

CHAPTER THREE

1. Edmund M. Blunt, *Blunt's Stranger's Guide to the City of New-York* (New York, 1817), 189–90, 195.

2. Ward Stafford, *The New Missionary Field: A Report to the Female Missionary Society for the Poor of the City of New-York, and Its Vicinity* (New York, 1817), 6–7, 55. Stafford did not count the Zion Protestant Episcopal Church in Mott Street, then being rebuilt after a fire, in his calculation.

3. Blunt, *Stranger's Guide*, 40–1, 47, 165. Patricia Cline Cohen has argued for the ascendancy of quantification as a primary means of advancing knowledge in the early nineteenth century. As knowledge came to be understood as composed of facts, counting became the preferred means of analysis because it produced hard numbers. "Statistical knowledge was deeply gratifying," she writes, "because it was presumed to be objective, unimpeachable truth." Patricia Cline Cohen, *A Calculating People: The Spread of Numeracy in Early America* (Chicago: University of Chicago Press, 1982), 206.

4. Weeden's calculations are low. If the population in 1820 was 123,706 and in 1825 it was 166,086, the population was probably closer to 149,000 in 1823. Ira Rosenwaike, *Population History of New York City* (Syracuse: Syracuse University Press, 1972), 36. Jonathan Weeden, "A Summary

View of the Houses for Public Worship, in the City and County of New-York, A.D. 1823" (New York, 1823); chart reprinted in *Evangelical and Literary Magazine* 6 (August 1823): 444–48.

5. See Jay P. Dolan, *The Immigrant Church: New York's Irish and German Catholics, 1815–1865* (Baltimore, MD: Johns Hopkins University Press, 1975), 11; Jonathan Greenleaf, *A History of the Churches, of All Denominations, in the City of New York, from the First Settlement to the Year 1846* (New York, 1846), 335–36.

6. Edwin G. Burrows and Mike Wallace, *Gotham: A History of New York City to 1898* (New York: Oxford University Press, 1999), 444.

7. Ibid., 419–22; Hilary Ballon, *The Greatest Grid: The Master Plan of Manhattan, 1811–2011* (New York: Museum of the City of New York; Columbia University Press, 2012), 27–55.

8. Ryan K. Smith, *Gothic Arches, Latin Crosses: Anti-Catholicism and American Church Design in the Nineteenth Century* (Chapel Hill: University of North Carolina Press, 2006). The exception to this rule did not come until 1857 when the Second Wesleyan Church on Mulberry Street moved uptown and renamed itself St. Paul's Methodist Episcopal Church.

9. See the appendix for a list of these publications.

10. John S. Stone, *A Memoir of the Life of Rev. James Milnor, D.D.* (New York, 1849), part 3.

11. Dorothy C. Barck, ed., *Letters from John Pintard to His Daughter, Eliza Noel Pintard Davidson*, vol. 2 (New York: Published for the New-York Historical Society, 1940–41), 39.

12. Stafford, *New Missionary Field*, 17–18.

13. See Franklin Bowditch Dexter, *Biographical Sketches of the Graduates of Yale College*, vol. 6 (New Haven: Yale University Press, 1912), 496–99.

14. Stafford, *New Missionary Field*, 5, 18.

15. Even in the better-settled wards, the ratio of residents to church buildings often numbered in the thousands instead of the hundreds. Blunt, *Stranger's Guide*, 44.

16. Stafford, *New Missionary Field*, 6–7.

17. Ibid., 7.

18. Ibid., 13.

19. Ibid., 11.

20. Ibid., 22–23.

21. Dell Upton, "Another City: The Urban Cultural Landscape in the Early Republic," in *Everyday Life in the Early Republic*, ed. Catherine E. Hutchins (Winterthur, DE: Henry Francis du Pont Winterthur Museum, 1994), 65; Upton, "The City as Material Culture," in Anne Elizabeth Yentsch and Mary C. Beaudrey, eds., *The Art and Mystery of Historical Archaeology: Essays in Honor of James Deetz* (Boca Raton, FL: CRC Press, 1992): 51–71. See also Elizabeth Blackmar, *Manhattan for Rent, 1785–1850* (Ithaca, NY: Cornell University Press, 1989), 77, 95–100, and Diane Shaw, *City Building on the Eastern Frontier: Sorting the New Nineteenth-Century City* (Baltimore: Johns Hopkins University Press, 2004), 26–27.

22. Upton, "Another City," 64–65. Historians have long been interested in the shadow landscapes of New York. See, for example, Timothy J. Gilfoyle, *City of Eros: New York City, Prostitution, and the Commercialization of Sex, 1790–1920* (New York: W. W. Norton, 1992) and Christine Stansell, *City of Women: Sex and Class in New York, 1789–1860* (Urbana: University of Illinois Press, 1987).

23. Stafford, *New Missionary Field*, 11.

24. Ibid., 23.

25. Ibid., 28–29.

26. Ibid., 27.

27. The colonial city functioned, as Sam Bass Warner Jr. has famously argued, as a "walking city." Historians have subsequently read a range of meanings into Warner's conception, arguing that integrated work and living spaces and spatial compactness contributed to deference and social harmony among the merchants, artisans, and laborers who inhabited it. See Sam Bass Warner Jr., *Streetcar Suburbs: The Process of Growth in Boston, 1870–1900* (Cambridge, MA: Harvard University

Press, 1978), 15–18. For a counter view, see Betsy Blackmar "Rewalking the 'Walking City': Housing and Property Relations in NYC, 1780–1840," *Radical History Review* 21 (1979): 131–48.

28. See Paul Boyer, *Urban Masses and Moral Order in America, 1820–1920* (Cambridge, MA: Harvard University Press, 1978), especially the preface and part 1.

29. Stafford, *New Missionary Field*, 27, 31. Historians have also made much of the ways in which the grid promoted surveillance, especially within prisons, almshouses, and other rehabilitative structures. See Michel Foucault, *Discipline and Punish: The Birth of the Prison* (New York: Pantheon Books, 1978), Michael Ignatieff, *A Just Measure of Pain: The Penitentiary in the Industrial Revolution* (New York: Pantheon Books, 1978), and David J. Rothman, *The Discovery of the Asylum: Social Order and Disorder in the New Republic* (Boston: Little, Brown and Company, 1971).

30. Stafford, *New Missionary Field*, 44–46.

31. Ibid., 48–50.

32. In February 1816, the New York Sunday School Union was formed. See the *Proceedings of the First Quarterly Meeting of the New York Sunday School Union Society* (New York, 1816), 14. In May, the New York Bible Society (formed in 1809) announced its national aspirations by helping found, and becoming an auxiliary to, the American Bible Society. See the American Bible Society, *First Annual Report* (New York, 1817).

33. Raymond Mohl, for example, cites that between April 1, 1814, and April 1, 1815, more than one-fifth of the city's residents sought some form of public relief. "Humanitarianism in the Preindustrial City: The New York Society for the Prevention of Pauperism, 1817–1823," *Journal of American History* 57 (December 1970): 578.

34. Ibid., 582.

35. Burrows and Wallace, *Gotham*, 493–95. See also Mohl, "Humanitarianism"; Carroll Smith-Rosenberg, *Religion and the Rise of the American City: The New York City Mission Movement, 1812–1870* (Ithaca, NY: Cornell University Press, 1971), 27, 39; and Raymond A. Mohl, *Poverty in New York, 1783–1825* (New York: Oxford University Press, 1971), 241–58.

36. *Second Anniversary Report of the Female Missionary Society for the Poor of the City of New York and its Vicinity* (New York, 1818). Over a third (185/501) of the women who had subscribed to the Society were listed under the names of their husbands, many of whose occupations could be discerned from *Longworth's New York Register, and City Directory* (New York, 1818).

37. Matthew La Rue Perrine, *Women Have a Work to Do in the House of God: A Discourse Delivered at the First Annual Meeting of the Female Missionary Society for the Poor in the City of New-York and Its Vicinity* (New York, 1817), 3.

38. Stafford, *New Missionary Field*, 41.

39. Gardiner Spring, *Memoir of Samuel John Mills* (Boston, 1829), 11.

40. Edwin F. Hatfield, *Patient Continuance in Well-Doing: A Memoir of Elihu W. Baldwin, D.D.* (New York, 1843), 133.

41. Gardiner Spring, *Personal Reminiscences of the Life and Times of Gardiner Spring* (New York, 1866), 304.

42. See *History of the Young Men's Missionary Society of New York: Containing a Correct Account of the Recent Controversy, Respecting Hopkinsian Doctrines* ([New York], 1817), 9–12.

43. *History of the Young Men's Missionary Society*, 18.

44. See *A Brief View of Facts which Gave Rise to the New-York Evangelical Missionary Society of Young Men* (New York, 1817).

45. Much of this area originated in the ancestral estate of Col. Henry Rutgers or the confiscated farms of the loyalist Delancey Family. Burrows and Wallace, *Gotham*, 389; Eric Homberger, *Historic Atlas of New York City* (New York: Henry Holt, 1994), 60–61; and Blackmar, *Manhattan for Rent*, 101–2.

46. Baldwin organized the Seventh Presbyterian Church on March 27, 1818, in a room in a house on Grand Street belonging to William Badeau, with whom he lived. Hatfield, *Patient Continuance*, 200.

47. Hatfield, *Patient Continuance*, 174–200, quote 218. See also *Third Annual Report of the Board of Directors of the Young Men's Missionary Society of New-York* (New York, 1818), 15–18.

48. Hatfield, *Patient Continuance*, 218, 227.

49. According to *Longsworth's New York Register, and City Directory* (1818), Catherine Street had ten grocers out of thirty-eight recorded occupations. Walking to church one Sabbath morning, Staffordcounted twenty-six open "tippling and fruit shops" in a short distance. Stafford, *New Missionary Field*, 13–15.

50. Spring, *Memoir of Samuel John Mills*, 111.

51. Stafford, *New Missionary Field*, 15.

52. Hatfield, *Patient Continuance*, 184. For more on the area, see Gilfoyle, *City of Eros*, 31–33, 51–53.

53. T. M. Dawson, *Semi-Centennial Sermon of the Seventh Presbyterian Church* (New York, 1868). 8.

54. Hatfield, *Patient Continuance*, 181–82.

55. These included a hatter, a cartman, the wife of a grocer, a shovel-maker, the wife of a smith, a carpenter, and a teacher. They were joined in subsequent years by a laborer, a rope maker, a mason, a shoemaker, and several more teachers. Seventh Presbyterian Church, Register, 1818–1858, PHS.

56. Between 1818 and 1834, women made up 60–80 percent of new church members each year. Seventh Presbyterian Church, Register.

57. Missionary William Gray promised that they were not abandoning their previous mission field and that Sunday schools would remain open. See "Female Missionary Society for the Poor of the City of New York and Its Vicinity," *Religious Intelligencer* 8, no. 9 (August 2, 1823): 132.

58. This seems hyperbolic considering the nearest Unitarian and Universalist congregations were on the other side of town. Hatfield, *Patient Continuance*, 264.

59. Hatfield, *Patient Continuance*, 270. On Baptist and Methodist meetinghouses founded subsequently in the area, see Greenleaf, *History of the Churches*, 146, 288.

60. Seventh Presbyterian Church, Session Records, 1818–1835, V MI46 N48ssr, PHS, entries for July 7, 1820; Jan 25, July 11, Oct 5, Nov 21, 1821; and July 17, 1822.

61. On the new Seventh Presbyterian Church, see Hatfield, *Patient Continuance*, 274–80.

62. Seventh Presbyterian Church, "Session Records," entries for December 14, 1826; January 5, February 25, March 9 and 16, and June 13, 1827.

63. The Church's session minutes typically record the names of those joining the church and, if they joined by letter of dismission, the name of the church that issued it. See Seventh Presbyterian Church, Session Records.

64. Seventh Presbyterian Church, Session Records, April 1825 and March 1828. The speed with which the session approached Hale made him uncomfortable, which his biographer later recorded in his memoirs. See Joseph Thompson, *Memoir of David Hale, Late Editor of the "Journal of Commerce" with Selections from His Miscellaneous Writings* (Hartford, 1850), 59–61.

65. Hatfield, *Patient Continuance*, 269; Edwin F. Hatfield, *Twenty Years in the Seventh Presbyterian Church, New-York City* (New York, 1855), 28.

66. See excerpts from the Fifth Annual Report of the NYEMS in *Christian Watchman* 3 (January 19, 1822): 23. For more on Cornish's career, see David E. Swift, *Black Prophets of Justice: Activist Clergy before the Civil War* (Baton Rouge: Louisiana State University Press, 1989). For more on New York's antebellum African American community, see Shane White, "Black Life in Freedom: Creating a Popular Culture"; Carla L. Peterson, "Black Life in Freedom: Creating an Elite Culture"; and Craig Steven Wilder, "Black Life in Freedom: Creating a Civic Culture," in *Slavery in New York*, ed. Ira Berlin and Leslie M. Harris (New York: New Press, 2005), 147–237; and Leslie Harris, *In the Shadow of Slavery: African Americans in New York City, 1626–1863* (Chicago: University of Chicago Press, 2003), chaps. 3 and 4.

67. The house of worship stood at Elm and Canal Streets, was 50 feet by 62 feet, and was built completely of brick. It cost $14,000 to build. Greenleaf, *History of the Churches*, 152–53.

68. See review of Sereno D. Clark's *The New England Ministry Sixty Years Ago: The Memoir of John Woodbridge, D.D.* (Boston, 1877) in "New Publications," *New York Evangelist* 68 (December 20, 1877): 2.

69. Blackmar, *Manhattan for Rent*, 213–16.

70. Paul Gilje, *Liberty on the Waterfront: American Maritime Culture in the Age of Revolution* (Philadelphia: University of Pennsylvania Press, 2004); Robert Greenhalgh Albion, *The Rise of New York Port, 1815–1860* (Hamden, CT: Archon, 1961).

71. Phillip Lopate, *Waterfront: A Journey around Manhattan* (New York: Crown, 2004), 221.

72. Brian Rouleau, "Dead Men Do Tell Tales: Folklore, Fraternity, and the Forecastle." *Early American Studies: An Interdisciplinary Journal* 5 (Spring, 2007): 30–62.

73. Edward D. Griffin, *The Claims of Seamen: A Sermon Preached November 7, 1819, in the Brick Church, New-York for the Benefit of the Marine Missionary Society of That City* (New York, 1819), 7.

74. These included the Marine Bible Society (1817), the Society for Promoting the Gospel among Seamen in the Port of New York (1818, better known as the New York Port Society), the New York Marine Missionary Society (1818), and the New York Bethel Union (1821). For a brief summary of the history of each, see "Seamen's Friend Society," *Sailor's Magazine, and Naval Journal* (July 1831): 333–41. Subsequent national organizations included the United Domestic Missionary Society (1822) and the American Seaman's Friend Society (1826).

75. *The Constitution of the New York Missionary Society* (New York, 1817), 5.

76. Griffin, *Claims of Seamen*, 13–22, quotes 13, 20, 22. See also John Romeyn, *A Sermon Delivered in the Middle Dutch Church on the Evening of the Lord's Day, March 21, 1819 for the Benefit of the New-York Marine Missionary Society* (New York, 1819).

77. The occupations of the forty-one officers and managers that can be traced break down as follows: ship captain (21), merchant (6), unidentified (6), lawyer (2), shipchandler (2), doctor (1), fur store owner (1), hatter (1), notary (1). "Marine Bible Society of New York," *Christian Herald* 2 (March 22, 1817): 413, and *Longworth's New York Register, and City Directory* for 1818 and 1819.

78. See New York Marine Bible Society, "Fifth Annual Report, read at the Anniversary Meeting, 11th April 1821," *CHSM* 8 (June 2, 1821): 59.

79. Christopher Prince, Diary (1819–1821), V H2 P935d, PHS, entry for May 3, 1819.

80. See Griffin, *Claims of Seamen*, 19.

81. Ward Stafford, *Important to Seamen. Extracts from a Report Entitled the New Missionary Field* (New York, 1817).

82. Stafford, *New Missionary Field*, 36.

83. Chase's dedication to preaching to sailors necessitated a permanent pulpit, which went against the norm of Methodist appointments, to the chagrin of some of his fellow ministers. See Henry Chase, Diary, Henry Chase Papers, BV New York City—Marriages, NYHS, entries for January 12 and 14 and February 9, 1825. On his efforts to secure a permanent pulpit from the Methodist Conference, see May 13, 1825; April 27 and 28 and May 12, 13, 19, and 20, 1826; and May 9 and 10, 1827.

84. Journal of the Bethel Flag, *CHSM* 8 (July 21, 1821): 137–38.

85. Journal of the Bethel Flag, *CHSM* 8 (July 7, 1821): 128.

86. The *Christian Herald* was founded in March 1816 by John Caldwell, the son of a Presbyterian minister. After his death in 1821, *Seaman's Magazine* was added to the title. See "Biographical Sketch of Mr. John E. Caldwell," *CHSM* 5 (March 20, 1819): 760–64. For more on the magazine, see Gaylord Albaugh, *History and Annotated Bibliography of American Religious Periodicals and Newspapers: Established from 1730 and 1830*, vol. 1 (Worcester, MA: American Antiquarian Society, 1994): 145–48. Quote about the new title from "Introduction," *CHSM* 8 (1822): iii–iv.

87. Journal of the Bethel Flag, *CHSM* 9 (June 15, 1822): 96. For other descriptions of awnings being put up see *CHSM* 8 (July 7, 1821): 121; and 8 (September 1, 1821): 253. I am thankful to Brian Rouleau for his insight into the mechanics of this transformation of the ship's deck.

88. Journal of the Bethel Flag, *CHSM* 8 (September 1, 1821): 253.

89. Ibid., 254.

90. Journal of the Bethel Flag, *CHSM* 8 (October 6, 1821): 317–18; see also *CHSM* 8 (March 2, 1822): 639; 8 (April 20, 1822): 733–34; and 9 (June 15, 1822): 96.

91. Journal of the Bethel Flag, *CHSM* 8 (October 6, 1821): 318; and 8 (September 1, 1821): 253.

92. Blackmar, *Manhattan for Rent*, 87–93; Brian Luskey, *On the Make: Clerks and the Quest for Capital in Nineteenth-Century America* (New York: NYU Press, 2011). On tensions between boardinghouse owners and sailors, see Gilje, *Liberty on the Waterfront*, 207–12.

93. The largest prayer meeting chronicled in Under the Bethel Flag numbered "100 ears." More often the number averaged between ten and thirty. See *CHSM* 9 (April 25, 1823): 703.

94. Chase, Diary, entry for December 18, 1822.

95. Journal of the Bethel Flag, *CHSM* 9 (April 19, 1823): 701–4.

96. Journal of the Bethel Flag, *CHSM* 9 (April 23, 1823): 702.

97. Chase, Diary, entry for May 31, 1828.

98. Chase went on to explain that "those who have families, and whose occupation is along the shore, I have found at their homes. There I visited them, left tracts, gave advice, reproved, exhorted, and warned them as their cases and circumstances might seem to require." "Report of the Rev. Henry Chase, to the Board of the Society for Promoting the Gospel among Seamen," *CHSM* 8 (August 18, 1821): 217–18.

99. Ibid., 218.

100. Chase, Diary, entry for November 18, 1821.

101. Ibid., entry for December 18, 1821.

102. See visit to 96 Henry Street in Ibid. When Chase revisited Mrs. Smith a month later, he had to comfort her and her family over the "unfavourable news from the ship" that her husband had been lost at sea.

103. Ibid., entries for January 2, 3, and 7, 1823.

104. Mrs. Smith's mother ended up lingering on beyond the winter of 1823. See Ibid., entries for January 5, 6, 8, 10, 11, 13, 17, 22, 23, 29, and February 12 and 24, 1823.

105. Miss Starr appears to have recovered. Ibid., entries for January 9, 10, 11, and 12, 1823.

106. Stafford, *New Missionary Field*, 35.

107. Prince, Diary, entry for October 13, 1820.

108. Another image, published just before a new meetinghouse opened, reveals that a center door was added at some later point. See "The Mariner's Church, Roosevelt Street, New-York," *National Magazine* 4 (February 1854): 112–13.

109. "Society for Promoting the Gospel among Seamen in the Port of New-York, Annual Report, Presented June, 1821," *CHSM* 8 (July 7, 1821): 124.

110. Prince, Diary, entry for June 11, 1820.

111. Chase, Diary, entries for January 3 and 12, 1823.

112. Dexter, *Biographical Sketches*, 499.

CHAPTER FOUR

1. Richard Brooks, *The Diary of Michael Floy, Jr., Bowery Village, 1833–1837* (New Haven, CT: Yale University Press, 1941), 84. The only extant copy of the tract I have located is at AAS, which is a later printing. See [Michael Floy Jr.], *Memoir of John Mather, Jun. A Sunday School Scholar Attached to the Bowery Village Sunday School Association, to which are added The Life and Happy Death of Rosetta Edgar* (New York, 1837).

2. On the place of the deathbed narrative in evangelical literature, see Henry D. Rack, "Evangelical Endings: Death-Beds in Evangelical Biography," *Bulletin of the John Rylands University*

Library of Manchester 74, no. 2 (Spring 1992): 39–56; and D. Bruce Hindmarsh, "'My Chains Fell Off, My Heart Was Free': Early Methodist Conversion Narrative in England," *Church History* 68 (December 1999): 910–29, esp. 927.

3. See Candy Gunther Brown, *The Word in the World: Evangelical Writing, Publishing, and Reading in America, 1789–1880* (Chapel Hill: University of North Carolina Press, 2004), 10.

4. Paul S. Boyer, *Urban Masses and Moral Order in America, 1820–1920* (Cambridge, MA: Harvard University Press, 1978). Despite being a brilliant exploration of the connections between evangelical publishing and the market, David Nord begins with the assumption that religion and the market had to be at odds. See David Paul Nord, *Faith in Reading: Religious Publishing and the Birth of Mass Media in America* (New York: Oxford University Press, 2004). See also Mark A. Noll, ed., *God and Mammon: Protestants, Money, and the Market, 1790–1860* (Oxford: Oxford University Press, 2001).

5. See John M. Giggie and Diane Winston, eds., *Faith in the Market: Religion and the Rise of Urban Commercial Culture* (New Brunswick, NJ: Rutgers University Press, 2002), 4. For more on relationship between religion and commercial culture, see Colleen McDannell, *Material Christianity: Religion and Popular Culture in America* (New Haven, CT: Yale University Press, 1995); R. Laurence Moore, *Selling God: American Religion in the Marketplace of Culture* (New York: Oxford University Press, 1994); David Morgan, *Protestants and Pictures: Religion, Visual Culture, and the Age of American Mass Production* (New York: Oxford University Press, 1999); and Nord, *Faith in Reading.*

6. Cornelius Davis, "Introduction," *New-York Missionary Magazine and Repository of Religious Intelligence* (New York, 1800), 1.

7. This was down from a high of twenty in 1813. See Clarence S. Bingham, *History and Bibliography of American Newspapers, 1690–1820* (Worcester, MA: American Antiquarian Society, 1947) 1:606–707; Edward Connery Latham, comp., *Chronological Tables of American Newspapers, 1690–1820* (Barre, MA: American Antiquarian Society and Barre Publishers, [1972]).

8. Benedict Anderson, *Imagined Communities: Reflections on the Origin and Spread of Nationalism* (1983; New York: Verso, 1991); Loughran, *Republic in Print*, 9–10.

9. On the important role of partisan politics in shaping the expansion of the public sphere in the Early Republic, see Jeffrey Pasley, *"The Tyranny of Printers": Newspaper Politics in the Early American Republic* (Charlottesville: University Press of Virginia, 2001).

10. Sidney I. Pomerantz, *New York: An American City, 1783–1803* (New York: Columbia University Press, 1938), 454–56; William Beer, *Checklist of American Periodicals, 1741–1800* (Worcester, MA; American Antiquarian Society, 1923); Benjamin M. Lewis, *A History and Bibliography of American Magazines, 1800–1810* (PhD dissertation, University of Michigan, 1956). Fueled by nationalism and republicanism, American authors attempted to create a distinctive American literature in the late 1780s and 1790s. See James N. Green, "The Rise of Book Publishing," in *A History of the Book In America, Vol. 2: An Extensive Republic: Print Culture and Society in the New Nation, 1790–1840*, ed. Robert Gross and Mary Kelley (Chapel Hill: University of North Carolina Press, 2010), 102–9; and Michael Warner, *The Letters of the Republic: Publication and the Public Sphere in Eighteenth Century America* (Cambridge, MA: Harvard University Press, 1990), chap. 5.

11. The term "sect" denoted a distinct group, or as Noah Webster defined it in 1806, "a body of men united in certain tenets or beliefs." The term is often used opposed to the more widely used nineteenth-century term "denomination" with its connotations of complex, organized religious structures. See Noah Webster, *A Compendious Dictionary of the English Language* (New Haven, 1806), 270, as quoted in Sam Haselby, "The Origins of Religious Nationalism, 1787–1832," (PhD dissertation, Columbia University, 2006), 278, 291.

12. "A Letter from the Baptists, to Their Dissenting Sister, Who Had Lately Joined the Universalists *and* Her Reply," *Free Universal Magazine* I (1793): 122–25. For more on Universalism, see Sidney E. Ahlstrom, *A Religious History of the American People* (New Haven: Yale University Press, 1972), 481–83.

13. For more on the history of the magazine, see Gaylord Albaugh, *History and Annotated Bibliography of American Religious Periodicals and Newspapers, Established from 1730 through 1830* (Worcester, MA: American Antiquarian Society, 1994), 401–3.

14. Trish Loughran, *The Republic in Print: Print Culture in the Age of U.S. Nation Building* (New York: Columbia University Press, 2007), 22.

15. Jeffrey L. Pasley, "The Two National Gazettes: Newspapers and the Embodiment of American Political Parties," *Early American Literature* 35 (2000): 55–56.

16. William Beer calculates that of ninety-six magazines published in the United States between 1741 and 1800, sixty-eight did not survive one year, sixteen expired in under two years, three under three years, and six under four years. Beer, *Checklist*, 4–5. See also Frank Luther Mott, *A History of American Magazines, 1741–1850* (Cambridge, MA: Harvard University Press, 1957), chap. 3.

17. Loughran, *Republic in Print*, 19–20.

18. Ibid., 6.

19. See Amanda Porterfield, *Conceived in Doubt: Religion and Politics in the New American Nation* (Chicago: University of Chicago Press, 2012).

20. "Introduction," *United States Christian Magazine* 1 (1795): 1.

21. "Introduction," *Christian's Magazine* 1 (1806): vi, xi.

22. On Whitefield's deployment of print, see Frank Lambert, *"Pedlar in Divinity": George Whitefield and the Transatlantic Revivals, 1737–1770* (Princeton, NJ: Princeton University Press, 1994), and *Inventing the "Great Awakening"* (Princeton, NJ: Princeton University Press, 1999); and Harry Stout, *The Divine Dramatist: George Whitefield and the Rise of Modern Evangelicalism* (Grand Rapids, MI: Wm. B. Eerdmans, 1991).

23. "Dedication," *Experienced Christian's Magazine* I (May 1796): 3.

24. "An Account of the Life and Death of Polycarp, Who Was Bishop (or Angel) of the Church of Smyrna, at the Time When St. John Was in the Isle of Patmos" (7–11) and "An Account of the Experience and Death of Mrs. Bartine of New York," (22–25) appeared in the first number of *The Experienced Christian's Magazine* (May 1796).

25. "Letter to the Editor," *Experienced Christian's Magazine* I (August 1796): 121.

26. "To the Patrons of the Experienced Christian's Magazine," *Experienced Christian's Magazine* II (April 1806): 283–85.

27. The literature on the public sphere is voluminous, but a good place to start is Jurgen Habermas, *The Structural Transformation of the Public Sphere: An Inquiry into a Category of Bourgeois Society* (Cambridge, MA: MIT Press, 1991). For a helpful introduction, see Craig Calhoun, "Introduction: Habermas and the Public Sphere," in *Habermas and the Public Sphere*, ed. Craig Calhoun (Cambridge, MA: MIT Press, 1992), 1–38; John L. Brooke, "Consent, Civil Society, and the Public Sphere in the Age of Revolution and the Early American Republic" in *Beyond the Founders: New Approaches to the Political History of the Early American Republic*, ed. Jeffrey L. Pasley, Andrew W. Robertson, and David Waldstreicher (Chapel Hill: University of North Carolina Press, 2004), 207–50; and John L. Brooke, *Columbia Rising: Civil Life on the Upper Hudson from the Revolution to the Age of Jackson* (Chapel Hill: University of North Carolina Press, 2013).

28. Letter to the Editor, *Theological Magazine* 3 (December 1798, January and February 1799): 470–71.

29. "Remarks on the Several Classes of Readers," *Theological Magazine* 2 (September and October 1796): 31–33.

30. Sperans, "On the Coming of the Redeemer's Kingdom," *New-York Missionary Magazine* 1 (1800): 257. Davis, "Preface," *New-York Missionary Magazine* IV: [i].

31. "The Black Prince," *New York Missionary Magazine* I (1800): 139–50; and "Account of the Conversion of Levi P——and Catharina M——, from the Jewish Religion to Christianity," *New York Missionary Magazine* III (1802): 185–88.

32. Sperans, "On the Coming," 259.

33. See Loughran, *Republic in Print*, 11–12, for more on this idea.

34. Mott, *History*, 199. For more on the *Port Folio*, see Edward Chielens, "The Port Folio" in *American Literary Magazines: The Eighteenth and Nineteenth Centuries*, ed. Edward Chielens (New York: Greenwood, 1986), 319–23.

35. "Number of Copies Subscribed For" bound in after the title page of the copy of the first volume of the *New-York Missionary Magazine, and Repository of Religious Intelligence for the Year 1800* in the collection of the PHS.

36. Davis, "Preface," *New-York Missionary Magazine* I (1803): [i–ii].

37. Davis explicitly addressed this issue in the preface to the third volume of the *Theological Magazine* (1799, p. 3).

38. Sperans, "On the Coming," 258.

39. Davis, "Preface," *New York Missionary Magazine* IV (1804).

40. *The First Annual Report of the New York Tract Society* (New York, 1813), 3.

41. When publishers in the latter regions tried to effect regional distribution agreements on jointly printed texts, New York's existence as a free trade zone between them often foiled their efforts. Green, "Rise of Book Publishing," 110.

42. See Green, "Rise of Book Publishing," 112–19, on technological advances, and 119–23 on geographic competition between the leading publishing centers.

43. On the importance of the Erie Canal to New York's economy, see Edwin G. Burrows and Mike Wallace, *Gotham: A History of New York City to 1898* (New York: Oxford University Press, 1999), chap. 27, and Robert G. Albion, *The Rise of New York Port, 1815–1860* (Hamden, CT: Archon Books, 1961), chap. 5.

44. *Compendium of the Enumeration of the Inhabitants and Statistics of the United States* (Washington, DC, 1841), 139.

45. William Jones, *The Jubilee Memorial of the Religious Tract Society* (London, 1849), chaps. 1–2.

46. Henry Forster Burder, *Memoir of the Rev. George Burder* (New York and Boston, 1833), 196.

47. "An Address to Christians, Recommending the Distribution of Cheap Religious Tracts," *New-York Missionary Magazine, and Repository of Religious Intelligence* 3 (1802): 361–72.

48. Divie Bethune, Diary (October 9, 1803, to January 6, 1805), WCL, entries for October 14 and November 18, 1804.

49. Rev. John Stanford also wrote, printed, and distributed tracts, including the eight-page "Way of Salvation" in 1794. See Charles G. Sommers, *Memoir of the Rev. John Stanford, D.D.* (New York, 1835), 16, 125–27, 142, 195–96, 280, 301.

50. Bethune was listed as a Manager and Life Subscriber to both the NYBS and NYTS. See *The Annual Report of the New-York Bible Society* (New York, 1810), 14, 15; *The First Annual Report of the New-York Religious Tract Society*, 10; and *The Third Annual Report of the New-York Religious Tract Society* (New York, 1815), 12.

51. Nord, *Faith in Reading*, 42–43.

52. The NYTS, for example, reported in 1815 that they distributed tracts to New England (12,960), New York State (11,395), New York City (5,335), New Jersey (1,727), Pennsylvania (1,208), Tennessee (387), and to itinerants (2,373) and steamboats (5,089) that connected many of these regions. See *The Third Annual of the New-York Religious Tract Society*, 5–6.

53. The adoption of stereotype printing put American Bible and tract publishers well in advance of the nation's commercial printers. On the adoption of stereotyped plates and the founding of the American Bible Society, see Paul C. Gutjahr, *An American Bible: A History of the Good Book in the United States* (Stanford, CA: Stanford University Press, 1999), 29–31; and Nord, *Faith in Reading*, 45–52. On Matthew Carey's decision to print Bibles from standing type, see Green, "Rise of Book Publishing," 97–98.

54. Elias Boudinot, *An Answer to the Objections of the Managers of the Philadelphia Bible-Society against a Meeting of Delegates from the Bible Societies in the Union to Agree on Some Plan to Disseminate the Bible in Parts without the United States* (Burlington, NJ, [1815]), 10, quoted in Haselby, "Origins," 308.

55. Haselby, "Origins," 307–13. For more on evangelical innovations in business, see Noll, ed., *God and Mammon*.

56. See Henry Otis Dwight, *The Centennial History of the American Bible Society* (New York, 1916), 21–23.

57. ABS, *First Annual Report* (New York, 1817), [iii].

58. Dwight, *Centennial History*, 32.

59. See *A Brief History of the American Tract Society, Instituted at Boston, 1814, and Its Relations to the American Tract Society at New York, Instituted 1825*. (Boston, 1857), 22–23.

60. *The Address of the Executive Committee of the American Tract Society to the Christian Public*, Tract 1 [June, 1825], 10, as quoted in Lawrance Thompson, "The Printing and Publishing Activities of the American Tract Society from 1825 to 1850," *Papers of the Bibliographical Society of America* 35 (Second Quarter 1941): 86–87.

61. The American Tract Society was headquartered in New York City until 1978, when it relocated to Garland, Texas. The American Bible Society is still headquartered in New York City.

62. For descriptions of these new specialized environments see W. P. Strickland, *History of the American Bible Society, Revised, and Brought Down to the Present Time* (New York, 1856), chap. 5; and ATS, *First Annual Report of the American Tract Society* (New York, 1826), 18–19.

63. The structure cost $22,500 and was paid for by private donations so that money would not be diverted from the distribution fund. Dwight, *Centennial History*, 67–68, 192.

64. ATS, *First Annual Report*, 18–19.

65. Dwight, *Centennial History*, 192–94.

66. For an overview of tracts published between 1825 and 1859, see *Sketch of the Origins and Character of the Principal Series of Tracts of the American Tract Society* (New York, 1859). For more on Baldwin's experience of writing a tract, see Edwin F. Hatfield, *Patient Continuance in Well-Doing: A Memoir of Elihu W. Baldwin, D.D.* (New York, 1843), 138–41.

67. Frustration with the system of voluntary distribution paved the way for the rise of colportage, a national distribution system based on salaried employees and managers in 1841. See Nord, *Faith in Reading*, chap. 5.

68. Ibid., 82–88.

69. Diane Ravitch, *The Great School Wars: New York City, 1805–1873* (New York: Basic Books, 1974); Tracy Fessenden, *Culture and Redemption: Religion, the Secular, and American Literature* (Princeton, NJ: Princeton University Press, 2007), chap. 3; Jon Gjerde, *Catholicism and the Shaping of Nineteenth-Century America* (Cambridge: Cambridge University Press, 2012).

70. See Haselby, "Origins."

71. John Henry Hobart, *A Pastoral Letter to the Laity of the Protestant Episcopal Church in the State of New-York, on the Subject of Bible and Common Prayer Book Societies* (New York, 1815), 5–6. On Hobart's larger objection to the ABS, see Dwight, *Centennial History*, 36–37.

72. The ABS published *Extracts from the Correspondence of the American Bible Magazine* (1818–1843) and the ATS the monthly *American Tract Magazine* (1825–1842) for their supporters, but only as updates on their activities. Albaugh, *History*, 51–52, 388–91.

73. See "The Press of New York," *Episcopal Recorder* 26, no. 42 (December 30, 1848): 168.

74. Leslie Harris, *In the Shadow of Slavery: African Americans in New York City, 1626–1863* (Chicago: University of Chicago Press, 2003), chap. 4.

75. James Penn Pilkington, *The Methodist Publishing House: A History, Volume 1* (Nashville, TN: Abingdon, 1968), prologue, chaps. 1 and 2, and *Since 1789: The Story of the Methodist Publishing House* (Nashville, TN: Abingdon, 1964). For the British origins of the Methodist Book Concern see Isabel Rivers, "Wesley as Editor and Publisher," in *The Cambridge Companion to John Wesley*, ed. Randy L. Maddox and Jason E. Vickers (Cambridge: Cambridge University Press, 2010), and "Religious Publishing," in *The Cambridge History of the Book in Britain*, vol. 5, 1695–1830, ed. Michael Suarez and Michael Turner (Cambridge: Cambridge University Press, 2009), 577–600; and Rich-

ard P. Heitzenrater, *Wesley and the People Called Methodists* (Nashville, TN: Abingdon Press, 1995), 156–57.

76. Bangs also was responsible for the publishing of two magazines aimed at younger audiences, *Youth's Instructor and Guardian* (1823–1832) and the *Child's Magazine* (1828–1842). See Albaugh, *History*, 107–8, 112–14, 597, 604–7, 1061–63.

77. Pilkington, *Methodist Publishing House*, 188, 232–40.

78. See Nord, *Faith in Reading*, 155–57, as well as J. Newton Brown, *History of the American Baptist Publication Society, from Its Origin in 1824, to Its Thirty-Second Anniversary in 1856* (Philadelphia, 1856); and Willard M. Rice, *History of the Presbyterian Board of Publication and Sabbath-School Work* (Philadelphia, [1889]).

79. David Max Eichhorn, *Evangelizing the American Jew* (Middle Village, NY: Jonathan David, 1978), 43–52; Howard B. Rock, *Haven of Liberty: New York Jews in the New World, 1654–1865* (New York: New York University Press, 2012), 110–11.

80. Robert Ernst, *Immigrant Life in New York City, 1825–1863* (New York: Octagon, 1979), 151.

81. George C. Smith, *The Life and Letters of James Osgood Andrew* (Nashville, TN, 1882), 98, as quoted in Pilkington, *Methodist Publishing House*, 164.

82. John Nelson Norwood, *The Schism in the Methodist Episcopal Church 1844: A Study of Slavery and Ecclesiastical Politics* (Alfred, NY: Alfred University, the Alfred Press, 1923), quote 67; Smith, *In His Image*, 94–114; and Goen, *Broken Churches*, 78–87.

83. Unlike the Methodists and Presbyterians, the Baptists had no single national governing body. Their schism, then, occurred within the national voluntary associations that oversaw their tract, Bible, and missionary operations. Smith, *In His Image*, 115–27; Goen, *Broken Churches*, 90–98.

84. As quoted in Goen, *Broken Churches*, 101.

85. Other examples include the New York publishers Robert Carter & Brothers and A. D. F. Randolph working with the Presbyterians. Brown, *Word*, 65–66, 74–78.

86. Ibid., 75–78.

87. See Michael Denning, *Mechanic Accents: Dime Novels and Working Class Culture in America* (London: Verso, 1998).

88. Brooks, *Diary*, 7, 123, and 235.

89. The rest of his outfit accommodated other reading necessities, such as his testament, pens and pencils, and India rubber. Brooks, *Diary*, 8.

90. See Brown, *Word*, introduction, quote 8.

91. Brooks, *Diary*, 107.

92. George L. Prentiss, ed. *The Life and Letters of Elizabeth Prentiss* (New York: Anson D. F. Randolph, 1882), 26–29.

93. Brooks, *Diary*, 31. See also pp. 9 (purchasing books from Irishman), 59 (his brother considers leaving the Methodist Book Concern), and 68 (book auction).

94. This was likely an edition of Joseph Alleine and Richard Baxter, *The Solemn Warnings of the Dead, or, An Admonition to Unconverted Sinners by Joseph Alleine; and, A Call to the Unconverted by Richard Baxter*, a Methodist Episcopal imprint which went through nine editions in New York and Philadelphia between 1792 and 1818.

95. Brooks, *Diary*, 15.

96. Ibid.

97. Watts's hymns were widely reprinted and favored by evangelicals in early America, although, interestingly, this hymn is not one included in the official hymnbooks produced by the Methodist Book Concern. For the full text, see Isaac Watts, *Hymns and Spiritual Songs, in Three Books* (Boston, 1801), 175.

98. Brooks, *Diary*, 17.

99. The ATS had no hesitancy in editing these texts to remove "controversial" or "sectarian" views. Brown, *Word*, 86–87.

100. Floy singled out Jonathan Edwards, William Penn, and George Whitefield as having particular influence on him. See Brooks, *Diary*, 42, 143, 146, 154.

101. Ibid., 104–5.

102. Stephen A. Marini, "Religious Change in Revolutionary Society, 1750–1790: Historiography, Contexts, Processes, Patterns," paper presented to the Boston Area Early American Studies Seminar, April 5, 2007, 34–39, quote 38. See also Mark Noll, *America's God: From Jonathan Edwards to Abraham Lincoln* (Oxford: Oxford University Press, 2002).

103. Brooks, *Diary*, 150.

104. Ibid., 46. See also 102.

105. Ibid., 186–87.

106. Ibid., 200.

107. Ibid., 189–90. For more on Martyn, see John Sargent, *Memoir of the Rev. Henry Martyn, B.D.* (London, 1816); and Avril A. Powell, "Henry Martyn," in *Oxford Dictionary of National Biography*, ed. H. C. G. Matthew and Brian Harrison (Oxford: Oxford University Press, 2004), 37: 36–37.

108. On the early history of the Bowery Village Methodist Episcopal church and meetinghouse, see J. B. Wakeley, *Lost Chapters Recovered from the Early History of American Methodism* (New York, 1858), 523–31; F. Bottome, *Bowery Village Methodist Episcopal Church: A Discourse* (New York, 1864); and *1786–1886 Centennial Anniversary—"Two-Mile Stone," "Bowery Village," now Seventh Street M.E. Church, New York City* ([New York], [1886]).

109. Brooks, *Diary*, 25.

110. Ibid.: for singing association, 22; for the camp meeting outing, 174–75, 179–81; for the benevolent society, 122–23, 131, 135–36.

111. Post, who did not show up to deliver the reward (or even teach his Sunday school class) for two Sundays proved equally livid at Floy's actions. Ibid., 54.

112. See *Methodist Magazine* 23 (1800): 291, as quoted in Rack, "Evangelical Endings," 44.

113. Rack, "Evangelical Endings," 42–49. The popularization of free will over predestination among Methodists shifted this dynamic somewhat. It provided a different kind of stress, as people feared that salvation might just as easily be lost as gained.

114. Brooks, *Diary*, 84–85.

115. While I generally agree with Scott Casper's interpretation of Floy, I depart from his belief that the shift from biographies of religious to secular figures meant that he was looking for something different in these texts. Rather I see a continuity in the criteria that he brings to bear on them. See Scott E. Casper, *Constructing American Lives: Biography & Culture in Nineteenth-Century America* (Chapel Hill: University of North Carolina Press, 1999), 125–34.

116. Brooks, *Diary*, 19.

117. The biography is James Sigston's *Memoir of the Life and Ministry of William Bramwell, with Extracts from His Correspondence* (London, 1821). See also Henry D. Rack, "William Bramwell," in *Oxford Dictionary of National Biography*, ed. H. C. G. Matthew and Brian Harrison (Oxford: Oxford University Press, 2004), 7:329. Brooks, *Diary*, 106–7.

118. Brooks, *Diary*, 233.

119. Floy carefully laid out his time as Mather's Sunday school teacher, as well as that of his subsequent teachers. On Sunday school literature, see Cornelia S. King, "Sunday School Lessons: The Moral Training in Periodical Fiction Published by the American Sunday-School Union, 1824–1853" (master's thesis, Temple University, Philadelphia, [1989]).

120. Floy, "Memoir of John Mather," 172. For Floy's feeling about the spiritual experience of children, see Brooks, *Diary*, 181–83.

121. Brooks, *Diary*, 85–86.

122. Farnam's narrative appeared the following week in the paper. See "Memoir of Rosetta Edgar, a Member of the Adult African Sabbath School of the M.E. Church New-York," *CAJ* 8 (June 27, 1834): 174. On Floy's experience writing the narrative and reactions to it, see Brooks, *Diary*, 85–87, 100–101.

123. See R. Gordon Kelly, *Mother Was a Lady: Self and Society in Selected America Children's Periodicals, 1865–1890* (Westport, CT: Greenwood, 1974), xiii–xiv, and Anne Scott MacLeod, *A Moral Tale: Children's Fiction and American Culture, 1820–1860* (Hamden, CT: Archon, 1975).

124. Brooks, *Diary*, 263.

125. See Kyle B. Roberts, "Locating Popular Religion in the Evangelical Tract: The Roots and Routes of *The Dairyman's Daughter*," *Early American Studies* 4, no. 1 (Spring 2006): 233–70.

126. *Eleventh Annual Report of the American Tract Society* (New York, 1836), 9–10.

127. Daniel Tyerman, *The Dairyman* (New York, n.d.).

128. See, for example, "Are Tracts Fiction? Verification of the Dairyman's Daughter," *Religious Intelligencer* 12 (September 8, 1827), 236.

129. This occurred in 1822. See "Legh Richmond" in Sir Leslie Stephen and Sir Sidney Lee, eds., *The Dictionary of National Biography* (London: Oxford University Press, 1917), 16:1144.

130. The chair is mentioned only in the description of a visit originally published in the *Christian Guardian* in 1821. See "A Visit to the Grave of the Dairyman's Daughter," *Theological Repertory, and Churchman's Guide* 3 (1821), 366. For a description of the chair, see Rev. Charles S. Robinson, quoted in Edwin Noah Hanby, "The Dairyman's Daughter's Chair" (n.p., n.d.), Collection of the American Tract Society, Garland, Texas.

131. Cathy N. Davidson, "The Life and Times of *Charlotte Temple*: The Biography of a Book" in *Reading in America: Literature & Social History*, ed. Cathy N. Davidson (Baltimore: Johns Hopkins University Press, 1989), 168–69.

CHAPTER FIVE

1. Lewis Tappan, Diary (February 16, 1828, to November 6, 1829), Tappan Papers, LOC, July 20, 1828.

2. Finney made less of an impression on evangelical clergy. See Gardiner Spring, *Personal Reminiscences of the Life and Times of Gardiner Spring* (New York, 1866), 226–29.

3. Tappan, Diary, February 16, 1828, and April 6, 1828.

4. The only modern full-length biography of Lewis Tappan is Bertram Wyatt-Brown, *Lewis Tappan and the Evangelical War against Slavery* (Cleveland, OH: Case Western Reserve University Press, 1969), quote viii. Tappan often appears in larger studies of the abolitionist movement, such as Gilbert H. Barnes, *The Antislavery Impulse, 1830–1844* (New York: D. Appleton-Century, 1933); and Lawrence J. Friedman, *Gregarious Saints: Self and Community in American Abolitionism, 1830–1870* (New York: Cambridge University Press, 1982).

5. Tappan, Diary, March 11, 1829 (tract work), and April 14 and 19 and December 20, 1828 (Sabbath cause).

6. Ibid., March 9 and 16, 1828.

7. See Jonathan Greenleaf, *A History of the Churches, of All Denominations, in the City of New York, from the First Settlement to the Year 1846* (New York, 1846), 151–52. Allen Street increased from 39 members in 1821 to 89 in 1830, one of the most dismal growth rates of any Presbyterian church in the city. See "Records of the Presbytery of New York," vols. II and III, MF Pos 593.r.2, PHS, as well as *Minutes of the General Assembly of the Presbyterian Church in the United States with an Appendix* (Philadelphia, 1825).

8. Tappan, Diary, November 30, 1828. For more on his involvement with the church, see May 13 and July 9, 16, and 22, 1828.

9. Lewis Tappan, "History of the Free Churches in the City of New York," in *A Narrative of the Visit to the American Churches by Deputation from the Congregational Union of England and Wales*, ed. Andrew Reed and James Matheson, vol. 2 (London, 1836), 371.

10. For example, the Cedar Street Presbyterian congregation raised over $40,000 in November 1808 to pay off the money advanced to purchase the land and erect a structure. See Warner Van

Norden, *The Fatness of Thy House, 1807–1924* (New York: Scribner, 1954), 3, 17. On seventeenth-century New England pew seating, see Robert J. Dinkin, "Seating the Meetinghouse in Early Massachusetts," *New England Quarterly* 43 (1970): 450–64.

11. Tappan, "History of the Free Churches," 380. Ironically, Methodists began to move away from these policies in the 1830s. See chap. 7.

12. See Lewis Tappan, *The Life of Arthur Tappan* (New York, 1870), 59–61, 70, quote 61. Lewis believed Arthur's return to a credit-based system later in life compromised his success and led to his bankruptcy in 1837. See pp. 295–97.

13. Ibid., 64. For more on Arthur as a businessman, see chaps. 5–7.

14. Joseph P. Thompson, *Memoir of David Hale, Late Editor of the "Journal of Commerce" with Selections from His Miscellaneous Writings* (Hartford, CT, 1850), 48.

15. Tappan, Diary, January 7, 14, and 15, 1829.

16. One Episcopalian writer calculated that a church of three hundred members paying what amounts to two cents a day could provide enough funding ($2,200) to support a church for a year. "The Free Church System," *Episcopal Recorder* 10 (April 7, 1832): 3.

17. Tappan, "History of the Free Churches," 379. For a counterexample, see Boyer, *Urban Masses and Moral Order in Early America* (Cambridge, MA: Harvard University Press, 1978).

18. See Garth M. Rosell and Richard A. G. Dupuis, eds., *The Memoirs of Charles G. Finney: The Complete Restored Text* (Grand Rapids, MI: Academie Books, 1989), 285n23, 286n26.

19. Philetus, "Revival of Religion in the Union Presbyterian Church in the City of New York," *New York Evangelist* 1 (May 29, 1830): 35.

20. Works that have portrayed Finney as "the perfect Jacksonian democrat, the enemy of aristocratic Calvinism," in the words of Allen C. Guelzo, include Whitney Cross, *The Burned Over District: The Social and Intellectual History of Religion in Western New York, 1800–1850* (New York, 1928); Perry Miller, *The Life of the Mind in America: From the Revolution to the Civil War* (New York: Harcourt, Brace and World, 1965); Timothy L. Smith, *Revivalism and Social Reform: American Protestantism on the Eve of the Civil War* (Nashville: Abingdon, 1978); and Johnson, *Shopkeeper's Millennium.* From a theological standpoint, Charles Hambrick-Stowe and Allen Guelzo argue, Finney is better understood as a product of the rival Calvinisms of Princeton and New England than as a rabid Anti-Calvinist Arminian who arose sui generis on the New York frontier. See Charles Hambrick-Stowe, *Charles G. Finney and the Spirit of American Evangelicalism* (Grand Rapids, MI: William B. Eerdmans, 1996), vii (quote), chap. 6; and Allen C. Guelzo, "An Heir or a Rebel? Charles Grandison Finney and the New England Theology," *Journal of the Early Republic* 17, no. 1 (Spring 1997): 61–94.

21. Charles G. Finney, "Sinners Bound to Change Their Own Hearts," *Sermons on Various Subjects* (New York, 1834), 3–28.

22. Guelzo, "An Heir or a Rebel?"; Hambrick-Stowe, *Finney*, chap. 4.

23. George Cragin, "The Free Church of Old Times," *Free Church Circular* 2 (February 7, 1850): 20.

24. The church was organized under the First Presbytery of New York on September 22, 1830. Tappan, "History of the Free Churches," 372. The following year it joined the more revivalist-friendly Third Presbytery. Historical Records Survey, *Inventory of the Church Archives of New York City* (New York, 1940), 31–32.

25. On Finney and other evangelicals' efforts to sidestep the issue, see Hambrick-Stowe, *Finney*, 90, 91, 112; and Paul Johnson, *A Shopkeeper's Millennium: Society and Revivalism in Rochester, NY, 1815–1837* (New York: Hill and Wang, 1978), chap. 3.

26. Tappan, "History of the Free Churches," 371–76, and *Church Manual, No. II, for the Communicants of the Free Presbyterian Church, City of New York* (New York, 1832), 3–4.

27. From Finney's *Memoir*, as quoted in Rosell and Dupuis, *Charles Finney*, 354.

28. See Rosell and Dupuis, *Charles Finney*, 353–57, quote 360; Tappan, "History of the Free Churches," 374–76; and Bradley Wright Griffin, "A Faith Performed: A Performance Analysis of

the Revivals Performed by Charles Grandison Finney at the Chatham Street Theatre, 1832–1836," (PhD dissertation, University of Texas at Austin, 2005).

29. Third Free Presbyterian later moved to the Eighth Ward on the northern edge of settlement. Rosell and Dupuis, *Charles Finney*, 359n15. Fourth Free Presbyterian met for a time in an old Brewery in the Fourth Ward at the corner of Madison and Catherine Streets and later purchased lots to erect a church in the same area. Greenleaf, *History*, 192–93; Tappan, "History of the Free Churches," 375–76. Fourth Free Presbyterian also rented out "a line of stores in the basement story on Catherine Street," Greenleaf, *History*, 177.

30. Greenleaf, *History*, 178.

31. Finney, *Revival Lectures* (Grand Rapids, MI: Fleming H. Revell, n.d.), 4–5.

32. See Finney, "Lecture XIV: Measures to Promote Revival" in *Lectures on Revivals*, as quoted in Hambrick-Stowe, *Finney*, 109. Despite the novelty the name suggested, the "new measures" had antecedents in evangelical practice.

33. Cragin, "Free Churches," 20, as quoted in Rosell and Dupuis, *Charles Finney*, 297n73; Keith J. Hardman, "Joel Parker," in *American National Biography*, ed. John A. Garraty and Mark C. Carnes (New York: Oxford University Press, 1999), 17:32–33.

34. Rosell and Dupuis, *Charles Finney*, 357–58.

35. Ibid., 359n15.

36. Ibid., 366n43. See also Hambrick-Stowe, *Finney*, 148–49.

37. Samuel A. Seaman, *Annals of New York Methodism, Being a History of the Methodist Episcopal Church in the City of New York, from A.D. 1766 to A.D. 1890* (New York, 1892), 250, 252–56.

38. S. D. Alexander, *The Presbytery of New York, 1738–1888* (New York, 1888), 82–83.

39. Tappan, "History of the Free Churches," 373.

40. *Church Manual*, 34–35.

41. This policy also involved a certain amount of surveillance, as Visitors were asked to keep a record of every one in their division who was present and absent at communion. *Church Manual*, 36–38.

42. Rosell and Dupuis, *Charles Finney*, 360.

43. Ibid., 361.

44. Cragin, "Free Church," 60; Tappan, "History of the Free Churches," 375.

45. Johnson, *Shopkeeper's Millennium*, 103.

46. Rosell and Dupuis, *Charles Finney*, 362. In this statement, Finney echoes an assessment Tappan made years earlier. Tappan, "History of the Free Churches," 379.

47. It also challenges Paul Boyer's conclusion that urban Protestantism's only success was among "the more settled and comfortable ranks." Boyer, *Urban Masses*, 10–11.

48. Between September 1830 and March 1832, 86 out of 110 men and 190 out of 215 women joined without a spouse. See *Church Manual*, 9–33.

49. See "Episcopal City Mission," in *New York Evangelist* 2 (November 12, 1831): 338. The Church of the Nativity (1834) and the Church of the Redemption (1836) were both were short-lived. See Greenleaf, *History*, 95, 99.

50. Hunt's narrative is reprinted in Tappan, *Arthur Tappan*, 283–87, quote 287. For the record of Hunt's joining the First Free Presbyterian Church, see *Church Manual*.

51. On the rising prevalence of alcohol in early America, see W. J. Rorabaugh, *The Alcoholic Republic: An American Tradition* (New York: Oxford University Press, 1979); Ronald G. Walters, *American Reformers, 1815–1860*, rev. ed. (New York: Hill and Wang, 1997), chap. 6; and for a gendered reading, Bruce Dorsey, *Reforming Men and Women: Gender in the Antebellum City* (Ithaca, NY: Cornell University Press, 2002), chap. 3.

52. Charles G. Finney, "Evidences of Regeneration," in *Lectures on Systematic Theology* (1878), as quoted in Anne C. Loveland, "Evangelicalism and 'Immediate Emancipation' in American Antislavery Thought," *Journal of Southern History* 32 (May 1966): 178–79. For more on Finney's

adoption of Hopkins's New Divinity ideas, see Hambrick-Stowe, *Finney*, 30–31, 80–82; and Guelzo, "An Heir or a Rebel?" 80.

53. Sabbitarianism, anti-Masonry, abolition, and women's rights proved too politically charged and potentially divisive in Rochester, for example, but temperance was a perfect fit. See Hambrick-Stowe, *Finney*, 110–13; and Johnson, *Shopkeeper's Millennium*, chap. 4.

54. *Church Manual*, 43.

55. Ibid., 8; Tappan, "History of the Free Churches," 379.

56. See *Church Manual*, 43–46.

57. On colonization and antislavery, see Leslie Harris, *In the Shadow of Slavery: African Americans in New York City, 1626–1863* (Chicago: University of Chicago Press, 2003), chap. 6; Manisha Sinha, "Black Abolitionism: The Assault on Southern Slavery and the Struggle for Racial Equality," in *Slavery in New York*, ed. Ira Berlin and Leslie M. Harris (New York: New Press, 2005), 241–62.

58. Tappan, *Arthur Tappan*, chap. 20; Wyatt-Brown, *Lewis Tappan*, chaps. 6 and 10.

59. Wyatt-Brown, *Lewis Tappan*, 81–84.

60. Finney departed New York soon after on a voyage for his health, not returning to New York until November 1834. Rosell and Dupuis, *Charles Finney*, 362. On the Tappans' early abolitionist activities, see Tappan, *Arthur Tappan*, chaps. 8–10.

61. Edwin G. Burrows and Mike Wallace, *Gotham: A History of New York City to 1898* (New York: Oxford University Press, 1999), 556.

62. Tappan, *Arthur Tappan*, 203.

63. Burrows and Wallace, *Gotham*, 556–60.

64. Paul Gilje interprets the attacks as an attempt to destroy the black community over labor competition in *The Road to Mobocracy: Popular Disorder in New York City, 1763–1834* (Chapel Hill: University of North Carolina Press, 1987), 162–69. Graham Russell Hodges agrees but also sees racism in play. Graham Russell Hodges, *Root and Branch: African-Americans in New York and East Jersey, 1613–1863* (Chapel Hill: University of North Carolina Press, 1999): 227–28. See also Burrows and Wallace, *Gotham*, 557–58.

65. Of forty different potential targets for the fourth night of rioting, most were private residences of leading evangelicals (18), homes of black entrepreneurs (10), or institutions of black evangelicals (5). A few represented the state (3), and a few do not seem to follow any pattern (4).

66. As quoted in Hambrick-Stowe, *Finney*, 149.

67. As quoted in Tappan, *Arthur Tappan*, 218.

68. Harris, *Shadow*, 199–201.

69. As quoted in Hambrick-Stowe, *Finney*, 148, 150.

70. Rosell and Dupuis, *Charles Finney*, 371–77.

71. The first mention of antislavery in the *Revival Lectures* does not come until the fifteen lecture, 325–27.

72. Tappan, Diary, February 25, 1836, and April 26, 1836.

73. Ibid., February 26 and March 5 and 9, 1836.

74. Ibid., March 3, 1836.

75. Ibid., March 22, 1836. See also March 31 and April 2 and 3, 1836.

76. Ibid., April 24 and May 1, 1836.

77. On the Panic of 1837 see Jessica Lepler, *The Many Panics of 1837: People, Politics, and the Creation of a Transatlantic Financial Crisis* (Cambridge: Cambridge University Press, 2013); Charles Sellers, *The Market Revolution: Jacksonian America, 1815–1846* (New York: Oxford University Press, 1994); and Daniel Walker Howe, *What Hath God Wrought: The Transformation of America, 1815–1848* (New York: Oxford University Press, 2009).

78. Arthur Tappan soon after retired to New Haven, attempting several business ventures, none of which met with much success. See Tappan, *Arthur Tappan*, chaps. 17 and 19. On the losses of other evangelicals, see L. Nelson Nichols, *History of the Broadway Tabernacle of New York City* (New Haven, CT: Tuttle, Morehouse, and Taylor, 1940), 65–68.

79. Many pages of Tappan's diary are covered in newspaper clippings and the few written entries focus on family matters. There are no written entries from mid-October 1836 to May 11, 1837; May 29 to July 30, 1837; and October 1837 to May 1838.

80. While stressing Arthur's heroic efforts to "make the blow fall as lightly as possible upon others," Lewis blamed Arthur's increased dependence on credit, despite his earlier policy of cash transactions only, for weakening the firm. Tappan, *Arthur Tappan*, 279–82, 294–98, quote 281.

81. Robert Greenhalgh Albion, *The Rise of the New York Port, 1815–1860* (Hamden, CT: Archon, 1961), 390. On the Panic's impact on the working class community, see Sean Wilentz, *Chants Democratic: New York City and the Rise of the American Working Class, 1788–1850* (New York: Oxford University Press, 1984), chap. 8; and Burrows and Wallace, *Gotham*, 616–18.

82. Charles G. Finney, "Lecture XIII: Being in Debt," *Oberlin Evangelist* 1 (July 31, 1839): 130, as quoted in Mark Noll, "Introduction," in *God and Mammon: Protestants, Money, and the Market, 1790–1860*, ed. Mark Noll (New York: Oxford University Press, 2002), 14. On evangelical efforts to alleviate temporal suffering, see Burrows and Wallace, *Gotham*, 619–21.

83. Joseph P. Thompson, *The Last Sabbath in the Broadway Tabernacle* (New York, 1857), 17.

84. Tappan's diary is again oddly silent, providing no indication of his feelings about the demise of a church he had been so instrumental in founding.

85. Nichols, *History*, 60; and Susan Hayes Ward, *The History of the Broadway Tabernacle Church, from Its Organization in 1840 to the Close of 1900* (New York: [Trow Print], 1901), 28.

86. The price tag was more than five times the cost of next most expensive, the Fourth Free Presbyterian Church, which opened in 1836 at a cost of $13,000. Greenleaf, *History*, 177; and Ward, *History*, 28.

87. Rosell and Dupuis, *Charles Finney*, 367; and Nichols, *History*, 58–59. On the important influence of the Broadway Tabernacle on Protestant church architecture, see Jeanne Halgren Kilde, *When Church Became Theater: The Transformation of Evangelical Architecture and Worship in Nineteenth-Century America* (New York: Oxford University Press, 2002); and Anne C. Loveland and Otis B. Wheeler, *From Meetinghouse to Megachurch: A Material and Cultural History* (Columbia: University of Missouri Press, 2003).

88. For the negative response of an evangelical paper in Boston, see "Congregational Church in N. York," *Boston Recorder* 21 (March 25, 1836): 50. On communion practice, see Ward, *History*, 38.

89. Rosell and Dupuis, *Charles Finney*, 371; and Nichols, *History*, 61. On the charged power of the term "amalgamation" see Harris, *Shadow*, 192.

90. Hardman, "Joel Parker," 32.

91. Tappan, Diary, August 28, 1838.

92. See Lewis Tappan, *Proceedings of the Session of Broadway Tabernacle, against Lewis Tappan, with the Action of the Presbytery and General Assembly* (New York, 1839), 8. For a critical take on Parker in the press at the time, see H. W. Davison, "Ecclesiastical Juggling," *Liberator* 8 (October 5, 1838): 158, and Lewis Tappan's response, "Rev. Joel Parker," *Liberator* 8 (October 19, 1838): 166.

93. Tappan, *Proceedings*, 8.

94. Ibid., 9–11; and Tappan, Diary, December 16, 1838.

95. For the account of the actual trial, see Tappan, *Proceedings*, 11–33.

96. Tappan, Diary, June 29, 1839.

97. Ward, *History*, 43.

98. Tappan, Diary, July 21, 1839.

99. Thompson, *David Hale*, 97.

100. "The Free Church System," *New York Evangelist* 10 (June 22, 1839): 98. The Broadway Tabernacle abandoned their free pews soon after Joel Parker was installed in the autumn of 1838. [Joseph Thompson], *History of the Broadway Tabernacle Church, with Some Account of the Building, and Events Contained Therewith* (New York, 1846), 5; Ward, *History*, 36.

101. Thompson, *David Hale*, 65–78, quotes 66, 75.

102. On Hale's early life, see Thompson, *David Hale*, 11–46; On Tappan's childhood in Northampton and life in Boston before coming to New York, see Wyatt-Brown, *Lewis Tappan*, chaps. 1–2.

103. Hale's dislike of the antislavery movement was well known in New York. See Thompson, *David Hale*, 63. See also his "Abolition in the Churches," *Journal of Commerce* (February 2, 1839); "Slavery and the Ecclesiastical Bodies," *Journal of Commerce* (June 17, 1846); and "Use of Abolitionism," *Journal of Commerce* (May 14, 1847), all reprinted in Thompson, *David Hale*, 213, 233–36.

104. Thompson, *David Hale*, 108–9.

105. Ibid., 61.

106. Ibid., 64.

107. Nichols, *History*, 76. For the substance of the remarks that Hale published a few days after this meeting, see Thompson, *David Hale*, 79–83, quote 80.

108. Thompson, *David Hale*, 79.

109. Ward, *History*, 45.

110. Thompson, *David Hale*, 141.

111. A Congregational church typically folded when the minister died or left the congregation. See Greenleaf, *History*, 352–59.

112. Nichols, *History*, 80.

113. Thompson, *David Hale*, 29, 31.

114. Nichols, *History*, 82; and Thompson, *David Hale*, 55.

115. Nichols, *History*, 83–84; and Greenleaf, *History*, 356, 361–62.

116. Nichols, *History*, 85.

117. Hale served as a committeeman in 1840, 1841, and 1843 and as a trustee in 1840–1841 and from 1844 to his death in 1849. See Ward, *History*, 250, 254.

118. On Andrews's life before and time at the Tabernacle, see Nichols, *History*, chap. 5.

119. Literature on the evolution of New England meetinghouses is extensive. See Ola Elizabeth Winslow, *Meetinghouse Hill* (New York: MacMillan, 1952); Edmund W. Sinnett, *Meetinghouse and Church in Early New England* (New York: McGraw-Hill, 1963); Marian C. Donnelly, *The New England Meetinghouses of the Seventeenth-Century* (Middletown, CT: Wesleyan University Press, 1968); and Peter Benes and Phillips D. Zimmerman, *New England Meeting House & Church: 1630–1850* (Boston, MA: Boston University; Currier Gallery of Art [for the Dublin Seminar for New England Folklife], 1979).

120. See "Trustees Records of the Broadway Tabernacle Church, 1840," October 26, 1840, Box 2, BTC NYHS.

121. Thompson, *Last Sabbath*, 19.

122. Ward, *History*, 45–47; and Nichols, *History*, 79–80. Hale and the trustees agreed on a ten-year lease beginning July 1, 1840, which carefully spelled out that the church had use of the "Great Room or Auditory" on the Sabbath and the study, the "lecture room in basement," and the sexton's apartment at any time. Hale reserved the right to use the great room every other day of the week. Copy of original lease in "Account of David Hale with Broadway Tabernacle Church," Box 44, BTC NYHS.

123. Ward, *History*, 79–80.

124. "The Broadway Tabenacle [*sic*], New York," *Christian Register* 23 (April 20, 1844): 62. Hale apparently drew the line at Universalists, much to their dismay. See "Affairs in New York City," *Trumpet and Universalist Magazine* 17 (March 8, 1845): 150; "Affairs in New York City," *Trumpet and Universalist Magazine* 17 (March 15, 1845): 153; and "David Hale and the Tabernacle," *Trumpet and Universalist Magazine* 17 (April 26, 1845): 177. See also Ward, *History*, 69.

125. David Hale, "To the Editor of the *Evangelist*," *New York Evangelist* 15 (April 11, 1844): 58. Hale's long letter was written in response to a piece in an earlier issue that took issue with the mixed use of the Tabernacle. See Scrutator, "Broadway Tabernacle," *New York Evangelist* 15 (March 28, 1844): 51.

126. At an April 1841 meeting, the trustees asked Hale to post a bill in the anteroom or hall of

the church "indicating what part of the house is open to strangers." See "Trustees Records of the Broadway Tabernacle Society, 1840," Box 2, BTC NYHS.

127. "Records of the Broadway Tabernacle Congregation, from the Date of Organization, October 20, 1840," Box 2, BTC NYHS.

128. [Thompson], *History*, 13; and Nichols, *History*, 85.

129. "Resolution on Collections for Charities in the Church," November 9, 1841, in [BTC] Journal (1840–1865), Box 1, BTC NYHS.

130. Specific church members tried to challenge this official stance, but Hale remained intractable. [BTC] Journal, May 1, 1843, and November 4, 1845.

131. Calculated from "Chronological List of Members," Ward, *History*, 263–66.

132. See "Records of the Committee of Broadway Tabernacle Church, New York, Commencing March 1843," Box 5, BTC NYHS, I:13–14.

133. Ibid., I:26.

134. Obituaries of Hale celebrated his philanthropy. "Death of David Hale, Esq." *New York Evangelist* 20 (January 25, 1849): 14 and "Death of Mr. David Hale," *Independent* 1 (January 25, 1849): 30. For a list of the Congregational churches Hale helped found, see Ward, *History*, app. F.

135. [BTC] Journal, February 27, 1843.

136. As quoted in Nichols, *History*, 88.

137. Andrews was remembered as a powerful speaker but could not sustain the energy of the spring 1843 revival. The rate of new members fell off and did not recover until the arrival of the next minister in March 1845. Ward, History, 63; Nichols, History, 93; and BTC NYHS, Box 44.

138. "Records of the Broadway Tabernacle Congregation, from the Date of the Organization," Box 2, BTC NYHS, August 6, 1844.

139. On Thompson's childhood and life before the Tabernacle, see Ward, *History*, 72, and John E. Todd, *In Memoriam: Rev. Joseph P. Thompson, D.D.* (n.p., n.d.).

140. Joseph Thompson, New Haven, to David Hale and the Ministerial Search Committee, New York City, December 25, 1844, Box 44, BTC NYHS.

141. As quoted in Ward, *History*, 75.

142. See [BTC] Journal, February 25 (quote) and March 11, 1845 (voting); for drafting the deed of conveyance for the structure, see "Trustees Records of the Broadway Tabernacle," February 27, 1845; and for the selling of the pews and other matters involving the entire congregation, see "Records of the Broadway Tabernacle Congregation," January 6, February 11, and March 11, 1845.

143. [Thompson], *History*, 43–45.

144. For an interesting exploration of abolitionism as a religion for those dissatisfied with evangelicalism, see Loveland, "Evangelicalism."

145. John William Ward, *Andrew Jackson: Symbol for an Age* (New York: Oxford University Press, 1962).

CHAPTER SIX

1. Phoebe Palmer, *Promise of the Father; or, A Neglected Specialty of the Last Days* (Boston, 1985), preface.

2. For more on Beecher, see Debby Applegate, *The Most Famous Man in America: The Biography of Henry Ward Beecher* (New York: Doubleday, 2006).

3. See Kathryn Long, "Consecrated Respectability: Phoebe Palmer and the Refinement of American Methodism," in Nathan O. Hatch and John H. Wigger, eds., *Methodism and the Shaping of American Culture* (Nashville, TN: Kingswood Books, 2001), 282. On the eclipse of Palmer's fame, see Charles Edwin Jones, "The Inverted Shadow of Phoebe Palmer," *Wesleyan Theological Journal* 31 (Fall 1996): 120–31. The most important modern-day studies of Palmer are Harold E. Raser, *Phoebe Palmer: Her Life and Thought* (Lewiston/Queenston: Edwin Mellen, 1987) and Charles Edward White, *The*

Beauty of Holiness: Phoebe Palmer as Theologian, Revivalist, Feminist, and Humanitarian (Grand Rapids: Zondervan, 1986). On Palmer's writings, see Thomas C. Oden, ed., *Phoebe Palmer: Selected Writings* (New York: Paulist Press, c.1998). Palmer is also remembered as a crucial bridge between eighteenth-century Wesleyan Methodism and twentieth-century Pentecostalism.

4. Richard Wheatley, *The Life and Letters of Mrs. Phoebe Palmer* (New York, 1881), 16–17.

5. This process is well documented in Elizabeth Blackmar, *Manhattan for Rent, 1785–1850* (Ithaca: Cornell University Press, 1989), and Sean Wilentz, *Chants Democratic: New York City & the Rise of the American Working Class, 1788–1850* (New York: Oxford University Press, 1984), chap. 1. The Worralls lived at 37 Duane Street in 1826 and at 83 Duane Street in 1829 according to *Longworth's American Almanac, New-York Register, and City Directory* (New York, 1826 and 1829).

6. On Henry Worrall's ability to provide for his family, see John A Roche, *The Life of Mrs Sarah A Lankford Palmer* (New York, 1898), 18.

7. Wheatley, *Life*, 20–21.

8. See the work of Methodists Mary Mason and Mary Morgan in 1813 in *Consecrated Talents; or, The Life of Mrs. Mary W. Mason, with an Introduction by Bishop Janes*. (New York, 1870), 36; and Presbyterians Joanna Graham Bethune and her mother Isabella Marshall Graham in George W. Bethune, D.D. *Memoirs of Mrs. Joanna Bethune* (New York, 1863), chap. 10.

9. Anne M Boylan, *Sunday School: The Formation of an American Institution, 1790–1880* (New Haven: Yale University Press, 1988), 16–18.

10. Boylan, *Sunday School*, chap. 1, 78. For more on the New-York Sunday School Union, see Edwin Burrows and Mike Wallace, *Gotham: A History of New York City to 1898* (New York: Oxford University Press, 1999), 498–501.

11. Class meetings were rigidly separated by gender, age, and race in the early part of the nineteenth century. See Philip Hardt, *The Soul of Methodism: The Class Meeting in New York Methodism* (Lanham, MD: University Press of America, 2000). On the experience of race in class meetings, see Kyle Bulthius, *Four Steeples over the City Streets: Religion and Society in New York's Early Republic Congregations* (New York: New York University Press, 2014), 265–66.

12. On the structure and goals of the camp meeting, see Dee Andrews, *The Methodists and Revolutionary America, 1760–1800: The Shaping of an Evangelical Culture* (Princeton, NJ: Princeton University Press, 2000), 76–84.

13. Burrows and Wallace, *Gotham*, 497.

14. There is a vast literature on antebellum urban reform movements. Particularly helpful are Barbara J. Berg, *The Remembered Gate: Origins of American Feminism: The Woman and the City, 1800–1860* (New York: Oxford University Press, 1978); Bruce Dorsey, *Reforming Men & Women: Gender in the Antebellum City* (Ithaca, NY: Cornell University Press, 2002); Lori D. Ginzberg, *Women and the Work of Benevolence: Morality, Politics, and Class in the Nineteenth-Century United States* (New Haven, CT: Yale University Press, 1990); Nancy A. Hewitt, *Women's Activism and Social Change: Rochester, New York, 1822–1872* (Ithaca: Cornell University Press, 1984); Mary P. Ryan, *Cradle of the Middle Class: The Family in Oneida County, New York, 1790–1865* (Cambridge: Cambridge University Press, 1981); and Carroll Smith-Rosenberg, "Beauty, the Beast, and the Militant Woman: A Case Study in Sex Roles and Social Stress in Jacksonian America," *American Quarterly* 23 (1971): 562–84.

15. Wheatley, *Life*, 16.

16. Helpful in formulating this understanding is Mary Kelley, *Learning to Stand and Speak: Women, Education, and Public Life in America's Republic* (Chapel Hill, NC: University of North Carolina Press, 2006), Introduction.

17. Roche, *Sarah Lankford Palmer*, 19–20.

18. *Mary; or, The Young Christian. An Authentic Narrative, by One Who Was Intimately Acquainted with Her from Her Infancy* (New York, n.d.), 10–11. For the history of this book, see Oden, ed., *Selected Writings*, 144–45.

19. *Mary*, 12. Amanda Porterfield explores this issue in eighteenth-century Northampton,

Massachusetts in *Female Piety in Puritan New England: The Emergence of Religious Humanism* (New York: Oxford University Press, 1992).

20. Wheatley, *Life and Letters*, 18. This is echoed in Rev. John A. Roche, "Mrs. Phoebe Palmer," *The Ladies' Repository* 26 (February 1866): 26.

21. Walter first considered entering the ministry but ultimately decided "that no calling on earth could be more Christlike, in its aims and purposes than that of a pious physician." *Guide to Holiness* 53 (1868), 5, as quoted in White, *Beauty*, 4.

22. New York City directories list Palmer at 244 Rivington Street in 1829, at 129 Allen Street in 1831 and '32, and at 54 Rivington Street from as early as 1835 onward. See *Longworth's American Almanac*.

23. Wheatley, *Life*, 25.

24. Palmer's nursemaid had been left to care for the infant when Phoebe went to entertain a guest in the parlor. The nurse burned her hand filling a lighted oil lamp and, in panic, threw it into the infant's cradle. Badly burned, the infant survived only a few hours. White, *Beauty*, 7–8.

25. Wheatley, *Life*, 26, 31.

26. Phoebe Palmer, *The Way of Holiness with Notes by the Way: Being a Narrative of Religious Experience Resulting from a Determination to be a Bible Christian* (New York, 1867), 17.

27. Briane K. Turley, *A Wheel within a Wheel: Southern Methodism and the Georgia Holiness Association* (Macon, GA: Mercer University Press, 1999), 18–21. See also Timothy L. Smith, "John Wesley and the Second Blessing," *Wesleyan Theological Journal* 21 (Spring–Fall 1986), 137–39.

28. Leading advocates include Methodists Nathan Bangs and Timothy Merritt, Congregationalists Asa Mahan and Thomas Upham, and Presbyterian Charles Grandison Finney. Phoebe Palmer had a very public and longstanding debate with the Western New York Methodist minister Hiram Mattison. See Raser, *Phoebe Palmer*, 57.On rising interest in perfectionism, see Melvin Easterday Dieter, *The Holiness Revival of the Nineteenth Century* (Metuchen, NJ: Scarecrow, 1980), 4; John Leland Peters, *Christian Perfection and American Methodism* (New York: Abingdon, 1956), 114–15.

29. Roche, *Sarah Lankford Palmer*, 30.

30. Ibid., 33.

31. Wheatley, *Life*, 29.

32. Ibid., 30, 36.

33. Paul C. Gutjahr, *An American Bible: A History of the Good Book in the United States* (Stanford, CA: Stanford University Press, 1999); Mark Noll, *America's God: From Jonathan Edwards to Abraham Lincoln* (New York: Oxford University Press, 2002), chap. 1.

34. Wheatley, *Life*, 39.

35. Ibid., 47.

36. "Holiness. What Is Gospel Holiness, or Sanctification?" *CAJ* 16 (October 20, 1841): 37. Raser, *Phoebe Palmer*, 153–61.

37. Wheatley, *Life*, 40.

38. See Barbara Welter, "The Cult of True Womanhood: 1820–1860," *American Quarterly* 18, no. 2 (1966) 151–74; Mary Ryan, *Cradle of the Middle Class: The Family in Oneida County, New York, 1790–1865* (Cambridge: Cambridge University Press, 1981); Nancy Cott, *The Bonds of Womanhood: "Women's Sphere" in New England, 1780–1835* (New Haven, CT: Yale University Press, 1977); Jeanne Boydston, *Home and Work: Housework, Wages, and the Ideology of Labor in the Early Republic* (New York: Oxford University Press, 1993); Carroll Smith-Rosenberg, *Disorderly Conduct: Visions of Gender in Victorian America* (New York: Alfred A. Knopf, 1985); Patricia Cline Cohen, *The Murder of Helen Jewett: The Life and Death of a Prostitute in Nineteenth-Century New York* (New York: Alfred A. Knopf, 1998).

39. "Letter from a Lady to Her Friend," *Guide to Christian Perfection* 1 (December 1839): 125–29; 1 (January 1840):145–50; and 1 (March 1840): 290–14. See Edwards, *Beauty*, 262n6.

40. "Holiness," *CAJ* 16 (October 13 and 20, 1841; November 3, 10, and 24, 1841). For a detailed analysis of Palmer's religious thinking in this series, see Raser, *Phoebe Palmer*, 152–64.

41. *CAJ* 17 (December 28, 1842): 77; 17 (January 4, 1843): 81; 17 (January 11, 1843): 85; 17 (January 18, 1843): 89; and 17 (January 25, 1843): 93. Reprinted in *Guide to Christian Perfection* 4 (March 1843): 200–204; 4 (April 1843): 220–24; 4 (May and June 1843): 269–74; 5 (July 1843): 7–14; and 5 (August 1843): 39–43.

42. Palmer went on to sell 52,000 copies of *The Way* in the United States. White, *Beauty*, 28; Anne Loveland, "Domesticity and Religion in the Antebellum Period: The Career of Phoebe Palmer," *Historian* 39 (May 1977), 456. Palmer also wrote "Notes by the Way" which was packaged with *The Way of Holiness* to provide readers with more information about her theology.

43. Palmer, *Way*, 17. "Methodist" is redacted in later editions of *The Way*.

44. Palmer pointed to three simple words from 1 Peter 1:16—"be ye holy"—as providing the key to the heavenly journey. Ibid., 20, 28.

45. Palmer, *Way*, 34.

46. Ibid., 46.

47. Ibid., 47–48.

48. Ibid., 49–50.

49. Palmer, "Refining Processes: 'I have chosen thee.' 'Great Trials,' Great Triumphs" in Oden, ed., *Selected Writings*, 322–25. For an explanation of this text, see Kendra Weddle Irons, "Phoebe Palmer: Chosen, Tried, Triumphant—An Examination of Her Calling in Light of Current Research," *Methodist History* 37 (1998): 28–36.

50. Lucy Lind Hogan, "Negotiating Personhood, Womanhood, and Spiritual Equality: Phoebe Palmer's Defense of the Preaching of Women," *ATQ (The American Transcendental Quarterly)* 14 (September 2000), 214–15.

51. The most famous articulation of this idea is Welter, "Cult of True Womanhood," 151–74.

52. See Catherine Brekus, *Strangers and Pilgrims: Female Preaching in America, 1740–1845* (Chapel Hill, NC: University of North Carolina Press, 1998).

53. Hogan, "Negotiating Personhood," 215.

54. Ibid., 220–21.

55. Much of this poetry was gathered into the posthumous publication *A Mother's Gift; or, A Wreath for My Darlings* (New York, 1875). See also White, *Beauty*, 27.

56. See *Recollections and Gathered Fragments of Mrs Lydia N Cox of Williamsburg, L.I.* (New York, 1845) and *The Useful Disciple; or, A Narrative of Mrs Mary Gardner* (London, 1857).

57. George Hughes, *Fragrant Memories of the Tuesday Meeting and the Guide to Holiness, and Their Fifty Years' Work for Jesus* (New York, [1886]), 182. Story is quoted in White, *Beauty*, 28.

58. White, *Beauty*, 92–94; Raser, *Phoebe Palmer*, 71–73.

59. Walter Clarker Palmer Jr. (1842–1885) converted at age ten but never experienced sanctification. See White, *Beauty*, 30, 58–59.

60. Wheatley, *Life*, 238. See also, *Fragrant Memories*, chap. 1.

61. Sarah and her husband, Thomas Lankford, shared the Rivington Street house with the Palmers during these early years of the Tuesday Meeting before they moved up to Caldwell-on-the-Hudson in April 1840. In 1865 the Palmers moved to 23 St Mark's Place and in 1870 to 316 East 15th Street, taking the meeting with them. White, *Beauty*, 35, 100.

62. Reprinted from the *Guide to Holiness* and the *Promise of the Father* in Wheatley, *Life*, 253.

63. Wheatley, *Life*, 239–41.

64. Raser, *Phoebe Palmer*, 50.

65. Wheatley, *Life*, 268; see also 248–49.

66. Ibid., 247.

67. Long, "Consecrated Respectability," 281–307, quote 284.

68. Wheatley, *Life*, 243.

69. Ibid., 246. Palmer saw her sister Sarah as one that could aspire to that level of leadership.

70. See ibid., for examples in Brunswick, Maine (239), Philadelphia (276), and Rock Island City (247–48).

71. Palmer recorded in her diary on April 11, 1845: "Both parlors have been filled with a crowd much like tent-meetings and camp-meetings." Ibid., 244–45.

72. The camp meeting at Sing Sing, Long Island, was established in 1831, although it traced its origins back to Westchester County in 1804. See *Ossining Remembered* (Charleston, SC: Arcardia, 1999), 97; "The Sing-Sing Camp-Meeting.; Great Gathering of Methodists How they Live and What They Do: The Origin of Camp-Meetings; Tenting on the Old Camp Ground; Scenes and Incidents," *New York Times* , August 22, 1865, 8.

73. Brekus, *Strangers and Pilgrims*, 139–42, 267–69.

74. Wheatley, *Life*, 264.

75. Ibid., 290–8, quote 298.

76. Ibid., 309.

77. Ibid., 285.

78. Ibid., 321.

79. Palmer most frequency mentions her sister Sarah as her traveling companion, especially for long trips to Philadelphia and upstate New York. See, for example, ibid., 275.

80. From 1853 onward, Walter dedicated his holiday month to "physical and spiritual recuperation in evangelical expeditions" in Canada. Ibid., 300–301.

81. Ibid., 206–10, 215–18, 230–32, quote 232.

82. Carroll Smith-Rosenberg, *Religion and the Rise of the American City: The New York City Mission Movement, 1812–1870* (Ithaca, NY: Cornell University Press, 1971), 171–73, 185, 188–203, 206–10, 215; Leslie Harris, *In the Shadow of Slavery: African Americans in New York City, 1626–1863* (Chicago: University of Chicago Press, 2003), 6, 135, 147–67.

83. Originally published in "A Mission at the Five Points" *CAJ* 25 (July 11, 1850): 111. Reprinted in Ladies of the Mission, *The Old Brewery, and the New Mission House at Five Points* (New York, 1854), 36.

84. Rosenwaike, *Population History*, 36, 40–43.

85. Harris, *Shadow*, 250.

86. The classic text on antebellum Protestant anti-Catholic sentiment is Ray Allen Billington, *The Protestant Crusade, 1800–1860: A Study of the Origins of American Nativism* (New York: Macmillan, 1938).

87. "Constitution of the Ladies' Home Missionary Society of the M.E. Church for the City of New-York, formed April 1844" *CAJ* 18 (May 15, 1844):159.

88. The formation of an incorporated church typically marked the end of the LHMS's financial support and involvement. On these churches, see Samuel A. Seaman, *Annals of New York Methodism: Being a History of the Methodist Episcopal Church in the City of New York from A.D. 1766 to A.D. 1890* (New York, 1892), 333–34, 338–39, 341–43.

89. Wheatley, *Life*, 223–24.

90. John M. Hartmann, "New-York Ladies' Home Missionary Society," *CAJ* 19 (April 16, 1845): 143; Imogen Mercein, "A Pleas for the Home Mission of the City of New York", *CAJ* 20 (January 21, 1846): 96; Seaman, *Annals*, 392–94.

91. C. W. Doering, "The German Bethel Ship," *CAJ* 24 (April 12, 1849): 59; "Ladies Home Mission," *CAJ* 25 (May 16, 1850): 77.

92. *Old Brewery*, 34. For the larger history of Five Points, see Tyler Anbinder, *Five Points: The Nineteenth-Century New York City Neighborhood That Invented Tap Dance, Stole Elections, and Became the World's Most Notorious Slum* (New York: Free Press, 2001).

93. Phoebe Palmer's biographer credited the inspiration for the mission to an idea that came to her during the funeral procession for her father. Official histories of the mission do not substantiate

that attribution. Wheatley, *Life*, 224. The official history of the LHMS's efforts at Five Points credited inspiration to the similar work of Thomas Chalmers in Edinburgh. *Old Brewery* 22–30.

94. "Ladies' Home Missionary Society," *CAJ* 24 (May 17, 1849): 78; Anbinder, *Five Points*, 244.

95. Wheatley, *Life*, 225.

96. Imogen Mercein, "A Mission at the Five Points," *CAJ* 25 (July 11, 1850): 111. See also, Smith-Rosenberg, *Religion*, 227.

97. Louis M. Pease, "Five Points Mission," *CAJ* 26 (February 13, 1851): 28.

98. "The Five Points," *CAJ* 25 (September 5, 1850): 142; *Old Brewery*, 40.

99. Imogen Mercein, "The Ladies Home Missionary Society," *CAJ* 26 (June 5, 1851): 91. On Pease's feelings of being overwhelmed, see "Efforts at the Five Points," *CAJ* 27, January 29, 1852, 19.

100. *Old Brewery*, 47–49.

101. *Old Brewery*, 80; Imogen Mercein, "Dedication at the Five Points," *CAJ* 28 (June 30, 1853): 102. The LHMS made clear its desire to add, when funds became available, a workroom, a hospital, a reading room, and more apartments. *Old Brewery*, 303–4.

102. Diane Ravitch, *The Great School Wars: New York City, 1805–1873* (New York: Basic Books, 1974), chaps. 1–8; on evangelical clashes with Public School Society, see 21–22, 26. On Roman Catholic responses, see Jay P. Dolan, *The Immigrant Church: New York's Irish and German Catholics, 1815–1865* (Baltimore, MD: Johns Hopkins University Press, 1975), 100–110.

103. Imogen Mercein, "Triumphant Death at the Five Points' Mission," *CAJ* 27 (April 1, 1852): 53; reprinted in *Old Brewery*, 103–7.

104. "Ripe Fruit of Missionary Labour at the 'Five Points' Gathered into the Garner Above," *CAJ* 28 (October 20, 1853): 166; reprinted in *Old Brewery*, 130–35.

105. Jay P. Dolan, "Catholicism and American Culture: Strategies for Survival," in Jonathan D. Sarna, ed., *Minority Faiths and the American Protestant Mainstream* (Urbana: University of Illinois Press, 1998), 70.

106. "The Freeman's Journal and Catholic Register," *CAJ* 27 (November 11, 1852): 82. See also "The Five Points Mission," *CAJ* 28 (October 13, 1853): 162; "Five Points Mission," *CAJ* 28 (December 8, 1853): 194.

107. *Old Brewery*, 127.

108. Ibid., 195–97.

109. On the challenges facing the city's Catholic Church, see Dolan, *Immigrant Church*.

110. Smith-Rosenberg, *Religion*, 232–33.

111. See "The Freeman's Journal and Catholic Register," *CAJ* 27 (November 11, 1852): 82; "The Five Points Mission," *CAJ* 28 (October 13, 1853): 162; and "Five Points Mission," *CAJ* 28 (February 23, 1854): 30.

112. Smith-Rosenberg, *Religion*, 186.

113. Imogen Mercein, "Dedication at the Five Points," *CAJ* 28 (June 30, 1853): 102.

114. "Five Points Mission," *CAJ* 28 (December 8, 1853): 194.

115. *Old Brewery*, 132.

116. In "The One Infirmity Conquered," Pease is presented as having introduced the protagonist into an environment in his House of Industry that led to the loss of her health and possessions. *Old Brewery*, 204–13; also 57.

117. "The Twenty-Shilling Piece," *CAJ* 28 (September 15, 1853): 145, "The Five Points Mission," *CAJ* 28 (October 13, 1853): quote 162; "Five Points Mission," *CAJ* 28 (December 8, 1853): 194.

118. Seaman, *Annals*, 402–5.

119. Smith-Rosenberg, *Religion*, 238–42.

120. Wheatley, *Life*, 227.

121. *Old Brewery*, 88–90.

122. Phoebe Palmer, *Israel's Speedy Restoration and Conversion Contemplated; or, Signs of the Times in Familiar Letters* (New York, 1854).

123. David Max Eichhorn, *Evangelizing the American Jew* (Middle Village, NY: Jonathan David, 1978), 2, 78, 108–9, 115, 118–23, 125, 128–31. Eichhorn does not discuss Palmer's Ladies' Jewish Association and Industrial Tea Meeting. See Wheatley, *Life*, 227–29.

124. Wheatley, *Life*, 213–14.

125. Ibid., 228.

126. C. C. Goen, *Broken Churches, Broken Nation: Denominational Schisms and the Coming of the American Civil War* (Macon, GA: Mercer University Press, 1985).

127. This typically worked out to between a 2 percent and a 4 percent increase. The *Almanac of the Methodist Episcopal Church* for 1856 reported 800,327 members, up from 799,431 in 1855. For a reporting of numbers between 1853 and 1861, see table I in appendix B in Kathryn Long, *The Revival of 1857–58: Interpreting an American Religious Awakening* (New York: Oxford University Press, 1998), 144.

128. "Religious Bodies in the United States," *CAJ* 32 (February 12, 1857).

129. This decline might have reflected displacements from traditional Methodist strongholds with rapid migration across the continent or spiritual declension in a period of economic boom.

130. James V. Watson, *Helps to the Promotion of Revivals* (New York, 1856), was advertised in an issue of the *CAJ* between the third and fourth installments of Palmer's "Laity" series.

131. Watson, *Helps*, 14.

132. [Phoebe Palmer], "A Laity for the Times," *CAJ* 32 (February 12, 1857).

133. All quotes from "A Laity for the Times," *CAJ* 32 (February 19, 1857).

134. "A Laity for the Times," *CAJ* 32 (March 12, 1857).

135. Palmer deliberately chose not to label her speaking on religious topics to crowds as "preaching." Catherine Brekus argues that this reflects her middle-class background and a distancing from working class female preachers. Nevertheless, what Palmer actually did before gathered crowds for over thirty years was, in fact, preaching. See Brekus, *Strangers and Pilgrims*, 338.

136. Wheatley, *Life*, 323.

137. Ibid., 330.

138. The most comprehensive account is Long, *Revival*. See also John Corrigan, *Business of the Heart: Religion and Emotion in the Nineteenth Century* (Berkeley: University of California Press, 2002); Timothy L. Smith, *Revivalism and Social Reform: American Protestantism on the Eve of the Civil War* (Nashville, TN: Abingdon, 1978), chap. 4.

139. On the Panic, see Burrows and Wallace, *Gotham*, chap. 47.

140. Both had reverberations in other urban centers: by November, the YMCA had initiated a prayer meeting in Philadelphia, and the following month, Charles Grandison Finney initiated a four-month residency in Boston.

141. On the coverage of the revival by the secular press, see Long, *Revival*, chap. 2.

142. Applegate, *Most Famous Man*, 294–99.

143. "A Laity for the Times," *CAJ* 32 (March 12, 1857).

144. The *Independent* was more popularly known as "Beecher's paper" for its regular columns by the popular Brooklyn preacher.

145. In fact, Cheever proved an even greater foe than Beecher, and the two would have a falling out a few years later.

146. "The Two Revivals," *Independent* 10 (March 4, 1858): 1. See also, Long, *Revival*, 113–14.

147. "The Revival," *Independent* 10 (March 11, 1858), as quoted in Long, *Revival*, 93.

148. For more on this divide, see Long, *Revival*, chap. 6.

149. "City Intelligence: More Trouble in Dr. Cheevers' Church," *The New York Herald* 7876 (March 27, 1858): 5. Many of the dismissed congregants transferred their membership to the Broadway Tabernacle.

150. Applegate, *Most Famous Man*, 294–300.

151. Smith, *Revivalism*, 211–12, as quoted in Raser, *Phoebe Palmer*, 223.

152. Long, *Revival*, chap. 4. On the appeal of evangelicalism to women and African Americans, see the appendix.

153. Palmer, *Promise of the Father*, 1. Anne Loveland argues for an inherent conflict in Palmer's theology between domestic and religious duties. In her interpretation, Palmer recognized women's domestic obligations but did not see them restricting her to the domestic sphere. See Loveland, "Domesticity and Religion in the Antebellum Period," 455–71.

154. Palmer, *Promise*, 29.

155. Ibid., 165.

156. Ibid., 162–63.

CHAPTER SEVEN

1. "Great Excitement in John Street. Trouble among Methodists," *New York Daily Tribune* 16 (July 26, 1856): 5; "A Muss among the Methodists—The John Street Church Difficulty," *Weekly Herald* 20 (July 26, 1856): 233; "The John Street Methodist Church. The Fight Gets into the Streets," *New York Daily Times* 5 (July 26, 1856): 8. The city's religious papers remained largely silent on the incident.

2. "The John Street Church Difficulties.—A Free Fight," *New York Dispatch* 11 (July 27, 1856): 5.

3. The Churches of England, Scotland, France, and Holland all had houses of worship in the colonial city.

4. On the founding of John Street, see Nathan Bangs, *The Substance of a Sermon Preached on the Opening of the Methodist Church in John-street, in the City of New York* (New York, 1818), 8–10, and *A Short Historical Account of the Early Society of Methodists Established in the City of New York in the Year 1763* (New York, 1824), 3–5; J. B. Wakeley, *Lost Chapters Recovered from the Early History of American Methodism* (New York, 1858), chaps. 2–4; Samuel A. Seaman, *Annals of New York Methodism, Being a History of the Methodist Episcopal Church in the City of New York, from A.D. 1766 to A.D. 1890* (New York, 1892), chaps. 2 and 3. For more recent treatments of John Street's founding, see Dee Andrews, *The Methodists and Revolutionary America, 1760–1800: The Shaping of an Evangelical Culture* (Princeton, NJ: Princeton University Press, 2000), 35–38; and Kyle Bulthius, *Four Steeples over the City: Religion and Society in New York's Early Republic Congregations* (New York: New York University Press, 2014), 36.

5. Nineteenth-century historian Jonathan Greenleaf credits the Baptists with using that space before the Methodists; Greenleaf, *A History of the Churches, of All Denominations, in the City of New York, from the First Settlement to the Year 1846* (New York, 1846), 225.

6. Wakeley says the structure stood until 1854; Wakeley, *Lost Chapters*, chap. 5. More recently Raynor R. Rogers has argued that the structure was radically altered in 1854 and stood until 1910; Rogers, *The Story of Old John Street Church* (New York: John Street Press, 1984), 6.

7. Seaman, *Annals*, 25. On Wesley's innovations in sacred space, see George W. Dolbey, *The Architectural Expression of Methodism: The First Hundred Years* (London: Epworth, 1964).

8. Originally the structure had no galleries, but the increase in worshippers necessitated their addition in 1778. *Short Historical Account*, 7; Wakeley, *Lost Chapters*, 108–9; Seaman, *Annals*, 36–41.

9. The earliest published attribution to Heck is in Bangs, *Substance*, 11–12. Wakeley built on this in *Lost Chapters*, 65–67. Rogers points out that Palatine Methodists simply built what they knew in *John Street Church*, 10.

10. *Short Historical Account*, 7.

11. Richard Allen, *The Life, Experience, and Gospel Labors of the Rt Rev Richard Allen* (Philadelphia, 1880), 18. On the broader appeal of Methodism in postrevolutionary America, see Nathan Hatch, *The Democratization of American Christianity* (New Haven, CT: Yale University Press, 1989), and John H. Wigger, *Taking Heaven by Storm: Methodism and the Rise of Popular Christianity in America* (New York: Oxford University Press, 1998).

12. David Hempton, *Methodism: Empire of the Spirit* (New Haven, CT: Yale University Press, 2005), chap. 6.

13. Ibid., chap. 4.

14. Wakeley devotes four chapters to the history of Peter and Molly Williams in *Lost Chapters*, 438–79.

15. See Bulthius, *Four Steeples*, 125–28.

16. For membership numbers, see Seaman, *Annals*, 82, 207–8; for the decision to rebuild, 203. See also, Kyle Bulthius, "Preacher Politics and People Power: Congregational Conflicts in New York City, 1810–1830," *Church History* 78 (June 2009): 270–72.

17. *Short Historical Account*, 7; Wakeley, *Lost Chapters*, 581–82.

18. Seaman, *Annals*, 205–6.

19. On New York's systematic landscape, see Dell Upton, "Inventing the Metropolis: Civilization and Urbanity in Antebellum New York," in Catherine Hoover Voorsanger and John K. Howat, eds., *Art and the Empire City, New York, 1825–1861* (New Haven, CT: Yale University Press, 2000), 3-45, quote 11–12.

20. The Bowery Church built its first dedicated church from the frame of the original John Street meetinghouse. F. Bottome, *Bowery Village Methodist Episcopal Church* (New York, 1864), 6–20.

21. For the histories of these churches, see Seaman, *Annals*, chaps. 10–17, and *A Familiar Conversational History of the Evangelical Churches of New-York* (New York, 1839), 200–214; and Greenleaf, *History*, 281–330.

22. *Short Historical Account*, 5.

23. Seaman, *Annals*, 112, 144, 180, 182.

24. Ibid., 195–98.

25. Ibid., 206, 209, 212.

26. Samuel Stilwell, *Historical Sketches of the Rise and Progress of the Methodist Society in the City of New York* (New York, 1821), 42.

27. Ibid., 12.

28. Ibid., 16–23. See also Seaman, *Annals*, 217–31, and Bulthius, "Preacher Politics," 270–75.

29. Seaman, *Annals*, 219.

30. Ibid., 230.

31. Joshua Soule, *The Substance of a Discourse, Delivered in the New Methodist Meeting House in John-Street, New-York: On the Evening of the 4th of January, 1818* (New York, 1818), 30–31.

32. Bangs, *Substance*, 30.

33. See Edwin G. Burrows and Mike Wallace, *Gotham: A History of New York City to 1898* (New York: Oxford University Press, 1999), 429–32, 435-39, 450–51; Robert Greenhalgh Albion, *The Rise of New York Port, 1815–1860* (Hamden, CT: Archon, 1961); Carol Sheriff, *The Artificial River: The Erie Canal and the Paradox of Progress, 1817–1862* ([New York]: Hill and Wang, 1996).

34. Burrows and Wallace, *Gotham*, 611–8; Jessica M. Lepler, *The Many Panics of 1837: People, Politics, and the Creation of a Transatlantic Financial Crisis* (New York: Cambridge University Press, 2013).

35. Federal and state censuses reveal, in finer grain, population growth from 4 to 6 percent every five years during this period, with the exception of 1835–40, reflecting the detrimental effects of the panic. The overall population of the city increased from 123,706 in 1820 to 312,710 in 1840. Ira Rosenwaike, *Population History of New York City* (Syracuse, NY: Syracuse University Press, 1972), 36.

36. Rosenwaike, *Population History*, 36, 44–45. See also Graham Russell Gao Hodges, *Root and Branch: African Americans in New York and East Jersey, 1613–1863* (Chapel Hill: University of North Carolina Press, 1999), and Leslie M. Harris, *In the Shadow of Slavery: African Americans in New York City, 1626–1863* (Chicago: University of Chicago Press, 2003).

37. Eric Homberger, *The Historical Atlas of New York City, A Visual Celebration of Nearly 400 Years of New York City's History* (New York: Henry Holt, 1994), 69.

38. Homberger, *Atlas,* 77; Burrows and Wallace, *Gotham,* 564–67.

39. See Nan A Rothschild, *New York City Neighborhoods: The 18th Century* (San Diego: Academic Press, 1990), chap. 1; Elizabeth Blackmar, "Rewalking the 'Walking City': Housing and Property Relations in NYC, 1780–1840," *Radical History Review* 21 (1979): 131–48; Elizabeth Blackmar, *Manhattan for Rent, 1785–1850* (Ithaca, NY: Cornell University Press, 1989); Kenneth A. Scherzer, *The Unbounded Community: Neighborhood Life and Social Structure in New York City, 1830–1875* (Durham, NC: Duke University Press, 1992).

40. Burrows and Wallace, *Gotham,* 391–92; Tyler Anbinder, *Five Points: The Nineteenth Century Neighborhood That Invented Tap Dance, Stole Elections, and Became the World's Most Notorious Slum* (New York: Free Press, 2001).

41. Burrows and Wallace, *Gotham,* 596–601; Homberger, *Atlas,* 78–79.

42. Seaman, *Annals,* 279–80.

43. See *Minutes of the Annual Conferences of the Methodist Episcopal Church, for the Years 1829–1839,* vol. 2 (New York, 1840).

44. Deborah Dash Moore, *Urban Origins of American Judaism* (Athens: University of Georgia Press, 2014), 23.

45. On the histories of these churches, see Seamans, *Annals,* 296–99, 300–321.

46. Even though not everyone agreed with this departure from Methodist practice, it would become increasingly common in the years to come. Despite their best efforts, the debt at the Second Wesleyan Chapel grew to be such an embarrassment that they permitted the mortgage to be foreclosed on. See Seaman, *Annals,* 321–26.

47. See Greenleaf, *History,* on the Methodist Society (306–8), Methodist Protestants (308–10), Welsh Methodists (310–14), Primitive Methodists (314–16), Wesleyan Methodists (317–20), and the African Methodist Churches (320–29). On the city's complex landscape of African American churches, see Christopher Rush, *A Short Account of the Rise and Progress of the African M.E. Church in America* (New York, 1843; republished 1866).

48. On Clement Moore's opening up of this neighborhood for settlement, see Burrows and Wallace, *Gotham,* 447–48. Methodist class meetings met in scattered settlements along the North River above Greenwich beginning in the 1820s. A more permanent site for worship was established in the house of a lay member on 18th Street, and then a frame church went up on 20th Street between Seventh and Eighth Avenues in 1830. It moved around the corner to 18th Street and Eighth Avenue in 1836. By that point Baptists had opened a Sunday School on 16th Street, moved to a frame church in 18th Street in 1833, and moved back to 16th Street in 1838. Presbyterians worshipped in a schoolhouse on 17th Street, a rented storefront on Eighth Avenue, and finally, in 1834, moved to a church on 18th Street. St. Peter's Protestant Episcopal formed a chapel in 1831 and a full church in 1838. See Seaman, *Annals,* 318–21; Greenleaf, *History,* 89–90, 189–90, 262–64.

49. Episcopalians opened St. Mary's at Manhattanville, St. Ann's at Fort Washington, St. Matthew's in Yorkville, and St. Andrew's in Harlem during this period. See Greenleaf, *History,* 74–78, 87–88.

50. These included the old German Reformed Church in 1822 (to found the South Baptist Church), a former Presbyterian Church on Provost Street in 1825, and a former Universalist Society Church in 1837 (to found the short-lived West Baptist Church). Greenleaf, *History,* 246–47, 250–51, 266–67.

51. Ibid., 193–94.

52. These include All Saints, 1819; Evangelist, 1831; Epiphany, 1833; and Nativity, 1834. Ibid., 90–97.

53. John Street Methodist Episcopal Church Board of Trustees, Minutes, 1838–1867, JSMEC, March 9, 1840. See also Rogers, *John Street Church,* 30–31.

54. Seaman, *Annals,* 280; Rogers, *John Street Church,* 32.

55. Debt incurred by the board of trustees rose from over $78,000 in 1833 to nearly $90,000 in 1834. Seaman, *Annals,* 270, 271.

56. Ibid., 274–76. On John Street's share of the debt, see Board of Trustees, Minutes, 1838–1867, November 22, 1838.

57. *CAJ* 15 (1840): 27, as quoted in Seaman, *Annals*, 280.

58. Burrows and Wallace, *Gotham*, 471.

59. The author of *A Familiar Conversational History* studiously avoided giving any consideration to the history of the city's non-Protestant churches and hoped the book would be used in Sunday schools. See 10, 18, quote 11.

60. Wakeley, *Lost Chapters*, 576.

61. *A Short Historical Account*, frontispiece.

62. J. B. Wakeley had Smith create the illustrations for *Lost Chapters*; see page 41. On Smith's career as a painter, see Arthur Bruce Moss, "Joseph Beekman Smith, Methodist Artist, and the Original Painting of John Street Church," *Methodist History* 3 (July 1965): 28–30.

63. This might be most evident in Smith's inclusion of John Street's heroic first generation in his images of the first meetinghouse and the lack of recognizable people connected with their building in his paintings of the second and third meetinghouses.

64. Collapse of the Ohio Life Insurance and Trust Company in August started the chain reaction that led to the Panic of 1857. See Burrows and Wallace, *Gotham*, 649–70, 843–45.

65. Burrows and Wallace, *Gotham*, 735–7; Rosenwaike, *Population History*, 35–43.

66. Rosenwaike, *Population History*, 36, 44–45. On African Americans as targets for urban violence, see Burrows and Wallace, *Gotham*, 854–58; Iver Bernstein, *The New York Draft Riots: Their Significance for American Society and Politics in the Age of the Civil War* (New York: Oxford University Press, 1990).

67. Homberger, *Atlas*, 77.

68. Burrows and Wallace, *Gotham*, 714–17, 726–30.

69. Eric Homberger, *Scenes from the Life of a City: Corruption and Conscience in Old New York* (New Haven, CT: Yale University Press, 1994), chap. 1.

70. William Perris, *Maps of the City of New York Surveyed under Direction of Insurance Companies of Said City*, vol. 1 (New York, 1857), plate 6.

71. William Perris, *Maps of the City of New York Surveyed under Direction of Insurance Companies of Said City, West 22nd to West 52nd Street* (New York, 1859), plate 91.

72. See the May 14, 1849, motion (unanimously passed) to "sell the stores no 42 and 48 John Street for not less than twenty-thousand dollars each with reservation of light for the church." Board of Trustees, Minutes, 1838–67, May 14, 1849.

73. Seaman, *Annals*, 279. The revival was part of a citywide uptick in interest in evangelicalism in the midst of the recession, which saw the number of members in Methodist churches increase by 44 percent, from 6,787 in 1841 to 9,780 in 1843. Burrows and Wallace, *Gotham*, 628–29. Methodist membership numbers can be found in *Minutes of the Annual Conferences of the Methodist Episcopal Church, for the Years 1839–1845*, vol. 3 (New York, 1840).

74. See John Street Methodist Episcopal Church, Register, 1842–54, Item 240, MER NYPL. On the history of Methodist class meetings, see Philip F. Hardt, *The Soul of Methodism: The Class Meeting in Early New York City Methodism* (Lanham, MD: University Press of America, 2000).

75. *Minutes of the Annual Conferences*, vol. 6 (1856).

76. On the failure of Methodists to devise particularly effective strategies for converting non-Protestants, see David Hempton, *The Religion of the People: Methodism and Popular Religion, c. 1750–1900* (London: Routledge, 1996), chap. 2; see also chapter 6 of this book.

77. "Legal Record," *Evening Post*, May 10, 1855, 2.

78. "City Intelligence," *New York Herald*, April 29, 1856, 1.

79. Seaman, *Annals*, 341–42, 344–46, 347–48, 352–53.

80. By 1860 there were congregations in the following wards north of 14th Street (from south to north): 16 (2), 18 (1), 20 (2), 21 (1), 22 (3), 19 (2), and 12 (3).

81. Fifth Avenue Baptist began in 1855 on Fifth Avenue and 35th Street but the church was not able to afford the cost of the pricey thoroughfare and moved three years later.

82. Just off of Fifth Avenue were Madison Avenue Presbyterian and Fourth Avenue Presbyterian (1855) on the corner of 22nd Street. Reconstructed from 1840s and '50s city directories and from Historical Records Survey, *Inventory of the Church Archives of New York City: The Presbyterian Church* (New York: Work Projects Administration, 1940).

83. Reconstructed from Historical Records Survey, *Inventory of the Church Archives of New York City, Volume 2: Protestant Episcopal Church in the United States of America, Diocese of New York* (New York: Work Projects Administration, December 1940). See also David Dunlap, *From Abyssinian to Zion: A Guide to Manhattan's Houses of Worship* (New York: Columbia University Press, 2004).

84. Seaman, *Annals*, 391–94, 336–39; Greenleaf, *History*, 301–2.

85. These include the Bloomingdale German Mission (1852 to at least 1860), the Centre Street Mission (1852–1856), the Five Points Mission (1853 onward), the German Home Mission (1847–1848), Manhattanville Mission (1853 to 1858), the North River Mission (1846–1849), Swedish Mission (1850 to at least 1859), Washington Street German Mission (1852–1856), and Welsh Mission (1855–1860). All reported low numbers of members. See *Minutes of the Annual Conferences* for 1840–1860.

86. The Dutch Reformed opened a Mission Church in a schoolroom on Allen Street in 1835 (and later a small church on Forsyth and Houston), the Third German mission on Duane Street in 1855, and Fourth German on W. 28th Street in 1860. Protestant Episcopals founded St. Timothy's in 1837 and St. Simon's in 1844. Baptists opened their First German Mission in 1850 followed by a second one, on the other side of the city, in 1853. Presbyterians accepted the Second German Evangelical Mission Church into the Presbytery from the Dutch Reformed Consistory in 1852. Greenleaf, *History*, 48, 102–3, 193–94.

87. On the Protestant Episcopal Missionary Society for Seamen in the City and Port of New York (originally the Young Men's Auxiliary Society, a subsidiary of the City Mission Society), see *Inventory: Protestant Episcopal Church*, 90–91. Presbyterians took the longest, opening the Church of the Sea and Land in 1864. Greenleaf, *History*, 270; *Inventory: Presbyterian Church*, 72.

88. The City Missionary Society was organized in 1831 "to provide by building, purchase, hiring or otherwise, as many churches at different points in the City of New York, as they may deem proper, in which churches the seats shall be free, and to provide suitable clergymen to act as missionaries in the said churches." Missions aimed at specific ethnic populations included St. Saveur's (French, 1842–1849), St. Simon's (German, 1843–1858), St. George the Martyr (British, 1845–1900), and Church of the Circumcision (Jews, 1846–1848).

> The few missions founded after this point tended to target geographic regions, like Holy Martyrs on Forsyth Street (1846–1894), the Astor Place Mission (1855), and the Madison Street Free Chapel (1857–1897).
>
> St. Jude's Episcopal Free Church (1842–1853) was in the Chapel of New York University until it moved to Sixth Avenue near 4th Street. Transfiguration (1849–present) was first in the home of a layman before moving to 1 East 29th Street. *Inventory: Protestant Episcopal Church*, 78–79, 87–89, 93–96, 102.

89. Evidence that the number for Catholics is inflated can been seen in the reported numbers for 1865, which were only half that (54,170). There are reasons why Catholics might have played up their religious identity in the mid-1850s, which was a high-water mark for nativism in the city.

90. See the Garden Street or South Dutch Church, for example. *Familiar Conversational History*, 100; Greenleaf, *History*, 21.

91. The congregation of the Duane Street Presbyterian Church, which had already moved uptown from Cedar Street in 1835, moved again to Fifth Avenue at the corner of 19th Street in 1852. *Inventory: Presbyterian Church*, 39.

92. "City Intelligence," *New York Herald*, April 29, 1856, 1. On the sale to the *New York Times*, see Burrows and Wallace, *Gotham*, 717.

93. Ryan Smith, *Gothic Arches, Latin Crosses: Anti-Catholicism and American Church Designs in the Nineteenth Century* (Chapel Hill: University of North Carolina Press, 2006).

94. Seaman, *Annals*, 323–26, quote 325–26.

95. In all, every major Protestant denomination had seen at least one—and in the case of the Presbyterians, eight—of its downtown churches relocate uptown. Thompson lists Presbyterian (8), Dutch Reformed (5), Protestant Episcopal (3), Baptist (2), Methodist (2), Moravian (1), African (1), and Universalist (1) churches. Joseph P. Thompson, *The Last Sabbath in the Broadway Tabernacle* (New York, 1857), 4–6, 37–38.

96. Thompson, *Last Sabbath*, 38.

97. For example, in July 1849, the trustees resolved to look for a site between 12th and 23rd Streets and Fourth and Sixth Avenues. By the following February they had found, and by April purchased, a plot on the corner of 14th Street and Irving Place for $18,000. Yet in December 1851 they had resolved to sell the lot at auction. By May 1852 it had been sold for $20,343. See Board of Trustees, Minutes, 1838–1867, July 19, 1849; February 20, 1850; April 8, 1850; December 8, 1851; and May 3, 1852. See also "Home Department," *Spectator*, March 4, 1850, 1.

98. "Legal Record," *Evening Post*, May 10, 1855, 2.

99. "John-street Methodist Episcopal Church—The Split," *New York Daily Times*, August 28, 1855, 1.

100. "Supreme Court—Special Term. Before Hon Judge Roosevelt. A Religious Corporation Award," *New York Herald*, April 29, 1856, 4.

101. "To be in Fashion, or Not? John-street Church," *New York Daily News*, November 29, 1855, 4.

102. "Supreme Court—Special Term. Before Hon Judge Roosevelt. A Religious Corporation Award," *New York Herald*, April 29, 1856, 4.

103. "John Street Church," *Sun*, July 26, 1856, 3.

104. "A Muss among the Methodists—The John Street Church Difficulty," *The Weekly Herald*, July 26, 1856, 233.

105. "Obituary for Mrs. Mary McPherson," in "Record of the John Street Methodist Episcopal Church beginning April 18, 1869," JSMEC.

106. "Great Excitement in John Street. Trouble among Methodists," *New York Daily Tribune*, July 26, 1856, 5.

107. "Settlement of the John-street Church Difficulty," *New York Times*, January 27, 1858, 4; Board of Trustees, Minutes, 1838–1867, January 21, 1858.

108. Wakeley, *Lost Chapters*, vi.

109. "News of the Day," *New York Times*, February 23, 1858; "The Great Awakening," *New York Times*, March 22, 1858, 4. Kathryn Long, *The Revival of 1857–58: Interpreting an American Religious Awakening* (Oxford: Oxford University Press, 1998).

110. "Minutes of Stewards and Leaders," Item 244, MER NYPL, 95.

CONCLUSION

1. For all its aura of objectivity, map making is a subjective process, dependent on the decisions of the cartographer. See John W. Reps, *Views and Viewmakers of Urban America: Lithographs of Towns and Cities in the United States and Canada, Notes on the Artists and Publishers, and a Union Catalog of Their Work, 1825–1925* (Columbia: University of Missouri Press, 1984), 21. On Bornet's image, see Marilyn Symmes, *Impressions of New York: Prints from the New York Historical Society* (New York: Princeton Architectural Press, 2005), 107–9.

2. Numbers 22:23. Samuel A. Seaman, *Annals of New York Methodism, Being a History of the Methodist Episcopal Church in the City of New York, from A.D. 1766 to A.D. 1890* (New York, 1892), 205–6; Divie Bethune Diary (September 29, 1822–July 27, 1823), WCL, entry for December 22, 1822;

Alexis C. Madrigal, "The First Long Distance Telegraph Message, Sent This Day in 1844, 'What Hath God Wrought?'" *Atlantic*, May 24, 2014, http://www.theatlantic.com/technology/archive/2013/05/the-first-long-distance-telegraph-message-sent-this-day-in-1844-what-hath-god-wrought/276226/.

3. Until 1892, the tallest building in the city was the 284-foot spire of Trinity Church. Eric Homberger, *The Historical Atlas of New York City* (New York: Henry Holt, 1994), 104.

4. Homberger, *Atlas*, chap. 6; Ira Rosenwaike, *Population History of New York City* (Syracuse, NY: Syracuse University Press, 1972), chap. 4; Edwin G. Burrows and Mike Wallace, *Gotham: A History of New York City to 1898* (New York: Oxford University Press, 1999), pts. 4 and 5.

5. In all, 736 houses of worship are listed in *Trow's General Directory of the Boroughs of Manhattan and Bronx* (New York, 1901), 32–39.

6. Jon Butler, "Religion in the City: Faith That Could Not Be," *U.S. Catholic Historian* 22, no. 2 (Spring 2004), 57.

7. As Butler notes, the story of urban evangelicalism after the Civil War is still being written. See, for example, Burrows and Wallace, *Gotham*, chaps. 65 and 66; Genna Rae McNeil, Houston Bryan Roberson, Quinton Hosford Dixie, and Kevin McGruder, *Witness: Two Hundred Years of African-American Faith and Practice at the Abyssinian Baptist Church of Harlem, New York* (Grand Rapids, MI: William B. Eerdmans, 2014); Butler, "Religion in the City," 51–53; and Matthew Bowman, *The Urban Pulpit: New York City and the Fate of Liberal Evangelicalism* (New York: Oxford University Press, 2014).

8. Jay P. Dolan, *The Immigrant Church: New York's Irish and German Catholics, 1815–1865* (Baltimore, MD: Johns Hopkins University Press, 1975).

APPENDIX

1. [Anonymous], "Review of *A History of the Churches of All Denominations, in the City of New York*," *Biblical Repertory and Princeton Review* 18 (October 1846): 609. For the testimonials, see Jonathan Greenleaf, *A History of the Churches of All Denominations, in the City of New York* (New York, 1846), 1–7.

2. Roger Finke and Rodney Stark, *The Churching of America: Winners and Losers in Our Religious Economy* (New Brunswick, NJ: Rutgers University Press, 1992; 2nd ed., 2005); Edwin S. Gaustad and Philip L. Barlow, *New Historical Atlas of Religion in America* (New York: Oxford University Press, 2000). More recently, Lincoln Mullen has proposed to digitally map large-scale congregational data; see Mullen, "Mapping Boston's Religions: Next Steps in Mapping U.S. Religious History," http://lincolnmullen.com/projects/asch-2015/.

3. Terry D. Bilhartz, *Urban Religion and the Second Great Awakening: Church and Society in Early National Baltimore* (Rutherford, NJ: Fairleigh Dickinson University Press, 1986). Another example that uses religious data as one of several factors of analysis is Kenneth A. Scherzer, *The Unbounded Community: Neighborhood Life and Social Structure in New York City, 1830–1875* (Durham, NC: Duke University Press, 1992), chap. 6.

4. Bilhartz, *Urban Religion*, 142.

5. For example, *A Familiar Conversational History of the Evangelical Churches of New-York* (New York, 1839), covered the major Protestant denominations and paid little heed to African, Roman Catholic, Jewish, Unitarian, Universalist, German, and Welsh churches.

6. See Roger Finke and Rodney Stark, "Turning Pews into People: Estimating 19th Century Church Membership," *Journal for the Scientific Study of Religion* 25 (June 1986): 180–92; and Finke and Stark, *Churching of America*, 12–22.

7. An invaluable resource for locating church records are the guides produced by the Historical Records Survey of the Works Projects Administration in the late 1930s and early 1940s. These exhaustive surveys document surviving records in the city's churches at the time. See Historical Records Survey, *Inventory of the Church Archives of New York City: Presbyterian Church in the United*

States of America (March 1940); *Protestant Episcopal Church in the United States of America, Diocese of New York, Manhattan, Bronx, Richmond* (1940); *Lutherans* (1940); *Reformed Church in America* (1939); *Catholic Church* (1941); *Methodist Church* (1940); and *Religious Society of Friends* (1940). Many of these records have been subsequently gathered into major repositories including PHS, MER NYPL, United Methodist Archives and History Center at Drew University, and the American Baptist Historical Society at Mercer University.

8. See *Familiar Conversational History*, 20–21.

9. Richard Pointer, *Protestant Pluralism and the New York Experience: A Study in Eighteenth-Century Religious Diversity* (Bloomington: Indiana University Press, 1988), 82–90, 104. For a counterargument, see Sidney Mead, *The Lively Experiment* (New York: Harper & Row, 1963).

10. Jon Butler, *Awash in a Sea of Faith: Christianizing the American People* (Cambridge, MA: Harvard University Press, 1990), chaps. 7 and 9. For an argument that puts the rise of organized religious activity earlier in the eighteenth century, see Patricia U. Bonomi, *Under the Cope of Heaven: Religion, Society, and Politics in Colonial America* (New York: Oxford University Press, 1986; rev. ed., 2003).

11. Mixed-evangelical denominations include the Protestant Episcopal and Reformed Dutch churches. Both were open to a range of devotional approaches and would have included evangelical and nonevangelical congregations.

12. Butler, *Awash*, chap. 8.

13. Paul E. Johnson and Sean Wilentz, *The Kingdom of Matthias: A Story of Sex and Salvation in Nineteenth-Century America* (New York: Oxford University Press, 1994).

14. This compares favorably with the ratios Terry Bilhartz calculated for Baltimore in 1810 (1:1,788) and 1820 (1:1,957). A lack of large-scale foreign immigration and an expanding series of revivals, which resulted in new church building, lowered that ratio to an impressive 1:1,091 in 1830. See Bilhartz, *Urban Religion*, 97.

15. For a useful reminder that institutional development could at times outpace the successes (and often failures) of proselytizing efforts, see Butler, *Awash*, 268, 270.

16. See John Henry Hobart, *The Candidate for Confirmation Instructed in a Sermon Explaining the Office of Confirmation, a Catechism* (New York, 1816), 10.

17. Philip F. Hardt, *The Soul of Methodism: The Class Meeting in Early New York City Methodism* (Lanham, MD: University Press of America, 2000).

18. Patricia U. Bonomi and Peter R. Eisenstadt, "Church Adherence in the Eighteenth-Century British American Colonies," *William and Mary Quarterly* 39 (April 1982), 252.

19. The churches' congregational total is consistently five or six times the number of families, suggesting a father, mother, and four children, a standard size for an early nineteenth-century New York family. See *The Acts and Proceedings of the General Synod of the Reformed Dutch Church, in North America* (Albany, 1817–1819).

20. The percentage of communicants within the New York Collegiate Churches averaged from 42 percent to 53 percent of congregants, while the more conservative Garden Street Church averaged only 10 percent to 16 percent. The very high percentage for the Northwest Church (78 percent) reflects the high incidence of revivalism within the church, as they added many new members each year.

21. Bilhartz, *Urban Religion*, 142.

22. The Presbytery of New York, for example, did not require congregations to submit annual statistics until 1806 and did not print statistics until after 1825. Some membership records from 1806 through 1825 can be found in the following manuscript volumes: "Records of the Presbytery of New York, So Far as They Are Extant, prior to the Year 1810. Copied from the Originals, in the Possession of the Presbytery of Newark. By Order of the Presbytery of New York, October 1, 1847" [MF Pos 593.r.1], "The Records of the Presbytery of New York, Jan 9, 1810–Nov 23, 1815" [MF Pos 593.r.2], "Records of the Presbytery of New York Vol II—From Nov 28, 1815 to April 2, 1822" [MF Pos 593.r.2], and "Records of the Presbytery of New York Vol III—From April 15, 1822 to August 13,

1828" [MF Pos 593.r.2], all PHS. After 1825, see the annual publication of the *Minutes of the General Assembly of the Presbyterian Church in the United States with an Appendix* (Philadelphia, 1825–1860).

Minutes of the Annual Conferences of the Methodist Episcopal Church (New York, 1840–1860) contains membership numbers for New York Methodists from 1773–1860.

New York's Baptist churches zealously guarded their congregational autonomy but did join regional associations that reported membership numbers. Frustratingly, New York City congregations did not all belong to the same association. Membership numbers can be found in the published reports of the New York Association (1784–at least 1840), the Warwick Association (1791–1804), and the Hudson River Association (1816–at least 1845).

23. This happened, for example, to the Methodists in 1821 when Zion and Asbury, the two African American congregations, removed to form the independent African Methodist Episcopal Zion Church and when William Stilwell led out 350 white Methodists of the "plain, prudent sort" to form an independent Methodist Society. Kyle Bulthius, "Preacher Politics and People Power: Congregational Conflicts in New York City, 1810–1830," *Church History* 78 (June 2009): 261–82.

24. Baptists have had the least effective national structures owing to their traditional congregational orientation. Few repositories have copies of the annual reports for the associations to which New York congregations belonged.

25. Rosenwaike, *Population History*, 52–53; *Census of the State of New York* (Albany, 1857).

26. The list is in Douglas A. Levien, *Debates on the Trinity Church Bill* (Albany, 1857), 9. The numbers of communicants come from *Journal of the Conventions of the Diocese of New York* (New York, 1857), 154–79.

27. Where editors chose to list these churches is another issue. Sometimes they are all listed separately under "Colored," but more often they are listed with their respective denominations.

28. These included 2 Baptist, 1 Congregational, 9 Methodist, 1 nondenominational, 2 Presbyterian, 4 Protestant Episcopal, and 1 Reformed Dutch.

29. In 1816, the New York District reported 1,769 white and 803 black members, 31 percent of the overall number.

30. By 1856, the New York District ceased breaking out membership by race altogether.

31. According to the 1845 state census there were 12,913. See Rosenwaike, *Population History of New York City* (Syracuse, NY: Syracuse University Press, 1972), 36. Using the 1840 census as a guide for population distribution, 18 percent of the black population was under the age of ten, thus reducing the adult population in 1845 to an estimated 10,589.

32. On the local appeal of evangelicalism to African Americans, see Graham Russell Hodges, *Root and Branch: African Americans in New York and East Jersey, 1613–1863* (Chapel Hill: University of North Carolina Press, 1999), 119–28, 146–47, 180–85, 213–15; 238–39. On the broader appeal, see Mechal Sobel, *Trabelin On': The Slave Journey to an Afro-Baptist Faith* (Princeton, NJ: Princeton University Press, 1988); and Sylvia R. Frey and Betty Wood, *Come Shouting to Zion: African American Protestantism in the American South and British Caribbean to 1830* (Chapel Hill: University of North Carolina Press, 1999).

33. Dee Andrews, *The Methodists and Revolutionary America, 1760–1800: The Shaping of an Evangelical Culture* (Princeton, NJ: Princeton University Press, 2000), chap. 4. See also, Susan Juster, *Disorderly Women: Sexual Politics and Evangelicalism in Revolutionary New England* (Ithaca, NY: Cornell University Press, 1994). For an older interpretation that stresses networks and support over rebellion, see Nancy Cott, "Young Women and the Second Great Awakening," *Feminist Studies* 3 (Fall 1975): 15–29; and Cott, *The Bonds of Womanhood* (New Haven, CT: Yale University Press, 1977).

34. Christine Leigh Heyrman, *Southern Cross: The Beginnings of the Bible Belt* (Chapel Hill: University of North Carolina Press, 1998).

35. Ann Braude, "Women's History *Is* American Religious History," in *Retelling U.S. Religious History*, ed. Thomas A. Tweed (Berkeley: University of California Press, 1997).

Index

Page numbers in italic refer to figures and tables.

HISTORICAL STUDIES OF URBAN AMERICA

Edited by Lilia Fernández, Timothy J. Gilfoyle, and Amanda I. Seligman

James R. Grossman, editor emeritus

Series titles, continued from front matter

Mike Amezcua, *Making Mexican Chicago: From Postwar Settlement to the Age of Gentrification*

Arnold R. Hirsch, *Making the Second Ghetto: Race and Housing in Chicago, 1940–1960*, With a New Afterword by N. D. B. Connolly

William Sites, *Sun Ra's Chicago: Afrofuturism and the City*

David Schley, *Steam City: Railroads, Urban Space, and Corporate Capitalism in Nineteenth-Century Baltimore*

Rebecca K. Marchiel, *After Redlining: The Urban Reinvestment Movement in the Era of Financial Deregulation*

Steven T. Moga, *Urban Lowlands: A History of Neighborhoods, Poverty, and Planning*

Andrew S. Baer, *Beyond the Usual Beating: The Jon Burge Police Torture Scandal and Social Movements for Police Accountability in Chicago*

Matthew Vaz, *Running the Numbers: Race, Police, and the History of Urban Gambling*

Ann Durkin Keating, *The World of Juliette Kinzie: Chicago before the Fire*

Jeffrey S. Adler, *Murder in New Orleans: The Creation of Jim Crow Policing*

David A. Gamson, *The Importance of Being Urban: Designing the Progressive School District, 1890–1940*

Kara Murphy Schlichting, *New York Recentered: Building the Metropolis from the Shore*

Mark Wild, *Renewal: Liberal Protestants and the American City after World War II*

Meredith Oda, *The Gateway to the Pacific: Japanese Americans and the Remaking of San Francisco*

Sean Dinces, *Bulls Markets: Chicago's Basketball Business and the New Inequality*

Julia Guarneri, *Newsprint Metropolis: City Papers and the Making of Modern Americans*

Amanda I. Seligman, *Chicago's Block Clubs: How Neighbors Shape the City*

Timothy B. Neary, *Crossing Parish Boundaries: Race, Sports, and Catholic Youth in Chicago, 1914–1954*

Julia Rabig, *The Fixers: Devolution, Development, and Civil Society in Newark, 1960–1990*

Aaron Shkuda, *The Lofts of SoHo: Gentrification, Art, and Industry in New York, 1950–1980*

Mark Krasovic, *The Newark Frontier: Community Action in the Great Society*

Ansley T. Erickson, *Making the Unequal Metropolis: School Desegregation and Its Limits*

Andrew L. Slap and Frank Towers, eds., *Confederate Cities: The Urban South during the Civil War Era*

Evan Friss, *The Cycling City: Bicycles and Urban America in the 1890s*

Ocean Howell, *Making the Mission: Planning and Ethnicity in San Francisco*

Benjamin Looker, *A Nation of Neighborhoods: Imagining Cities, Communities, and Democracy in Postwar America*

Nancy H. Kwak, *A World of Homeowners: American Power and the Politics of Housing Aid*

Andrew R. Highsmith, *Demolition Means Progress: Flint, Michigan, and the Fate of the American Metropolis*

Lila Corwin Berman, *Metropolitan Jews: Politics, Race, and Religion in Postwar Detroit*

Gillian O'Brien, *Blood Runs Green: The Murder That Transfixed Gilded Age Chicago*

Marta Gutman, *A City for Children: Women, Architecture, and the Charitable Landscapes of Oakland, 1850–1950*

N. D. B. Connolly, *A World More Concrete: Real Estate and the Remaking of Jim Crow South Florida*

Cindy R. Lobel, *Urban Appetites: Food and Culture in Nineteenth-Century New York*

Jeffrey Helgeson, *Crucibles of Black Empowerment: Chicago's Neighborhood Politics from the New Deal to Harold Washington*

Christopher Lowen Agee, *The Streets of San Francisco: Policing and the Creation of a Cosmopolitan Liberal Politics, 1950–1972*

Camilo José Vergara, *Harlem: The Unmaking of a Ghetto*

Sarah Jo Peterson, *Planning the Home Front: Building Bombers and Communities at Willow Run*

Lawrence J. Vale, *Purging the Poorest: Public Housing and the Design Politics of Twice-Cleared Communities*

Lilia Fernández, *Brown in the Windy City: Mexicans and Puerto Ricans in Postwar Chicago*